The Illustrated Collector's Guide To Alice Cooper

Dale Sherman

All photographs used for cover artwork, the color section, and above, by and courtesy of Ken Ballard and kindly provided by Brian Nelson, except where noted. Cover design by Collector's Guide Publishing, Inc.

All rights reserved under article two of the Berne Copyright Convention (1971)
No part of this book may be reproduced or transmitted in any form or by any means, electronic or mechanical, including photocopying, recording, or by any information storage and retrieval system without permission in writing from the publisher.
We acknowledge the financial support of the Government of Canada through the Book Publishing Industry Development Program for our publishing activities.
Published by Collector's Guide Publishing Inc., Box 62034,
Burlington, Ontario, Canada, L7R 4K2
Printed and bound in Canada by Webcom Ltd. of Toronto
The Illustrated Collector's Guide To Alice Cooper / Dale Sherman
ISBN 1-896522-46-7

The Illustrated Collector's Guide To Alice Cooper

Dale Sherman

P.O. Box 406795
Louisville KY 40204
justabob@iglou.com

To Jill

Columbus, Ohio, 1998. Photo courtesy of Kevin Workman

~~~ Contents ~~~

Introduction 7
Reading Guide 9
Chapter 1: 1964 - 1974
   Part 1 — "I Hear My Name" 13
   Part 2 — Recordings 1964 - 1974 17
   Part 3 — Tours 1964 - 1974 66
   Part 4 — Film and Television 1969 - 1974 78
   Part 5 — Books 1969 - 1974 87
Chapter 2: 1975 - 1979
   Part 1 — "Devil's Food" 91
   Part 2 — Recordings 1975 - 1979 92
   Part 3 — Tours 1975 - 1979 118
   Part 4 — Films and Television 1975 - 1979 126
   Part 5 — Books and Comics 1975 - 1979 138
Chapter 3: 1980 - 1982
   Part 1 — "Six Is Having Problems . . ." 140
   Part 2 — Recordings 1980 - 1982 140
   Part 3 — Tours 1980 - 1982 156
   Part 4 — Films and Television 1980 - 1982 160
   Part 5 — Books and Comics 1980 - 1982 164
Chapter 4: 1984 - 1990
   Part 1 — "He's Back!" 165
   Part 2 — Recordings 1984 - 1990 165
   Part 3 — Tours 1984 - 1990 185
   Part 4 — Films and Television 1984 - 1990 195
   Part 5 — Books and Comics 1984 - 1990 202
Chapter 5: 1991 - 1998
   Part 1 — "It's Me" 204
   Part 2 — Recordings - 1991 in into the future 206
   Part 3 — Tours 1991 - 1998 220
   Part 4 — Films and Television 1991 - 1998 233
   Part 5 — Books and Comics 1991 - 1998 241
Chapter 6: "Luney Tune"
   Part 1 — The 1969 Concert Albums 244
   Part 2 — Compilation Albums 253
   Part 3 — Soundtrack Albums 265
   Part 4 — Guest Appearances 270
   Part 5 — Performances by the Alice Cooper Group Members 273
   Part 6 — Bootleg Albums 280
Chapter 7: Acknowledgments 299

Photo courtesy of Ken Ballard

~~~ Introduction ~~~

I remember the first time I encountered Alice.

It was the Fall of 1976. I was twelve, I had a bad case of Bronchitis, and it had hit me so badly that I never wanted to get out of bed again. Which was fine, as I needed the rest. Only problem was, I was bored out of my mind. With only one television in the house — a large one in the living room — I didn't get to waste the time away staring at soap operas and game shows. My stack of comic books had been read too many times even before I was sick. With nothing else to do, my only source of relief from the boredom came through the radio.

Which was of no help. You see, I didn't listen to the rock stations growing up. My Dad was from a Reformed Mennonite background, and both my parents were Nat King Cole fans. My older brother was listening mostly to instrumental rock bands at the time (although that would soon change.) So I spent my time with the radio on either an easy-listening station or a Christian music station. It was what I had always listened to when going to sleep at night. Naturally, I thought it would help me when I was sick.

After about two non-stop days of this music — while suffering from the Bronchitis and the side effects of the medication — I was ready to crawl out of my skin. I just couldn't take it anymore. It was becoming "music to die by." It began to make me nervous. Finally, I switched the radio over to WING-AM, a local rock station, to get away from it. Someone had told me that the morning DJ was fun to listen to, so I settled back to hear what was being played on the rock stations for the first REAL time in my life.

The first song I heard was called I Never Cry.

I was stunned. I actually liked this song and understood what the singer was talking about. Oh sure, I know, some Cooper fans are cringing right now and thinking "Oh, no! The writer is a fan of Alice's ballads!" But, why not? These were great songs just as much as the hard-edge material that he was doing, and continues to do to this day. What really struck me was the notion that the evil man in the bizarre makeup and the tough guy attitude had come up with a song that dealt with the Man's side of heartbreak.

It got me hooked. Not only on Alice, but on rock music itself. For the rest of the time I was sick, and for all the years thereafter, I kept on listening to rock and roll (although I do still pull out one of my Dad's old Nat King Cole on albums occasionally.) Soon after, my brother brought home a copy of Queen's NEWS OF THE WORLD, and Todd Rundgren's SOMETHING / ANYTHING, and it was just never again the same. The brighter the colors, the harder the music, and the more theatrical the show, the better it was it by me. And in my mind, Alice was at the pinnacle. Without that chance turn of the dial, and without that chance song being played, my whole life would have ended up differently. Literally.

And Alice came along another time to drastically change my life.

November 6, 1986. Columbus, Ohio. I got a call from a friend of mine asking if I wanted to go see an Alice Cooper show that night. I'd never had the chance to see Alice live and he was coming on strong with his THE NIGHTMARE RETURNS tour that year, so I immediately said yes.

When I got to Vets that night, my friend introduced me to some of her friends from college. In the group was a girl that instantly caught my eye. I was a shy guy, certainly not a womanizer, but I did want to have at least the chance to talk to the girl that night. So I managed to maneuver myself into a seat next to her during the show. We talked and got to know each other a tiny bit.

After the show, we stood outside in the cold for a bit, waiting on other friends that had to sit in a different area of the theater. Seeing as how the girl was shivering in the cold, I gave her my coat. It was the start of a friendship more than twelve years ago and Jill and I haven't been separated since. So, Alice played an important part in my life again. Without him, I would never have met my wife.

So, what am I getting to here? Just that I owe where I am in my life, perhaps in an off-centered way, to Alice. He was very influential in my life in ways that I never thought of until I began working on this book.

That's just it. It never occurred to me just how Alice influenced my life until I actually thought about it. But it doesn't stop there. Just as Alice was influential in my life, he was influential in rock music, and in theatrics overall. Yes, one can't deny that other people were doing theatrical rock before Alice, but there was no one that took that mantle and created a monster that ruled the pop world, the media world, the public's imagination as Alice did. At an age in rock music where it was becoming pedestrian and "love the one you're with," Alice was jumping up and down in the background saying "forget all that pretentious stuff, let's put on a show!" More importantly, his success with over-the-top theatrics enabled so many others to build upon such actions and to change the face of rock music throughout the 1970's, 1980's and 1990's. Yet, people tend to look at theatrical bands, and at Alice in particular, as if they were just a cast-off freak show relative to the "important" music of the day. Certainly the rock critics and writers felt this way and still do.

And, that's a shame. To really understand any event in history, you have to understand the popular culture of its times. To look at rock music from the 1970's on without looking at the influence of Alice Cooper is like studying the erosion of land by a geologist and missing the Grand Canyon.

Alice's career spans a period of over thirty years. In those decades, Alice has experimented with hard-rock, heavy metal, punk and new wave, besides pop standards and ballads. His popularity may have had highs and lows, but his success has continued throughout the years. This book is not only a chance to examine Alice's career in some small way, but also to celebrate his career with a look through the many albums, videos, books and tours that have contributed to his success over the years.

Above all, this book is for the fans — to see what's out there, what to look for and, hopefully, to share a thought or two from a fellow fan that may be worth noting the next time you pull out some of Alice's music to listen to.

Beyond that serious hope, there is only the music. And the show.

Columbus, Ohio, 1998. Photo courtesy of Kevin Workman

~~~ Reading Guide ~~~

The purpose of this book is to give Alice Cooper fans a way to reflect on the many albums, singles, videos, tours and books about the band and the man which have come out over the years. Normally, this would lead to a book that would be written as: 1) a biography with a brief, limited discography, or, 2) a reference guide that covered nothing but the recordings released over the years and with no hint as to the rich history of the man beyond those official products. Either method could be frustrating for fans, especially since a book dealing with Alice's entire career has not been published since the 1970's.

The Illustrated Collector's Guide To Alice Cooper is written with both types of fans in mind — the collector who already knows the history of Alice Cooper, and the fan who wants to try and place Alice's career in perspective with those albums, videos, books and tours. Chapters One through Five cover Alice's history and his official discography. Each chapter is broken down into sections (labeled parts), and each part deals with a different aspect of Alice's career. The sections are:

Part 1 - An overview of Alice's career during the years covered by the chapter.
Part 2 - Official recordings released by Alice's label (both domestic and foreign) in the years covered by the chapter.
Part 3 - Tours performed in the years covered by the chapter.
Part 4 - Film and Television appearances in the years covered by the chapter.
Part 5 - Books and Comic Books made in the years covered by the chapter.

By doing the book in this fashion, we can cover Alice's official discography effectively — but it still leaves a good portion of his career overlooked. Chapter 6 has been written to satisfy those fans who want to learn more about Alice's guest appearances on other performers' albums, compilations and even bootlegs. Chapter 6 is also broken in sections in order to more easily locate specific items (see that chapter for more details on the breakdown between sections.)

Releases are covered in many different forms in this book — however, the book is not an "end-all" to all variations of albums, etc. Discographies for some countries are incomplete and other countries, such as Taiwan, were just impossible to cover in any viable form at this time. The US, UK, Germany, France and Australia are covered in-depth, with many other important foreign releases covered as well.

As more information is gathered, future editions of the book will be able to cover additional entries in the history of Alice Cooper. With Alice's career looking ready for another leap in popularity, there will be plenty more albums, singles and tours to add in the future.

Hope you enjoy the trip.

RECORD Data Layout:

In an attempt to make the album listings informative for the casual reader, and helpful for the collector, album entries in Chapters 1 through 5 are presented in the follow manner:

The **Main Entry** for an album or single will read as:
Album Title: Album title
Recorded: Date and location of recording.
Production: Production, engineering and mixing information.
Personnel: Performer(s).
Song List: Song List (tracks and songwriters) information.
Notes about the album.

Subsequent Entries are for different pressings of an album are listed under each Main Entry, and will read as:
Album Title: Album title.
Released: Album release date and record company information.
Catalog No.: Catalog number.
Media: Media (Vinyl, Cassette, 8-Track and/or CD) of release.

Followed by Notes concerning that particular pressing of the album.

This entry method will allow for an album's recording information to be covered directly, and any significant differences between pressings (foreign or domestic) to be covered within the same part of the book as the recording history.

Single Release Albums
In some cases, an album has only had one release. If so, then the catalog number, release date and record company information will appear under the album title as one entry instead of broken into smaller entries (the Spiders and Nazz singles are a good example of this type of entry.)

All albums and singles covered in Chapters One through Five are official entries in the Alice Cooper catalog. Compilation albums, bootlegs and other recordings that have involved Alice are presented in Chapter 6 (details as to what distinguishes an album as not being part of the "official" discography are given there as well.) Foreign releases are noted when possible, and if information is available to show a unique aspect of the foreign release, it is noted as well. While several countries are represented here, there are not many entries for Canada due to fact that Canadian releases normally mirrored US releases right down to the catalog number. They were also normally released at or near the same point in time as the US releases. However, there are important Canadian releases (such as a string of CD reissues in the late 1990's) that are specifically listed since they are unique.

Singles and EPs
Single Title: Single (or EP) title.
Released: Single (or EP) release date and record company information.
Catalog No.: Catalog number.
Media: Media (Vinyl, Cassette, 8-Track and/or CD) of release.

Record Media
Other media besides vinyl were common for albums in the 1970's (although most collectors tend to prefer vinyl.) The 70's were the glory days of both 8-track tapes and Reel-to-Reel, while audio cassettes were normally looked upon as the black sheep of the family. For those who are too young to remember the '70's (or too fried at the time), here's a bit of a primer describing the other media formats:

1) **8-Tracks** were tapes built into plastic containers about the size of a small paperback. These were inserted into a tape deck much like most audio cassette car stereos today, except that a large portion of the tape stuck out of the machine and was constantly at risk of being knocked about if anyone brushed up against the deck.

    8-tracks were popular because the sound quality was better than audio cassette at the time and because it was incredibly simple to replace the radio in your car with an 8-track player in no time flat. However, 8-tracks had numerous problems — the tapes were bulky; the limited space per track meant that songs often faded out midway at the end of one track then faded back in to continue on the next track (there were four stereo tracks altogether); and, most important, 8-track players had a tendency to eat tapes on a regular basis. It was these problems, and the advancements made with audio cassettes, that lead to the death of 8-track by the beginning of the 1980's (**FLUSH THE FASHION** is the last Alice Cooper album known to have been released on 8-track.)

    8-track really didn't become big until the very early 1970's, so it is only with albums such as **LOVE IT TO DEATH** that 8-track tape versions were released at the same time as the vinyl albums.

2) **Reel-To-Reel** was a media popular before the arrival of 8-track (you can almost follow a line of succession in the preferred media — 1960-70: Reel-to-Reel, 1970-80: 8-track, and 1980 onward: CD's.) The sound quality over vinyl was generally considered better, and it allowed for more stereo reproduction than commonly available on vinyl in the 1960's and early 1970's. One additional advantage for the conspirator in all of us was that it allowed for music to be played backward readily without the risk of royally destroying a vinyl album.

    Unfortunately, Reel-to-Reel was normally only made available for classical music and other "highbrow" musical forms. While rock and pop music did get released on the format, the equipment could be expensive and one had to spend time threading the tape through the machine properly before listening to the music (and then do the same again to hear the other side.) Reel-to-Reel also had a tendency to snap if too much tension was placed on the tape (and you could end up splicing tapes together all night instead of listening to music.)

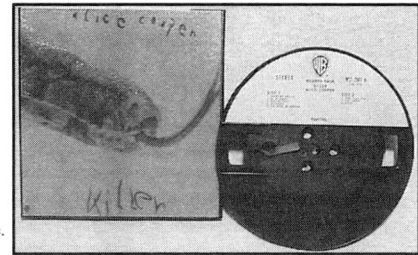

The Killer amlbum on Reel-to-Reel tape.

The most common place to purchase Reel-to-Reel was not in the stores, but through the record clubs such as Columbia House. The list of Alice Cooper Reel-to-Reels is limited for this reason alone, but much mid-1970's catalogue was released on this media before it died.

3) **Audio cassettes**, as stated above, were considered the lowest form of tape-life on the planet back in the 1970's. It wasn't until the 1980's (and the public's acceptance of boom-boxes with audio cassette capability) that audio cassettes finally began to win people over. Why the problems with cassettes in the 1970's? — because, out of the three tape formats one could buy over vinyl, audio cassettes were considered the weakest in sound quality and the tapes themselves were normally so cheap that warping and snapping of the tapes was quite common (so common, that it was more likely to find a broken tape blowing in the breeze along the side of the road than one actually working in a player.) That changed in the 1980's when technology was able to advance the sound quality to an acceptable level, and with the demise of vinyl, made them the cheapest format on which to buy new music.

Many Cooper albums were reissued on cassette in the 1970's with no information to show that they were reissues (normally the cassettes merely list the copyright year of the initial release and not of the year of reissue.) One thing that collectors should keep in mind is that all of the Cooper cassettes up to and including MUSCLE OF LOVE were not originally released in the now-standard "flip-out" cassette cases, but in plastic slip-boxes that held the tape in place through friction.

Mid-70's reissue of four Alice Cooper albums on cassette. Note that the uncensored cover was used for LOVE IT TO DEATH.

Reading Guide

Compact Discs are covered in greater detail in Chapter 3.

TOUR Data Layout:
The following information is presented for each tour:

Tour Name:	The official tour name if there was one, otherwise the name commonly used.
Tour Period:	The beginning and end dates of the tour, or a single date for non-tour shows.
Performers:	The band members plus any additional performers that took part in the tour or show.
Opening Act:	Gives either the act(s) that Alice Cooper opened for or the act(s) which opened for them or him, as applicable.
Set List:	The songs normally performed during the tour (when known.)

Notes about the tour.

Single (non-tour) shows are listed by date and location, and include any relevant notes.

Concerts known to be recorded — as a bootleg, for radio or for official release — are noted, as are shows that were filmed. This is not presented as a necessarily complete list of all shows ever recorded or filmed, but merely a mention of those shows that are known to have been preserved. As we'll see in later chapters, with the advances in technology in the early 1980's, more shows were being filmed and audio-recordings became increasingly high-tech.

FILMS AND TELEVISION Data Layout:
The following information is presented for each film or television appearance:

Film Title:	Film (movie, etc.) titles or name of television program.
Film Type:	This category includes feature films, full length movies, music videos, documentaries and television appearances.
Created:	Date and location of filming or taping.
Music:	Music in the film or TV appearance which Alice Cooper performed or to which he contributed.

BOOK AND COMIC BOOK Data Layout:
The following information is presented for each book or comic book:

Book Title:	Book or comic book title.
Published:	Publication date, Publisher (and ISBN if applicable and known.)
Author:	Author(s), collaborators and artists, as applicable.
Content:	A brief description of the content or content type.

Alice not "in character" on the cover
of the French single for You and Me.

Reading Guide

~~~ Chapter 1: 1964 - 1974 ~~~

Yes, my child, the rain is falling hard outside.
But it's here to cleanse the world.
And the fists of lightning and bursts of thunder
are only there to toughen the world up
for what is to come.

But, never you mind the danger outside,
you're here within. Where the darkness
is just a warm cover to hide behind
and keep you safe from the storm.

Now put your head back on the pillow
and listen to my story.
Listen carefully and listen quickly.

Because the storm is really about to begin.

Part 1 — "I Hear My Name"

If one wants to become a rock star, location is everything.

With the expansion of the auto industry that came with the end of the Second World War, the auto makers had made Detroit, Michigan a major city. Detroit was also a city on the verge of becoming a hotbed of music after the war. With the American sounds of Motown, and later the early punk movements of performers like the MC5 and Iggy Pop, little by little Detroit became known for its music. Located in the midlands of America — unlike the sun-baked fantasy lands of Los Angeles, California, or the self-indulgent darkness of New York City — Detroit also voiced the grim reality and the scattered hopes of America. So if one wanted to come from a city that really said "American Music," Detroit was a definite town to keep in mind.

It was in this heartland of American that Vincent Damon Furnier was born on February 4, 1948, though he would only see Detroit off and on for many years to come. The Furnier family consisted of parents Ether and Ella, Vince and his older sister Nicola. The family was constantly on the move during Vince's early years, as his father went wherever he could find a job while studying to be a minister. By the time Vince was one year old, the family had already moved from Detroit to Los Angeles and back again, and then at the age of three the family moved to Phoenix, Arizona for a couple of years. Detroit was a return destination for the family as Vince turned five years old and the family would stay there until 1956 when they would again move back to Los Angeles. In May 1961, his father became ordained and the family moved, this time for good, to Phoenix, Arizona. So, while the story begins in Detroit, most of the story occurs in an unlikely spot for the beginnings of a rock star, Phoenix.

Vince went to school in Phoenix and eventually ended up at Cortez High School where he became involved with the track team and with the school newspaper. These two venues of extracurricular activities at school would lead to the band that would eventually become the Alice Cooper Group. Drawn into organizing talent for a Letterman's talent show in October 1964, Vince asked fellow track runners, Dennis Dunaway (born December 9, 1948) and John Speer if they wanted to do a parody of the Beatles during the show. After some taunting back and forth, the two decided to join Vince, along with the track coach, Emmet Smith. Needing someone who actually could play an instrument, Vince went to his friend Glen Buxton (born November 11, 1947) who not only worked on the school newspaper as a photographer, but also played guitar. Buxton agreed to be in the band and the Earwigs were formed.

Although the appearance was mainly a joke (each member wore a Beatles' wig and sang song parodies about track), the excitement of being on stage was enough to hook the high school students into wanting to do it regularly. Taking up with guitarist John Tatum, they formed a band and by 1965 changed their name to the Spiders. The Spiders consisted of Vince on vocals and harmonica, Glen Buxton, Dennis Dunaway and John Tatum on guitar, and John Speer on drums. Having by this time learned how to play their instruments, the band had actively been involved in "battle of the bands" competitions in the Phoenix area and appeared as a

Cover of the ALICE COOPER COMPLETE song book.

house band at the VIP Lounge, and in a production of BYE BYE BIRDIE in November 1965. So the band was becoming known around the area, and it was during the summer of 1965 that the owner of the VIP Lounge, Jack Curtis, financed a single by the band, Hitch Hike backed by Why Don't You Love Me.

In the summer of 1966, John Tatum had decided to leave the band, although the others still wanted to carry on. To do so, the band needed to find a replacement quickly. Although they advertised for a replacement, the only response they got was from was a friend of Dennis', Michael Bruce (born March 16, 1948.) The band already knew Bruce for his work in a Beatles-cover-band called the Trolls, and knew that he had recorded a couple of singles with his band the Wildflowers; but the main deciding factor may have been that Bruce had a van and could carry equipment around to the shows. Nevertheless, Bruce was in and the band would go back into the studio with Jack Curtis to record a new single in the summer of 1966, Don't Blow Your Mind (a song that would be part of the band's set-list for several years) backed with No Price Tag.

By 1967 the band had decided to change their name to the Nazz and had recorded another single, Wonder Who's Loving Her Now, backed with Lay Down and Die, Goodbye (a song that would be recorded by the band for the EASY ACTION album in 1970.) It was then that they decided to try their luck in Los Angeles and the fivesome moved there from Phoenix. Once there, drummer Neal Smith replaced John Speer in December 1967. The Nazz members had known Smith (born September 23, 1947) back in Phoenix as a drummer in a couple of local bands — the Surf Tones and the Holy Grail — and Smith had moved to Los Angeles at the same time as the others.

With the band now in its final form (Vince, Michael, Glen, Dennis and Neal), they began playing clubs in the L.A. area, and then became the house band at the Cheetah. It was soon apparent, however, that they would need to make another change. A band from Philadelphia was beginning to become known with the name the Nazz (a band that featured a young Todd Rundgren, who would work with Alice eventually in 1979 on the ROADIE soundtrack album), so the band needed a new name.

Although the story had been told a million times of how the band arrived at the name of Alice Cooper after consulting an Ouija board, the real origin of the name is much more mundane. It really just came about as a name Vince arrived at as simple, easy to remember, and one that sounded like a name of a female folk-singer. One twist of the name was to get unsuspecting audience-members to arrive at the show expecting to see a blond, female folk-singer, only to end up with five grungy-looking guys playing hard rock music. After some minor disagreements about the name, especially from Smith who thought the name was ridiculous, they decided to go with Alice Cooper and played their first show with that name on March 16, 1968. Soon after, Vince decided to use the band's name as his own stage name. This was not because having one of the guys in the band named Alice would upset people, but because Vince worried how fame with the band would affect his father's ministry if his name came out. Thus, going by the name Alice effectively (or, at least, for a bit of time) killed two birds with one stone.

The band continued playing at the Cheetah, and extended their stage performance to more than just playing their instruments, by becoming increasingly aggressive on stage with props, and by reacting to the audience. They soon became known as the "band to hate." People would line up for shows just to see how bad the band really was.

It was at the Cheetah in the summer of 1968 that two individuals who would become involved with the band first saw the Alice Cooper Group — one who would help shape the immediate future of the band, the other who would be connected with Alice right up to the present day. The setting was the Lenny Bruce Memorial Party held at the Cheetah. Present at the party was Frank Zappa, known for his work with the Mothers of

Invention, and as an accomplished musician and businessman in the area. Also there was Shep Gordon, who, along with partner Joe Greenberg, were contemplating the idea of trying to find a band they could manage. What interested both Gordon and Zappa was the band's ability to drive out the audience from the Cheetah and clear out the club within ten minutes of stepping on stage. It was this abundance of negative energy from the audience that fascinated these two individuals and motivated them to get involved with the band.

With Zappa, it meant having the band do an audition for a new label he was starting at the time called Straight. He was looking for performers and bands to put on the label and thought the Alice Cooper Group may have had what he wanted for Straight (along with such others as Captain Beefheart and the GTOs.) Once Gordon found out that the band was being considered for the label and was to be signed, he recommended himself and Greenberg as managers for the band so that they would get a fair deal when signing a contract with Zappa. It was the start of a relationship between Alice Cooper and Shep Gordon that has lasted throughout Alice's career, but it was almost the end from Zappa's side of the fence. When the band turned down his idea to change the name of the band to Alice Cookies and become more of a comedy group, Zappa's interest waned considerably.

Still, the band was signed and their first album, PRETTIES FOR YOU, was released in 1969. The album was called "listenable" by Lester Bangs in ROLLING STONE magazine, while the ARIZONA REPUBLIC referred to the music strangely as "a happy, bright, optimistic attitude about life." Either way, the Alice Cooper Group now had an album and began touring around the country. It was during this time that they made their first appearance on film with the infamous "chicken incident" which was recorded at a 1969 Toronto festival. The band began to get a name for itself, but it did little to generate any interest in record sales.

The band was signed for three albums with Straight and 1970 saw the release of EASY ACTION and more touring. However, money was running dry as Zappa considered selling the label to Warner Brothers and the band members found themselves moving from gig to gig, trying to support themselves while waiting to work on the next album. 1970 also saw Joe Greenburg decide to move on to other things, leaving Shep Gordon as the sole manager of the band. The band also made a change by moving to Pontiac, Michigan, where they would stay until after the completion of the SCHOOL'S OUT album in 1972. Pontiac may have seemed like an odd choice, but it turned out to be an excellent move. Not only was Detroit a central location with respect to the band's constant touring around the country, it was also a central location for the Mid-West — an area where, once gained, an audience was loyal for life.

Their next album, the final one under their Straight contract, would be the one to break the band to the public. 1971 saw the release of LOVE IT TO DEATH, and the single I'm Eighteen. 1971 also saw the Alice Cooper Group working with a new producer, Bob Ezrin, who would help turn the tide for the band and help develop to the conceptual nature of the music. Ezrin would not only produce this and several other albums by the Alice Cooper Group, but would continue to work with Alice in his solo career off and on up to the present.

With I'm Eighteen becoming a hit, and the band now firmly under the Warner label, they began to take their theatrical nature on stage and build a coherent show around the music they were playing in concert. It was still not to the point of being like some of Alice's tours from later in the 1970's, but the beginning of the "Killer Alice" with the deranged makeup on his face was beginning to take shape.

KILLER followed in late 1971, which did well, but SCHOOL'S OUT would be the album to secure the Alice Cooper Group's place in the history of rock music, building on the success of I'm Eighteen. It was after this point that the band would become more than just a band to see in concert. They started becoming a household name. In the forefront was the lead singer, Alice Cooper, who was also the band's spokesman. The shows also became more theatrical and fell into the normal format of Alice as "Killer Alice," committing crimes against the people and ultimately paying the price through execution. It was at this point that they also began to use Joe Gannon for designs of the stage and other elements of their performance. Gannon would work with Alice from then up to the present as well.

Following SCHOOL'S OUT was an essential album, BILLION DOLLAR BABIES, and the tour that came on its heels was one of the Alice Cooper's biggest successes. After that, they had money, fame and power, but, as with many a band, the members began becoming dissatisfied with their roles and splintering off. While everyone agreed that Alice made a perfect and logical frontman for the band, the other band members each wanted their chance in the limelight as well. When the MUSCLE OF LOVE album following up BILLION DOLLAR BABIES didn't push the band's image farther, nor their bank accounts higher, band members began to question what they wanted to do next. It was also becoming apparent that Alice himself was getting a bit tired of doing

Part 1: I Hear My Name

Inside cover of the ALICE COOPER COMPLETE song book.

the same show and wanted a break from the constant touring and recording that had held the band together since the mid-1960's. He also wanted to make the shows even more theatrical in nature, while the other band members wanted a break from the constant special effects and additional performers on stage.

After a brief tour in South American in 1974, the Alice Cooper Group decided to take a break. For Neal Smith and Michael Bruce that meant a chance to work on solo material for albums of their own (see Chapter 6 for more details), while for Alice it would mean some time off before considering his own ideas for what to do with his career.

Some thought this meant that Alice was planning on retiring — They were wrong.

Part 2 — Recordings 1964 - 1974

During the years that the Alice Cooper Group struggled through name and member changes, they recorded two singles under the name Spiders and one as the Nazz. There were also recordings done by future member Michael Bruce during these years with a band called Wildflowers, which are covered in Chapter 6.

While these singles provided some local success for the band, only a small number of the original 45 singles were produced in 1965 through 1967 (a pirated version of these singles exists called The Spiders Vs. The Nazz.) Dealing with these early singles is easy (they came and went in a flash at a local level) although finding them is a bit of a chore.

After these early singles, however, presenting a discogpraphy becomes a bit of a challenge. Not only are there several albums and singles to cover from over the years, but there have been variations in packaging and even mixing over the years. Foreign versions of albums add to the challenge since they present variations of their own from country to country (see the entries for KILLER or SCHOOL'S OUT for a better understanding of this phenomenon.)

It should be pointed out that it was not until the release of I'm Eighteen and the LOVE IT TO DEATH album that Warner Brothers decided to expand the market for Alice Cooper beyond the US, the UK and Japan. Once both the single and the album became successful, however, the catalog included many other countries. PRETTIES FOR YOU and EASY ACTION, were not immediately reprinted and it was years before these two albums appeared in the rest of the world.

A look at the Alice Cooper material released during 1964 through 1974 provides an interesting time capsule not only of Alice's career, but of the rock music of that era overall. At the time that Alice was just starting to break through, most bands were expected to release at least one album a year, and sometimes two or more. This certainly explains the wealth of material that the Alice Cooper Group pumped out between 1969 and 1973 — seven albums of new material, with at least two of the earlier albums reissued to interest fans who did not catch onto the Alice Cooper Group until after LOVE IT TO DEATH (not to mention the special SCHOOL DAYS reissue of PRETTIES FOR YOU and EASY ACTION released in March 1973 in the UK.) Neither Alice nor any other member of the band has been as prolific since.

Pirated 45 of the Spiders and Nazz singles.

One enticing aspect of these albums was the special designs and extra "treats" included with each release. Instead of just a record in a sleeve, even the very first album, PRETTIES FOR YOU, contained something extra for fans to consider while listening to the album. True, that extra element for that first album was only a gatefold cover with some additional photos of the band. but considering the cost of using a gatefold sleeve for a single vinyl disc, credit goes to Warner Brothers and Straight for willing to shell out the cash for some additional flashiness.

Extras like a gatefold cover were a bit of the norm at the time, and certainly experimentation in album cover design was becoming widespread at Warner in the early 1970's (one need look no farther than a few Bearsville releases from Warner.) But Alice could always be relied on for at least one additional surprise with every new album. It could be something as simple as a lyric sheet, or as marvelous as the "build your own school desk" from SCHOOL'S OUT or the "pop-up book" of FROM THE INSIDE.

For the Cooper connoisseur who must have the first edition of PRETTIES FOR YOU, the label used by Straight changed over the years before Warner Brothers absorbed them. The first label used was pink in color with "Straight" printed several times horizontally down the center of the label. As the row goes down, the name changes color, ranging from white, to black, pink, orange and then yellow. The second "Straight" label was actually a green Warner Brothers label with the Straight logo (the name of the company and a drawing of a straight ruler) sectioned off to one side, either to the right or left of the track listing. This was followed a few years later with the revised Warner Brothers label that was a painting of a road with palm trees off to the left and right of the street. Commonly referred to by fans as the "palm tree" label, this was an artist's depiction of the streets of Burbank where Warner Brothers is located. By the late 1970's / early 1980's, Warner had dropped the "palm tree" label in favor of a simple greyish-white label with the Warner Brothers' logo in full color at the top above the track listings and title of the album.

Finally, the early days of the band saw some songs written and performed that would become lost to time. These include at least three songs performed during the Nazz period — Everything is Orange, Travel Agent and Animal Pajamas — of which only Animal Pajamas would survive as long as the early days of the Alice Cooper Group. There is also known to be a song called Come With Us Now (written by Michael Bruce and performed at one of the 1969 Whisky A Go Go shows) that Bruce updated and performed on a CD single by Ant-Bee (Billy James) under the title Child of the Moon. There are no doubt many others, but these three songs are known to have existed outside the band's normal recording history.

Single Title: **Why Don't You Love Me? / Hitch Hike**
Released: 1965 by Mascott.
Catalog No.: 112
Media: 7" vinyl.
Personnel: Recorded by The Spiders.

Why Don't You Love Me was originally a hit for the The Mersey Beats. Hitch Hike was a hit for Marvin Gaye. Both sides of this single, along with Don't Blow Your Mind and an instrumental version of Why Don't You Love Me, were reissued in 1998 (see entry below).

Single Title: **Don't Blow Your Mind / No Price Tag**
Released: 1966 by Santa Cruz.
Catalog No.: SCR. 10.003
Media: 7" vinyl.
Personnel: Recorded by The Spiders.

Produced by The Spiders. Recorded by the band with no producer, Don't Blow Your Mind was written by the entire band. The track would become a minor hit on the Tucson radio station KFIF. A live version of Don't Blow Your Mind can be found on THE TORONTO ROCK 'N' ROLL REVIVAL 1969, VOLUME IV and has many reissues under the title of Freak Out Song (see entry below for more details.) Michael Bruce had joined The Spiders by this time, replacing John Tatum in the band. Don't Blow Your Mind would be reissued as part of a four track single with Why Don't You Love Me (both the original and an instrumental version of the song) and Hitch Hike in 1998 (see entry below).

Single Title: **Why Don't You Love Me / Don't Blow Your Mind / Hitch Hike / Why Don't You Love Me (instrumental)**
Released: 1998 by Sundazed Music.
Catalog No.: SEP 141
Media: 7" vinyl.
Personnel: Recorded by the Spiders.

This reissued of the two Spiders singles was the first legitimate reissue of these tracks since their first appearance back in 1965 and 1966. The single, however, is not endorsed by any of the former band members. Although No Price Tag is not on the reissue, an alternative instrumental version of Why Don't You Love Me appears in its place. The single comes in a color picture sleeve, with a posed photo of the band from after Michael Bruce had joined.

Single Title: **Wonder Who's Loving Her Now / Lay Down and Die, Goodbye**
Released: 1967 by the Very label.
Catalog No.: 001
Media: 7" vinyl.
Personnel: Recorded by the Nazz.

Part of a live version of Lay Down and Die, Goodbye can be found on THE TORONTO ROCK 'N' ROLL REVIVAL 1969, VOLUME IV album and its many reissues listed as Group Instrumental and as I've Written Home To Mother (see Chapter 6.) It would also be rerecorded for the EASY ACTION album release in 1970.

Album Title: **PRETTIES FOR YOU**
Recorded: 1968 at Whitney Studios in Burbank, California.

Production:	Produced by Ian Underwood and Herb Cohen. Engineered by Dick Kune. Mixed by Herb Cohen, with assistance from Frank Zappa (or, so the story goes.)
Personnel:	Alice Cooper Group
Song List:	Titanic Overture / 10 Minutes Before the Worm / Sing Low, Sweet Cheerio / Today Mueller / Living / Fields of Regret / No Longer Umpire / Levity Ball (Live at the Cheetah) / B.B. on Mars / Reflected / Apple Bush / Earwigs to Eternity / Changing, Arranging (All songs listed as written by the band and no individual credits appear.)

The first album released for the Alice Cooper Group simply lists the band as Alice Cooper. In fact, the band's picture does not even appear on the front cover. Instead, a painting by an artist named Ed Beardsley appears. The painting used was not done specifically for the album, but was one that Frank Zappa had hanging in his home at the time. Why it was used instead of something remotely connected to the band in some fashion is any one's guess, except Zappa fans who had come to expect that type of nonsensical thinking in his work.

The first Alice Cooper album: PRETTIES FOR YOU

An attempt was made to get the rights to Dali's painting "Geopoliticus' Child" for the cover. But, negotiations never got very far and so an alternative had to be found. As it occurred, the Beardsley painting used had its share of controversy anyway, thanks to the appearance of a woman in the painting who is raising her skit so that her panties are showing. Although extremely mild even in the days of its release, the record company decided to help keep American clean by putting a small brown sticker over the woman's underwear in early editions of the album.

There is a photo by Ed Caraeff of the band on the back of the album cover, and — as would be the rule for all of the original and many rereleases of the Alice Cooper Group albums on vinyl — the packaging of the album itself was somewhat unique. Using a gatefold cover for a single vinyl disc — something also done with EASY ACTION, LOVE IT TO DEATH, KILLERS and BILLION DOLLAR BABIES — the inside gatefold contained additional photos of the band members, also taken by Ed Caraeff. While later reissues of the album eliminated the gatefold, the CD reissues from 1989 did include these photos in the booklet that came with the packaging.

In Alice's autobiography, ME ALICE, he states that the recording for this album was done in November 1971. This, of course, is incorrect. It is best to assume that he meant November 1968. The band went into the studios expecting to have some time to warm up and get into the feel of the studio before actually cutting the album. Instead, the album was finished within a week and the band was out the door with only a hope that it would sound okay. Demos and rehearsals do exist from these recordings and have been floating around fan circles for a while.

Rumors have been around for years that Zappa himself produced and / or mixed this album. Michael Bruce even stated in his book, NO MORE MR. NICE GUY, that Zappa was to produce the album, but backed out at the last minute. In fact, Zappa appeared only briefly in the studio and may have briefly helped with some mixing on the album, but it was the responsibility of both Ian Underwood and Herb Cohen to get the album in the can and ready for release. The Alice Cooper producer credit listed is simply inaccurate.

As to why the album then sat around for nearly six months before being released has to do mainly with problems on the record company's side of the production. Between mixing problems and legal problems (over rights) to be ironed out, there was no hope of releasing the album until the Spring of the following year. In many discographies put together by fans, the album is listed as coming out in December 1969. This can't be correct since there are reviews of the album dated as early as May 1969, and an interview with Alice and Neal Smith from July 1969 where they discuss the album cover and the production of the album. Alice does go on to say in the biography that the band first saw the album (and the cover used, for that matter) in March 1969 while performing in Vancouver, British Columbia. This would certainly be in line with the reviews and interviews mentioned above, so March 1969 is likely to be the correct release date. The album is also mentioned in a full-page ad from Straight in ROLLING STONE (July 26, 1969, the ad is listed as "#4 in a series of Bullshit Record Hypes from STRAIGHT") as coming out soon after the creation of the label in March 1969. The same issue of ROLLING STONE featured a review of the album by Lester Bangs who called it "listenable," but also "totally dispensable."

The song **Today Mueller** got its name from a friend of the band whose nickname was Tootie. As they developed the song, the lyrics changed from Tootie to Today. As to **B.B. on Mars**, the title came by way of Dennis Dunaway, and the song is about an actual B. B. pellet on Mars and not about a person, as might be expected.

Levity Ball is listed as a live track from the Cheetah club in the Los Angeles area. This club was not only a regular club for the band to hit in the early days, but was also the site in which Frank Zappa first saw the band empty the club within two minutes flat.

About 45-minutes worth of demos and rehearsals for this album exists in fan circles, and include mainly variations to the lyrics of the tracks from the album, along with the track **Nobody Likes Me**.

PRETTIES FOR YOU was later released in 1973 in a double vinyl set with EASY ACTION under the title SCHOOL DAYS in the UK and in Germany. See the entry under SCHOOL DAYS for more information. Two songs, **Titanic Overture** and **Refrigerator Heaven** also appeared on the sampler album ZAPPED in 1969 (see Chapter 6 for more details.)

PRETTIES FOR YOU reached No. 193 on the Billboard charts.

Album Title: **PRETTIES FOR YOU**
Released: March 1969 by Straight. Distributed by Bizarre, a division of Warner Brothers.
Catalog No.: STS 1051
Media: Vinyl and cassette.

As stated above, the original pressing of this album was issued with a gatefold cover that displayed additional photos of the band members. The inner sleeve of the album was a black paper sleeve with an advertisement and coupon for a sampler album called ZAPPED. The Straight label used is orange instead of the typical pink label used on future releases.

Album Title: **PRETTIES FOR YOU**
Released: December 1969 by Straight. Distributed by Bizarre, a division of Warner Brothers.
Catalog No.: STS 1051

Released on a purple variation of the originally pink Straight label, PRETTIES FOR YOU appeared in the UK eight months after it's release in the US. The UK release date has been used in some discographies as the date for the US release, which is incorrect.

Album Title: **PRETTIES FOR YOU**
Released: 1971 by Warner Brothers.
Catalog No.: WS 1840
Media: Vinyl, Cassette and 8-Track.

Warner Brothers reissued the album pressed once Alice started getting some recognition thanks to the success of I'm Eighteen and the LOVE IT TO DEATH album. Released with the latter Green Warner Brothers label. The Straight logo can be seen off in the right-hand side of the track listings on the label.

Album Title: **PRETTIES FOR YOU**
Released: 1989 by Retro-Enigma Records.
Catalog No.: 7 73362-2 (CD) and 7 73362-2 (cassette)
Media: CD and Cassette.

Although many rock albums were hastily reissued in the late 1980's in a slipshod fashion to cash in on the growing CD market, the first CD reissue of PRETTIES FOR YOU was something almost unheard of at the time — a CD reissue put together with some care and polish. The CD packaging included a reproduction of the entire vinyl album original packaging, including the photos that were in the gatefold cover. The CD came, for the first time, in the normal "long box" cardboard packaging, which included a sticker stating additional information about the album. The US rerelease on the Rhino label soon followed it.

Enigma reissued much of the Cooper catalog on CD during the late 1980's, and all were issued in the long box packaging that was the standard for the time. This included not just the official catalog from PRETTIES FOR YOU through ALICE COOPER GOES TO HELL, but also THE ALICE COOPER SHOW, RAISE YOUR FIST AND YELL and the "best of" PRINCE OF DARKNESS album.

Album Title: **PRETTIES FOR YOU**
Released: 1989 by Rhino / Bizarre.
Catalog No.: R2 70351
Media: CD

Nicely packaged by Rhino, the booklet with the CD contains the same artwork and photos as were with the original vinyl version of the album. Still, the Enigma editions that came out the same year were hard to beat.

Single Title: **Reflected / Living**
Released: March 1969 by Straight, a division of Bizarre, Inc.
Catalog No.: ST 101
Media: 7" vinyl single

Promo copies of the single are the only ones known to exist. Unfortunately, counterfeits also exist, so collectors should take care when purchasing this single. As with the album, Alice Cooper is listed as the producer and writer of the song. A photo of this single can be found in Michael Bruce's book NO MORE MR. NICE GUY.

Album Title: **EASY ACTION**
Recorded: 1969 at Sunset Studios, Hollywood, CA.
Production: Produced by David Briggs for Alive Productions. Executive Producer was Herb Cohen. Engineered by Barry Keene.
Personnel: All music, lyrics and arrangements by Alice Cooper, Michael Bruce, Glen Buxton, Dennis Dunaway and Neal Smith. Additional performers: David Briggs (piano on Shoe Salesman.)
Song List: Mr. and Misdemeanor / Shoe Salesman / Still No Air / Below Your Means / Return of The Spiders (For Gene Vincent) / Laughing at Me / Refrigerator Heaven / Lay Down and Die, Goodbye / Beautiful Flyaway

Lorrie Sullivan did cover photos, with John Williams doing the art directions on the album. As with PRETTIES FOR YOU, the first few pressings and reissues of the album came in a gatefold sleeve, with additional black and white photos of the band members inside. Interestingly enough, it's already evident that Alice himself is becoming the focus of the group — out of eight photos in the gatefold cover, four are of Alice alone.

Original STRAIGHT version of Easy Action.

Tom Smothers of the Smothers Brothers says "You can turn me off" in the song **Beautiful Flyaway**, which was taken from a broadcast of the Brothers' television series. While Alice does sing on this track, it is actually Michael Bruce singing lead on both this song and on **Below Your Means**.

In the lyrics of **Mr. and Misdemeanor**, a person by the name of Kenneth Pasarelli is mentioned. Pasarelli was actually an old friend of the band and had played bass with Tommy Bolin in a band called Zepher. He would reappear in 1978 on FROM THE INSIDE.

Lay Down and Die, Goodbye was a second try for the band, being earlier recorded and released back in 1967 as the B-side of Wonder Who's Loving Her Now. It was also a song that the band had played in concert off and on since that time.

Return of the Spiders was dedicated to Gene Vincent, who the band had played with during the Toronto '69 concert. After the release of LOVE IT TO DEATH in 1971, only Return of the Spiders would be done in concert, and only as the encore during the LOVE IT TO DEATH tour. In fact, after the LOVE IT TO DEATH tour, none of the songs from either EASY ACTION or PRETTIES FOR YOU would be performed live by Alice again.

The bootleg album EARLY HITS OF ALICE COOPER is actually just a hastily-reedited version of EASY ACTION and of questionable quality. EASY ACTION was also reissued as part of a double-vinyl set with a reissue of PRETTIES FOR YOU under the title SCHOOL DAYS (released in Germany and the UK) in 1973. A demo from the EASY ACTION sessions has also circulated in fandom of a song called Below Your Means.

EASY ACTION, which was promoted in BILLBOARD as being released by "Alice Sooper," did not reach the Top 200 on the Billboard Charts.

Album Title: **EASY ACTION**
Released: May 1970 by Straight Records. Distributed by Bizarre Records, a division of Warner Brothers.
Catalog No.: ST 1061
Media: Vinyl.

Original US release. Issued with the pink Straight label.

Album Title: **EASY ACTION**
Released: June 1970 by Straight, UK. Distributed by Bizarre, a division of Warner Brothers.
Catalog No.: STS 1061
Media: Vinyl.

Original UK release. Issued with the pink Straight label.

Album Title: **EASY ACTION**
Released: July 1970 by Straight, Japan.
Catalog No.: Unknown.
Media: Vinyl.

Original Japanese release was on the Straight label. A sampler album with a white sleeve was also released for this album in Japan.

Album Title: **EASY ACTION**
Released: Reissued 1971 by Warner Brothers.
Catalog No.: WS 1845
Media: Vinyl.

First US reissue. Released with the later Green Warner Brothers label. The Straight logo can be seen off in the right-hand side of the track listings on the label. A later reissue of this album under the same catalog number reversed the color-scheme of the title on the cover, changing it from white letters with black shading, to black letters with white shading. The album was once again reissued in the late 1970's with the "Palm Tree" label, but with the same catalog number.

Album Title: **EASY ACTION**
Released: Late 1970's by Warner Brothers, South Africa.
Catalog No.: Unknown.
Media: Vinyl.

This album made its first appearance in the official South African catalog as a two-vinyl set with SCHOOL'S OUT as the second disc in the set.

Album Title: **EASY ACTION**
Released: Late 1970's by Warner Brothers, Canada.

Catalog No.: CWX 1845
Media: Vinyl and Cassette.

Album Title: **EASY ACTION**
Released: 1989 by Enigma Retro.
Catalog No.: 1877-73391-2 (CD) and 1877-73391-4 (cassette)
Media: CD and Cassette.

First CD reissue. As with PRETTIES FOR YOU, the CD came in the, at-the-time, traditional long box with the cover art for the front and back of the album appearing on the front and back respectively of the box. The long box also came with a sticker that listed additional information about the album and the band. Soon to be followed in the US by the Rhino reissue.

Album Title: **EASY ACTION**
Released: 1989 by Rhino / Bizarre.
Catalog No.: R2 70350 (CD)
Media: CD and Cassette.

Both the Enigma and Rhino releases are out of print and becoming harder to find.

CD reissue of EASY ACTION.

Single Title: **Shoe Salesman / Return of the Spiders**
Released: Never released, although promo copies of the single from 1970 exist. Warner Brothers is the only company listed on this promo single.
Catalog No.: 7398
Media: 7" vinyl single

As with the Reflected single from PRETTIES FOR YOU, only promotional copies of this single exist. In his book NO MORE MR. NICE GUY Michael Bruce states that the single for Hallowed Be My Name was released as a single instead, but that track was not recorded until 1970 for the LOVE IT TO DEATH album.

Album Title: **LOVE IT TO DEATH**
Recorded: December 1970 at the RCA Mid-America Recording Center, Chicago, Illinois.
Production: Produced by Jack Richardson and Bob Ezrin for Nimbus 9 Productions. Executive Producer was Jack Richardson. Session engineer was Brian Christian. Mastering engineer was Randy Kling. Additional technician: Bill Conners (recording) and Charles Carnel (environmental control.)
Personnel: Additional performers: Bob Ezrin (listed as "Toronto Bob Ezrin") on keyboards for Caught in A Dream, Long Way to Go, Hallowed by My Name, Second Coming and Ballad of Dwight Fry.
Song List: Caught in A Dream (Michael Bruce) / I'm Eighteen (Michael Bruce, Alice Cooper, Dennis Dunaway, Neal Smith and Glen Buxton) / Long Way to Go (Bruce) / Black Juju (Dunaway) / Is It My Body (Bruce, Cooper, Dunaway, Smith and Buxton) / Hallowed Be My Name (Smith) / Second Coming (Cooper) / Ballad of Dwight Fry (Buxton and Cooper) / Sun Arise (Rolf Harris and Butler)

This was the last album released by Straight under their deal with Warner Brothers. Soon after this album's release, the company was bought out by Warner and all of the artists became part of the main WB label instead of an affiliated label. In fact, while the album cover states Straight, the labels used on the vinyl disc inside were the normal green WB labels (at least in the US.) After a short time under the original Straight catalog number, the album was reissued (when I'm Eighteen became a hit) with a new WB catalog number.

This album is usually remembered first off because of its cover and the controversy caused by a casually-placed thumb by Alice in the front cover photo. While it may look evident that Alice is merely keeping his robe closed with one hand, to a casual glance by a person with a vivid imagination (or dirty mind) it looked like Alice was exposing himself. This would not do for WB when the time came for the album to be reissued — which came swiftly once I'm Eighteen had been released as the second single from the album and had begun to hit it big on the charts. The problem, of course, was — what to do about the cover?

The first bright idea from WB was simply to block out the offending part of the photo by putting a thick white

Part 2: Recordings

strip clear across the photo, and, to make it look more symmetrical, place the a similar thick white strip clear across the top of the photo as well (giving the cover a "letterboxed" look.) The same was done to the back cover photo (although there wasn't anything to censor there) to make the album look like it was supposed to be printed this way. A huge black banner was then slapped into the upper-right-hand corner of the front cover which announced that the song I'm Eighteen appeared on the album.

While this reissue was hitting the stands, WB had the original photo painted (not airbrushed, as cleanup work on photos is often done) so that the offending thumb disappeared and Alice's coat / robe stayed closed on it's own. This new version of the cover was then used for the third reissue of the album, again with the banner about I'm Eighteen. Finally, later in the 1970's, the album was released again, this time with the censored cover, but with no banner. Ironically enough, the CD version of this album, released in 1989, also contains the censored cover, while the many cassette versions over the years have been remarkable in containing the uncensored cover in all its glory — causing no problems and eliciting no complaints (WB must have thought that the cassette version of the photo was too small to be noticed.)

The back cover is another photo of the band, along with the listing of song titles. Both front and back cover photos were done by Roger Prigent, who is listed only as "Prigent" on the album.

As usual for Alice Cooper original studio releases, the album came in a gatefold cover, which opened up to display photos shot by Dave Griffith. The main photo, which that takes up the majority of the cover, is of Alice's eyes with mascara drawn around the eyes to give the appearance of spiders (or extended eyelashes.) This is the very first appearance on album cover of makeup on Alice's face, which would be reduced to a sinister clown-strip over both eyes within a couple of years. Alice's pupils have been replaced in the photo with additional photos by Griffith of the band members (each pupil having a differently staged shot.) Griffith also shot a variety of photos of the band in posed shots on a brass bed in a white room. Excepting one photo which appeared in CIRCUS Magazine, these photos have been filed away unused.

The original album came in the typical Straight black paper sleeve, which changed with the reissues to a paper sleeve advertising WB, then to a white paper sleeve, and finally to the dreaded clear plastic sleeve.

But enough about the packaging. Another important first with this album was the appearance of an individual who would contribute the band, and to Alice as a solo performer, for years to come — Bob Ezrin. Jack Richardson is listed as co-producer of the album. This credit is given because the album was produced by his company, Nimbus 9 Productions, and Bob Ezrin was a relatively unknown talent at the time. Ezrin was associated with Nimbus 9 Productions and was brought in as the band began work on the album. It was with Ezrin's help that the Alice Cooper Group began to focus their attention on creating an album's worth of music which gelled as a whole, instead of the hit and miss feeling of the first two studio albums. With Ezrin also contributing to the musical structure of many tracks, the music started getting away from the merely odd staging and lyrics of the earlier albums, and instead into a darker, more threatening and nightmarish view of the world. In fact, Ezrin's conceptual ideas for albums — a practice which extended to many other bands that he has produced over the years — were to be a driving force on all of the albums he would record with Alice Cooper. This would also influence Alice as an artist, with the stage shows becoming more conceptual in nature. Ezrin also played keyboards on five tracks from the album, a role he adopted on later albums for Alice as well.

LOVE IT TO DEATH was also be the first album to really give each member of the band a chance to shine in the liner notes and track listings. Instead of the generic "written and performed by Alice Cooper" tag that appeared on the first two albums, a breakdown was given for each member on what they played on the album, and individual song credits. It was at this point as well that royalties began to be broken down to each songwriter as well, and a split began to emerge when some band members received more money for their many contributions than those who only contributed to one or two songs for an album.

LOVE IT TO DEATH saw the release of the single which would become one of Alice's biggest hits, I'm Eighteen, and also contained several other tracks that would show up in concert years after the album's initial release, such as Long Way to Go, Is It My Body and the very popular Ballad of Dwight Fry. Caught in a Dream ended up becoming the second single off the album, backed by Hallowed Be My Name.

I'm Eighteen was originally called I Wish I Was 18 Again and came out of a jam that the band occasion did in their early days, which explains why it was originally more than eight minutes long — they had always constructed it as an in-concert jam, something that they were still doing in their shows at this point in time. When thy began working with Ezrin, it was decided to cut the song down to size for use as a possible single (and to make it more manageable) and Alice had already rewritten most of the lyrics to those that are remembered today. As a side note, when Ezrin first heard the song, he believed the title was "I'm Edgy" due to misunderstanding what Alice was singing. I'm Eighteen become the first single off of the album, backed by Is It My Body, which was later extended when the band performed it in concert with a section called My Very Own. Long Way to Go, another great song from the album, includes the lyrics which became the title of the album.

Black Juju was another song that came out of an extended jam and was named for a dog that hung around the farm where the band was staying at that time in Pontiac, Michigan. In his book NO MORE MR. NICE GUY Michael Bruce admitted that his organ part in Black Juju was a variation on the Pink Floyd track Set the Controls for the Heart of the Sun.

Hallowed Be My Name is sometimes mistakenly listed in discographies as "Hallowed Be Thy Name". It became the B-side of the second single off of the album.

Second Coming was the only track on the album written solely by Alice, although Ezrin contributed some additional orchestration (as he did with nearly all of the tracks on the album.)

Ballad of Dwight Fry has risen to nearly the same status as I'm Eighteen in the eyes of Alice Cooper fans — and certainly in the eyes of fans who have seen Alice in concert. The song is named (or, rather, misnamed) for the 1930's actor Dwight Frye, who appeared in such films as the original FRANKENSTEIN with Boris Karloff and DRACULA with Bela Lugosi. Frye is probably best remembered for his DRACULA role (he played Dracula's assistant Renfield, who ends up in an insane asylum eating bugs and waiting for his "master".) For many concerts from the days of LOVE IT TO DEATH onward, Ballad would be a centerpiece production number with Alice appearing in a strait jacket and wrestling to escape. The child's voice heard at the beginning of the album track is actually that of a woman, by the name was Monica, who was a friend of the band. Michael Bruce normally did the voice live. In concert, Cindy Smith — Neal Smith's sister and later the wife of Dennis Dunaway — took on the role of the nurse who helps Alice with his strait jacket, a role she would play for quite some time before moving on to be the "dancing tooth" of Unfinished Sweet fame.

Sun Arise was the only song on the album not written by the band members. It is, in fact, a song that was a major hit in the UK during the 1960's for Rolf Harris, an Australian entertainer who also co-wrote the song.

Demos from the LOVE IT TO DEATH sessions have circulated in fandom for some time now. Most interesting are the many different takes of the song You Drive Me Nervous, which later turned up on the KILLER album. A variation of the lyrics for Ballad of Dwight Fry also appears in the demo tapes.

Thanks to the success of I'm Eighteen, LOVE IT TO DEATH rose to No. 35 on the America charts and No. 28 on the UK charts — the band's first successful album with respect to sales — and was certified Gold on November 6, 1972. LOVE IT TO DEATH was later reissued with the album KILLER on cassette under the title TWO ON ONE (catalog number 23861-4.) Little information is known beyond this for the cassette reissue.

Album Title: **LOVE IT TO DEATH**
Released: March 1971 by Straight Records. Distributed by Warner Brothers, Inc.
Catalog No.: ST 1065 (vinyl)
Media: Vinyl, Cassette and 8-Track.

The first issue of this album included the infamous "is that a thumb?" photo cover. Because I'm Eighteen wasn't released as a single, and wasn't foreseen becoming the huge hit that it did, the original issue of this album doesn't contain the banner which advertises the single. Thus the original cover has the uncensored cover and has no banner in the top right-hand corner. For more information about the alternative covers, check the main album listing above.

Album Title: **LOVE IT TO DEATH**
Released: June 1971 by Straight, UK. Distributed by Warner Brothers.
Catalog No.: STS 1065
Media: Vinyl.

Original UK release of the album. Uncensored cover still in place and the pink Straight logo still being used.

Album Title: **LOVE IT TO DEATH**
Released: June 1971 by Straight, Japan.
Catalog No.: P 8049W
Media: Vinyl.

A promo version of this album also exists on a blue Straight label.

Album Title: **LOVE IT TO DEATH**
Released: December 1971 by Warner Brothers.
Catalog No.: WS 1883 (vinyl) and M5 1883 (cassette)
Media: Vinyl, Cassette and 8-Track.

This was the first Warner Brothers reissue done after WB bought out Straight and was also the first attempt at resolving the "thumb" problem on the album cover. This was resolved at first by simply putting a white band at the top and bottom of the album cover. For consistency, the same white band was placed on the back cover as well. A banner was printed at the top right-hand corner advertising the fact that the single 18 appears on the album.

An artist was then brought in to retouch the photo to remove Alice's thumb. This was done by actually repainting the photograph and not by airbrushing (which was more common.) The retouched cover was then used for further reissues, but the banner for 18 was dropped.

Another issue of the album was released a few months later with the retouched photo, but with the banner reappearing. This one is probably the most common of the versions. Oddly enough, when the CD was finally released in October 1990, the retouched photo was still the one being used. Stranger still, while all of this brouhaha was going on with the vinyl album, no one bothered changing the artwork for the cassette version of the album. The thumb version of the cover is evident on most, if not all, cassette releases.

Through all of these editions, the gatefold cover survived. It was only with later pressings into the late 1970's that the album cover was redesigned as a single sleeve.

Album Title: **LOVE IT TO DEATH**
Released: June 1971 by Straight, Germany.
Catalog No.: 06292463
Media: Vinyl.

One of the rare Alice Cooper releases on the Straight label in a country other than the US or the UK. It came in the standard gatefold cover, but the opening for the vinyl was on the outside of the sleeve instead of in the middle.

Album Title: **LOVE IT TO DEATH**
Released: September 9, 1972 by Warner Brothers, UK.
Catalog No.: K 46177 (vinyl) and K4 46177 (cassette)
Media: Vinyl and Cassette.

Rereleased in the UK with the green Warner Brothers label instead of Straight. The gatefold cover was still used. The cover for the cassette opened to display only one of Alice's eyes from the gatefold of the vinyl album. This featured white lettering on a black background, with the cassette being on a blue label. The cassette was later reissued in the UK (catalog number ZCK4 46177) with black lettering on a white background. The cassette for the reissue came on a light green cassette label.

Album Title: **LOVE IT TO DEATH**
Released: September 1972 by Warner Brothers, Italy.
Catalog No.: 46177
Media: Vinyl.

The first Alice Cooper album released in Italy, it shared the same catalog number as its UK counterpart. This would be true for many albums and singles over the years, with the same catalog number on both the UK and Italian releases.

Album Title: LOVE IT TO DEATH
Released: October 1972 by Warner Brothers, Argentina.
Catalog No.: 112960
Media: Vinyl.

The first Alice Cooper album to be released in Argentina.

Album Title: LOVE IT TO DEATH
Released: October 1972 by Warner Brothers, Australia.
Catalog No.: WS-1883
Media: Vinyl.

The first Alice Cooper album to be released in Australia, this had the same catalog number as its US counterpart. Australian and US catalog numbers matched on many releases throughout the Warner Brothers years and beyond. LOVE IT TO DEATH did not chart in Australia.

Album Title: LOVE IT TO DEATH
Released: October 1972 by Warner Brothers, Brazil.
Catalog No.: WS 1883
Media: Vinyl.

First Alice Cooper album released in Brazil.

Album Title: LOVE IT TO DEATH
Released: October 1972 by Warner Brothers, France.
Catalog No.: 46177
Media: Vinyl.

The first Alice Cooper album to be released in France. It came in the standard gatefold sleeve.

Album Title: LOVE IT TO DEATH
Released: October 1972 by Warner Brothers, Germany.
Catalog No.: K46177
Media: Vinyl.

Came in the gatefold cover with the Straight and Warner Brothers logos, along with the "Includes 18" banner, but the cover was censored.

Album Title: LOVE IT TO DEATH
Released: October 1972 by Warner Brothers, Italy.
Catalog No.: K46177
Media: Vinyl.

Came in a single sleeve instead of a gatefold.

Album Title: LOVE IT TO DEATH
Released: October 1972 by Warner Brothers, Japan.
Catalog No.: P-8094W
Media: Vinyl.

Came with obi for "Rock Age." Very difficult album to find, even in collectors' circles.

Album Title: LOVE IT TO DEATH
Released: October 24, 1990 by Warner Brothers.
Catalog No.: WB 1883-2 (CD) and WB 1883-4 (cassette)
Media: CD and Cassette.

This is first CD pressing of the album in the US. Released a week after another reissue on cassette on October 17, 1990. The retouched "no-thumb" photo cover is used.

Album Title: **LOVE IT TO DEATH**
Released: 1990 Warner Brothers, Australia.
Catalog No.: WAR 18832
Media: CD

The first CD release of the album in Australia.

Album Title: **LOVE IT TO DEATH**
Released: January 1, 1991 by Warner Brothers, Germany.
Catalog No.: WEA 9271872
Media: CD

The censored cover was used.

Album Title: **LOVE IT TO DEATH**
Released: January 1, 1991 by Warner Brothers, Germany for French release.
Catalog No.: 7599-27187-2 (CD) and 7599-27187-4 (cassette)
Media: CD and Cassette.

The censored cover was used. As with most French CD reissues of the Alice Cooper albums, these discs were manufactured in Germany and then shipped to France.

Album Title: **LOVE IT TO DEATH**
Released: September 1997 by Warner Brothers, Japan.
Catalog No.: WPCP 3488
Media: CD.

The censored cover was used. Part of the "Forever Young Series" of reissues done specifically for the Japanese market. Each album in the series came with an obi (a strip of paper that wrapped vertically around the CD) which gave additional information about the album and what other albums were available in the series.

Album Title: **LOVE IT TO DEATH**
Released: October 3, 1997 by Warner Brothers, Canada.
Catalog No.: WARN CD 01883
Media: CD.

The censored cover was used.

Single Title: **I'm Eighteen / Is It My Body**
Released: March 1971 by Straight. Distributed by Warner Brothers.
Catalog No.: 7449
Media: 7" Vinyl single.

This was the commercially available version of the single listed above on the typical green WB label with the Straight logo in the upper right-hand portion of the label.

Is It My Body was incorrectly listed on both the original pressing of this 7" single and on the subsequent reissue later in the year. On the first pressing the song is listed simply as "Body," while the second pressing lists the song as "(This Is My) Body." Both pressings have the same catalog number.

I'm Eighteen went on to hit No. 21, with eight weeks on the American charts.

Single Title: **I'm Eighteen / Is It My Body**
Released: April 1971 by Straight. Distributed by Warner Brothers, UK.
Catalog No.: STRS 7209
Media: 7" Vinyl single.

This was the first Alice Cooper single released in the UK. The song didn't make the UK charts, and no other singles from LOVE IT TO DEATH were released in the UK. A promo version of this single is available under the same catalog number. It was also released in Italy under this catalog number.

Single Title: **I'm Eighteen / Is It My Body**
Released: April 1971 by Straight, Japan.
Catalog No.: P-1036W
Media: 7" Vinyl single.

This was the first Alice Cooper single released in Japan. Is It My Body is listed as "Body".

Single Title: **I'm Eighteen / Is It My Body**
Released: 1972 by Warner Brothers, Australia.
Catalog No.: WB-7449
Media: 7" Vinyl single.

The first single released in Australia for Alice Cooper. Although on the Straight label in the UK and US, this single was released on the Warner Brothers label. The single didn't chart in Australia.

Single Title: **I'm Eighteen / Is It My Body**
Released: 1972 by Warner Brothers, Brazil.
Catalog No.: WCS 35023
Media: 7" Vinyl single.

This was the first Alice Cooper single released in Brazil.

Single Title: **I'm Eighteen / Is It My Body**
Released: 1972 by Warner Brothers, Germany.
Catalog No.: 1C 006-92345
Media: 7" Vinyl single.

This was the first Alice Cooper single released in Germany.

Single Title: **I'm Eighteen / Caught in a Dream**
Released: Late 1970's by Warner Brothers.
Catalog No.: 7141
Media: 7" Vinyl single.

Although listing a catalog number lower than that of the first I'm Eighteen single, this was a later reissue of I'm Eighteen on the Warner Brothers "palm tree" label (which WB switched to from their green label in mid-1973.) I'm Eighteen would later be reissued as the B-side to School's Out in the late 1980's as part of the American Pie series on Warner Special Products (basically a "greatest hits" on 7" vinyl series.)

Single Title: **Caught in a Dream / Hallowed Be My Name**
Released: June 1971 by Warner Brothers.
Catalog No.: 7490
Media: 7" Vinyl single.

The second single from the LOVE IT TO DEATH album, this didn't do as well as I'm Eighteen, although Caught in a Dream did reach No. 94 on the US charts.

Single Title: **Caught in a Dream / Hallowed Be My Name**
Released: June 1971 by Warner Brothers, Australia.
Catalog No.: WB-7490
Media: 7" Vinyl single.

Second single released for Alice in Australia. It didn't chart and no other singles were released in Australia until School's Out in the summer of 1972.

Single Title: **Caught in a Dream / Hallowed Be My Name**
Released: June 1971 by Warner Brothers, Japan.
Catalog No.: P-1055W
Media: 7" Vinyl single.

Second single released for Alice in Japan. A promo version of the A-side also exists.

EP Title:	**Caught in a Dream / Hallowed Be My Name / Is It My Body / Long Way to Go**
Released:	1971, company unknown, Thailand.
Catalog No.:	M.037
Media:	12" Vinyl single.

One of the numerous EPs released in Thailand of questionable official status.

Album Title:	**KILLER**
Recorded:	Fall 1971 at the RCA Mid-America Recording Center, Chicago, IL.
Production:	Produced by Bob Ezrin for Nimbus 9 Productions. Executive Producer was Jack Richardson. Recording engineer was Brian Christian. Mastering by Randy Kling. Additional technician: Brian Christian (recording) and Joe Lopes (technical.) String and horn orchestrations by Bob Ezrin.
Personnel:	Additional performers: Bob Ezrin (mini-Moog on Killer and keyboards.) Rick Derringer (guitar on Under My Wheels and Yeah,Yeah,Yeah.)
Song List:	Under My Wheels (Bruce, Dunaway and Ezrin) / Be My Lover (Bruce) / Halo of Flies (Cooper, Smith, Dunaway, Bruce and Buxton) / Desperado (Cooper and Bruce) / You Drive Me Nervous (Cooper, Bruce and Ezrin) / Yeah,Yeah,Yeah (Cooper and Bruce) / Dead Babies (Cooper, Smith, Buxton, Bruce and Dunaway) / Killer (Bruce and Dunaway)

With Warner Brothers now in charge of the roster of bands and performers that infiltrated the Straight label, it was time to clean house at the record company. As such, speculation would lead one to wonder what would have happened to the Alice Cooper Group at that time if LOVE IT TO DEATH and I'm Eighteen hadn't hit it as big as they did. Fortunately, that wasn't the case, and speculate was all that the naysayers could do at that point.

Instead, the band began touring for the LOVE IT TO DEATH tour throughout the spring and summer of 1971. During this time they also started preparing songs for the follow-up album which would be recorded between some later LOVE IT TO DEATH concert dates in the fall of 1971. Not wanting to mess with success, the band and the label agreed to do the follow-up album again at the RCA Mid-America Recording Center in Chicago and, again, with Bob Ezrin from Nimbus 9 Productions producing (Randy Kling, who mastered the recordings for LOVE IT TO DEATH, also returned.) Jack Richardson was executive producer again, but that goes without saying, since he was the head of Nimbus 9 Productions.

During the recording of the album, the band came up with a cover design for the album which was later scrapped because of its complexity. At first wanting to call the album KILLER - CONVICTED, the album cover was to show a stack of newspapers tied in a bundle with the front page screaming the album's title as the headlines and a picture of Alice as the killer under the headline. When the idea was deemed non-functional, it was decided to use a simpler idea of Neal Smith's boa constrictor on the cover. The snaked, named Kachina, had been given to Neal during the LOVE IT TO DEATH tour and had become part of the show. As songs from the upcoming KILLER album were added to the LOVE IT TO DEATH set list, Kachina would be brought out during Be My Lover for Alice to hold and wrap around himself (a practice that Alice stayed with for many tours to follow.) The back cover was a posed color photo of the band members with a deep red tint. A similar band photo from the same session can also be seen on the cover of Michael Bruce's book NO MORE MR. NICE GUY and on the front cover of the KILLER tour book. A latter reissue of the album featured the same back cover photo, only this time with a deep green tint to the photograph. Both the front and back photos were done by Pete Turner.

A gatefold cover was developed for KILLER which folded out to display the cover photo and additional track listings, and also contained a 1972 calendar that could be removed at the perforated edge of the gatefold (and pinned up on the wall or thrown in the trash, as one was inclined.) The calendar was a month-by-month calendar printed on one sheet, with a photo decorating the top of Alice hanging dead from a noose. This photo of Alice was so popular that it was used repeatedly over the years for later merchandise. The calendar was also updated for 1973 and 1974 when Warner Brothers reissued the album in those years. After that, the album was released minus the calendar and gatefold cover altogether (until the initial CD release in the US.) When the album was released in Mexico (under the title ASESINO) it was decided to use the calendar shot (instead of the snake) for the front cover of the album for fear of upsetting people (because of the religious implications of the snake.) It should be pointed out as well that many foreign countries (Uruguay, Argentina, Malaysia) didn't include the calendar at all with the album, which is certainly understandable in the context of image, translations and budget. The original German release of KILLER did come with the calendar, but used white lettering on the cover instead of black.

The green WB label was used for the first release KILLER for its and its first reissue. The later reprints switched to the "Palm Tree" WB label.

Although only two songs from KILLER were released as singles, the album contained several songs that would become standards of Alice's concerts over the years. These included such favorites as Under My Wheels, Be My Lover, Desperado and Dead Babies, with even Halo of Flies popping up now and then — meaning more than half of the tracks from KILLER became concert standards. Rehearsals and demos from the KILLER recordings are known to exist in fan circles, with Desperado being the standout in this material because of its many different lyrical changes (made before the song was in final form.) Desperado, a song Michael Bruce has referred to as "Desert Night Thing," was a song Alice had written with his friend Jim Morrison in mind, and some of the lyrics are very good at invoking the image of Morrison visually.

Halo of Flies took shape in the studio and came from an earlier unfinished song of Bruce's called The More I Want to Know You along with bits and pieces from the other band members. Alice was the one who took the pieces and arranged the song into what would ultimately appear on the album. As reported over the years, Alice's girlfriend at the time, Cindy Lang, came up with the title for the track.

KILLER was released in November 1971 with a tour that kept the band busy until May of the following year. It was the first album from the band to be certified Gold, which occurred on January 28, 1972, and they were presented with the plaques for this achievement at the WB headquarters in Burbank, California once they got back

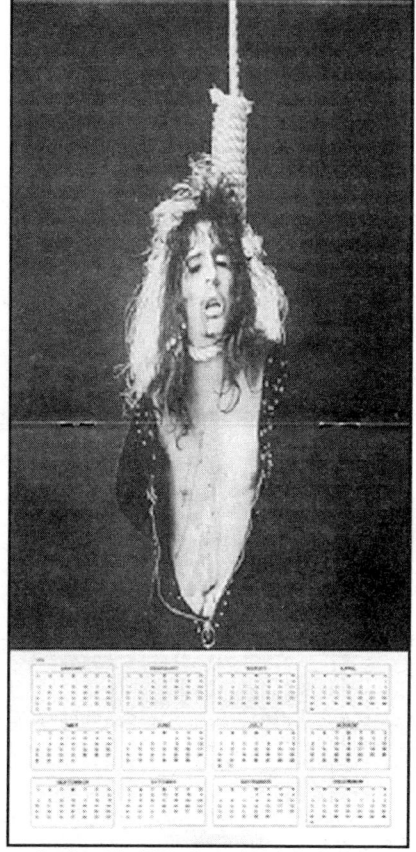

Reprint of the 1972 calendar included with Killer.

from the tour in May 1972 (although the discs used for the presentation were actually copies of Jimi Hendrix's RAINBOW BRIDGE album.) KILLER was one of three Alice Cooper albums certified Platinum on October 13, 1986 (the other two were BILLION DOLLAR BABIES and ALICE COOPER'S GREATEST HITS.)

KILLER reached #21 on the US charts, and #27 with 18 weeks on the UK charts. It was later reissued with the album LOVE IT TO DEATH on a cassette titled TWO ON ONE (catalog number 23861-4.)

Album Title: **KILLER**
Released: November 1971 by Warner Brothers, Inc.
Catalog No.: BS 2567 (vinyl) and M5 2567 (cassette)
Media: Vinyl, Cassette, Reel-to-Reel and 8-Track.

This was the first Alice Cooper album released solely under Warner Brothers. See the previous entry for more details about the packaging design. This version of the album included the red tinted back cover. The cassette, however, shows the cover with more of a purple tint. As standard for the Warner Brothers cassettes, only general track information is contained on the inside of the cassette cover.

Album Title: **KILLER**
Released: February 5, 1972 by Warner Brothers, UK
Catalog No.: K 56005
Media: Vinyl and Cassette.

Same as the US edition, including the gatefold and the calendar. Although some discographies list this album as coming out in December 1971, February 1972 is most definitely the month of release as the band began turing in the UK and Europe in support of the album soon after February.

Album Title: **KILLER**
Released: February 1972 by Warner Brothers, Argentina.
Catalog No.: 14030-2
Media: Vinyl.

The album was released with no calendar.

Album Title: **KILLER**
Released: February 1972 by Warner Brothers, Australia.
Catalog No.: BS-2567
Media: Vinyl.

Same as the original US release. KILLER did not chart in Australia.

Album Title: **KILLER**
Released: February 1972 by Warner Brothers, Brazil.
Catalog No.: 85006
Media: Vinyl.

Came with the calendar.

Album Title: **KILLER**
Released: February 1972 by Warner Brothers, France.
Catalog No.: 56005
Media: Vinyl.

Released in both mono and stereo versions under the same catalog number.

Album Title: **KILLER**
Released: February 1972 by Warner Brothers, Germany.
Catalog No.: WB 46121
Media: Vinyl.

The album came with the calendar, but the lettering on the front cover is white instead of black.

Album Title: **KILLER**
Released: February 1972 by Warner Brothers, Japan.
Catalog No.: Unknown.
Media: Vinyl.

Came with the calendar.

Album Title: **KILLER (a.k.a. ASESINO)**
Released: 1972 by Warner Brothers, Mexico.
Catalog No.: LWB 5090
Media: Vinyl.

As mentioned in the main entry for this title, it was decided to use the calendar shot as the front cover of the album instead of the snake due to fear of upsetting people with the religious implications of the snake.

Album Title: **KILLER**
Released: Late-1970's by Warner Brothers, UK.
Catalog No.: K56005
Media: Vinyl.

Same red tinted cover and green tinted inner sleeve, but without the calender attachment. The cream colored Warner Brothers label pegs this as a late 1970's / early 1980's reissue.

Album Title: **KILLER**
Released: May 1, 1989 by Warner Brothers, Germany.
Catalog No.: 927255-2 (CD) and 927255-4 (cassette)

Media: CD and Cassette.

First French / German reissue of the album in the CD format.

Album Title: **KILLER**
Released: October 25, 1990 by Warner Brothers.
Catalog No.: WB 2567-2 (CD) and WB 2567-4 (cassette)
Media: CD and Cassette.

First CD reissue of KILLER in the US. It was released one week after the cassette reissue, under the same catalog number, on October 17, 1990. A black and white version of the 1972 calendar was included as the centerfold in the booklet with the CD. A page in the booklet also discusses the band, with a short paragraph about the album.

CD reissue of KILLER showing the back and front covers of the album.

Album Title: **KILLER**
Released: 1990 by Warner Brothers, Australia.
Catalog No.: WAR 9272552
Media: CD.

This is the first CD release of the album in Australia.

Album Title: **KILLER**
Released: September 1997 by Warner Brothers, Japan.
Catalog No.: WPCP-3489
Media: CD.

Part of the special "Forever Young Series" that WB released in Japan. The album came with an obi that listed the album's title as well as additional albums available in the series.

Album Title: **KILLER**
Released: October 3, 1997 by Warner Brothers, Canada.
Catalog No.: CD 02567
Media: CD.

Latest reissue of the album. Part of a mass reissuing of the Alice Cooper catalog in Canada.

Single Title: **Under My Wheels / Desperado**
Released: November 1971 by Warner Brothers.
Catalog No.: 7529
Media: 7" Vinyl single.

The first single from KILLER, which is considered a classic by Cooper fans, didn't reach as high as I'm

Eighteen, getting only to the No. 59 slot on the US charts.

Single Title: **Under My Wheels / Desperado**
Released: December 1971 by Warner Brothers, UK.
Catalog No.: K 16127
Media: 7" Vinyl single.

Although KILLER was not to be released in the UK until February 1972, the first single from the album was released a couple of months early in support of Alice performing in concert in London during November 1971.

Single Title: **Under My Wheels / Desperado**
Released: December 1971 by Warner Brothers, France.
Catalog No.: 16127
Media: 7" Vinyl single.

Picture sleeve.

Single Title: **Under My Wheels / Desperado**
Released: December 1971 by Warner Brothers, Germany.
Catalog No.: WB 16127
Media: 7" Vinyl single.

Although released with the same catalog number as its UK counterpart, the German version of this single came in a color picture sleeve. The photo is an alternative shot from the LOVE IT TO DEATH album cover photo session.

Single Title: **Under My Wheels / Desperado**
Released: December 1971 by Warner Brothers, Japan.
Catalog No.: P-1097W
Media: 7" Vinyl single.

Picture Sleeve.

German single for Under My Wheels.

Single Title: **Be My Lover / Yeah, Yeah, Yeah**
Released: January 1972 by Warner Brothers.
Catalog No.: 7568
Media: 7" Vinyl single.

Second single from the KILLER album with the typical green Warner label used in the early 1970's. While it did better than Under My Wheels, the song did not reach the top 40, achieving only No. 49 on the US charts.

Single Title: **Be My Lover / You Drive Me Nervous**
Released: February 1972 by Warner Brothers, UK.
Catalog No.: K 16154
Media: 7" Vinyl single.

Single released in the UK at the same time KILLER was released, it followed the US pattern by not ranking very well on the charts. It wouldn't be until School's Out, released in June 1972, that Cooper would break the top 40 in the UK (and in a big way, as will be seen.)

US single for Be My Lover

Single Title: **Be My Lover / Yeah, Yeah, Yeah**
Released: 1972 by Warner Brothers, Brazil.
Catalog No.: WBCS 7030

Chapter 1: 1964 - 1974

Media: 7" Vinyl single.

A promo version of the A-side also appeared under the same catalog number.

Single Title: **Be My Lover / Yeah,Yeah,Yeah**
Released: 1972 by Warner Brothers, Germany.
Catalog No.:   WB 16158
Media: 7" Vinyl single.

Picture sleeve.

Single Title: **Be My Lover / Yeah,Yeah,Yeah**
Released: 1972 by Warner Brothers, Portugal.
Catalog No.:   N-63-15
Media: 7" Vinyl single.

This came in a green colored picture sleeve, and with a black and white version of the same photo that appears on the German Under My Wheels single listed above.

Single Title: **Under My Wheels / Halo of Flies**
Released: 1973 by Warner Brothers, Holland.
Catalog No.:   16296
Media: 7" vinyl single.

Portugal single for Be My Lover.

A late-issue pressing of Halo of Flies and Under My Wheels. It came in a photo sleeve of Alice in concert with a yellow banner in the left-hand corner stating that the single is a "special release for Holland." At the bottom left-hand corner the cover states that the single is a "DJ's choice," while in the lower right-hand corner it states that the single was "number 8 in radio veronica's top-100."

Holland late issue pressing of Under My Wheels.

Single Title: **Nobody Likes Me**
Catalog No.:   none given.
Media: 7" cardboard cutout from the back of the KILLER tour book.

This was a single printed on the back of the KILLER tour book and could be bought at the shows on that tour. The song was a studio recording of this track, which is still unavailable commercially (although live versions of this song can be found on the LIVE AT THE WHISKY A GO GO 1969 album and the various Toronto Rock 'N' Roll Festival 1969 albums.)

Nobody Likes Me was done in concert from 1968 through 1970 and was recorded in the studio during that time. Although recorded, it never appeared on any of the official albums.

Album Title: **SCHOOL'S OUT**
Recorded: Recorded periodically between March - June 1972 at The Record Plant, New York and the Galecie Estate in Greenwich, Connecticut (referred to as the Alice Cooper Mansion in the liner notes.)
Production: Produced by Bob Ezrin for Nimbus 9 Productions. An Alive Enterprises Inc. Production. Recording engineers were Roy Cicala and Shelly Yakus. Recording technician: Danny Turbeville,

Personnel:	Frank Hubach and Dennis Ferrante. String and horn orchestrations by Bob Ezrin. Additional performers: Bob Ezrin (mini-Moog and keyboards.) Dick Wagner (guitar on My Stars.) Rockin' Reggie Vincent (additional guitar and vocals.)
Song List:	School's Out (Cooper, Bruce, Buxton, Dunaway and Smith) / Luney Tune (Dunaway and Cooper) / Gutter Cat Vs. the Jets (Buxton, Dunaway, Leonard Bernstein and Steven Soundheim) / Street Fight (Cooper, Bruce, Buxton, Dunaway and Smith) / Blue Turk (Bruce and Cooper) / My Stars (Cooper and Ezrin) / Public Animal #9 (Bruce and Cooper) / Alma Mater (Smith) / Grande Finale (Mack David, Elmer Bernstein, Ezrin, Cooper, Smith, Dunaway, Buxton and Bruce)

With the success of the KILLER album and tour, the band was finally getting the recognition that they had for years been dreaming of. On the downside, they were also being pressured to tour and record consistently and on short order, as compared to their schedule of less than three years earlier, when songs for an album were worked on in concert for several months before being recorded in the studio.

Instead, they were brought into Studio Instrument Rentals in Los Angeles, California to rehearse the next album and the tour that was immediately to follow. After a couple of weeks of rehearsal (when the band also received their first Gold Album award for KILLER) they went east to record the SCHOOL'S OUT at the Record Plant in New York. Some minor recordings were also done at the mansion in Connecticut were the band stayed during this period.

The main single from the album, School's Out was a song which the band began working on during the KILLER tour and was actually performed as an instrumental break after Long Way to Go before its lyrics were written. The School's Out track was recorded during a break in the KILLER tour and the single was released in early April, two months before its appearance on the SCHOOL'S OUT album. The School's Out single was the first Top Ten hit for the band and helped make the album a Top Ten hit as well. Along with I'm Eighteen and No More Mr. Nice Guy, School's Out became one of the songs most closely associated with Alice over the years. School's Out was the only single issued from the SCHOOL'S OUT album, quite unlike previous Alice Cooper albums which each spawned multiple singles.

Alice has explained that the phrase "School's Out" came to him from an old Bowery Boys movie (a series of B-movies, that ran from the late 1930's through the 1940's, about a gang of kids who get into all types of trouble.) However, this has never been substantiated, and it's possible that Alice may have not actually heard the phrase there. Still, Alice's claim that the phrase means "to wise up" is a good one, and certainly the song is more about school being out than "wising up" anyway, so ultimately it does little to hurt the song if it's not true.

My Stars included the phrase "Klaatu barada Nikto" in the background vocals. This is the phrase used to stop Gort from destroying the Earth in the classic science fiction movie THE DAY THE EARTH STOOD STILL.

Gutter Cat Vs. the Jets was a track that Dennis Dunaway and Glen Buxton spent several months developing before work began in the studios with Bob Ezrin. Once there, Ezrin suggested adding material from the Broadway musical WEST SIDE STORY into the mix. This explains why the individuals behind WEST SIDE STORY — Leonard Bernstein and Stephen Sondheim — both get writing credits on the track. Using this bit from WEST SIDE STORY would be further extended into the concerts themselves (as one can see by checking out the tour information for SCHOOL'S OUT in Part 3 below) and into further references on later Alice Cooper albums. References to the film and novel A CLOCKWORK ORANGE also appeared in the song around the time of the TRASH tour when Alice would revert to singing "Singin' in the Rain" during concert version of this track. Gutter Cats was originally written as "Gutter Pussy," then changed. An acetate of the School's Out single shows the original title for Gutter Cats as the B-side (with it being crossed out and the proper title written in it's place.) In concert, Street Fight usually ended up as an extension of Gutter Cat Vs. the Jets.

Grande Finale, a track not listed on the album's back or inside covers, was put together in the studio by Bob Ezrin to emphasize the conceptual nature of the album. This is a device that Ezrin used on several subsequent albums which he produced, including into Pink Floyd's THE WALL and KISS' DESTROYER.

Demos from SCHOOL'S OUT recording sessions have long been circulating in fandom, including a song recorded but never used by the band titled Evil.

The album design for SCHOOL'S OUT is certainly the most eccentric of the entire official discography (although BILLION DOLLAR BABIES comes a close second in that category.) Designed by Wilkes & Braum, Inc. and put together by Sound Packaging Corporation, this album cover also went through several small changes throughout the first year of its release. The cover is designed to look and open like an old school desk, with a cover surface that the pupil would write on, built on a hinge so that the lid could be opened and books, pens and other school material could be placed inside. As most schools in the US changed from these types of school desks to either long tables or flat desks with no compartments during the 1970's, it is actually more of an antique now than at the time of the album's release.

Unlike most covers today, which would put the desk into the picture using airbrush or a computer, the SCHOOL'S OUT desk was actually carved up to include the album logo in the upper right-hand corner, and the names and initials of the band members carved (by the band members themselves) into the surface. This desk is now part of the Hard Rock Cafe's circulating display material, and in 1998 the Hard Rock used the desk as the basis for their Summer menu. The menu looked like

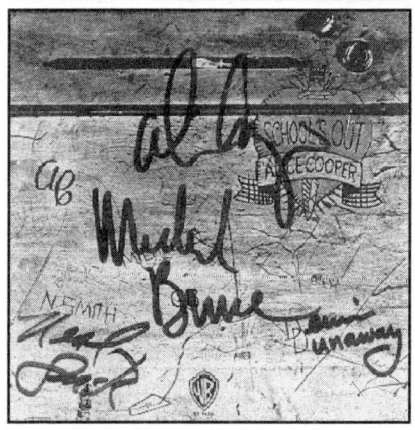

Autographed copy of SCHOOL'S OUT
(from the Bryan Erikson collection.)

the album cover and opened in the same manner, with the contents inside being the menu items and rock-related memorabilia (including an Alice Cooper ticket stub from September 23, 1981.)

The cover was constructed so that the lid of the desk could be opened to reveal not only the vinyl album inside, but also album credits (made up to look like a school test), various items that would have been thrown into the desk (including marbles, a slingshot, a switchblade, and what appears to be a comic book but is actually an issue of MAD Magazine that has a great parody of Liberace called "Lovely Liberace") and a photo of the band "taped" up to the top of the lid. The photography of the desk — both inside and out — was done by Robert Offer, while the photo of the band was done by Roger Prigent. Prigent also shot the front and back cover photos of the band for the LOVE IT TO DEATH album. A similar photo of the band was used on the picture sleeve for the US single of School's Out which came out in April (and on the pirated The Spiders Vs. the Nazz single.)

The back of the album cover was designed to look like the bottom of the desk (including gum-wads) and portions were perforated so that the buyer could fold out the back of the album and turn the cover into an actual standing desk. Most fans got the notion of the album cover and, not wanting to mess with it, tended to leave the album alone, so finding the album without the back of the cover being destroyed is relatively easy.

The album was released in the US and the UK as described above. There are variations as to how the back of the album appears:
- Germany and Brazil pressings show the inside of the school desk on the back cover.
- FIN DE CLASS, the Venezuela pressing, shows a picture of the band with the heart logo.
- SE ACABBO' LA ESCUELA, the Mexican pressing, shows the photo from the front cover on the back.
- The Japanese pressing promotes other albums available, including Bobby Sherman and Joe Cocker.
- The Argentina pressing shows the bottom of the desk, but the legs do not pop out.
- South African and New Zealand pressings show the bottom of the desk, but with the photo of the band from the inside of the desk "taped" to the desk.

It should be pointed out that the liner notes inside the desk list the songs in the wrong order (which may be why the sides and track order are given as part of the test inside.) Public Animal #9 is listed as simply Public Animal, while Street Fight is not even listed. This was also the first album to list Alive Enterprises in the liner notes.

More difficult to find is the original pressing of the album which included the next little "extra" that came with the packaging — a pair of see-through paper panties (in beige, pink, blue and white) wrapped around the vinyl album itself. It should be pointed out that, while the panties were put on the records instead of the normal paper sleeves, each piece of vinyl was first wrapped in a protective plastic sleeve before the panties were put on. There have also been numerous stories about how the panties did not meet Federal Trade Commission standards on clothing and were confiscated at customs in Canada for this reason. Of course, such stories merely made the band look even more like renegades to teenage fans, so the fact that it occurred (and, if Bob Greene in his book BILLION DOLLAR BABY is to be believed, was perpetrated by Alice's manager Shep Gordon who called the FTC to report the unfitness of the panties) merely turned out to be good publicity for

Part 2: Recordings

the band over all.

REPORT CARD

School's Out	3:26
Luney Tune	3:36
Gutter Cat	4:39
Street Fight	:55
Blue Turk	5:29
My Stars	5:46
Public Animal 9	3:53
Alma Mater	3:39
Grande Finale	4:36
Oral English	
School Music	
Appearance	
Courtesy	

Report Card, which came with the first pressing of SCHOOL'S OUT.

Additional panties would later be dropped into the audience at the July 22, 1972 concert at the Hollywood Bowl. The panties disappeared from the album after the first pressing and a standard paper sleeve was used for later reissues.

One last item was included in the first pressing that has turned up missing from many copies found today by collectors. A 4" by 6" report card was included, which gave the track listings and playing times for all songs on the album. Gutter Cat Vs. the Jets is listed as Gutter Cats on the report card, and Public Animal #9 is listed as Public Animal 9. The report card came only with the initial release of the album and went the way of the panties when the album was reissued later that same year.

SCHOOL'S OUT was later reissued with EASY ACTION in South African as part of a two-vinyl set under the title EASY ACTION (see that album's entries for more information.)

SCHOOL'S OUT reached No. 2 on the US album charts and No. 4 on the UK charts. It also reached Gold status on July 10, 1972. It was later reissued on cassette with BILLION DOLLAR BABIES as part of a TWO ON ONE packaging in Europe (catalog number 23846-4.)

Album Title: **SCHOOL'S OUT**
Released: June 1972 by Warner Brothers.
Catalog No.: BS 2623
Media: Vinyl, 8-Track, Cassette and Reel-to-Reel.

As mentioned above, the first pressing of this album came with the paper panties and a report card, but the back of the album cover is missing the track listing that can be seen on all reissues. The area where the track listing should go is clearly defined on the back of the album, however. Oddly enough, the album would later be reissued in the late 1970's / early 1980's with the back cover again missing the track listing. The initial pressing of the album is a tad darker in color than the reissue that occurred in 1974. It also came with the green WB label.

Album Title: **SCHOOL'S OUT**
Released: July 22, 1972 by Warner Brothers, UK.
Catalog No.: K 56007
Media: Vinyl and Cassette.

The initial UK release of the album also came with the paper panties and the green WB label.

Album Title: **SCHOOL'S OUT**
Released: July 1972 by Warner Brothers, Australia.
Catalog No.: BS-2623
Media: Vinyl.

The initial Australian release came in the flip-top sleeve and with the paper panties. The album reach No. 5 on the Australian charts, the first album to do so.

Album Title: **SCHOOL'S OUT**
Released: July 1972 by Warner Brothers, France.
Catalog No.: 56007
Media: Vinyl.

Came with the flip-top sleeve and the paper panties.

Album Title: **SCHOOL'S OUT**
Released: 1972 by Warner Brothers, Germany.
Catalog No.: WB 56007
Media: Vinyl.

Came in flip-top sleeve and with paper panties. The back of the album cover displays the inside of the school desk.

Album Title: **SCHOOL'S OUT**
Released: 1972 by Warner Brothers, Japan.
Catalog No.: P-8227W
Media: Vinyl.

Came in flip-top sleeve and with paper panties. The back album cover is an ad promoting other albums available, including Bobby Sherman and Joe Cocker.

Album Title: **SCHOOL'S OUT**
Released: 1972 by Warner Brothers, South Africa.
Catalog No.: BS 2623
Media: Vinyl.

The back cover of the album shows the bottom of the desk, but instead of a track listing, the photo of the band from inside the desk is displayed.

Album Title: **SCHOOL'S OUT**
Released: Reissued 1974 by Warner Brothers.
Catalog No.: BS 2623
Media: Vinyl.

While the panties around the vinyl discs were a fun idea, there was no way WB was going to continue to reissue the album in that manner forever. Instead, with this first reissuing of the album, WB replaced the panties and plastic sleeve with a normal square-shaped paper sleeve. This sleeve, as was typical with WB at the time, advertised many of their promotional "sampler" albums available through WB by mail-order, several of which included Alice Cooper tracks in the mix (see Chapter 6 for more details about these albums.)

Also dropped was the report card, while the track listing on the back of the album was added. This list was either painted or airbrushed in for the reissue, and not carved into the desk as the information on the front of the album is. **Street Fight** is not listed on the back of the album. This reissue used the mid-1970's "Palm Tree" WB label.

Album Title: **SCHOOL'S OUT**
Released: Late 1970's by Warner Brothers.
Catalog No.: BS 2623
Media: Vinyl.

This final vinyl reissue of the album in the US not only had the track listing missing from the back of the album, but was also redesigned so that the cover is a standard sleeve and doesn't open up like a desk as on previous pressings. This reissue used the late 1970's beige / white WB label.

Album Title: **SCHOOL'S OUT**
Released: Late 1970's by Warner Brothers, France and distributed to France and Germany.
Catalog No.: WB 56007 (BS2623); also states "Germany Z - France WE 341" on the cover.
Media: Vinyl.

Featured the beige / white WB label. However, the album still opened up as the original packaging did.

Album Title: **SCHOOL'S OUT**
Released: Early 1980's by Warner Brothers, France. Distributed by WEA Filipacchi Music
Catalog No.: 456-007

Media: Cassette.

The full album was cover on the cassette with a bright yellow border.

Album Title: SCHOOL'S OUT
Released: Early 1980's by Warner Brothers, France and distributed to France and Germany.
Catalog No.: K456 007; also states "Germany G - France WE 321" on the cover.
Media: Vinyl and chrome Cassette.

In the early 1980's, the album was released one last time for the French / German market, only this time with a normal sleeve instead of the desk. This last reissue is packaged by WEA as a "Prime Cuts" edition of the album. The back cover shows the contents of the desk from the inside view of the original desk packaging. The cover for the cassette displayed only the contents from the desk.

Album Title: SCHOOL'S OUT
Released: September 16, 1988 by Warner Brothers, Germany.
Catalog No.: WEA 927260-2 (CD) and WEA 927260-4 (cassette)
Media: CD and Cassette.

The first French / German reissue of the album on CD. The cassette version was released February 23, 1988.

Album Title: SCHOOL'S OUT
Released: October 24, 1990 by Warner Brothers.
Catalog No.: WB 2623.2 (CD) and WB 2623.4 (cassette)
Media: CD and Cassette.

The first CD pressing of the album in the US. Released a week after another reissue of the album on cassette on October 17, 1990.

Album Title: SCHOOL'S OUT
Released: 1990 by Warner Brothers, Australia.
Catalog No.: WAR 9272602
Media: CD.

The first CD release of the album in Australia.

Album Title: SCHOOL'S OUT
Released: September 1997 by Warner Brothers, Japan.
Catalog No.: WPCP-3490
Media: CD.

Part of the special "Forever Young Series" that WB released in Japan. The album came with an obi that listed the album's title and additional albums available in the series.

Album Title: SCHOOL'S OUT
Released: October 3, 1997 by Warner Brothers, Canada.
Catalog No.: WARN CD 02623
Media: CD.

The latest reissue of the album, part of mass reissuing of the Alice Cooper catalog in Canada.

Album Title: SCHOOL'S OUT
Released: February 1, 1998 by Warner Brothers, Australia.
Catalog No.: 927260-2
Media: CD.

Part of a group of Alice Cooper albums reissued on CD for the Australian market. Notice that the Australian edition carries the same catalog number as the French / German reissue.

Single Title: **School's Out** (stereo) / **School's Out** (mono)
Released: May 1972 by Warner Brothers.
Catalog No.: 7596
Media: 7" promotional Vinyl.

Promotional radio-only release of the first single from the SCHOOL'S OUT album. As stations were beginning to play rock music on FM channels where stereo could be heard, promotional singles and albums of this type with both mono and stereo versions of songs were quite common. By this time, Warner had switched to their "palm tree" label.

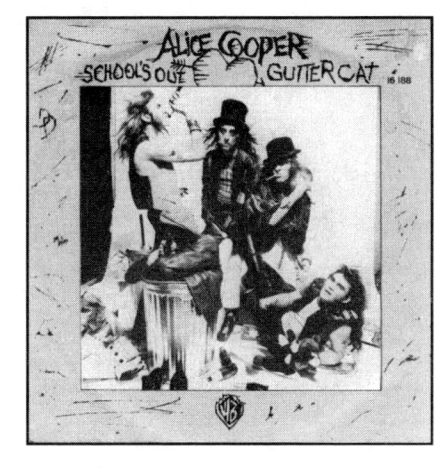

US promo single for School's Out.

Single Title: **School's Out / Gutter Cat Vs. the Jets**
Released: May 1972 by Warner Brothers.
Catalog No.: 7596
Media: 7" Vinyl single.

The first single from the album of the same name, School's Out was actually released a month before the finished album. This wouldn't be a once-only occurrence, as other singles over the years were released before the albums on which they subsequently appeared. As mentioned above, the original working title for the B-side, Gutter Cat Vs. the Jets was Gutter Pussy and an acetate of this single was pressed with the original title crossed out and "Guttercats" written in its place.

The first single in the US to feature a photo cover instead of a normal single sleeve, it featured the photo used inside the SCHOOL'S OUT album cover. The Photo was by Roger Prigent. School's Out reached No. 7 with ten weeks on the US charts. School's Out would also become one of Alice's most famous songs, and has been remade and reissued in countless forms over the years.

Single Title: **School's Out / Gutter Cat Vs. the Jets**
Released: June 1972 by Warner Brothers, UK.
Catalog No.: K 16188
Media: 7" Vinyl.

Picture sleeve, same as US release. School's Out would be the band's first number one single in the UK.

Single Title: **School's Out / Gutter Cat Vs. the Jets**
Released: June 1972 by Warner Brothers, Australia.
Catalog No.: WB-7596
Media: 7" Vinyl.

School's Out reached No. 39 on the Australian charts, and was the first single released since Caught in a Dream back in 1971.

Single Title: **School's Out / Gutter Cat Vs. the Jets**
Released: June 1972 by Warner Brothers, France.
Catalog No.: 16188
Media: 7" Vinyl.

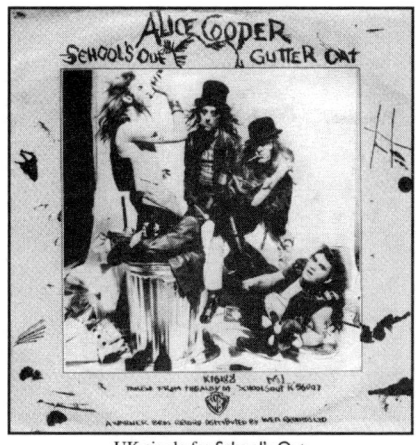

UK single for School's Out.

Picture sleeve, same as the US release.

Single Title: **School's Out / Gutter Cat Vs. the Jets**
Released: June 1972 by Warner Brothers, Germany.
Catalog No.: WB 16188
Media: 7" Vinyl.

This single also came in a picture sleeve, which was a close-up version of the KILLER calendar shot.

Single Title: **School's Out / Gutter Cat Vs. the Jets**
Released: June 1972 by Warner Brothers, Italy.
Catalog No.: JB 34
Media: 7" Vinyl.

One of the few Italian Alice Cooper singles not to follow the catalog number of the UK release.

Single Title: **School's Out / Gutter Cat Vs. the Jets**
Released: June 1972 by Warner Brothers, Japan.
Catalog No.: P-1143W
Media: 7" Vinyl.

Picture sleeve.

Single Title: **School's Out / Gutter Cat Vs. the Jets**
Released: June 1972 by Warner Brothers, Yugoslavia.
Catalog No.: K 16188
Media: 7" Vinyl.

Picture sleeve, same as the US and French release.

Single Title: **School's Out / Elected**
Released: February 1976 by Warner Brothers, UK.
Catalog No.: K 16287
Media: 7" Vinyl.

Reissue single, came with a picture sleeve of the desk as seen on the cover of the SCHOOL'S OUT album.

Single Title: **School's Out/ Elected**
Released: 1985 by Warner Brothers, Germany.
Catalog No.: OG 9519
Media: 7" Vinyl.

Reissued single, released under the Warner Brothers' "Old Gold" label.

Single Title: **School's Out / I'm Eighteen**
Released: 1988 by American Pie, a division of Warner Special Products.
Catalog No.: 9012
Media: 7" Vinyl.

Reissue of School's Out done in the late 1980's as part of a series of the "golden oldies" reissues on 7" vinyl. (Mentioned here to avoid confusion with the regular releases.)

German single for School's Out.

UK reissue single for School's Out.

American Pie reissue of I'm Eighteen and School's Out.

Chapter 1: 1964 - 1974

Single Title: **Elected / Luney Tune**
Released: September 1972 by Warner Brothers.
Catalog No.: WB 7631
Media: 7" Vinyl.

This song was recorded in August 1972 for the BILLION DOLLAR BABIES album. It was released to correspond with the upcoming presidential election occurring that November (which Nixon would win by a landslide, for those interested.) Most of the other songs for BILLION DOLLAR BABIES were still in the works, which explains why the B-side is a track from SCHOOL'S OUT. Releasing the song so far ahead of the album was a calculated risk and it peaked at No. 26 with six weeks on the US charts. It's this mixture of tracks from two different albums that explains why this single appears here in the discography and not following BILLION DOLLAR BABIES. A film was made to promote the single as well, a first for the band. (See Part 4 for more details.)

Single Title: **Elected / Luney Tune**
Released: October 1972 by Warner Brothers, UK.
Catalog No.: K 16214
Media: 7" Vinyl.

Another picture sleeve, only this time of the infamous photo of Alice wearing his snake. Although the single was released five months before the album it would appear on, it reached No. 4 on the UK charts (doing much better than in the US.)

Single Title: **Elected / Luney Tune**
Released: October 1972
by Warner Brothers, Australia.
Catalog No.: WB-7631
Media: 7" Vinyl.

Elected reached No. 83 on the Australian charts.

UK single for Elected using the infamous 'snake' photo.

Single Title: **Elected / Luney Tune**
Released: October 1972 by Warner Brothers, Brazil.
Catalog No.: WBCS 7030
Media: 7" Vinyl.

A promo single of the A-side was also released.

Single Title: **Elected / Luney Tune**
Released: October 1972 by Warner Brothers, France.
Catalog No.: 16214
Media: 7" Vinyl.

Two different picture sleeves were released for this record in France.

Single Title: **Elected / Luney Tune**
Released: October 1972 by Warner Brothers, Germany.
Catalog No.: WB16214
Media: 7" Vinyl.

This single came in another picture sleeve, this one a doctored photo of a bored Alice being sworn in as President. Alice is photograph wearing the same "Christmas wrapping" clothes that can be seen on the cover of the PRIME CUTS videocassette (which was also used for a poster of Alice in 1972 / 1973.)

German single for Elected.

Part 2: Recordings

Single Title: **Elected / Luney Tune**
Released: October 1972 by Warner Brothers, Holland.
Catalog No.: 16214
Media: 7" Vinyl.

Picture sleeve.

Single Title: **Elected / Luney Tune**
Released: October 1972 by Warner Brothers, Italy.
Catalog No.: K 16214
Media: 7" Vinyl.

Same as the UK release.

Single Title: **Elected / Luney Tune**
Released: October 1972 by Warner Brothers, Japan.
Catalog No.: P-1173W
Media: 7" Vinyl.

Picture sleeve, gatefold cover.

Single Title: **Elected / Luney Tune**
Released: October 1972 by Warner Brothers, Portugal.
Catalog No.: N-S-63-23
Media: 7" Vinyl.

Picture sleeve.

Single Title: **Elected / Luney Tune**
Released: October 1972 by Warner Brothers, Yugoslavia.
Catalog No.: K 16214
Media: 7" Vinyl.

Picture sleeve.

Single Title: **Elected / Luney Tune**
Released: 1980 by Warner Brothers, Holland.
Catalog No.: WB 17.536
Media: 7" Vinyl.

Picture sleeve. Part of the Warner Brothers "Oldies Series."

EP Title: **SCHOOL'S OUT EP**
Released: October 1972 by Warner Brothers, UK.
Catalog No.: Unknown.
Media: 12" Vinyl.
Song List: Caught in a Dream / Be My Lover / School's Out / Elected

A relatively unknown phenomenon in the US for rock music by the 1970's, extended play albums were a chance for fans to get the singles from a given album in a cheaper form (instead of paying full-price for an album, you got the just the hits.) This was also a good way to squeeze another dollar (or, rather, anything but a dollar) out of the fans who had to have everything that came out by the band. A similar disc would be done for BILLION DOLLAR BABIES in 1973, MUSCLE OF LOVE in 1974 and WELCOME TO MY NIGHTMARE in 1975.

The cover of the EP is red with the photo from the back

UK extended play for SCHOOL'S OUT. Note that the just released single **Elected** was included on this EP.

Chapter 1: 1964 - 1974

cover of LOVE IT TO DEATH appearing in a centered circle. The song titles appear above the band members in the photo.

Album Title:	**BILLION DOLLAR BABIES**
Recorded:	August and October 1972 at "The Cooper Mansion" in Greenwich, Connecticut; December 1972 at Morgan Studios, London, England; and December 1972 through January 1973 at the Record Plant, New York, NY.
Production:	Produced by Bob Ezrin for Nimbus 9 Productions, Ltd. An Alive Enterprises Inc. Production. "The Cooper Mansion" recordings engineered by Shelly Yakus and Frank Hubach. Morgan Studios recordings engineered by Robin Black and Peter Flanagan. Record Plant recordings engineered by Jack Douglas, Shelly Yakus and Ed Sprigg. Mastered by George Marino at The Cutting Room, New York, NY.
Personnel:	Additional Performers: Bob Ezrin (Piano.) Dick Wagner (Guitar on I Love the Dead.) Steve Hunter (Guitar on I Love the Dead and Generation Landslide among others.) Mick Mashbir (Guitar for most of the album.) Donavan Leitch (additional vocals on Billion Dollar Babies.)
Song List:	Hello Hooray (Rolf Kempf) / Raped and Freezin' (Bruce and Cooper) / Elected (Cooper, Smith, Dunaway, Bruce and Buxton) / Billion Dollar Babies (Cooper, Bruce and R Reggie) / Unfinished Sweet (Cooper, Bruce and Smith) / No More Mister Nice Guy (Bruce and Cooper) / Generation Landslide (Cooper, Bruce, Dunaway, Smith, Buxton) / Sick Things (Ezrin, Cooper and Bruce) / Mary-Ann (Bruce and Cooper) / I Love the Dead (Dick Wagner [not credited], Ezrin, and Cooper)

Coming on the heels of the "extras"-laden SCHOOL'S OUT, BILLION DOLLAR BABIES didn't disappoint Coop fans looking for things to pin up on their wall (whether the walls were padded or not.) The concept and design of the original vinyl version of the album were done by Drew at Pacific Eye & Ear and featured a gatefold cover created to look like a snake-skinned billfold. Opening the album gave fans a folded 22" x 10¾" Billion Dollar bill, which was a piece of art in itself. Featuring a photo of the band in the front center of the bill, the artwork on front and back also contained snakes, Alice being hung, a punk with a switchblade, naked women in makeup, a guy jumping out of a window, and the famous Medusa-head Alice.

The bill fit snugly in a precut strap on the right-hand side of the inner gatefold cover. To the left were perforated photos of each band member, along with photos of the band in concert and in an alternative shot of the inner sleeve cover. If the photos were removed, you would find the credits for the album listed on the inside of the gatefold sleeve. Surprisingly enough, many people didn't take out the photos, so copies of the album with these still intact are actually quite accessible. Finding a copy of the album with the billion-dollar bill, on the other hand, is not quite as easy — especially one that hasn't been manhandled to death over the years.

BILLION DOLLAR BABIES

The inner sleeve contained some full-color photos of the band, including the infamous "baby" photo by world renown photographer David Bailey. This photo — which showcased the band in white, standing in a white bedroom, with white doves in a cage in the background, white rabbits in the band members' hands and Alice holding a crying baby in Alice makeup on top of a pile of money — would become notorious as the most frequently used by Christian crusaders against rock music in later years. The baby was a girl named Lola Pfeiffer, the daughter of Carolyn Pfeiffer, a public relations representative who handled the band's PR in the UK at the time. The other side of the inner sleeve featured lyrics to the songs on the album — a first for an Alice Cooper album, and a standard from this point forward.

Besides the two photos by David Bailey, were photos by Lynn Goldsmith and Neal Preston. When reissued in the mid-1970's, the first thing to go was the dollar bill. A latter reissue, the last in the 1980's, featured the beige / white WB label on the record itself, with no dollar bill and no perforated edges to the photos on the inside gatefold. Since the only way to see the album credits was to take the photos out, with the photos no longer removable, the album ended up being reissued with no credits. Later reissues and foreign pressings would lose the rounded edges of the "wallet" and be issued in normal square album covers with additional snake skin added to take up the additional cover space.

According to Michael Bruce in his book NO MORE MISTER NICE GUY, the basic tracks for all songs except Hello Hooray and Generation Landside were recorded at the estate in Connecticut that the band was sharing at the time. Time was then spent at the Record Plant in New York before completing most of the album in England. It was then decided to add another track to the album and Generation Landslide was finished at the Record Plant in the last few days of recording.

By this time, Glen Buxton began having noticeable health problems, sometimes leaving him unable to perform in concert and in the studio. It was at this point that Mick Mashbir was asked to perform with the band on the album and the subsequent tour. Mashbir would continue in this role off and on through the remainder of the time that the Alice Cooper Group was together.

While in England, a jam session was held in the studio with guest performers such as Keith Moon, Rick Grech, Marc Bolan, Donavan and Harry Nilsson. Although hopes were that such a collection of talented performers would lead to some exciting tracks for the album, it instead ended up, to all concerned, as a drunken — all be it fun — waste of time (which seems the only logical conclusion since Moon and Nilsson particularly were notorious for their excessive drinking at the time.)

The only guest performer who made it onto the album was Donavan, who shares vocals with Alice on Billion Dollar Babies. While recordings remain of the "superstar" session, it's been suggested by those who have heard them that they're not worthy of being released in any form.

Elected is a revised version of "Reflected" from the band's first album, PRETTIES FOR YOU, which was rewritten between the US and European portions of the KILLER concert tour (and performed during the final days of the tour in Germany.) Elected was the first single off of the album to be released (coming actually nearly four months before the release of the album), and was also the first single to have a conceptual promotional film (or music video) made for it by the band. The film features predominately Alice in the role of campaigning for office through the streets of a busy city and at a rally. The film then cuts to Alice behind a desk, with money and phones decorating it, trying desperately to answer all the phones at once. As can be seen from the film, the focus is more on Alice Cooper, the man, and less on Alice Cooper, the group (in fact, a roller-skating chimpanzee is seen more in the film than the other band members.) This film would first been seen on American television during the infamous IN CONCERT appearance from 1972 (see entry in Part 4.)

Hello Hooray (for which a promotional film was also made) was the only song on the album not written or co-written by a member of the band, and was originally recorded by Judy Collins. There are also rumors that Mary-Ann was originally written as a protest song about the Vietnam War, with the original title being "Uncle Sam."

Raped and Freezin' carried its own problems (its title) and promo copies of the album given to radio stations were known to have been marked (and sometimes altered) to make sure that DJs didn't play the track on the air.

I Love the Dead was the first song co-written for Alice by guitarist Dick Wagner. In a fix for funds, Wagner readily sold his rights to the song, which is why he is not credited on the tune.

An album that many fans consider being THE classic album by the band, BILLION DOLLAR BABIES, reached No. 1 in both the US and the UK, and reached Gold status three months after its release. The album was certified Platinum on October 13, 1986.

BILLION DOLLAR BABIES was reissued in 1974 as a Quadraphonic release, with alternative music and lyrics in the remix. (See the entry below for more details.) Finally, BILLION DOLLAR BABIES was reissued in the latter 1970's on cassette with SCHOOL'S OUT as part of a TWO ON ONE package (catalog number 23846-4.)

Album Title: **BILLION DOLLAR BABIES**
Released: January 1973 by Warner Brothers Records, Inc.
Catalog No.: BS 2685
Media: Vinyl, Cassette, 8-Track and Reel-to-Reel.

The original pressing of this album was released with the green WB label. It was the last Cooper album to be released with this label. All reissues in 1974 through 1979 featured the "Palm Tree" label, followed by the beige / white WB from the later of 1980's onward. As mentioned above, the first pressing contained the perforated photos, the dollar bill and the inner sleeve with the color photo and lyrics. Also, as mentioned, the album had rounded edges on the cover to simulate those of a wallet.

Album Title: **BILLION DOLLAR BABIES**
Released: March 24, 1973 by Warner Brothers, UK.
Catalog No.: K 56013 (vinyl) and K456013 (cassette)
Media: Vinyl and Cassette.

Released in the same format as the US version, including the green WB label, the photos, the color sleeve and the dollar bill. The cassette cover also displayed the pictures from the inside of the vinyl gatefold cover, only in black and white.

Album Title: **BILLION DOLLAR BABIES**
Released: March 1974 by Warner Brothers, Australia.
Catalog No.: BS-2685
Media: Vinyl.

Came with the gatefold cover, the dollar bill and the perforated cards. The album reached No. 4 on the Australian charts.

Album Title: **BILLION DOLLAR BABIES**
Released: March 1974 by Warner Brothers, France.
Catalog No.: 56013
Media: Vinyl.

Came in a normal gatefold sleeve with perforated cards and the dollar bill.

Album Title: **BILLION DOLLAR BABIES**
Released: March 1974 by Warner Brothers, Germany.
Catalog No.: WB 56013
Media: Vinyl.

Came in a normal gatefold sleeve with perforated cards and the dollar bill.

Album Title: **BILLION DOLLAR BABIES**
Released: 1974 by Warner Brothers, Japan.
Catalog No.: P-8322W
Media: Vinyl.

First Japanese pressing of this album.

Album Title: **BILLION DOLLAR BABIES**
Released: 1974 by Warner Brothers, South Africa.
Catalog No.: BS 2685
Media: Vinyl.

Came in a gatefold cover.

Album Title: **BILLION DOLLAR BABIES**
Released: Late 1970's by Warner Brothers, UK.
Catalog No.: K56013 (BX 2685)
Media: Vinyl.

Reissue of the album in a square gatefold cover (no rounded corners as on the original pressing.) No bill was enclosed and the photos on the inside were not perforated. The back of the album did list album credits, which is very unique (none of the other later reissues on vinyl printed the credits elsewhere, leaving them off completely.) The album came with the beige / white WB label.

Album Title: **BILLION DOLLAR BABIES**
Released: Late 1970's by Warner Brothers, France. Distributed through France and Germany.
Catalog No.: K56013 (S 40 396)
Media: Vinyl.

Late 1970's reissue of the album for France and Germany. The album cover was a normal single sleeve.

Album Title: **BILLION DOLLAR BABIES**
Released: August 10, 1989 by Warner Brothers, Germany.
Catalog No.: WEA 927269-2, WEA 927269-4
Media: CD and Cassette.

First French / German reissue of the album on CD.

Album Title: **BILLION DOLLAR BABIES**
Released: October 24, 1990 by Warner Brothers.
Catalog No.: WB 2685.2 (CD) and WB 2685.4 (cassette)
Media: CD and Cassette.

First CD pressing of the album in the US. Released a week after another reissue of the album on cassette on October 17, 1990.

Album Title: **BILLION DOLLAR BABIES**
Released: 1990 by Warner Brothers, Australia.
Catalog No.: WAR 26852
Media: CD.

First CD release of the album in Australia.

Album Title: **BILLION DOLLAR BABIES**
Released: September 1997 by Warner Brothers, Japan.
Catalog No.: WPCP-3491
Media: CD.

Part of the special "Forever Young Series" WB released in Japan. The album came with an obi that listed the album's title and additional albums available in the series.

Album Title: **BILLION DOLLAR BABIES**
Released: October 3, 1997 by Warner Brothers, Canada.
Catalog No.: WARN CD 02685
Media: CD.

Latest reissue of the album, part of a mass reissuing of the Alice Cooper catalog in Canada.

Single Title: **Slick Black Limousine** (Dunaway) / excepts from the **BILLION DOLLAR BABIES** album
Released: February 1973 by New Music Express, London, England.
Catalog No.: LYN 2585
Media: 7" flexi-disc.
Personnel: Additional performer: Mick Mashbir (lead guitar, replacing Glen Buxton).

In honor of toping three fan polls in the well known music newspaper NEW MUSIC EXPRESS, the band decided to show its thanks by allowing NME to release a studio recorded track on a flexi-disc to be given away with copies of the February 17, 1973 issue of NEW MUSIC EXPRESS. The song, written by Dennis Dunaway, was recorded by the band during the BILLION DOLLAR BABIES recording sessions and featured Mick

Slick Black Limousine flexi-disc from NME.

Mashbir playing lead guitar with the rest of the band. It has not been released officially in any other form, but does exist on a few bootlegs. The February 17 issue of NME also contained a short article about the song and why the band was allowing it to appear with that particular issue of the newspaper.

Single Title:	**Hello, Hooray** (Mono) /
	Hello, Hooray (stereo)
Released:	January 1973 by Warner Brothers.
Catalog No.:	WB 7673
Media:	7" promotional Vinyl.

A radio-only promotional single released to correspond with the commercial release of the single. As with all promotional singles, the label used was a pure white WB label.

Single Title:	**Hello, Hooray / Generation Landslide**
Released:	February 1973 by Warner Brothers.
Catalog No.:	WB 7673
Media:	7" Vinyl.

While there was some initial talk of releasing **No More Mr. Nice Guy** as the first single, it was decided to go with Hello, Hooray. Hello, Hooray quickly fell off the charts after only three weeks, reaching No. 35 at its peak on the US.

Warner Brothers promo 45 for Hello, Hooray. Note that the song title is misspelled.

Single Title:	**Hello, Hooray / Generation Landslide**
Released:	February 1973 by Warner Brothers, UK.
Catalog No.:	K 16248
Media:	7" Vinyl.

The first UK single to be released almost simultaneously with its US counterpart, it would gain a much higher ranking there than in the States, reaching a high of No. 6 on the charts.

Single Title:	**Hello, Hooray / Generation Landslide**
Released:	February 1973 by Warner Brothers, Australia.
Catalog No.:	WB-7673
Media:	7" Vinyl.

Hello, Hooray reached No. 95 on the Australian charts.

Single Title:	**Hello, Hooray / Generation Landslide**
Released:	February 1973 by Warner Brothers, France.
Catalog No.:	16248
Media:	7" Vinyl.

The single was released in a picture sleeve of Alice in concert, in top hat, tails and ready to hit one of the giant balloons used during the show.

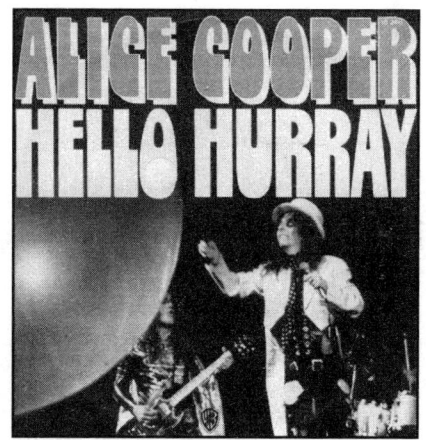

French single for Hello, Hooray.

Single Title:	**Hello, Hooray / Generation Landslide**
Released:	February 1973 by Warner Brothers, Germany.
Catalog No.:	WB 16248
Media:	7" Vinyl.

Picture sleeve, with photo of Alice in concert with a snake.

German single for Hello, Hooray.

Single Title: **Hello, Hooray / Generation Landslide**
Released: February 1973 by Warner Brothers, Holland.
Catalog No.: WB 16248
Media: 7" Vinyl.

Two different picture sleeves were used for this single.

Single Title: **Hello, Hooray / Generation Landslide**
Released: February 1973 by Warner Brothers, Italy.
Catalog No.: K 16248
Media: 7" Vinyl.

Same as the UK release with the same catalog number.

Single Title: **Hello, Hooray / Generation Landslide**
Released: February 1973 by Warner Brothers, Japan.
Catalog No.: P-1200W
Media: 7" Vinyl.

Picture sleeve.

Single Title: **Hello, Hooray / Generation Landslide**
Released: February 1973 by Warner Brothers, Portugal.
Catalog No.: N-S-63-31
Media: 7" Vinyl.

Holland single for Hello, Hooray.

Picture sleeve.

Single Title: **Hello, Hooray / Generation Landslide**
Released: February 1973 by Warner Brothers, Yugoslavia.
Catalog No.: K 16248
Media: 7" Vinyl.

Picture sleeve.

Single Title: **No More Mr. Nice Guy** (stereo) / **No More Mr. Nice Guy** (mono)
Released: April 1973 by Warner Brothers.
Catalog No.: WB 7691
Media: 7" promotional Vinyl.

A radio-only promotional single released to correspond with the commercial single. Released on the promo-only white WB label.

Single Title: **No More Mr. Nice Guy / Raped and Freezin'**
Released: April 1973 by Warner Brothers.
Catalog No.: WB 7691
Media: 7" Vinyl.

Released without a picture sleeve, No More Mr. Nice Guy would become a concert standard for Alice and one of the songs that Alice would be remembered for over the years. This would be the last single released with the green WB label. No More Mr. Nice Guy reached No. 25, with eight weeks on the US charts.

Single Title: **No More Mr. Nice Guy / Raped and Freezin'**
Released: April 1973 by Warner Brothers, UK.
Catalog No.: K 16262
Media: 7" Vinyl.

Same as the US release. No More Mr. Nice Guy reached No. 10 on the UK charts.

Single Title: **No More Mr. Nice Guy / Raped and Freezin'**
Released: April 1973 by Warner Brothers, Australia.
Catalog No.: WB-7691
Media: 7" Vinyl.

No More Mr. Nice Guy did not chart in Australia.

Single Title: **No More Mr. Nice Guy / Raped and Freezin'**
Released: April 1973 by Warner Brothers, Brazil.
Catalog No.: WBCS 7049
Media: 7" Vinyl.

A promo single of the A-side was also released.

Single Title: **No More Mr. Nice Guy / Raped and Freezin'**
Released: April 1973 by Warner Brothers, France.
Catalog No.: 16262
Media: 7" Vinyl.

Picture sleeve of the BILLION DOLLAR BABIES wallet cover, with a close-up of the gold coin encircled by a string of pearls from the cover.

Single Title: **No More Mr. Nice Guy / Raped and Freezin'**
Released: April 1973 by Warner Brothers, Germany.
Catalog No.: 16262
Media: 7" Vinyl.

Picture sleeve.

Single Title: **No More Mr. Nice Guy / Raped and Freezin'**
Released: April 1973 by Warner Brothers, Holland.
Catalog No.: 16262
Media: 7" Vinyl.

Picture sleeve.

French single for No More Mr. Nice Guy.

Single Title: **No More Mr. Nice Guy / Raped and Freezin'**
Released: April 1973 by Warner Brothers, Italy.
Catalog No.: K 16262
Media: 7" Vinyl.

Same as the US release.

Single Title: **No More Mr. Nice Guy / Raped and Freezin'**
Released: April 1973 by Warner Brothers, Japan.
Catalog No.: P12222W
Media: 7" Vinyl.

Picture sleeve.

Single Title: **No More Mr. Nice Guy / Raped and Freezin'**
Released: April 1973 by Warner Brothers, Portugal.
Catalog No.: N-S-63-40
Media: 7" Vinyl.

Picture sleeve.

Single Title: **Billion Dollar Babies** (stereo) / **Billion Dollar Babies** (mono)
Released: July 1973 by Warner Brothers.
Catalog No.: 7724
Media: 7" promotional Vinyl.

A radio-only promotional single released to correspond with the commercial of the single. Released on the promo-only white WB label.

Single Title: **Billion Dollar Babies / Mary-Ann**
Released: July 1973 by Warner Brothers.
Catalog No.: 7724
Media: 7" Vinyl.

The first Alice Cooper single to be released on the "Palm Tree" WB label, it was also the first single in quite a while not to have a UK counterpart. Billion Dollar Babies reached No. 57 on the US charts.

Single Title: **Billion Dollar Babies / Halo of Flies**
Released: August 1973 by Warner Brothers, France.
Catalog No.: 16307
Media: 7" Vinyl.

This single comes in a beautiful picture sleeve that shows Alice in concert with Neal Smith behind the drums (Smith is obscured behind the title information.) The catalog number is printed as 16 307 on the sleeve and 16307 on the label. Halo of Flies is the complete version (rather lengthy for a single.) Why a song from KILLER is used for the B-side of the Billion Dollar Babies single is another question, however.

French single for Billion Dollar Babies.

Chapter 1: 1964 - 1974

Single Title: **Billion Dollar Babies / Halo of Flies**
Released: August 1973 by Warner Brothers, Germany.
Catalog No.: WB 16307
Media: 7" Vinyl.

This single came in picture sleeve showing the snakeskin wallet and the gold BILLION DOLLAR BABIES coin (a slight variation of the sleeve used for the French No More Mr. Nice Guy single released earlier in the year.) As with the French single release of the A-side, Halo of Flies is again the B-side.

German single for Billion Dollar Babies.

Single Title: **Billion Dollar Babies / Mary Ann**
Released: August 1973 by Warner Brothers, Portugal.
Catalog No.: N-S-65-47
Media: 7" Vinyl.

Black and white photo of Alice on the purple-colored single sleeve.

Portugal single for Billion Dollar Babies.

Single Title: **School's Out / No More Mr. Nice Guy / Elected / Billion Dollar Babies**
Released: July 1973 by Warner Brothers, UK.
Catalog No.: K16409
Media: 7" Vinyl.

EP Title: **BILLION DOLLAR BABIES EP**
Released: July 1973 by Warner Brothers.
Catalog No.: LLP 208
Media: 7" Vinyl.
Song List: Billion Dollar Babies / No More Mr. Nice Guy / Mary-Ann / Raped and Freezin'

The cover of the EP shows the inner sleeve photo from the album. The words "ALICE COOPER - BILLION DOLLAR BABIES" appear above that and "Stereo Album" appears in the upper right- and left-hand corners of the EP cover. See the entry for SCHOOL'S OUT EP listed above for more details.

Album Title: **BILLION DOLLAR BABIES - QUADRADISC**
Released: 1974 by Warner Brothers.
Catalog No.: QS 0638
Media: Vinyl.
Production: Remixed by Jack Richardson for Nimbus 9 Productions.

By the beginning 1970's, young people were getting deadly serious about their stereo equipment. The best needles, the best tweeters, the ability to turn your house into one giant speaker — anything and everything was important to the rock music fan who had the money to spend. Although one speaker was for a long time deemed acceptable for listening to music, mono was now being frowned upon. The next question was — could stereo be turned into something more? Why stop at two speakers when you could make it four speakers? Quadraphonic sound was introduced into the rock age, but only lasted a few years, once the record companies realized that most people were quite happy with two speakers, thank you very much.

Two Alice Cooper albums were reissued in quadraphonic during the 1970's: BILLION DOLLAR BABIES and MUSCLE OF LOVE. The most noteworthy aspect of the quadraphonic releases was that they were remixed, making them unique entities in the Alice Cooper catalog.

Evidently, alternative recordings were sometimes used for the quadraphonic releases, and remixing altered tracks to emphasize various instruments and vocals that couldn't easily be heard on the stereo versions. Mary-Ann, for instance, sounds different, while Raped and Freezin' includes alternative lyrics. Sick Things not only has a vastly different beginning, but also an extended drum ending, while additional guitar work can be heard on I Love the Dead. Of course, listening to these quadraphonic albums on a stereo player you don't really hear the album as it was recorded, since the playback mix won't be what was heard by the people doing the remix.

The quadraphonic version of BILLION DOLLAR BABIES was ripped-off in its entirety as a bogus "demos and rehearsals" bootleg called FEARLESS, which has been reissued under various other titles since then (see Chapter 6 for more details.)

Album Title: **SCHOOL DAYS**
Recorded: Recorded in 1968 and 1969 as the albums PRETTIES FOR YOU and EASY ACTION.
Released: March 1973 by Warner Brothers, France, Germany, UK and Australia.
Catalog No.: WB 66 021/1 and WB 66 021/2 for vinyl and WB 44 6021/1 and WB 44 6021/2 for cassette (German and French release); K 56013 (UK vinyl release), K4666021 (UK cassette release); and 2WS-2549 (Australian vinyl release.)
Media: Double-Vinyl and double-Cassette.
Song List: Side One: Titanic Overture / 10 Minutes Before the Worm / Sing Low, Sweet Cheerio / Today Mueller / Living / Fields of Regret; Side Two: No Longer Umpire / Levity Ball / B. B. On Mars / Reflected / Apple Bush / Earwigs to Eternity / Changing, Arranging; Side Three: Mr. And Misdemeanor / Shoe Salesman / Still No Air / Below Your Means; Side Four: Return of the Spiders / Laughing at Me / Refrigerator Heaven / Beautiful Flyaway / Lay Down and Die, Goodbye

The album cover for this reissue of the first two studio albums features Alice himself prominently on the cover. In the four corners of the album are additional photos of the other band members (each in his own corner.) This Warner Brothers package has the "Palm Tree" Warner Brothers label on the vinyl. The packaging included text inside the gatefold cover with responses to questions by Alice. Also listed is additional information about the two albums, including when they were recorded and released, although the year of release for both albums is incorrectly given as 1970. The inner sleeves advertised numerous other artists and featured the cover artwork for LOVE IT TO DEATH, KILLER, SCHOOL'S OUT, BILLION DOLLAR BABIES and (oddly enough) SCHOOL DAYS.

This package was produced in response to the increased popularity of the band by 1973, and since Germany had never seen domestic releases for either PRETTIES FOR YOU or EASY ACTION, it was a opportunity to earn additional revenue from these two albums. Since the originals were long out of print in the UK, it made sense to release SCHOOL DAYS there as well. In the late 1970's, SCHOOL DAYS would occasional show up in the racks at used record stores in the US. As a reissue special package, the album did not chart.

Album Title: **MUSCLE OF LOVE**
Recorded: September - October 1973 at the Record Plant, New York City, New York; Sunset Sound, Hollywood, California (for the Pointer Sisters backing vocals on Teenage Lament '74 and Working Up a Sweat.) A & R Recording Studios, New York City, New York (for orchestrations) and "The Cooper Mansion," Greenwich, Connecticut.
Production: Produced by Jack Richardson and Jack Douglas for Nimbus 9 Productions, Ltd. An Alive Enterprises Inc. Production. Recording engineer was Phil Ramone (for orchestrations recorded at A & R Recording Studios) and Jack Douglas. Recording Technicians were Reed Stanley, Dennis Ferrante and Ed Sprigg. Mastered by Doug Sax at the Mastering Lab, Hollywood, California. Strings and Horns arranged by MacMillan.
Personnel: Additional Performers: Dick Wagner (Guitar.) Saul Prestopino (banjo on Crazy Little Child.) Bob Dolin (keyboards.) Mick Mashbir (Guitar, replacing Glen Buxton.) Backing vocals: Liza Minnelli (Teenage Lament '74 and Man With the Golden Gun), Noma and Sarah La Belle (Teenage Lament '74), Ronnie Spector (Teenage Lament '74), the Pointer Sisters (Teenage Lament '74 and Working Up a Sweat), Bob Greene (Hard Hearted Alice and Woman Machine.) Additional backing vocals by Stu Day, Bob Dolin, Dennis Ferrante, "The Big Cheese," Joe Gannon and Dave Libert with Dolly

Song List: Big Apple Dreamin' (Hippo) (Cooper, Bruce, Buxton, Dunaway and Smith) / Never Been Sold Before (Cooper, Bruce, Dunaway, Smith and Buxton) / Hard Hearted Alice (Cooper and Bruce) / Crazy Little Child (Cooper and Bruce) / Muscle of Love (Cooper and Bruce) / Man with the Golden Gun (Cooper, Bruce, Dunaway, Smith and Buxton) / Teenage Lament '74 (Cooper and Smith) / Woman Machine (Cooper, Bruce, Dunaway, Smith and Buxton)

There comes a time in every successful band's career when one album manages to get away from them. With the success that came Alice Cooper's way after SCHOOL'S OUT and BILLION DOLLAR BABIES (not to mention LOVE IT TO DEATH), the band was able to choose who they wanted to appear on their new album, and how the album was going to sound.

This led to an album where the band members rarely even saw each other in the studio. The bonus of having "guest stars" appear on the album was offset by the incredible logistics problems involved in having a choir for one song (Teenage Lament '74) being pieced together from recordings made over a period of several weeks and and at several different locations — the time and money involved led to a beautiful sounding choir, but produced nothing that uniquely presented any of the individual guest stars. While the publicity of such guest performers worked (take for example the photos of Liza Minnelli with Alice when she was in the studio for a short time), it did little to help shape the album into a whole in the manner of the three preceding studio albums. In fact, if anything, MUSCLE OF LOVE resembles the first two Cooper albums — EASY ACTION and PRETTIES FOR YOU — in that there is no coherent conceptual thread running through the album (some may argue that the album is about sex, but, even there, only about 50% of the album addresses that theme.) MUSCLE OF LOVE is also a detour from the horror-tinged makings of BILLION DOLLAR BABIES and SCHOOL'S OUT. Instead, this album's tracks go off in many different directions, which ultimately undermines the general feel of the album. That's certainly not to say that there aren't any great songs on the album, as there certainly are. It's just that the album rarely jibes into a consistency until somewhere after its midpoint.

When ideas were first being tossed around for the band to do a theatrical film (ultimately released as GOOD TO SEE YOU AGAIN, ALICE COOPER), the title MUSCLE OF LOVE was suggested, but not used. When the initial title of the new studio album, A KISS AND A FIST, was rejected, the album took on the film's original title.

The 'before' and 'after' photos from the inner sleeves of MUSCLE OF LOVE.

MUSCLE OF LOVE was the first Cooper album completely produced by Jack Richardson, who, as the head of Nimbus 9 Productions, contributed to the productions of LOVE IT TO DEATH, SCHOOL'S OUT, and BILLION DOLLAR BABIES (on the first two of which he acted as executive producer.) Bob Ezrin was originally slated to produce this album as he had the past three, but withdrew from the project after only a few days in the studio. Also in on the production was Jack Douglas, who would go on to work with many other rock performers over the years, including John Lennon and Aerosmith.

Both Bob Dolin and Mick Mashbir became more involved with the band for this album and on the short tour which followed. Dolin, on keyboards, was essentially taking over for the departed Ezrin, while Mashbir took over lead guitar from Glen Buxton. Dick Wagner, a musician who had become a regular fixture in the studio with Ezrin for some time, would go on to co-write some of the songs on WELCOME TO MY NIGHTMARE, and also to tour with Alice in the mid-1970's.

Teenage Lament '74 was the first single released from the album and would be the second and last conceptual music clip filmed by the band for promotional purposes. The film shows the band breaking out of jail, dressed in prison garb. After avoiding being captured, they arrive at a hall and finish the song on stage.

Big Apple Dreamin' (Hippo), as one might guess, is about New York. The song was originally titled Hippopotamus, to tie in with a New York club of the same name which the band would frequent when in the area.

In his book BILLION DOLLAR BABY, Bob Greene spends an entire chapter discussing his time in the studio recording backing vocals for **Never Been Sold Before** and **Woman Machine**. However, this doesn't necessarily mean that he can be heard on the album in its finished form (he could have been mixed out at a later point in time.)

Woman Machine grew out of a song performed in the Nazz days called **Mr. Machine**. The voice heard at the end of the track (which is also the end of the album) is that of Alice reading from the technical section of an Ampex tape recorder manual.

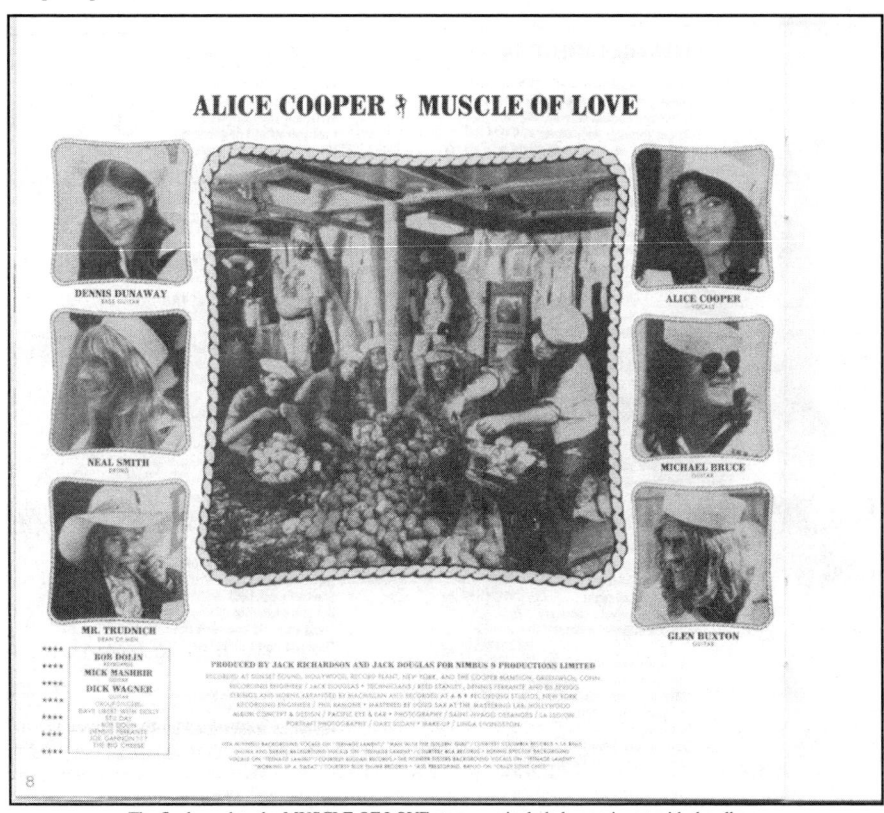

The final panel to the MUSCLE OF LOVE story was included as an insert with the album.

Man With the Golden Gun started as an idea by Alice to write a song to be used for the (at the time) next James Bond movie. This was made possible by the fact that the ending credits for the most recent Bond movie, LIVE AND LET DIE, stated that Bond would be back in THE MAN WITH THE GOLDEN GUN (such teasers were the norm for the Bond films — at least until they ran out of Bond novels and short story titles to base them on.) Perhaps, since the Bond producers had used Paul McCartney (a rock musician) for the theme song of LIVE AND LET DIE — and the fact that the band members were not only fans of the movie series, but had also developed a secret agent theme in their song **Halo of Flies** — Alice believed that after writing the song the Bond producers would just have to use it for the next film. Instead, Don Black, who co-wrote the themes for THUNDERBALL and DIAMONDS ARE FOREVER, was hired on and Lulu sang the theme (the movie was released in mid-December 1974.) In view of singers used for the previous Bond movies, Lulu certainly made more sense than the still-thought-of-as-a-freak Alice Cooper. It's a shame in a way, since not only is Man With the Golden Gun one of the more thoroughly developed songs on the album, but the orchestration is so reminiscent of the Bond themes that it would have fit perfectly into the mix if it had been chosen. Ironically, Alice would mention James Bond in Identity Crisis, the theme to his movie MONSTER DOG.

Of all the songs on the album, only two (Muscle of Love and Teenage Lament '74) would pop up in the set lists of concert tours after the brief tour in support of MUSCLE OF LOVE (and then not until 1990 and 1996 respectively.)

Demos from the MUSCLE OF LOVE recording sessions have, like most of those for the other early albums, been circulating in fandom for some time. Teenage Lament '74 has some different lyrics, while Muscle of Love is referred to as Respect for the Sleepers and had completely different lyrics in its early stages. Working Up a Sweat and Hard Hearted Alice also have many different lyrics, and Never Been Sold Before has different music. Finally, a song sung by Neal Smith called Baby, Please Don't Stop was recorded as a demo and would eventually be used by Smith on his solo project PLATINUM GOD (see Chapter 6 for more details.)

MUSCLE OF LOVE originally came in the most complex packaging of any Cooper album and was developed by the band's now-standard album cover designers, Pacific Eye and Ear. The outside of the packaging was an album-sized cardboard holder, printed to look like a shipping box. This was accomplished by printing "Fragile" and "Attention: This Carton Contains One (1) ALICE COOPER MUSCLE OF LOVE," and by including grease stain marks on the front cover (which may have deterred one or two fans from buying the album at the time in fear of getting damaged goods.)

The box opened up in back to reveal a full-color inner sleeve (no normal cardboard album sleeve was included) that pictured the band as sailors on leave outside the "Institute of Nude Wrestling." The photos are made to be looked at as a "before and after" situation, with the front cover showing the sailors on the town, while the back cover shows them semiconscious and bleeding after their night on the town. The two photos were by Saint-Jivago Desanges of La Legion. Other posed photos from this shoot would turn up in public later, including one of Neal Smith giving the finger to the camera in the magazine CIRCUS PIN UPS VOLUME 1, and a photo of all five band members doing a chorus line kick which appears as a poster in the background of one scene in the movie GOOD TO SEE YOU AGAIN, ALICE COOPER. The photos were considered scandalous in South Africa and the album was not released there until it was repackaged without the offending material.

Also included in the packaging was a fold-out that listed the song titles and album credits, along with additional portrait shots of the band members (and the short person in the inner sleeve photos, who is listed as Mr. Trudnich, Dean of Men, although that name was merely made up for the album insert) and a photo of the band in the galley of a ship, peeling potatoes and recovering from their hi-jinks of the night before. The portrait photos were by Gary Sloan. Linda Livingston is listed in the credits as doing make-up for the photos, a credit not seen on any of the previous Alice Cooper albums.

You were supposed to be able to take the album insert and fold it in such a way that it could be used as a book cover for school books. However, the directions were so meager that it's hard to see how anyone could've got it to work properly if they tried to use it in this fashion. It's hard to find the album with the insert intact, since once the package was opened, it became increasingly difficult to keep the album in proper shape without damaging the insert.

Foreign editions of MUSCLE OF LOVE were released in different formats. It's known that the original German and Brazilian editions of the album were released in a regular album sleeve, with the photos from the inner sleeve used for the cover, while, the Mexican and French versions were released in regular album sleeves using a reproduction of the box cover. The New Zealand edition of MUSCLE OF LOVE came in the box, but the printing on the box (including the water / grease stain at the bottom of the front cover) is darker and sharper than the US / UK edition. Finally, there are known misprints of the box cover which have the printing off center, causing some writing from the front cover to appear on the back and vice versa.

MUSCLE OF LOVE was the last new studio album to feature all five original members of the Alice Cooper Group. It was also the first Cooper album to be released on the "Palm Tree" Warner Brothers label (reissues and the SCHOOL DAYS package were also on the "Palm Tree" label, but MUSCLE OF LOVE was the first case of the initial release of a Cooper album appearing with this particular label.)

Two important reissues of this album have occurred since its initial release: a Quadraphonic remix (like the remix done for BILLION DOLLAR BABIES) was released in 1974 (see the entry below), and MUSCLE OF LOVE was later reissued as part of a two vinyl disc set with LACE AND WHISKEY in 1978 as A MAN CALLED ALICE

(see the entry below.)

MUSCLE OF LOVE reached No. 10 on the US charts and No. 34 on the UK charts, and was certified Gold within a month of its release.

Album Title: **MUSCLE OF LOVE**
Released: November 1973 by Warner Brothers.
Catalog No.: BS 2748
Media: Vinyl, 8-Track, Cassette and Reel-to-Reel.

As listed above, the packaging of this release is somewhat odd, and finding it complete and in good shape is a bit harder to do.

Album Title: **MUSCLE OF LOVE**
Released: January 12, 1974 by Warner Brothers, UK.
Catalog No.: K 56018
Media: Vinyl and Cassette.

Same as the US release.

Album Title: **MUSCLE OF LOVE**
Released: January 1974 by Warner Brothers, Argentina.
Catalog No.: 50-14165
Media: Vinyl.

Came in a cardboard box sleeve and with an additional insert.

Album Title: **MUSCLE OF LOVE**
Released: January 1974 by Warner Brothers, Australia.
Catalog No.: BS-2748
Media: Vinyl.

Same as the US release. The album reached No. 36 on the Australian charts.

Album Title: **MUSCLE OF LOVE**
Released: January 1974 by Warner Brothers, Germany.
Catalog No.: WB 56018
Media: Vinyl.

Album Title: **MUSCLE OF LOVE**
Released: January 1974 by Warner Brothers, Japan.
Catalog No.: P-8404W
Media: Vinyl.

Came in a standard cardboard box sleeve with an insert. Also came with obi.

Album Title: **MUSCLE OF LOVE**
Released: 1989 by Metal Blade.
Catalog No.: 9 26447-2 (CD) and 9 26447-4 (cassette)
Media: CD and Cassette.

First US release of the album on CD. Metal Blade put a bit of work into the production of these CD Cooper reissues — of which there are three (MUSCLE OF LOVE, LACE AND WHISKEY and FROM THE INSIDE) — and the album not only came with a booklet that featured many photos and liner credits used for the original vinyl release, but also with a page of notes from Alice himself about the making of the album. Unfortunately, with

Autographed MUSCLE OF LOVE CD.
From the Bryan Erikson collection.

the demise of Metal Blade, only these three albums were released.

Album Title: **MUSCLE OF LOVE**
Released: December 3, 1990 by Warner Brothers, Germany.
Catalog No.: 7599-26226-2, 7599-26226-4
Media: CD and Cassette.

First French / German reissue of the album on CD.

Album Title: **MUSCLE OF LOVE**
Released: 1990 by Warner Brothers, Australia.
Catalog No.: WAR 9262262
Media: CD.

First Australian reissue of the album on CD.

Album Title: **MUSCLE OF LOVE**
Released: September 1997 by Warner Brothers, Japan.
Catalog No.: WPCP-3495
Media: CD.

Part of the special "Forever Young Series" that WB released in Japan. The album came with an obi that listed the album's title and additional albums available in the series.

Single Title: **Teenage Lament '74** (stereo) /
Teenage Lament '74 (mono)
Released: November 1973 by Warner Brothers.
Catalog No.: WB 7762
Media: 7" Vinyl.

A radio-only promotional single released to correspond with the commercial single. Released on the promo-only white WB label.

Single Title: **Teenage Lament '74** /
Hard Hearted Alice
Released: November 1973 by Warner Brothers.
Catalog No.: WB 7762
Media: 7" Vinyl.

As with previous albums, the first single from MUSCLE OF LOVE was released a month ahead of the album. Teenage Lament '74 reached No. 48 on the US charts.

Single Title: **Teenage Lament '74** (stereo) /
Teenage Lament '74 (mono)
Released: November 1973 by Warner Brothers, UK.
Catalog No.: K 16345
Media: 7" Vinyl.

1990 Japanese album reissues.

A radio-only promotional single released to correspond with the commercial single. Released on the promo-only white WB label.

Single Title: **Teenage Lament '74 / Hard Hearted Alice**
Released: January 1974 by Warner Brothers, UK.
Catalog No.: K 16345
Media: 7" Vinyl.

Aside from the catalog number, this is the same as the US edition. Following the trend set by earlier singles, Teenage Lament '74 would do better in the UK than the US, reaching No. 12 on the UK charts.

Single Title: **Teenage Lament '74 / Hard Hearted Alice**
Released: January 1974 by Warner Brothers, Australia.
Catalog No.: WB-7762
Media: 7" Vinyl.

Teenage Lament '74 reached No. 89 on the Australian charts.

Single Title: **Teenage Lament '74 / Working Up a Sweat**
Released: January 1974 by Warner Brothers, Brazil.
Catalog No.: WBCS 7059
Media: 7" Vinyl.

Single Title: **Teenage Lament '74 / Working Up a Sweat**
Released: January 1974 by Warner Brothers, France.
Catalog No.: 16 344
Media: 7" Vinyl.

Released with a photo cover of the band members in their sailor suits from the MUSCLE OF LOVE album cover. In the photo they're shown leaning up against a wall.

Single Title: **Teenage Lament '74 / Working Up a Sweat**
Released: January 1974 by Warner Brothers, Germany.
Catalog No.: WB 16344
Media: 7" Vinyl.

Comes in a picture sleeve which is a reprint of the inside sleeve of the album (the "night before" photo.) In the bottom left-hand corner it lists that the songs are from the MUSCLE OF LOVE album, and gives the album's catalog number.

German single for Teenage Lament '74.

Single Title: **Teenage Lament '74 / Working Up a Sweat**
Released: January 1974 by Warner Brothers, Holland.
Catalog No.: WB 16344
Media: 7" Vinyl.

Picture sleeve.

Single Title: **Teenage Lament '74 / Working Up a Sweat**
Released: January 1974 by Warner Brothers, Italy.
Catalog No.: K16344
Media: 7" Vinyl.

Picture sleeve.

Single Title: **Teenage Lament '74 / Working Up a Sweat**
Released: January 1974 by Warner Brothers, Portugal.
Catalog No.: N-S-63-56
Media: 7" Vinyl.

Picture sleeve.

Single Title: **Muscle of Love** (stereo) / **Muscle of Love** (mono)
Released: February 1974 by Warner Brothers.
Catalog No.: WB 7783
Media: 7" promotional Vinyl.

A radio-only promotional single, released to correspond with the commercial release of the single, on the promo-only white WB label.

Single Title: **Muscle of Love / Crazy Little Child**
Released: February 1974 by Warner Brothers.
Catalog No.: WB 7783
Media: 7" Vinyl.

Not even released as a 7" single in the UK, this single would not reach the Top 200 in the US.

Single Title: **Muscle of Love / Crazy Little Child**
Released: February 1974 by Warner Brothers, Brazil.
Catalog No.: WBCS 7064
Media: 7" Vinyl.

A promo single of the A-side was also released.

Single Title: **Muscle of Love / Crazy Little Child**
Released: February 1974 by Warner Brothers, France.
Catalog No.: 16314
Media: 7" Vinyl.

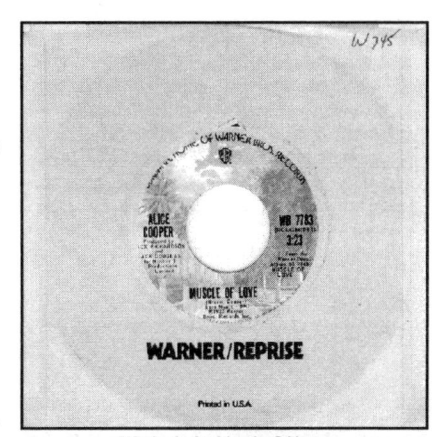

US single for Muscle Of Love.
Note the use of the "palm tree" Warner label.

Picture sleeve.

Single Title: **Muscle of Love / Crazy Little Child**
Released: February 1974 by Warner Brothers, Germany.
Catalog No.: WB 16374
Media: 7" Vinyl.

Picture sleeve.

Single Title: **Muscle of Love / Crazy Little Child**
Released: February 1974 by Warner Brothers, Holland.
Catalog No.: 16374
Media: 7" Vinyl.

Picture sleeve.

Single Title: **Muscle of Love / Crazy Little Child**
Released: February 1974 by Warner Brothers, Italy.
Catalog No.: WB 16374
Media: 7" Vinyl.

Released with a photo sleeve showing Alice with legs and arms like the Popeye cartoon character.

Single Title: **Muscle of Love / Crazy Little Child**
Released: February 1974 by Warner Brothers, Portugal.
Catalog No.: N-S-63-62
Media: 7" Vinyl.

Picture sleeve of the band in their sailor suits, leaning

Portugal single for Muscle Of Love.

against a wall. The photo is black and white on an orange-colored sleeve.

MUSCLE OF LOVE EP.

EP Title:	**MUSCLE OF LOVE EP**
Released:	February 1974 by Warner Brothers.
Catalog No.:	S 2748
Media:	10" Vinyl.
Song List:	Muscle of Love / Never Been Sold Before / Working Up a Sweat / Teenage Lament '74

This album comes with two songs from the MUSCLE OF LOVE album on each side. It comes in a cardboard sleeve that shows the inner sleeve photo of the band waiting to go into the Institute. At the top of the photo the words ALICE COOPER - MUSCLE OF LOVE appear and above the photo in the upper right and left-hand corners are the words "Stereo Album." See the entry for the SCHOOL'S OUT EP for more details about this type of release.

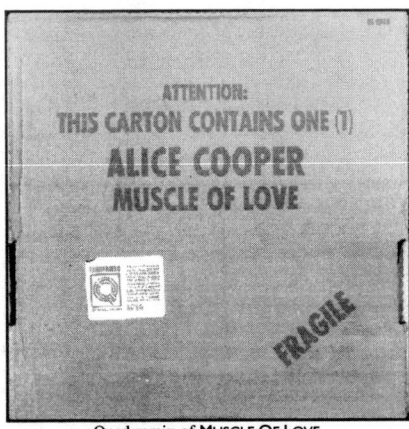

Quad remix of MUSCLE OF LOVE.

Album Title:	**MUSCLE OF LOVE - QUADRADISC**
Released:	March 1974 by Warner Brothers.
Catalog No.:	BS4 2748
Media:	Vinyl.

Following the success of BILLION DOLLAR BABIES, it was decided to do a Quadraphonic remixing for MUSCLE OF LOVE. Fans tempted to buy the Quadraphonic version to get different mixes and recordings (as were available on the Quad version of BILLION DOLLAR BABIES) should be advised that there are no major differences between this recording and the original mix of MUSCLE OF LOVE. While backing vocals are a bit higher on Man With the Golden Gun, the only significant difference is one vocal line from Alice. Otherwise, there are no real surprises on this remixed version. Jack Richardson did the remix (he also did the Quad remix of BILLION DOLLAR BABIES.) See the BILLION DOLLAR BABIES - QUADRADISC for more details concerning Quadraphonic.

Album Title:	**ALICE COOPER'S GREATEST HITS**
Recorded:	No new recordings done for the compilation album.
Production:	Remixing of some tracks done by Bob Ezrin in Spring 1974.
Personnel:	All songs produced, performed and written by those performers listed for each album from which the original tracks came.
Song List:	I'm Eighteen / Is It My Body / Desperado / Under My Wheels / Be My Lover / School's Out / Hello Hooray / Elected / No More Mr. Nice Guy / Billion Dollar Babies / Teenage Lament '74 / Muscle of Love

By this point in time, the band had separated to work on their solo projects and Warner Brothers had decided it was time to cash in a bit on the band by releasing a "greatest hits" compilation.

The packaging for this album was a bit more pedestrian than that of previous Alice Cooper official releases. That's not to say that what the album includes isn't worth mentioning. Pacific Eye & Ear came through again for Alice Cooper, with a cover by Drew Struzan that depicts the band as gangsters in the 1920's (although some of the movies stars hanging around would actually throw the time period into the mid-1930's.) Also featured on the cover are little reminders of past hits for the band, including a number "18" on a door, newspapers with the headline "School's Out" and magazines hanging at the newsstand behind the band with the BILLION DOLLAR BABIES logo and title (but, alas, no one under the wheels of the car.)

As mentioned, several movie stars from the 1930's are depicted on the cover, along with a piece of optical illusion that showcases five gangsters with machine guns ready to blast away at six individuals, just as occurred during the St. Valentine's Day Massacre in 1929 (a well-known gangland slaying that became national news.) Struzan would go on to do artwork for movie posters, including RAIDERS OF THE LOST ARK.

Inside the single sleeve album cover is an inner sleeve displaying artwork from Bill Garland. The artwork is a continuation of Struzan's artwork, and shows the band posing for the artist with their equipment (Bruce, Dunaway and Buxton have electric guitars, while Smith holds drum sticks and Alice holds a 1920's style microphone with the initials "A.C." on its side.) Behind them is a large group of movie stars (ranging from the early 1920's through the 1950's), most of whom are posed as if caught in the middle of a dance. A bit unusual is the fact that the open end of the sleeve is on the side instead of at the top as per usual. Also, on the back of the inner sleeve, are additional credits and a track listing. This is the first album to list the illustrators from Pacific Eye & Ear by name in the credits, while Bob Pleasant, Bob Gruen and Shep Gordon are listed in the "Special Thanks" credits.

While the album was being put together, Bob Ezrin decided to beef up the vocals and cut back on the rhythm guitar a bit for several tracks on GREATEST HITS. This is most noticeable on the three tracks from the KILLER album. Added studio effects are evident on the LOVE IT TO DEATH tracks as well.

ALICE COOPER'S GREATEST HITS reached No. 8 on the US charts. It was certified Gold on October 15, 1974 and certified Platinum on October 13, 1986.

Album Title: **ALICE COOPER'S GREATEST HITS**
Released: August 1974 by Warner Brothers.
Catalog No.: W 2803
Media: Vinyl, Cassette, 8-Track and Reel-to-Reel.

Printed with the "Palm Tree" Warner Brothers label. See the entry above for more details about the packaging of the album.

Album Title: **ALICE COOPER'S GREATEST HITS**
Released: August 1974 by Warner Brothers, UK.
Catalog No.: K 56043 (vinyl) and K456043 (cassette)
Media: Vinyl and Cassette.

The original issue of this album in the UK came in a gatefold cover that opened to show the entire inner sleeve painting as one piece (instead of being split between the front and back of the inner sleeve.) This also allowed the front cover to be seen in its entirety when the gatefold was opened. It came with an additional competition booklet. The album was reissued in the 1980's without the gatefold cover. This release came with an additional competition booklet. Some editions of the vinyl album came with the cassette's catalog number (the additional "4" in between "K" and "56043"), which was simply a misprint.

Album Title: **ALICE COOPER'S GREATEST HITS**
Released: August 1974 by Warner Brothers, Argentina.
Catalog No.: 14202
Media: Vinyl.

Album Title: **ALICE COOPER'S GREATEST HITS**
Released: August 1974 by Warner Brothers, Australia.
Catalog No.: W-2803
Media: Vinyl.

The Australian edition of this album came in a gatefold cover, with the entire inner sleeve painting inside the cover. GREATEST HITS reached No. 71 on the Australian charts.

Album Title: **ALICE COOPER'S GREATEST HITS**
Released: August 1974 by Warner Brothers, France.
Catalog No.: 56043
Media: Vinyl.

Album Title: **ALICE COOPER'S GREATEST HITS**
Released: August 1974 by Warner Brothers, Germany.

Catalog No.: WB 56043
Media: Vinyl.

Album Title: ALICE COOPER'S GREATEST HITS
Released: Late 1970's by Warner Brothers, France. Distributed to France and Germany.
Catalog No.: K 456 043 (Germany U - France WE 441)
Media: Cassette.

Album Title: ALICE COOPER'S GREATEST HITS
Released: Late 1970's by Warner Brothers.
Catalog No.: M5 3107
Media: Cassette.

Album Title: ALICE COOPER'S GREATEST HITS
Released: May 1, 1989 by Warner Brothers, Germany.
Catalog No.: WEA 927330-2 (CD) and WEA 927330-4 (cassette)
Media: CD and Cassette.

First French / German reissue of the album on CD. The German edition was the first to print the vinyl inner sleeve inside the booklet of the CD, but the first four movie stars on the left of the back sleeve are missing.

Album Title: ALICE COOPER'S GREATEST HITS
Released: June 1989 by Warner Brothers, UK.
Catalog No.: 256043
Media: CD.

First CD pressing of the album in the UK.

Album Title: ALICE COOPER'S GREATEST HITS
Released: October 24, 1990 by Warner Brothers.
Catalog No.: WB 3107.2 (CD) and WB 3107.4 (cassette)
Media: CD and Cassette.

First CD pressing of the album in the US. Released a week after another reissue of the album on cassette on October 17, 1990.

Album Title: ALICE COOPER'S GREATEST HITS
Released: May 1, 1989 by Warner Brothers, Australia.
Catalog No.: WMI 9273302
Media: CD.

First CD pressing of the album in Australia.

Album Title: ALICE COOPER'S GREATEST HITS
Released: September 1997 by Warner Brothers, Japan.
Catalog No.: WPCR-1245
Media: CD.

Part of the special "Forever Young Series" that WB released in Japan. The album came with an obi that listed the album's title and additional albums available in the series.

Album Title: ALICE COOPER'S GREATEST HITS
Released: October 3, 1997 by Warner Brothers, Canada.
Catalog No.: WARN CD 03107 (CD) and WARN CWX 2803 (cassette)
Media: CD and Cassette.

Latest reissue of the album, part of mass reissuing of the Alice Cooper catalog in Canada.

Single Title: **I'm Eighteen** (stereo) / **I'm Eighteen** (mono)
Released: August 1974 by Warner Brothers.
Catalog No.: WBS 8023

Media: 7" promotional Vinyl.

A radio-only promotional single, timed to correspond to the commercial release of the single, on the promo-only white WB label.

Single Title: **I'm Eighteen / Muscle of Love**
Released: August 1974 by Warner Brothers.
Catalog No.: WBS 8023
Media: 7" Vinyl.

Not even released as a 7" single in the UK, this single didn't reach the Top 200 in the US.

Single Title: **Under My Wheels / Desperado**
Released: August 1974 by Warner Brothers, UK.
Catalog No.: K 16127
Media: 7" Vinyl.

Originally released in the UK in December 1971, this was a reissue in support of the ALICE COOPER'S GREATEST HITS album. It didn't reach the charts in the UK.

Single Title: **Under My Wheels / Desperado**
Released: August 1974 by Warner Brothers, Germany.
Catalog No.: WB 16127
Media: 7" Vinyl.

Reissue of the 1971 single in support of the ALICE COOPER'S GREATEST HITS album. The German single came in a full color picture sleeve of Alice and the band from an alternative photo shot during the LOVE IT TO DEATH photo session.

EP Title: **SCHOOL'S OUT EP**
Released: February 1975 by Warner Brothers, UK.
Catalog No.: K 19409
Media: 12" Vinyl.
Song List: School's Out / Elected / No More Mr. Nice Guy / Billion Dollar Babies

Another EP release in the UK for Alice, this time in support of hits from the previous few years. This single came without a picture sleeve and is no relation to the SCHOOL'S OUT EP released in the UK during October 1972.

EP Title: **Nothing to Lose / Liar / Jet / Muscle of Love**
Released: 1974 by Warner Brothers, Thailand
Catalog No.: TKR-157
Media: 12" Vinyl.

A typical EP release from Thailand that includes tracks from many different performers on one disc. The vinyl comes in a full-color sleeve that shows Todd Rundgren from an episode of the television series THE MIDNIGHT SPECIAL. The tracks are from (in order of appearance) KISS, Queen, Wings and Alice Cooper.

Part 3 — Tours 1964 - 1974

The time period covered in this chapter shows the rise of the Alice Cooper Group from a band known only for being hated to the status of international stardom. The increases in both the complexity and the popularity of the tours throughout this decade show Alice growing from a local curiosity into a major trend setter within the rock genre.

Dates are listed in chronological order and are grouped according to tour name. Tour names are not necessarily the same as the (at the time) most recent album. As an example; the tour in support of MUSCLE OF LOVE was actually called THE BILLION DOLLAR BABIES HOLIDAY TOUR, and in Chapter 2 we'll see that the tour supporting FROM THE INSIDE was the MADHOUSE ROCK TOUR. Early gigs were not part of any particular tour, so these dates have been grouped together with the early album titles used for the set list. In all other instances the tour name given is the title of the album it was in support of (THE KILLER TOUR for the KILLER album, etc.)

The band was playing gigs before signing with Straight in 1968, but the details of many these dates are unfortunately lost in time (they were playing anywhere that they could get work.) Tour dates in the 1968 through 1971 period were somewhat sporadic because the band was still struggling to hit it big, even after two albums by 1971. In fact, when they were playing, it was mostly either in little clubs or as part of bigger festivals (such as the Toronto Rock 'N' Roll Festival in September 1969 or part of the Medicine Ball Caravan in 1970.)

Tour Name: **Earwigs / Spiders / Nazz tour dates**

Fall 1964 - Letterman Talent Show, Cortez High School
   First appearance of the Earwigs.
Early 1965 - Lis Hawks, Sweet Sixteen Birthday Party, Phoenix, AZ
   The Spiders' first paying gig.
June 1965 - Phoenix, AZ
   Battle of the Bands competition.
September 1965 - VIP Lounge, Phoenix, AZ
   The Spiders get a gig playing the lounge on weekends.
November 1965 - Phoenix Star Theater, Phoenix, AZ
   The Spiders were used in an altered production of the musical BYE BYE BIRDIE.
March 26, 1967 - Griffith Park, Los Angeles, CA
   A Festival show.
March 28, 1967 - Los Angeles, CA
   The band played a bar on Sunset Strip (name unknown.)
May 1967 - Gallup, NM
   High School Prom (school name and location unknown.)
May 1967 - Albuquerque, NM
   Another High School Prom. (Location and name of school unknown.)

Tour Name: **Alice Cooper dates before the PRETTIES FOR YOU tour:**
Tour Period: Dates between March 16, 1968 (first show as Alice Cooper) and May 1969 (the PRETTIES FOR YOU tour.)
Performers: Alice Cooper (lead vocals), Glen Buxton (lead guitar and vocals), Michael Bruce (rhythm guitar and vocals), Dennis Dunaway (guitar and vocals) and Neal Smith (drums and vocals.)
Opening Act: Opened for The Doors, among others.

The band had become Alice Cooper and was starting to get a reputation in the Los Angeles area. It was here that they began working on material that would later turn up on PRETTIES FOR YOU.

Once Alice Cooper was signed to Straight, the band, along with Zappa, were anxious to promote themselves for the forthcoming album. Thus, they began playing in other parts of the country (although mostly along the West Coast) between December 1968 and May 1969 when the "real" tour began.

March 16, 1968 - Earl Warren Fairgrounds, Santa Barbara, CA
   This was their first show as Alice Cooper. They opened for the Nitty Gritty Dirt Band and Blue Cheer. Posters for the concert listed the band as Nazz.
May 1, 1968 - Cheetah, Los Angeles, CA
   First Show at the Cheetah after changing their name to Alice Cooper.

November 1968 - Army Base in Denver, CO
November 8, 1968 - California State, Fullerton, CA
   Opened for Frank Zappa.
December 6, 1968 - Shrine Exposition Hall, Los Angeles, CA
December 7, 1968 - Shrine Exposition Hall, Los Angeles, CA
   Both Shrine concerts were done to promote acts newly-signed to Zappa's Straight label. Playing besides Alice Cooper were Frank Zappa and the Mothers of Invention, Captain Beefheart, the GTO's and Ethiopia.
January 2, 1969 - Whiskey A Go Go, Hollywood, CA
January 3, 1969 - Whiskey A Go Go, Hollywood, CA
January 4, 1969 - Whiskey A Go Go, Hollywood, CA
January 5, 1969 - Whiskey A Go Go, Hollywood, CA
   Opened for Led Zeppelin at all four shows.
December 1968 - Shrine Auditorium, Los Angeles, CA
January 1969 - Salt lake City, MS
January 1969 - University of Boulder, Boulder, CO
February 1969 - The Black Dome, Cincinnati, OH
March 1969 - Vancouver, British Columbia
March 1969 - Whisky a Go Go, Los Angeles, CA
   The Album ALICE COOPER LIVE AT THE WHISKY A GO GO 1969 was recorded during this concert, which was also a showcase to present Alice Cooper to Warner Brothers (WB passed on the band.)
March 15, 1969 - Cal State, Fullerton, CA
   Opened for Zappa with the Mothers of Invention.
March 30, 1969 - Avalon Ballroom, San Francisco, CA
   A 40-minute recording from this concert exists. It appears on the bootleg SNAKE, RATTLE AND ROLL.
April 1969 - Strawberry Fields Festival, Toronto, Canada
   At this show, Alice threw watermelon into the crowd, hitting a group of handicapped audience members in the front row.
April 19, 1969 - Seattle Centre Arena, Seattle, WA
   Opened for Zappa with the Mothers of Invention and the Guess Who.
May 20, 1969 - Kinetic Playground, Chicago, IL
May 23, 1969 - Coliseum, Phoenix, Arizona
   Opened for Iron Butterfly.

Poster for November 8, 1968 Alice Cooper Group performance opening for Frank Zappa.

Other performances:
   The Lenny Bruce Memorial Party, 1968. (At the Cheetah; the date is uncertain, but is most probably around June or July 1968.
   Opened for the Doors at The Cheetah, 1968 (on numerous occasions.)

Tour Name: **PRETTIES FOR YOU**
Tour Period: Between May 1969 (the beginning of the PRETTIES FOR YOU tour) and June 1970, with a few dates before that while waiting for the album to be released.
Performers: Alice Cooper (lead vocals), Glen Buxton (lead guitar and vocals), Michael Bruce (rhythm guitar and vocals), Dennis Dunaway (guitar and vocals) and Neal Smith (drums and vocals).
Opening Act: Opened for many different acts, mostly in festival situations (these acts are listed by their dates.)
Set List: (partial) Nobody Likes Me / Swing Low Sweet Cheerio / B.B. on Mars / Reflected / No Longer Umpire / Don't Blow Your Mind

RECORD WORD magazine, in their May 31, 1969 edition, printed that Alice Cooper was to embark on a tour of the country from June 3rd through to the beginning of July. Actual dates, however, are hard to find. The band played a variety of festival shows throughout the country in 1969 and 1970.

Alice Cooper concerts were going through a very experimental stage at this time, employing a greater-than-usual amount of audience feedback, and using anything lying around as a prop during the show. Most nights included feather pillows (generally stolen from motels) being ripped apart and thrown into the crowd, along with the attacks on the audience with fire extinguishers. The band's antics in the film DIARY OF A MAD HOUSEWIFE are typical of what they were doing on stage at the time.

The PRETTIES FOR YOU tour was also when band members began experimenting with makeup, although it wasn't until LOVE IT TO DEATH that makeup styles took on a set look, and it waited until BILLION DOLLAR BABIES before Alice finally settled on the "demented clown" makeup around the eyes.

June 3, 1969 - Salt Lake City, UT
June 6, 1969 - Felt Forum, New York City, NY
    Fourth on the bill.
June 7, 1969 - Felt Forum, New York City, NY
June 11, 1969 - Steve Paul's Scene, New York City, NY
June 12, 1969 - Steve Paul's Scene, New York City, NY
    Opened for Slim Harp and his backing band, House.
June 13, 1969 - Electric Factory, Philadelphia, PA
June 14, 1969 - Steve Paul's Scene, New York City, NY
June 15, 1969 - Steve Paul's Scene, New York City, NY
June 16, 1969 - Steve Paul's Scene, New York City, NY
July 4, 1969 - New York Pop Festival, Roosevelt Raceway, NY
July 5, 1969 - New York Pop Festival, Roosevelt Raceway, NY
July 13, 1969 - Tyrone Guthrie, Milwaukee, WI
    Opened for Zappa and the Mothers of Invention.
July 18, 1969 - Terrace Ballroom, (city unknown), UT
    Performed with Love and Fever Tree.
July 25, 1969 - Seattle Pop Festival, Seattle, Washington
    Part of a rock festival that included Led Zeppelin, The Byrds, The Doors, The Guess Who, Chicago, Tina Turner and many others.
July 26, 1969 - Eugene Pop Festival, Hayward Field, University of Oregon, Eugene, OR
    Part of a rock festival that included the Doors, the Byrds, Them and many others.
July 29, 1969 - Masonic Temple, Portland, OR
July 30, 1969 - Masonic Temple, Portland, OR
    Opened for Steve Miller and Total Eclipse.
August 3, 1969 - Mt. Clemens Pop Festival, Sportman's Park, Mt. Clemens, MI
    Performed with Rush, Up and many others.
August 9, 1969 - Goose Lake International Music Festival, Goose Lake Park, Jackson, Michigan.
    Part of rock festival that included The Stooges, Bob Seger, Jethro Tull, the Small Faces, Chicago and many others. A poster for the show can be found in Michael Bruce's book NO MORE MISTER NICE GUY.
August 14, 1969 - Eugene Armory, Eugene, OR
August 30, 1969 - Oregon State Fair, Salem, OR
    Performed with the Box Tops.
August 1969 - Vancouver, British Columbia
September 12, 1969 - Toronto Rock 'N' Roll Revival
    The Alice Cooper Group shared the bill at this music festival with acts such as Gene Vincent, Bo Diddley, Chuck Berry and John Lennon. The group's show was recorded and subsequently released on a variety of albums (see TORONTO ROCK 'N' ROLL REVIVAL, 1969, VOLUME IV in Chapter 6 for more details), and part of the concert was filmed and turned up as a short film called CHICKEN INCIDENT by Baker Penne and Desmond Letter Franklin (see Part 4 for more details.) As you can guess, this was the show that included the infamous "chicken incident" that has dogged Alice throughout his career.
September 14, 1969 - Raceway Park, Toledo, OH
October 30, 1969 - Fillmore West, San Francisco, CA
October 31, 1969 - Fillmore West, San Francisco, CA
November 1, 1969 - Fillmore West, San Francisco, CA

Poster for 1969 appearance of the Alice Cooper Group.

November 2, 1969 - Fillmore West, San Francisco, CA
   Opened for Ike and Tina Turner and It's A Beautiful Day.
December 31, 1969 - The Rock Pile, Toronto, Canada
January 17, 1970 - Rose Palace, Pasadena, CA
   Could possibly be January 18. Mentioned in the EASY ACTION press kit.
March 28, 1970 - Ludlow's Garage, Cincinnati, OH
   Performed with Clifton and Ten years After.
April 17, 1970 - Opera House, Detroit, MI
   Performed with the Stooges and the Jam Band.
April 26, 1970 - Cow Palace, San Francisco, CA
   Performed with Albert Collins, Chairman of the Board, Eric Burdon and War, and Haydn.
May 15, 1970 - New Old Fillmore, San Francisco, CA
   Performed with The Stooges, Flamin' Groovies, Commander Cody and Purple Earthquake.

Tour Name: **EASY ACTION**
Tour Period: Between June 1970 (the beginning of the EASY ACTION tour) and March 1971.
Performers: Alice Cooper (lead vocals), Glen Buxton (lead guitar and vocals), Michael Bruce (rhythm guitar and vocals), Dennis Dunaway (guitar and vocals) and Neal Smith (drums and vocals.)
Opening Act: Opened for many different acts, although the band was finally starting to step away from the supporting act role to headline at some smaller clubs and arenas.
Set List: Sun Arise / Mr. and Misdemeanor / Fields of Regret / I'm Eighteen / Levity Ball / Is It My Body / Nobody Likes Me / Black Juju

The touring for EASY ACTION shouldn't really be called a tour, per se, since there wasn't a set of dates put together strictly for the promotion of the album. Instead, the dates played were either as part of festivals or in small clubs, and even then it was more a case of scrounging around for work instead of people asking them to play somewhere. In fact, it wasn't until almost the release of the follow-up album, LOVE IT TO DEATH, that more dates started coming their way, which explains why the set list above includes such songs as I'm Eighteen, Is It My Body, Black Juju and Sun Arise. A recording of this older set list is available for the early 1971 Seattle, Washington show listed below.

June 13, 1970 - Crosley Field, Cincinnati, OH
   15 minutes from this performance at the Midsummer Rock Festival exists on audio and was filmed as well.
September 8, 1970 - Max's Kansas City, New York, NY
   Alice was reportedly arrested at this show for saying the word "tits" on stage.
September 9, 1970 - New York Action House, Long Island, NY
October 31, 1970 - Bowen Field House, Eastern Michigan University, Ypsilanti, MI
   Part of the Black Magic Rock and Roll festival, performing with Arthur Brown, Brownsville Station and many more.
November 25, 1970 - Fairgrounds Coliseum, Salt Lake City, UT
   Performed with Wishful Thinking.
April 17, 1971 - Opera House, Chicago, IL
   With the Stooges and The Jam Band.
April 24, 1971 - Taft Theater, Cincinnati, OH
   With the Stooges and The Jam Band.

Other Performances:
1970 - Chicago Underground, Chicago, IL
   A full concert is known to exist of this show on audio. I'm Eighteen is performed as an extended, bluesy version with different lyrics.

1971 - Paramount NW Theater, Seattle, WA
   The full show recorded from the sound board. Portions of this show can be found on bootlegs such as SNAKE, RATTLE AND ROLL, SICK and THE KING SNAKE USA 1969 / 1970.

Tour Name: **LOVE IT TO DEATH**
Tour Period: May 1971 through November 1971.
Performers: Alice Cooper (vocals), Michael Bruce (rhythm guitar and vocals), Neal Smith (drums and vocals), Dennis Dunaway (bass and vocals) and Glen Buxton (lead guitar.) Additional performers: Cindy Smith (as the nurse.)
Opening Act: Meat Loaf and Rare Earth, among others.

Set List: Sun Arise / Caught in a Dream / I'm Eighteen / Is It My Body / Second Coming / Ballad of Dwight Fry / Black Juju / Return of the Spiders

With the "third time's the charm" success of the LOVE IT TO DEATH album and the single I'm Eighteen, the band was finally ready to tour the country as a major headliner. Not only did LOVE IT TO DEATH spark more interest in the band than had been anticipated, but it was the basis for a tour that ultimately set the groundwork for all of the Alice Cooper tours that were to follow. Included on this tour was the first appearance of Alice fighting his way out of a strait-jacket (during the new song Ballad of Dwight Fry.) Another first for this tour was the appearance of Cindy as an additional theatrical performer (she was to become a regular on the Cooper stage.) Her role was that of the nurse taking care of Alice for the Ballad (a variation of the nurse theme was also later used on the NIGHTMARE RETURNS tour, among others.)

Alice's stage execution premiered during the LOVE IT TO DEATH tour, with the band building their own electric chair for Alice to be strapped into during the song Black Juju. Finally, it was during this tour, as well, that the snake made its first appearance wrapped around Alice for a tune or two.

Return of the Spiders was the only song from the first two albums to make a regular appearance in the set list during the tour. After the NIGHTMARE RETURNS tour ended, none of the tracks from the first two albums would again appear in concert.

May 3, 1971 - Carnegie Hall, New York, NY
May 6, 1971 - Town Hall, New York University, New York City, NY
    With the Holy Modal Rounders opening.
May 29, 1971 - Will Rogers Coliseum, Fort Worth, TX
    With John Mayall and Brownsville Station.
June 12, 1971 - Fillmore East, New York, NY
    This concert occurred two weeks before the Fillmore East was permanently closed.
June 18, 1971 - Toledo Sports Arena, Toledo, OH
    With the Amboy Dukes and Brownsville Station.
June 19, 1971 - Teen Scene '71 Rock Fair, Birmingham, AL
    A festival with Ted Nugent, Mountain and many others. Alice headlined Saturday of the three-day festival.
July 13, 1971 - Fairgrounds Arena, Oklahoma City, OK
July 14, 1971 - Venetian Room, Ambassador Hotel, Los Angeles, CA
July 23, 1971 - The Barn, Peoria, IL.
    The full show was recorded from the audience.
September 1971 - Richmond Arena, Richmond, VA
September 1971 - Fairgrounds, Tampa, FL
September 12, 1971 - Miami Sportatorium, Miami, FL
    The full show was recorded from the audience.
September 13, 1971 - Berkeley Theatre, Berkeley, CA
    Opened for Led Zeppelin and Pink Floyd.
September 22, 1971 - The Barn, Peoria, IL
    With Mike Quattro and the Jam Band.
September 24, 1971 - Winterland, San Francisco, CA
September 24, 1971 - Winterland, San Francisco, CA
    With Glass Harp and Cold Blood.
October 1971 - Richmond Arena, Richmond, VA
    Part of this show was recorded from the audience.
October 19, 1971 - Danny Veno Auditorium, Irving, TX
October 22, 1971 - Tivoli, Copenhagen, Denmark
October 25, 1971 - Tivoli, Copenhagen, Denmark
    Tea opened.
October 27, 1971 - Frankfurt, Germany
October 29, 1971 - Amsterdam, Holland
October 30, 1971 - Volkshaus, Zurich, Switzerland
    Tea opened.
November 2, 1971 - Olympia, Paris, France
November 4, 1971 - The Kinetic Circus, Birmingham, England
    This was the band's first appearance in the UK. By this time they were beginning to perform some of the material from KILLER on tour, since the album was to be released that month in the US. The single Under My Wheels was to be released in the UK in December. Still, the "official" KILLER tour did not start until

January 1972.
November 6, 1971 - The Rainbow, London, England.
November 7, 1971 - The Rainbow, London, England.
With Arthur Brown, Roger Ruskin and Spear. The November 6 show was recorded from the audience.

Tour Name: **KILLER**
Tour Period: The tour began at the Academy of Music in New York, NY in December 1971 and continued until June 30, 1972 at the Empire Pool, Wembley, England.
Performers: Alice Cooper (vocals), Michael Bruce (rhythm guitar and vocals), Neal Smith (drums and vocals), Dennis Dunaway (bass and vocals) and Glen Buxton (lead guitar.)
Additional performers: Cindy Smith (as the nurse.)
Opening Act: Little information is available about which bands opened in the US. Roxy Music opened in the UK during the last month of the tour.
Set List: Instrumental Into / Be My Lover / You Drive Me Nervous / Yeah,Yeah,Yeah / I'm Eighteen / Is It My Body / Halo of Flies / Dead Babies / Killer / Long Way to Go / Under My Wheels (See th notes below for more details about changes that occurred in the set list.)

While the singles from KILLER didn't do as well as I'm Eighteen (from LOVE IT TO DEATH), the new album itself sold better than the former, leaving the band in a good position for the tour that followed. With the KILLER tour (and the latter part of the LOVE IT TO DEATH tour) the band was now touring on a full-time basis. In the earlier days, when gigs outside the California area were hard to find, the band's appearances had been rather spotty — a show here, a festival there, and several days or even weeks off in between shows. With the success of their singles and albums, there was a major push to put the band in front of the American (and international) public as much as possible. This resulted in extensive tours with only short breaks during which they could work on the follow-up album. While it helped to spread the name of Alice Cooper across the country, it led directly to the breakup of the band because of the continuous pressure and nonstop activity. But these problems were still in the future, even though the root cause of their problems existed at the time of the KILLER tour.

The band continued the practice of shuffling new songs into the set list while they were still being worked on, so that a song could likely be heard in concert long before it was recorded. The song School's Out was worked on during the five months of the KILLER tour, and an early version could be heard during an instrumental break in Long Way to Go. Once its lyrics had been written and the song was recorded, School's Out was performed (in its completed version) after Long Way to Go in concert, and Is It My Body was played after School's Out (instead of midway through the show following I'm Eighteen.)

The KILLER tour was an extension of the ideas introduced for the LOVE IT TO DEATH tour. Alice was again executed for his crimes against society (this time at the end of a rope in the gallows built as part of the stage.) Unlike later tours, which had other performers from the show doing the job, for KILLER the other band members took Alice to his hanging. In fact, at this point, only Cindy Smith was a regular additional performer on stage, still in her nurse role as on the previous tour.

During this tour the snake that Alice held and wrapped around himself during Be My Lover became a regular feature as Kachina (from the KILLER album cover.) The giant balloons sent over the audience during that latter part of the show also made their first continuous appearance during this tour.

Among all of these firsts is a last — this was the last tour to feature Glen Buxton only on lead guitar. After this, beginning with the SCHOOL'S OUT tour, other guitarists would supplement Buxton.

The KILLER tour was also the point in time when Alice made the final changes to his stage makeup, this time to the black circles-and-diamonds "clown" makeup which would be his trademark from then on. Except during the SPECIAL FORCES period of the early 1980's, he used the "clown" makeup, with slight alterations, for all subsequent tours. The change from the "spider-eyes" makeup was intentional — it allowed Alice and the band to move away from the feminine image that was starting to run out of steam, and go in the direction of the darker, more sinister music and lyrics that began showing up in their albums with LOVE IT TO DEATH.

This tour was the first to feature a tour program sold at the show. Fans got an additional treat — on the back of the tour book was printed a cutout single that, once removed and put on a turntable, played a non-album track called Nobody Likes Me. This song goes back to the days of 1968 / 1969 when it was a regular in the set at Cooper concerts. For years, the KILLER tour book was the only way to find an official studio version of this song, although a pirated copy of the track has shown up on bootlegs. Both LIVE AT THE WHISKY A GO

GO 1969 and the numerous Toronto Rock 'N' Roll Festival 1969 albums feature live versions of this track.

Footage from the Montreal, Canada concert on the KILLER tour can be seen in the Canadian documentary ROCK-A-BYE.

November 20, 1971 - Saginaw, MI
    The warm-up show for the tour.
December 1, 1971 - Academy of Music, New York, NY
December 3, 1971 - Municipal Auditorium, New Orleans, LA
December 5, 1971 - Independence Hall, Baton Rouge, LA
December 8, 1971 - Ohio Theater, Columbus, OH
December 10, 1971 - Coliseum, Indianapolis, IN
December 11, 1971 - Hara Arena, Dayton, OH
    With Cactus and Atomic Rooster opening.
December 12, 1971 - Sports Arena, Toledo, OH
    The full concert was recorded from the audience.
December 13, 1971 - Civic Auditorium, Chicago, IL
December 14, 1971 - Civic Auditorium, Chicago, IL
    With Dr. John, Poco and Humble Pie.
December 16, 1971 - Cowtown Theater, Kansas City, MO
December 17, 1971 - St. Louis Arena, St. Louis, MO
    The show was recorded from the audience.
December 19, 1971 - Cobo Hall, Detroit, MI
December 25, 1971 - Pirates World, Miami, FL
December 26, 1971 - Pirates World, Miami, FL
December 27, 1971 - Civic Arena, Pittsburgh, PA
December 28, 1971 - Lyric Theater, Baltimore, MD
December 29, 1971 - Public Auditorium, Cleveland, OH
December 31, 1971 - Maple Leaf Gardens, Toronto, Canada
January 1, 1971 - Civic Center, Ottawa, Canada
January 2, 1971 - Palace Theatre, New York City, NY
    The show was recorded from the audience.
January 1971 - Roanoke, VA
January 1971 - Capitol Theater, Passaic, NJ
January 30, 1971 - Civic Center, Baltimore, MD
February 1972 - Spectrum Stadium, Philadelphia, PA
April 1 - 3, 1972 - Mar Y Sol Festival, Puerto Rico, West Indian Isles
    Alice played during this festival, but it's not known on which day(s) they played.
May 23, 1972 - The New Woods, Tifton, GA
May 26, 1972 - Tampa Bay Stadium, Tampa Bay, FL
    The show was recorded from the audience.
June 16, 1972 - Zembo Mosque, Harrisburg, PA
    With Brownsville Station and Mutt Lee. Two shows were done that night.
June 25, 1972 - Nazareth Speedway, PA
    Muscular Dystrophy Benefit.
June 30, 1972 - Wembley Pool, London England
    This show was advertised with a truck carrying a huge billboard of Alice, dressed only in his snake. As a publicity stunt, the trucked conk out in the middle of Piccadilly Circus during rush hour for all to see. Roxy Music opened the show.

Other Performances:
1972 - Electric Ballroom, Detroit MI
    This show was audio-recorded from the audience.

Tour Name: **SCHOOL'S OUT**
Tour Period: July 1972 - September 1972.
Performers: Alice Cooper (vocals), Michael Bruce (rhythm guitar and vocals), Neal Smith (drums and vocals), Dennis Dunaway (bass and vocals) and Glen Buxton (lead guitar.) Additional performers: Cindy Smith (as Alice's nurse).
Opening Act: The many opening bands for this tour are unknown, but it's known that Todd Rundgren opened at least five of the SCHOOL'S OUT tour shows. Rundgren would later help record and produce two

Set List: tracks for Alice on the ROADIE soundtrack album.
Instrumental Intro / Public Animal #9 / Caught in a Dream / Under My Wheels / Be My Lover / I'm Eighteen / Is It My Body / Halo of Flies / Gutter Cat Vs. the Jets / Street Fight / Killer / Long Way to Go / School's Out (Elected replaced Long Way to Go on the European portion of the tour.)

Coming on the heels of the KILLER tour, there weren't many changes to the theatrical part of the show. The production at that time was pretty much in the form it would maintain through both the BILLION DOLLAR BABIES and MUSCLE OF LOVE tours — Alice would continue being hung, and the snake and other paraphernalia from the KILLER tour would remain. (Alice lost his snake at a motel while performing in Nashville, Tennessee on the KILLER tour. It was later found in the plumbing of the building.)

Special effects tapes used in concert during the KILLER tour — baby cries, the "Street Fight" loop, etc. — have been circulating in fan circles for some time.

July 12, 1972 - Field House, Wichita, KS
July 13, 1972 - Fairgrounds Arena, Oklahoma City, OK
July 14, 1972 - Hector County Auditorium, Odessa, TX
July 15, 1972 - County Coliseum, El Paso, TX
July 17, 1972 - Fairground Speedway, Salt Lake City, UT
July 19, 1972 - Grant Stadium, Phoenix, AZ
July 22, 1972 - Sports Arena, San Diego, CA
July 23, 1972 - Hollywood Bowl, Los Angeles, CA
This was renowned for the dropping of several thousand pairs of paper panties onto the audience from a helicopter before the show. A montage of film footage from this show was later shown on the TV show TOP OF THE POPS, with School's Out played over it. The show was recorded professionally and has turned up on several bootlegs.
July 27, 1972 - Armory, Minneapolis, MN
July 28, 1972 - Amphitheater, Chicago, IL
Two shows were done, but it's not known whether they were both on the same night, or on consecutive days.
July 31, 1972 - Cobo Hall, Detroit, MI
August 5, 1972 - Rubber Bowl, Akron, OH
August 10, 1972 - Location is uncertain.
There is conflicting information concerning this date. One source states that Alice Cooper played the Garden State Summer Music Fair at Capitol Theatre in Passic, NJ, while another has them at the Roosevelt Stadium in Jersey City, NJ. Both sources list the J. Geils Band as opening the show.
September 2, 1972 - Toronto Varsity Arena, Toronto, Canada
The full show was recorded from the audience
September 21, 1972 - Hofstra University, Long Island, NY
A portion of the show was recorded for the IN CONCERT television series.
November 10, 1972 - Green's Playhouse, Glasgow, Scotland
The show was recorded from the audience.
November 13, 1972 - Olympia Theatre, Paris, France
Two shows were performed.
November 15, 1972 - Circus Krone, Munchen, Germany
November 17, 1972 - De Doelen, Rotterdam, Holland
November 18, 1972 - Concertgebouw, Amsterdam, Holland
November 19, 1972 - Ernst Merckhalle, Hamburg, Germany
The show was recorded from the audience.
November 20, 1972 - Olympen, Lund, Sweden
The show was recorded from the audience.
November 21, 1972 - KB Hallen, Copenhagen, Denmark
November 23, 1972 - Deutchlandhalle, Berlin, Germany
November 24, 1972 - Gruga Halle, Essen, Germany
November 25, 1972 - Gesthalle, Frankfurt, Germany
The show was recorded from the audience.
November 26, 1972 - Mehrzweckhalle, Zufingen, Switzerland

Tour Name: **THE ALICE COOPER SHOW TOUR (a.k.a., THE BILLION DOLLAR BABIES TOUR)**
Tour Period: March 10, 1973 through June 7, 1973.

Performers: Alice Cooper (vocals), Michael Bruce (rhythm guitar and vocals), Neal Smith (drums and vocals), Dennis Dunaway (bass and vocals) and Glen Buxton (lead guitar.) Additional performers: Mick Mashbir (lead guitar), Bob Dolin (keyboards), The Amazing Randi (executioner, dentist) and Cindy Smith (the "dancing tooth".)

Opening Act: Flo & Eddie were the opening act

Set List: Hello Hooray / Billion Dollar Baby / Elected / Eighteen / No More Mr. Nice Guy / My Stars / Raped and Freezin' / Unfinished Sweet / Night of Bald Mountain (except) / Sick Things / Dead Babies / I Love the Dead / School's Out / Under My Wheels / God Bless America (recording, Kate Smith sound-alike)

Although reported in Michael Bruce's book NO MORE MR. NICE GUY as beginning on March 5, 1973 in Rochester, NY, the first show for a paying audience was not until Philadelphia. The tour was originally slated to begin at the Palace Theater in New York (over a series of days in mid-February 1973.) The show was being prepared as a Broadway production and was to have been choreographed by Michael Bennet of the musical FOLLIES. These plans fell through when the Palace pulled out of the negotiations. It was then decided to move the shows over to the Broadway Theatre, but these plans also fell through when advance ticket orders for the show were, ironically enough, overwhelming (apparently, it was felt that security would be too costly for ensuring that the type of audience attracted wouldn't tear up the theater.) Instead, the "production show" plans were scrapped and a normal cross-country tour began in March at the Philadelphia Spectrum in Philadelphia, Pennsylvania.

The artwork used on promotional material and the tour poster for the BILLION DOLLAR BABIES tour was created by Prarie Prince of the rock band The Tubes. It featured the Cooper band in top hat and tails, dancing in mid-step.

Something new on this tour was Alice being executed by guillotine. Also featured was the band beating up a President Nixon look-alike during the final moments of the encore and God Bless America. (God Bless America was a tape recording of the Kate Smith classic (sung by a sound-alike) played over the sound system as the band made their final bows. This tour also saw the silent replacement of Glen Buxton on lead guitar by Mick Mashbir behind the scenes (not seen on the stage.) Mashbir continued in this role through the next tour and the South American tour as well.

The BILLION DOLLAR BABIES tour showcased Alice wearing leopard skin platform shoes on stage (first seen at the Omni show in Atlanta, Georgia.) Sometimes it seems that people remember those shoes more than the shows. The tour is also remembered (perhaps unfavorably in some corners) for the inclusion of Flo & Eddie as the opening act. Unfavorably because Flo & Eddie — two former members of the 1960's rock group The Turtles, who had also later worked with Frank Zappa — would be asked to accompany Alice alone to radio interviews while the rest of the band was preparing for the shows. Some clearly felt that this was an attempt to emphasize Alice over the other members of the band.

The band received some free press in the UK at this time because of attempts by a member of Parliament, Labour Party member Leo Abse of Pontypool, and the infamous Mary Whitehouse of TV censorship fame, to make sure the band didn't tour there for BILLION DOLLAR BABIES. As it stood, the band hadn't planned to tour there anyway, but didn't bothered correcting the wrong assumption since it made for good press.

And speaking of press, although Bob Greene's book about the band is titled BILLION DOLLAR BABY, it's not actually about this tour, but the one that followed it (in the winter of 1973 / 74 for the album MUSCLE OF LOVE. Having said that, however, since the later tour ended up being a follow-up tour for B$B — and was called THE BILLION DOLLAR BABIES HOLIDAY TOUR — the two tours are understandably confused anyhow. For more information, check out the next tour entry.)

March 5, 1973 - Capitol Theatre, Portchester, NY
    A special dress rehearsal and press-only show for the tour.
March 8, 1973 - Philadelphia Spectrum, Philadelphia, PA
    The actual first show of the tour.
March 9, 1973 - Philadelphia Spectrum, Philadelphia, PA
March 16, 1973 - Cum. City Memorial Auditorium, Fayetteville, NC
March 17, 1973 - Clemsen University, Clemsen, SC
March 18, 1973 - Coliseum, Charlotte, NC
March 20, 1973 - Coliseum, Jackson MS
March 23, 1973 - Omni, Atlanta, GA

March 24, 1973 - Carolina Coliseum, Columbia, SC
March 26 1973 - Boston Gardens, Boston, MA
   The show was recorded from the audience.
March 28, 1973 - Hershey, PA
March 30, 1973 - Convention Center, Indianapolis, Indiana
   Bob Greene discusses this show in Chapter 2 of his book BILLION DOLLAR BABY.
March 31, 1973 - Public Hall, Cleveland, OH
April 1, 1973 - The Gardens, Cincinnati, OH
April 2, 1973 - Convention Center, Louisville, KY
April 4, 1973 - Cobo Hall, Detroit, MI
April 5, 1973 - Cobo Hall, Detroit, MI
April 6, 1973 - Civic Arena, Pittsburgh, PA
   The show was recorded from the audience.
April 8, 1973 - Memorial Coliseum, Fort Wayne, IN
April 9, 1973 - Amphitheater, Chicago, IL
April 10, 1973 - Amphitheater, Chicago, IL
April 12, 1973 - Pershing, Lincoln, NE
April 13, 1973 - Municipal Auditorium, St. Louis, MO
April 14, 1973 - Mid-South Coliseum, Memphis, TN
April 15, 1973 - Kansas City Municipal Auditorium, Kansas City, MO
April 20, 1973 - Pirate's World, Miami, FL
April 21, 1973 - Pirate's World, Miami, FL
April 22, 1973 - Veterans Memorial, Jacksonville, FL
April 25, 1973 - Municipal Auditorium, Mobile, AL
April 26, 1973 - Memorial Auditorium, New Orleans, LA
April 27, 1973 - Hirsh Memorial Coliseum, Louis, TX
April 28, 1973 - Memorial Auditorium, Dallas, TX
April 29, 1973 - Sam Houston Coliseum, Houston, TX
   The Dallas and Houston shows were filmed for inclusion in the film GOOD TO SEE YOU AGAIN, ALICE COOPER. (see the Film entry for more details.) As expected, both shows were professionally recorded and have turned up on audio in fan circles.
April 30, 1973 - Corpus Christi, TX
   This show was recorded from the sound board.
May 1, 1973 - Fairgrounds Arena, Oklahoma City, OK
May 2, 1973 - Tulsa Assembly Center, Tulsa, OK
May 3, 1973 - Will Rogers Coliseum, Fort Worth, TX
May 4, 1973 - University of New Mexico, Albuquerque, NM
May 5, 1973 - Community Center, Tucson, AZ
May 10, 1973 - L. A. Forum, Los Angeles, CA
   The show was recorded from the sound board.
May 12, 1973 - Swing Auditorium, San Bernardino, CA
May 13, 1973 - Sports Arena, San Diego, CA
May 1973 - Crescent City, CA
   The show was recorded from the sound board.
May 17, 1973 - Denver Coliseum, Denver, CO
May 18, 1973 - Denver Coliseum, Denver, CO
May 19, 1973 - Salt lake Palace, Salt lake City, UT
May 20, 1973 - Las Vegas, NV
May 24, 1973 - Portland Memorial Coliseum, Portland, OR
   The show was recorded from the sound board.
May 25, 1973 - Seattle, WA
May 26, 1973 - Vancouver, British Columbia
May 30, 1973 - Metro Sports Arena, Minneapolis, MN
   The show recorded from the sound board.
May 31, 1973 - Milwaukee Arena, Milwaukee, WI
June 3, 1973 - Madison Square Garden, New York, NY
   This was originally supposed to have been the final show of the tour, but two additional shows were added. Part of the show recorded from the audience, only twenty minutes of which are known to exist.
June 5, 1973 - Vancouver, British Columbia
June 7, 1973 - Providence, RI
   Show recorded from the audience. During the encore, Flo & Eddie appeared on stage with the band and

performed Hard Day's Night.

Tour Name: **THE BILLION DOLLAR BABIES HOLIDAY TOUR**
Tour Period: December 1973.
Performers: Alice Cooper (vocals), Michael Bruce (rhythm guitar and vocals), Neal Smith (drums and vocals), Dennis Dunaway (bass and vocals) and Glen Buxton (lead guitar.)
Additional performers: Mick Mashbir (lead guitar), Bob Dolin (keyboards), The Amazing (James) Randi (executioner, dentist), Cindy Smith (the "dancing tooth") and Bob Greene (Santa.)
Opening Act: Stories (the first show only) and ZZ Top.
Set List: Hello, Hooray / Billion Dollar Babies / Elected / I'm Eighteen / Big Apple Dreaming (Hippo) / Muscle of Love / Hard Hearted Alice / My Stars / Unfinished Sweet / Sick Things / Dead Babies / I Love the Dead / School's Out / Working Up a Sweat

Besides five shows in South America in the spring of 1974, this was the last time that the band played together on a regular basis. It was certainly the last North American tour of the original band.

This tour is documented in Bob Greene's book BILLION DOLLAR BABY, and Greene became part of the production playing Santa Claus at the end of the show in much the same fashion as Richard M. Dixon played Nixon on the BILLION DOLLAR BABIES tour (presented during the encore so the that band could beat up on him. See the Book entry in Part 5 for more details about the book.) The tour was seen by the band, other performers, and people behind the scenes as just a continuation of the previous tour, and, except for some songs from MUSCLE OF LOVE being dropped into the set list (and Santa replacing Nixon), there was little difference to be seen. The Amazing Randi still guillotined Alice, and Cindy Smith was once again the "dancing tooth". It was, no doubt, primarily for this reason that the band members viewed the tour as a downer — because of the continual repetition — and also because it took them away from home for the holiday season. As is evident in Greene's book, the band members were reaching their breaking points, and were in need of some time away from each other.

Two dates were canceled during the tour: Tampa, Florida (due to weather conditions and because half the tour group was sick); and Binghamton, New York (because of concerns by the board of directors who ran the hall where Alice was to play.) In their stead came a show added after the tour began for December 13 in Toledo, Ohio, which was the setting for the worst incident of the tour. The audience was throwing things at the band during their set, and an M-80 (fireworks) went off right near a road member (which could have severely injured people). Additionally, Glen Buxton later claimed that he'd been hit in the knee with a ball-peen hammer during the show. The band stopped after two songs and later told the press that Michael Bruce had been hit by flying glass from the explosion, and had had glass removed from his eye by a doctor. This was done so that the cancellation was for more personal reasons.

Some fans may see canceling the show when the fireworks began going off as a cop-out, but similar incidents have provided good reason. Rock concerts in the early- to mid-1970's had the potential for much destructive violence, and there were known stories of other performers having been hurt on stage (Lesley West of Mountain once had his hair catch on fire on stage when an M-80 exploded next to his head, and Peter Criss of KISS was blown right off of his drum kit by the same type of fireworks. There are other stories as well.) Beyond these unfortunate incidents, the tour was played out any without major problems.

December 8, 1973 - Municipal Auditorium, Nashville, TN
The first show of the tour.
December 9, 1973 - Greensboro Coliseum, Greensboro, NC
December 11, 1973 - Dane County Expo Center, Madison, WI
December 12, 1973 - University of Michigan Field House, Ann Arbor, MI
December 13, 1973 - Toledo Sports Arena, Toledo, OH
The site of the M-80 story above where the band refused to continue after two songs because the audience had become uncontrollable.
December 14, 1973 - Maple Leaf Gardens, Toronto, Canada
Tour equipment was unavailable for this show because of mechanical problems with the truck. The following two shows suffered the same shortcomings. Makeshift material was put together for the show (Randi cut Alice's head with a sword instead of the guillotine.) A bootleg of this show was released in 1977 as IN TORONTO 1973. The recording includes a pre-gig announcement about the events of the Toledo show and requesting that there be no repeat of the event in Toronto.
December 15, 1973 - Onondaga County War Memorial, Syracuse, NY
Tour equipment was unavailable for this show.
December 16, 1973 - The Scope, Norfolk, NY

Tour equipment was unavailable for this show.
December 19, 1973 - Capital Centre, Largo, MD
December 26, 1973 - New Haven Coliseum, New Haven, CT
   The show was recorded from the audience.
December 27, 1973 - Montreal Forum, Montreal, Canada
December 29, 1973 - Utica Memorial Auditorium, Utica, NY
   The show was recorded from the audience.
December 31, 1973 - Memorial Auditorium, Buffalo, NY
   The last concert of the tour.

Tour Name: **South America - 1974**
Tour Period: March 30 - April 8, 1974 (five shows only.)
Performers: Alice Cooper (vocals), Michael Bruce (rhythm guitar and vocals), Neal Smith (drums and vocals), Dennis Dunaway (bass and vocals) and Glen Buxton (lead guitar.)
Additional performers: Mick Mashbir (lead guitar), Bob Dolin (keyboards), The Amazing Randi (executioner, dentist), Cindy Smith (the "dancing tooth".)
Opening Act: Unknown.
Set List: Hello, Hooray / Billion Dollar Babies / Elected / I'm Eighteen / Big Apple Dreaming (Hippo) / Muscle of Love / Hard Hearted Alice / My Stars / Unfinished Sweet / Sick Things / Dead Babies / I Love the Dead / School's Out / Working Up a Sweat

Following the BILLION DOLLAR BABIES HOLIDAY TOUR, the band regrouped in Los Angeles to film a couple of segments for the barely-released GOOD TO SEE YOU AGAIN, ALICE COOPER. After a short time off, they gathered again in late March to prepare for the South American tour set for early April.

South America was not a typical place for Alice Cooper (nor any North American rock band) to play, and Alice was one of the first to do so. Rock bands playing in Brazil faced a sports venue, with huge attendance and much apprehension about security and safety. Alice's appearance in South America was no exception.

The South American tour show was the same as the previous HOLIDAY TOUR, excepting, of course, for Santa getting beaten up during the finale. All of the performers and songs were the same. This was the last time that the five original Alice Cooper members performed together in front of an audience.

March 30, 1974 - Anhembi, Sao Paulo, Brazil.
   More than 70,000 people attended this show.
April 2, 1974 - Teatro, Sao Paulo, Brazil
   Concert hall setting.
April 5, 1974 - Canecao, Rio de Janeiro, Brazil.
   Club setting.
April 7, 1974 - Maracanacinho, Rio de Janeiro, Brazil
April 8, 1974 - Maracanacinho, Rio de Janeiro, Brazil
   Sports arena setting.

Part 4 — Film and Television 1969 - 1974

As the band underwent its transition from the Spiders to the Nazz, and then into Alice Cooper (and finally as the Alice Cooper Group), film and television were also going through a transition, in terms of what was permissible for the public to see. Not only were music groups like the Beatles allowing rock and roll fans to see them on the big screen, but it became obvious to Hollywood producers that rock music would be a big money maker. Sure, there was no accounting for taste — did Hollywood producers ever exhibit taste? — but Hollywood has always known profits when it saw them.

Once begun, there was an explosion of rock bands appearing on television, in the US it was on variety programs such as THE ED SULLIVAN SHOW and THE HOLLYWOOD PALACE. But television was willing to showcase bands only if they could be reigned-in and controlled. No "spending the night together" for the Rolling Stones, they could only spend some time together. At least Jim Morrison was able to get away with singing "higher", but if you look at the clip from the SULLIVAN show, it's apparent that Morrison just slips it in with the look of a sly fox instead of the pouncing of a wild beast. Other performers were getting their segments cut from shows, such as THE SMOTHERS BROTHERS SHOW, simply because the themes of their songs were against the conservative norm. But some were getting away with things simply because the network gray suits couldn't figure out what they were singing.

The Alice Cooper Group couldn't hide their controversial aspects. In changing their focus to being as theatrical and outrageous as possible, the very force that pushed them into the spotlight made them an obvious target for TV censors. The original visual recording outlet for the band was through film, and then mostly as guest shots to show off the outrageous nature of rock and roll music.

It wasn't until the band broke through with I'm Eighteen in 1971 that television found it could no longer ignore Alice Cooper. Even then, it was in foreign markets that the band first had major exposure on the tube. Notoriety also came via young film makers experimenting with new ideas (the film THE CHICKEN INCIDENT for example.) There was a planned Excedrin commercial in the 1970's that was to feature Alice Cooper (as Excedrin Headache #48) that never got past the drawing board because of the (then) extreme nature of the band. In the US, it was the 1972 TV appearance on IN CONCERT (their first network appearance) that resulted in the first real backlash against the band (on a national level) in the States. (For more about that outrage see the IN CONCERT entry below.)

With the various incidents involving the band, and with the references being made to them becoming more widespread, the Alice Cooper Group — and even more so Alice Cooper himself — became household words, and there was no way for the American networks to ignore them any longer. It's unfortunate that, just as the band was achieving fame as a group, the media's attention was centering on the lead singer alone. When the band members went their own separate ways in 1974, Alice, as a solo performer, went on to finish the 1970's with a popularity miles beyond that of the original band thanks to the exposure from television and films.

IN CONCERT video cassette.

Finally, (although not discussed in great detail here) there is the film footage shot by fans during concerts. Before the days of the video-camera, people sometimes took their own 8-millimeter cameras to concerts. Normally such films are silent, and the picture-quality is shaky at best. Amateur footage exists from several tours from the 1970's, though normally not more than a few minutes at time.

On the B$B tour, Michael Bruce sometimes took a camera with him and shot footage of the band himself, but, apparently, the quality is not any better than the fan produced material. The Michael Bruce footage is about three hours long and contains only glimpses of the band members at work and play.

Film Title:	**CHICKEN INCIDENT**
Film Type:	Short film.
Created:	Filmed September 12, 1969 at the Toronto Rock 'N' Roll Revival. Created by D. A. Pennebaker and Desmond Letter Franklin.

This is a short film (approximately 13 minutes in length) of the band performing during the 1969 TORONTO ROCK 'N' ROLL REVIVAL. The film shows clearly that the band was still at a very experimental stage, with musicians crawling around during the extended solos, and Alice attacking the audience with a feather pillow.

This was also the time and place of the much publicized "chicken incident" (hence the name of the film) where a live chicken somehow managed to get on stage, and Alice, not guessing what would occur, threw it into the audience. The audience then ripped the live chicken to pieces, probably assuming that it was just another stage prop. There has been speculation over the years, even from Alice himself, that the chicken being on stage was not entirely accidental — it was widely known that the band would often grab hold of any loose, nearby object and make it part of the show. However, it's a safe assumption that the band never planned bringing a chicken on stage, or thought it might be killed by throwing it into the audience (I mean, who needs a chicken that badly?) The "chicken incident" incident became part of Alice's history, and is even discussed during the PRIME CUTS video documentary.

The film used was shot for the full-length rock documentary of the TORONTO ROCK 'N' ROLL REVIVAL by D. A. Pennebaker, which was called TORONTO POP and released in 1970. The film was later re-edited, after legal proceedings required the deletion of all John Lennon footage, and reissued as KEEP ON ROCKIN' including footage of Jimi Hendrix and Janis Joplin taken from the earlier MONTEREY POP FESTIVAL. The footage of Alice was never used in the film, and once he became famous, it found its way into the college and underground markets. Pennebaker is listed in the short film's credits as Baker Penne.

Film Title:	**DIARY OF A MAD HOUSEWIFE**
Film Type:	Theatrical film.
Created:	Filmed Fall 1969. Released by Universal Pictures, January 1970.

Frank Perry directed this film based on the novel by Sue Faufman. Perry has had a career with incredible creative highs (with such films as this one, MAN ON A SWING and THE SWIMMER), and drastic lows (such as MONSIGNOR and MOMMIE DEAREST.)

Alice Cooper and the band show up in the background of one early scene (they're performing at a party), and the band is seen only sporadically during this party scene. Nevertheless, they end it themselves by going the typical Cooper route and getting out the fire extinguisher and the feather pillows and cutting loose on the partygoers. The entire scene is roughly five minutes in length. The song performed is not an Alice original, but a song composed by Mars Bonfire of Steppenwolf fame.

Film Title:	**Reflected** and **Levity Ball** footage
Film Type:	Videotape.
Created:	Filmed 1969.
Music:	Reflected and Levity Ball.

During the promotion of PRETTIES FOR YOU, Alice Cooper appeared on a television program and performed these two songs. On the good side, copies of this are floating around in fandom and are incredibly good for such old footage. On the bad side, little information is know about the show other than that it was for a local program in a city in Pennsylvania. Still, it's worth looking for, especially for fans of the band's very early work.

Film Title:	**MIDSUMMER ROCK**
Film Type:	Film.
Created:	Filmed June 13, 1970 at the Cincinnati Pop Festival in Cincinnati, OH.
Music:	Lay Down And Die, Goodbye and Black Juju.

A portion of the film shows the band performing at this rock festival. It's evident that the band is still evolving. Alice gets hit with a cake at one point. The sequence is roughly fourteen minutes in length.

Film Title:	**STONE PONY** footage
Film Type:	Video-tape.
Created:	Filmed in 1971 at the Stone Pony, San Francisco, CA.

Music:	Sun Arise / Caught in a Dream / I'm Eighteen / Is It My Body / Second Coming / Ballad of Dwight Fry / Black Juju (a portion only)

This is approximately 35 minutes of the band performing live at the Stone Pony. Like most video tape recordings at the time, it's in black and white. It's also the only live footage from the LOVE IT TO DEATH tour that has become available in fan-circles, and is nearly a complete show (missing part of Black Juju and all of Return of the Spiders.) This tape is sometimes mistakenly claimed as being filmed in either Texas or Detroit, Michigan, and arguments still persist that this footage may not be from the Stone Pony.

Film Title:	TUBEWORKS
Film Type:	Television series.
Created:	Filmed in the Spring 1971 for a Detroit television station.
Music:	Is It My Body (two versions), I'm Eighteen and Black Juju.

This was recorded while the band was getting ready for the LOVE IT TO DEATH tour, and it is a good example of how they were beginning to firm up. It also provides a chance to see Michael Bruce on keyboards (a somewhat rare sight in a live performance for film or television.) Clips from this show appear in the 1991 video documentary PRIME CUTS.

Film Title:	MEDICINE BALL CARAVAN (a.k.a. WE HAVE COME FOR YOUR DAUGHTERS)
Film Type:	Theatrical film.
Created:	Filmed in the Summer of 1971 during the festival tour of the same name.
Music:	Black Juju.

Movie poster for the film.

One of the stops that the band made during the LOVE IT TO DEATH tour was as part of the MEDICINE BALL CARAVAN FESTIVAL tour sponsored by Warner Brothers. Also on the tour were The Youngbloods, Delaney and Bonnie, B. B. King, David Peel, Doug Kershaw and Jefferson Airplane. The concept of this tour was that Warner Brothers would put several of their west coast rock bands (like the Grateful Dead and Jefferson Airplane) on an old bus and them have the travel across the country playing shows along the way. Warner would then sell a soundtrack album made from some of the concerts, and release a film documentary about the tour. This ways they killed two birds with one stone — promoting the West Coast bands across the country, and, making money off the soundtrack album and movie.

To help cut costs, and to show the communal side of the West Coast bands, performers shared stage equipment. Unfortunately, Alice Cooper was not everyone's favorite mother's son, and the band was often looked upon as having spit in the communal soup bowl. At one show, they were even denied guitars and amps until Marty Balin of Jefferson Airplane lent them Airplane's equipment. Then again, Alice didn't help matters by publicly reporting that they needed the equipment because "after all, we are the best band here."

Alice Cooper performed Black Juju live on stage during the movie, but the soundtrack album uses the LOVE IT TO DEATH studio recording of Black Juju with crowd noises added over it.

Film Title:	THE BEAT CLUB
Film Type:	German television series.
Created:	Filmed and broadcast in October 1971 on German television.
Music:	Under My Wheels and I'm Eighteen.

While the band was in Europe to promote KILLER, they made their first performance on this series (they came back in 1972 to do a couple of more songs.) THE BEAT CLUB was a rock series that was much like TOP OF

THE POPS and MIDNIGHT SPECIAL, with the exception that the bands normally performed with no audience in attendance.

Film Title:	**OLD GREY WHISTLE TEST**
Film Type:	UK television series.
Created:	Filmed and broadcast in November 1971 on British television.
Music:	**Under My Wheels** and **Is It My Body**.

In England during the LOVE IT TO DEATH tour, the band performed **Under My Wheels** from the album that was to be released in the UK within a few weeks. This was basically the crossover point from the LOVE IT TO DEATH tour to the KILLER tour. Outtakes from this appearance have been circulating in fandom for some time now. It was obvious from both the show and the outtakes that Alice was drunk during this appearance.

Film Title:	**BARRY RICHARDS SHOW**
Film Type:	European television series.
Created:	Filmed 1971.
Music:	**I'm Eighteen**.

The band performs this one song for an episode entitled "Turn On TV". The only known copy of this footage is in black and white.

Film Title:	Unknown footage of **Killer**.
Film Type:	Unknown.
Created:	Filmed 1971.
Music:	**Killer**.

Circulating in fan circles is black and white footage of the band performing **Killer**. Not complete.

Film Title:	**ROCK-A-BYE**
Film Type:	Television documentary.
Created:	Portions filmed in the Summer 1972 at the Montreal, Canada KILLER concert, backstage at the same show, and at the airport where Alice is being picked up for the show.
Music:	**Dead Babies** and **Long Way to Go**.

A documentary about music overall, the segment featuring Alice centers on some members of a Gay Liberation Front group who are waiting for Alice at the airport (and get rather threatening to Alice's entourage as he gets into a waiting car.) The band is also shown backstage getting ready for the show, and performing parts of two songs. Alice's hanging is also shown.

Some fans over the years have mistakenly assumed that the segment of Alice and the men falling over themselves trying to get at him was a comedy sketch from the GOOD TO SEE YOU AGAIN, ALICE COOPER movie. Footage from this documentary that is floating around fandom was actually videotaped off a theater screen where the film was showing.

Film Title:	**TOP OF THE POPS**
Film Type:	British television series.
Created:	Filmed and broadcast in June 1972, while the band was finishing the KILLER tour and about to begin the SCHOOL'S OUT tour.
Music:	**School's Out**.

As listed, this was recorded right before the end of the KILLER tour when Alice and the band went to London, England to perform at Wembley. They appear in the show, although they appear to be merely synching their movements to the prerecorded track.

Film Title:	**School's Out**
Film Type:	Promotional live footage.
Created:	Filmed July 22, 1972 at the Hollywood Bowl, Hollywood, CA.
Music:	**School's Out**.

This was shot during the SCHOOL'S OUT concert at the Hollywood Bowl (where thousands of pair of paper panties were thrown into the audience by helicopter.) The footage was then edited to have **School's Out** played over top of it. The film was shown to help promote the School's Out single, and one of the first places it appeared was on the British series TOP OF THE POPS.

Film Title:	**New York City 1972 / School's Out** footage
Film Type:	Live footage.
Created:	Filmed in September 1972 in New York City.
Music:	School's Out.

Live footage of the band performing School's Out in New York City, with an extensive jam occurring in the middle of the song.

Film Title:	**IN CONCERT**
Film Type:	US television series.
Created:	Premiered at 11:30 p.m. September 21, 1972 on the ABC (USA) TV Network as part of their late-night WIDE WORLD OF ENTERTAINMENT programming.
Music:	I'm Eighteen / Gutter Cat Vs the Jets / Killer / Elected / School's Out.

This was the opening episode for the new series created by Don Kirshner, who would later leave the series to create his own syndicated series called, of course, DON KIRSHNER'S ROCK CONCERT (Dick Clark took over the production reigns once Kirshner left.) The show was part of ABC's late night programming which used an Umbrella name of WIDE WORLD OF ENTERTAINMENT, and was shown on Friday nights opposite Johnny Carson and the TONIGHT SHOW.

This first episode became a real news maker when some local stations around the country refused to air it because Alice Cooper was on the program. Supposedly, some stations even pulled the program as it was airing, something rarely done for network television in the US.

The program allowed fans to see how part of the normal stage show from the SCHOOL'S OUT period was set up, including the staged fight between band members during Gutter Cat Vs. the Jets. Alice was also seen fighting off members of the crowd at the beginning of the program.

Also performing on the show that night were Curtis Mayfield, Seals and Croft, Bo Diddley and Jethro Tull. A bootleg of both Alice's and Tull's performance was released within a year of the show called IAN AND ALICE 9-71 (see entry in Chapter 6.)

Film Title:	**THE BEAT CLUB**
Film Type:	German television series.
Created:	Filmed and broadcast November 1972 on German television.
Music:	I'm Eighteen and Public Animal #9.

While Alice was in Europe for the SCHOOL'S OUT tour, the band returned to this television series to help promote the album. The footage of the band performing I'm Eighteen (with a very drunk Alice) can be found on several video cassettes including PRIME CUTS and the Rhino release HAVE A NICE DAY, VOLUME 2.

Film Title:	**JUKE BOX**
Film Type:	Television series.
Created:	Filmed during the SCHOOL'S OUT tour.

A half-hour look at the SCHOOL'S OUT tour, this was a documentary film by Freddie Hauser and is sometimes referred to in fan circles as the "Hauser" film.

Film Title:	**Hello, Hooray**
Film Type:	Promotional music clip.
Created:	Filmed January 1973 and shown on various rock music programs.

This is a promotional film of the band performing the song on a darkened stage. Alice wears only a bit of black mascara around his eyes for the video, and is shown wearing a white shirt and pants with a rather odd looking belt (which is almost a predecessor to his soon-to-be-standard cup.) Alice performs the song as if he is weary of the show already, while passersby get in the way of the camera and hand things off to him.

Film Title:	**GOOD TO SEE YOU AGAIN, ALICE COOPER**
Film Type:	Full-length movie.
Created:	This was filmed April 28, 1973 in Dallas, Texas (concert footage), April 1973 in Houston, Texas (concert footage) and February 1974 in Los Angeles, California (comedy sketches.) Additional footage for the re-edited version of the film is from a press conference with Alice, time period unknown. Presented by Penthouse Productions in association with Alive Enterprises. Executive producer was Shep Gordon. Produced by Herb Margolis and Joe Gannon. Conceived by Joe Gannon. Written by Fred Smoot, Shep Gordon and Joe Gannon.

The original film premiered in the Summer of 1974 in Binghamton, NY. It was re-edited and distributed Fall 1974. The unofficial German video of the re-edited version was released in 1986 (catalog number SV 8612-1.) The box for the video says that it is "exclusive for Germany, Austria and Switzerland. |
| Music: | See details below. |
| Performers: | Alice Cooper, Michael Bruce, Dennis Dunaway, Neal Smith and Glen Buxton. Also, Cindy Smith as the "dancing tooth" and James Randi as the Dentist and Executioner. Additional performers in original version: Fred Smoot (as the Director, Lone Ranger-type hero and as security guard), Jefferson Kewley (as Baron Krelve, the opera-Viking / henchman) and Pat McAllister (as producer, rancher and man in charge of box-office.) Additional performers in re-edited version: Fred Smoot (as Director) and Pat McAllister (as Producer.) |

This was to have been the film to break Alice Cooper into a new media — the movies. Frankly, it didn't happen. Made with the backing of Penthouse Magazine, the film was conceived by Joe Gannon, who had worked with the Alice Cooper Group since the days of BILLION DOLLAR BABIES and had designed the stage set for most of the Cooper shows since SCHOOL'S OUT.

The principle idea was to do a concert film that was a bit different by inserting comedy sketches of the band into the proceedings. The problem was that the sketches written just weren't very good. The failure seems to have fallen heavily on the shoulders of Fred Smoot, who appears as the Director during the first sketch (and throughout the film in the original version.) His attempts at trying to improvise many of his lines on camera falls extremely flat (although he does shine a bit better in the Lone Ranger material.) The film doesn't seem to know where it's going from sketch to sketch, and the ending of the film can be guessed after about twenty minutes. Worse, the comedy sketches go on far too long, and are extremely static. Although the concert footage is quite inventive for its camera angles, the same doesn't hold true for the comedy sketches, which are shot dead on and locked into place. It wouldn't be a surprise to find that audiences were soon bored with the movie.

Thoughts of doing a concert film with comedy sketches came as early as the summer of 1973, when Alice spoke to CIRCUS MAGAZINE about the idea. He also stated that filming for some comedy sketches had already occurred during the B$B tour. One was filmed while the band was in Houston, Texas and featured them in their tour plane using tacos to fight off Indians who attacked the plane with balloons full of stage blood. Another filmed segment showed a man eating cake and drinking Listerine, while another man's face rots away from syphilis. Strangely enough, these hilarious hi-jinks never made it into either version of the finished film. Also mentioned in the CIRCUS interview is the name of the film, which was to be called either PELVIC THRUST or MUSCLE OF LOVE (the latter which, of course, became the title of the last studio album by the original Alice Cooper Group.)

After the film's premiere in Binghamton, New York (the city that refused to allow Alice to perform during his BILLION DOLLAR BABIES HOLIDAY TOUR), the movie was pulled and re-edited to tighten up its pace. However, to do so, most of the comedy material was jettisoned, leaving a movie barely over an hour long. The length of the movie was boosted by including old movie clips into the mix that are supposed to relate to each other, or to the song being performed. Additional footage was taken from a press junket done by Alice during the BILLION DOLLAR BABIES tour, but the footage is so haphazard that it's difficult to decipher what Alice is talking about half the time.

The film was then re-released and made some quick runs across the country (mostly, it seems, as a midnight movie), then disappeared until the mid-1980's when a company in Germany released the re-edited version of the movie on tape. It's this version of the film that most fans are aware of, and copies have been circulating in fan circles for years now. Meanwhile, the original cut of the movie has also resurfaced in fan circles, no doubt from a fan's private film collection since the original reel changes are still in evidence. Among the posters produced for the film, rare items themselves, is one that shows Alice with flowers in his hair, along with a guillotine, King Tut, Richard Nixon, a snake, Betty Boop and Uncle Sam.

Footage apparently shot by Michael Bruce during the making of the movie has also shown up in fan circles. This footage, part of three hours worth of home movie material, is very short and is shot from very far away, and so would probably only be of interest to die-hard fans.

Along with Joe Gannon, Jefferson Kewley was involved with the film and would return to work with Alice over the years. He plays the Director's henchman in the film, and replaced Dick Wagner on the second leg of the LACE AND WHISKEY tour (the SCHOOL'S OUT FOR SUMMER 1978 TOUR) and also played some guitar on the FROM THE INSIDE album. Kewley plays a banjo in the sketch version of the movie and does very well considering he's doing so while riding backwards on a mule and wearing an operatic Viking's outfit (long story, you'll just have to see the movie.)

There are several minor changes in the film beyond the comedy sketches, and for fans who are unable to get the movie, the best thing to do is to examine the two movies against each other as detailed below.

German video release of
GOOD TO SEE YOU AGAIN, ALICE COOPER

Original Version: [Running Length: 1 hour, 36 minutes]
0:00:00 - The film opens with the band getting ready to perform in their white tuxes (a bit longer than in the re-edited version.) Finally, the pianist announces Alice who sings **Lady is a Tramp**.
- Alice stops singing when he realizes how stupid the whole setup is. As the band rip off their tuxes, the Director tells them to stop. Fed up, the band members overturn the piano, push the producer around, and stomp out to their waiting limo, but not before Alice orders the destruction of the set by a waiting bulldozer.
- The bulldozer then destroys the set (in a slightly longer sequence than in the re-edited version.)
0:06:39 - The Director vows vengeance against the band.
0:07:28 - As the limo pulls off, the Director runs out and continues to yell. He's met there by a man dressed as an Operatic Viking and pushing a two-man bike. As they talk (and "good to see you again" is said for the first of many times), they agree to go off in search of the band.
0:08:19 - Cut to the limo, which stops. Alice pokes his head out of the window and announces that the movie is going to be made their way.
0:08:24 - The opening credits of the film are shown over fast forward footage of a stage being setup for the show. **Never Been Sold Before** is heard on the soundtrack during this footage (The credits are in a different typeface than in the re-edited version, and credits are included for those actors who only appear in the original edit.)
0:10:13 - As the lights dim, Alice is announced and the band performs **Hello, Hooray**.
0:13:18 - **Billion Dollar Babies** is performed.
0:17:02 - Cut back to the Director as he sits in a doctor's office (listed as "Psychity" on the door.) The Director discusses his paranoia concerning Alice with a figure who has his back to the camera. As he discusses his problems, the film goes into a flashback.
0:18:52 - The only other comedy sketch in the entire movie to showcase the band. Riding bicycles, they stop at a toll booth in the middle of the countryside and steal a man's elephant (Yes, it's about as funny as it sounds.) The Director and the Viking show up soon afterwards and steal a camel to continue with their chase. (And, yes, this is also about as funny as it sounds.) The entire segment is nine minutes long and Alice and the band only appear for about two of those minutes.
0:26:52 - **Elected** and **I'm Eighteen**.
0:33:41 - Back at the Doctor's office, the Director describes another flashback which show him as a Lone

Ranger-type hero. After talking with a rancher, the Director and the Viking steal a horse and a mule (in tennis shoes) and head off after the band once again.

0:37:36 - **Raped and Freezin'**.
0:41:11 - **No More Mr. Nice Guy**.
0:44:55 - **My Stars**.
0:49:48 - **Unfinished Sweet**.
- During the song, the film cuts to Alice with his giant toothbrush chasing Cindy Smith, as the dancing tooth, through the streets of a big city. He's stopped by the Amazing Randi, as the Dentist, and knocked out cold.
0:55:14 - Back at the Doctor's office, the Director talks about the show and the snakes.
0:56:55 - After all this talk about snakes, the film cuts to the ending of **Sick Things** and doesn't show any snakes whatever.
0:58:26 - **Dead Babies**.
1:01:04 - **I Love the Dead**.
- This concert sequence shows Alice being put into the guillotine and beheaded by the Amazing Randi as the executioner.
1:05:48 - As Alice's head is shown in the concert sequence, the scene cuts to Alice in a cape and skeleton costume, stumbling around in a graveyard. He soon comes across a neon gravestone with his own name on it. Taking a nearby shovel, Alice smashes the gravestone in slow motion. This sequence would be refilmed (although the smashing of the gravestone would remain the same) for the WELCOME TO MY NIGHTMARE tour and concert film.
1:07:58 - Back at the Doctor's office, the Director talks a bit more about his thoughts of Alice.
1:08:34 - **School's Out**
- This concert sequence is intercut with the Director outside of the hall trying to sneak in, as a security guard, so that he can get into the box office and take off with the money from the show. After he finally convinces the person in the box office to take the loot and get in the waiting car driven by the Viking, the car self-destructs.
- Incidentally, if you look closely at the background during this scene, there are posters on the wall showing the band doing a chorus-line kick dressed in their "after-the-party" clothes from the MUSCLE OF LOVE album inner sleeve.
1:23:18 - The final portion of **School's Out**.
- This sequence is often referred to as the scene where a person from the audience beats up on Alice. Actually it's more like Alice beating the stuffing out of a person from the audience. Although it's been suggested that the beating was staged, all involved claim that it wasn't.
1:25:54 - **Under My Wheels**.
- The final concert sequence in the movie shows Alice and the band taking their bows, and Richard M. Dixon coming on stage as Nixon, whereupon the band beat him up.
1:34:10 - Back at the Doctor's office, the Director tries to calm down. The Doctor finally turns around to face the camera, takes off his glasses and, of course, it's Alice. He tells to the camera audience that it's "good to see you again" and the film freezes on his image as the ending credits roll. **Hard Hearted Alice** is played over the credits. The final credit reads "The End?".

Re-edited Version: [Running Time: 1 hour, 21 minutes, 10 seconds]
0:00:00 - The film begins with the MOVIETONE NEWS logo, and some short news clips from a newsreel, followed by an announcement made about "The People Vs. Alice Cooper" and then begins combining old movie footage with an interview of Alice.
0:05:19 - Alice sings **Lady Is a Tramp**.
- The confrontation with the Director is slightly shorter than in the original version, and the part with the Director outside after the limo leaves is taken out.
0:09:10 - As the bulldozer breaks down the set and the limo is about to take off, Alice pokes his head out the car window and announces that the movie is going to be made their way. In the original version, the limo had been driving for some time before Alice makes his announcement.
0:10:20 - The opening credits are given over the stage being set up in fast-motion while **Never Been Sold Before** is heard on the soundtrack. The typeface used for the credits is very different from the original and the credits that no longer apply in the re-edited film have been cut .
0:12:04 - As the lights dim, Alice is introduced and the band plays **Hello, Hooray**.
0:15:03 - More old movie footage and Alice interview.
0:16:14 - **Billion Dollar Babies**.
0:19:47 - More old movie footage and Alice interview.
0:21:24 - **Elected** and **I'm Eighteen**.
0:27:54 - More old movie footage and Alice interview.

0:28:54 - **Raped and Freezin'**.
0:32:10 - **No More Mr. Nice Guy**.
0:34:40 - More old movie footage and Alice interview.
0:36:31 - **My Stars**.
- This segment opens with a long intro playing while a light show is superimposed over the screen. This intro was not in the original version.
0:43:45 - More old movie footage and Alice interview.
0:44:39 - **Unfinished Sweet**.
- Instead of the dream sequence (Alice chasing the dancing tooth through the streets), the re-edited version shows clips from an old W. C. Fields short about a Dentist.
0:49:37 - More old movie footage and Alice interview.
0:50:15 - **Sick Things**.
- The song is complete, unlike in the original version, and includes stock footage of snakes.
0:53:10 - **Dead Babies**.
0:55:55 - More old movie footage and Alice interview.
0:56:34 - **I Love the Dead**.
1:01:06 - Footage of Alice in the graveyard (see 1:05:48 in the original version for the details.)
1:03:10 - More old movie footage and Alice interview.
1:03:47 - **School's Out** (complete.)
1:11:01 - More old movie footage and Alice interview.
1:11:58 - **Under My Wheels**.
1:18:09 - The final bows by the band as the **Star Spangled Banner** plays on the sound system. Richard M. Dixon comes out to be beaten up and the camera freezes on his hand reaching out of the fight with the "victory" sign.
1:20:04 - Over this freeze-frame shot, the ending credits play. The music is **Hard Hearted Alice**, and the credits finish with "The End???"

Columbus, Ohio, 1998. Photo courtesy of Kevin Workman

Chapter 1: 1964 - 1974

Part 5 — Books 1969 - 1974

One of the several ROLLING STONE covers featuring Alice.

Contrary to popular opinion, some rock fans do like to read. And given the chance, they like to read about their favorite performers. Of course, in concession to the non-believers, many books about rock starts have been written on the "Dick and Jane" level (See Alice with the baby doll. Chop, Alice, Chop.) It also seems to be a prerequisite that books about rock stars have plenty of pictures.

During the Alice Cooper Group's rise to fame in the early 1970's, there were two books that typified the material coming out about Alice (they're dealt with below.) Interested fans can also find interviews with Alice and short articles in books such as the CREEM magazine-related paperback ROCK REVOLUTIONS (1976, Popular Library, 445-03121-150), or in some of the songbooks of the band's music released over the years (which sometimes also include photos of Alice.) Although the ROLLING STONE book listed below is actually from 1975 (after the release of WELCOME TO MY NIGHTMARE), it's listed here because most of the book deals with the early days of the band up to the breakup of the original Alice Cooper Group.

Rare MUSCLE OF LOVE book released in 1974.

Book Title: **CIRCUS - ALICE COOPER**
Published: Summer 1974 by Popular Library.
Author: Steve Demorest.
Content: 160 pages with black and white photos throughout. Gives the history of the Alice Cooper Group up to and including the GREATEST HITS album.

Written at the height of the band's fame (around the time that the GREATEST HITS album appeared), this is the earliest available book about the band. Information contained in the book is taken from several interviews, some of which have had their accuracy questioned over the years.

Circus released two other volumes in the CIRCUS BOOKS series — one on Elton John and the other on Robert Plant. Well worth checking out for early information and photos not normally seen (mostly from the KILLER and BILLION DOLLAR BABIES tours.)

Cover for the CIRCUS paperback released in 1974.

Book Title: **BILLION DOLLAR BABY**
Published: Hard cover in November 1974 by Ahtheneum, ISBN 0-689-10616-5, $10.
Paperback in October 1975 by Signet Books, ISBN 0-451-06713-4, $1.95.
Author: Bob Greene.
Content: This is a story written in the first person by newspaper columnist Bob Greene, who toured with the band during their 1973 BILLION DOLLAR BABIES HOLIDAY TOUR. Greene also sang backup on two tracks from the MUSCLE OF LOVE album (Woman Machine and Hard Hearted Alice.)

Greene's idea for the book was represented to Alice's manager as a story telling what life on the road is like for rock and roll musicians. To help give Greene an insider's view of the lifestyle and changes involved, he was made part of the show, playing Santa Claus on stage during the encore. Santa gets beaten up by the band and carried off stage (much like impressionist Richard M. Dixon playing Nixon did each night during THE ALICE COOPER SHOW tour earlier in the year.

Greene's writing is interesting and gives fans a look at how the band functioned day in and day out while on tour. It's also a chance to see how the band members reacted to each other on a personal level. Much has been said over the years about incidents being created purely for the benefit Greene's book — that some of it was merely "playacting" — but there's little in the book that comes across as being terribly outrageous or phony.

On the downside, Greene was intent on showing that the violent nature of the show had a negative effect on the audience (which he refers to as being more like frenzied animals in a cage than young kids) and actually went on to say in PUBLISHER WEEKLY (Vol. 206, page 28, August 5, 1974) that the acts performed on stage "are designed to titillate the darker side of the teenage personality." Greene also blasted the band in the same article as being a fabrication of the managers and the record company, referring to the band's entire career as a "mechanical process."

Fortunately, Greene's intent for the book never really comes off since he seems to be having too much fun on tour with the band to be successful at exposing them. Instead, those parts in the book where Greene tries to state his case against the band seem counterproductive his goal. Overall, the book is quite good in showing how the original Alice Cooper Group was burning out in its final days, but readers should take any insights from Greene with a grain of salt.

Greene also wrote about Alice in newspaper column back in the 1980's. The article appeared in a collection of his articles called MIDWESTERN BOY ON HIS OWN. The article portrayed Alice as just being a family man who didn't really care for rock music that much and wanted to live a normal life. This, of course, turned out to be incorrect since Alice was soon recording and touring again.

The book was first published in hardback in November 1974 with a cover that had no photo of the band. Instead, the cover shows a music bar with additional information about the book (almost like one would find on a Hunter S. Thompson book) which reads "A provocative young journalist chronicles his adventures on tour as a performing member of the Alice Cooper Rock-and-Roll Band." When the book was released a year later in paperback, a drawing of Alice in makeup was used for the cover.

Hard cover edition of BILLION DOLLAR BABY.

Paperback edition of BILLION DOLLAR BABY.

There's little doubt that the book's airing of the band's laundry in public contributed to the breakup of the original band. The book is now hard to find and has not been reissued since 1975.

Book Title:	**ROLLING STONE SCRAPBOOK: ALICE COOPER**
Published:	1975 by Straight Arrow Publishers, Inc. A ROLLING STONE Special Project.
Author:	Various.
Content:	72 pages with (color and black & white) photos. It came with a 17" x 22" color poster of the band. The book contains reprints of articles and reviews on Alice Cooper from 1970 through 1975.

Although ROLLING STONE has never been a magazine to hold theatrical groups such as Alice Cooper in high esteem, they have never denied what was popular. Thus, RS decided to put together this large trade paperback in 1975 after the successful release of WELCOME TO MY NIGHTMARE.

The book is made up of article reprints from the magazine along with many photos of Alice and the band. A discography is included in the back of the book put together by Dave Marsh. Annie Leibovitz, who did the front cover and poster photos, was a renowned rock photographer who was still emerging at the time of the book's release.

While some of the material is typical slagging-off of a band, there's a lot of good stuff in the book. This book is quite hard to come by today.

Chapter 1: 1964 - 1974

~~~ Chapter 2: 1975 - 1979 ~~~
Part 1 — "Devil's Food"

"Welcome to My Nightmare" would have been an fitting epitaph in March 1975 when Alice began his first tour as a solo artist. As it stood, there were rumors that Alice was planning on retiring, or possibly becoming a movie star and forsaking the world of rock music altogether. There were also concerns by promoters and record industry people that Alice Cooper the solo performer could never live up to the success of Alice Cooper the band.

Alice, though, was a performer who wanted to perform. The time off after the MUSCLE OF LOVE tour lasted only so long and then Alice was ready to begin work once again. Seeing as how both Neal Smith and Michael Bruce were working on solo projects, there was certainly no reason why Alice couldn't do the same. With that in mind, he began putting together material for the album that would become WELCOME TO MY NIGHTMARE. But the project didn't end with just the album. There was also a tour to put together, a concert film to be made, and a television special to support the album. Plus, without the concerns of the Alice Cooper Group band members to hold him back, Alice was able to turn the entire concert experience into a theatrical story to end all stories.

The album and tour were a success, and they found an Alice once again refreshed and having fun with the music and the tours. He met the woman who would become his wife, Sheryl, on the tour when she became one of the dancers used in the show. To follow it up, Alice now began making appearances on television shows and in films, and was ready to begin work on the sequel album to WELCOME TO MY NIGHTMARE, ALICE COOPER GOES TO HELL. With the new album, Alice had prepared to do another tour, but fell sick and ended up canceling the tour. So, while the album did well, featuring the hit single I Never Cry, it was a disappointment to fans looking for another Alice Cooper tour.

After the release of ALICE COOPER GOES TO HELL, Alice began to push the theatrical envelope a bit wider by becoming a different character in the show — one completely different from the "Killer Alice" that everyone knew. To bring that character to life, Alice devoted a good chunk of the next album to his creation, and with the appearance of LACE AND WHISKEY, the character "Maurice Escargot, the toughest cop in town" was born.

With "Maurice" came a new tour that further extended the theatrical presentation by devoting most of the stage to a giant television set on which films were played throughout a good part of the show. While "Killer Alice" still appeared in the show, "Maurice" was introduced to the crowd as a new Alice persona.

The tour was successful, and the album did well featuring the single You and Me. Yet, "Maurice" never really hit a nerve with fans the way that "Killer" had. More importantly, Alice was fighting his own demons while on the tour with an increasingly serious alcohol problem making him miserable and deathly ill. Alice had known that his drinking was getting out of hand, but he'd thought that he was winning the battle. However, by the end of the tour, he knew he had to seek help, and in October 1977 he had himself committed to a hospital to dry out.

1978 was a great year for Alice, starting with his return from the hospital. He returned to the stage to show the world a tough, strong and alcohol-free Alice with a tour that was the "second leg" to the LACE AND WHISKEY tour. His stay in hospital had also given Alice ideas for his next album, which appeared before the end of the year, FROM THE INSIDE.

This album showed that Alice was far from running out of ideas, and the tour that followed was just as successful, if not more so, than any tour before it. By the end of the 1970's, Alice looked to be on top of the world. But the world was changing, and soon Alice would as well.

Part 2 — Recordings 1975 - 1979

After the short South American tour in April 1974, the band members went their separate ways to work on other projects. Neal Smith and Michael Bruce were both working on solo albums that they hoped would show them as performers in their own right, as opposed to the commodity that had become Alice Cooper. While this was happening, Alice himself was hatching plans for a solo album to be made in the Fall of 1974.

Of these three solo projects, only Alice's album WELCOME TO MY NIGHTMARE was released to the public soon after it was finished. It was the real start of Alice's career outside of the Alice Cooper Group. Bruce's album IN MY OWN WAY waited until 1996 before being released in the US (although some deals were discussed at the time of the original recordings being made in 1974, and there was a brief 1980 release on vinyl in Germany), while Smith's PLATINUM GOD album has yet to appear officially, even though it's quite good. See Chapter 6 for more details on the other Alice Cooper Group members and their solo projects.

With the success of WELCOME TO MY NIGHTMARE — it achieved Gold status within three months (and ultimately Platinum) and did better on the charts then any of the earlier Alice Cooper Group albums with the exception of BILLION DOLLAR BABIES and SCHOOL'S OUT — Alice's solo career was assured. He began a five year period that saw him reach beyond the public's acceptance of the original band, and he was becoming part of the American culture fabric.

It was also the start of a period where each new album became the focus for a concept, with WELCOME TO MY NIGHTMARE and the follow-up album ALICE COOPER GOES TO HELL being two parts of a single story based on the same character. Alice tried to branch beyond the well-known Alice Cooper character and into new territory with LACE AND WHISKEY, only to return to his original character, from a very different perspective, on FROM THE INSIDE.

After the release of ALICE COOPER'S GREATEST HITS in 1974, packaging for Alice's albums reverted to the industry standard jacket. Four of the five albums released between 1975 and 1978 came in the standard, single-disc jacket, with a glossy paper inner sleeve. Only FROM THE INSIDE had a jacket design as experimental as those done for the likes of BILLION DOLLAR BABIES and SCHOOL'S OUT. After FROM THE INSIDE, only the special edition of THE LAST TEMPTATION in 1994 came close to presenting "extras" with a US pressing that had typically appeared with the early Alice Cooper albums.

The material in this chapter shows a period when Alice fell into a rhythm with his studio albums — one album released each year between 1975 and 1978 (with a live album in between two studio albums.) However, it was probably this same routine that led to Alice burning out, both in concert and on his albums, and led to the emergence in 1980 of a new Alice Cooper for a new decade. But for now, the time in November 1974, and the place is Toronto, Canada. Alice, the killer, was drifting in the background, and Steven, the little boy, was just about to go to sleep.

Album Title: **WELCOME TO MY NIGHTMARE**
Recorded: November - December 1974 at Soundstage, Toronto, Canada; Record Plant East and Electric Lady, New York City, NY; and A & R Studios, New York City, NY.
Production: Produced by Bob Ezrin for My Own Production Company Ltd. Production Assistant was Michael Sherman. A Black Widow Inc. and KRU Ltd. Production. Engineered at Soundstage by Dave Palmer and Jim Frank; engineered at Record Plant East and Electric Lady by Ed Sprigg, Dave Palmer, Corky Stasiak and Rod O'Brien; engineered at A & R Studios by Phil Ramone (listed as "the incredible" Phil Ramone.) Mastered by Mike Reese at The Mastering Lab in Los Angeles, CA. Musical orchestrations arranged by Bob Ezrin and Allan MacMillan. Additional credits: Bob Brown is listed as "Second Unit Director", and Alive Enterprises Inc. is listed under "Direction".
Personnel: Alice Cooper (vocals.) Dick Wagner (lead guitar on Devil's Food, The Black Widow, Only Women Bleed, Department of Youth, Cold Ethyl, The Awakening and Escape; acoustic guitar on Welcome to My Nightmare and Years Ago; slide guitar on Only Women Bleed; and additional vocals.) Steve Hunter (lead guitar on Welcome to My Nightmare, Some Folks, Cold Ethyl [opening lead only], Steven and The Awakening; slide guitar on Cold Ethyl; and high-strung guitar on Only Women Bleed.) Johnny (Bee) Badanjek (drums on Welcome to My Nightmare, The Black Widow and Escape.) Whitey Glan (all other drums.) Tony Levin (bass on Welcome to My Nightmare, The Black Widow and Escape.) Prakash John (all other bass.) Jozef Chirowski (clar-

	inet on WELCOME TO MY NIGHTMARE; organ on Devil's Food, Cold Ethyl and Escape; keyboards on The Black Widow and Department of Youth; piano on Some Folks, Steven and The Awakening; Fender Rhodes on Only Women Bleed; Harpsichord on Years Ago; and additional vocals.) Bob Ezrin (piano on The Black Widow; Tack Piano on Some Folks; and Fender Rhodes on The Awakening.) Additional vocals were by Gerry Lyons, Michael Sherman, David Ezrin and The Summerhill Children's Choir. Additional Performers: Vincent Price (as the Curator on The Black Widow) and Trish McKinnon (as Mom on Years Ago.)
Song List:	Welcome to My Nightmare (Cooper and Dick Wagner) / Devil's Food (Cooper, Ezrin, and Kelley Jay) / The Black Widow (Cooper, Wagner and Ezrin) / Some Folks (Cooper, Shep Gordon, and Ezrin) / Only Women Bleed (Cooper and Wagner) / Department of Youth (Cooper, Wagner and Ezrin) / Cold Ethyl (Cooper and Ezrin) / Years Ago (Cooper and Wagner) / Steven (Cooper and Ezrin) / The Awakening (Cooper, Wagner and Ezrin) / Escape (Cooper, Kim Fowley and Marc Anthony)

After the Brazilian tour in April 1974, Alice took time off from touring to do some television work (see Part 4 below) and some vocals for the album FLASH FEARLESS VS. THE ZORG WOMEN, PARTS FIVE AND SIX (see Chapter 6.) After it became apparent that Neal Smith and Michael Bruce would be busy with their solo albums, Alice decided to begin work on his own solo project.

The first step was writing the songs, and he worked on several with guitarist Dick Wagner while both were vacationing in the Bahamas that summer. Wagner, who had worked on earlier Cooper albums, had spent 1973 and early 1974 working with Lou Reed on three albums (ROCK AND ROLL ANIMAL, BERLIN and LOU REED LIVE.) Also involved on the three Reed albums was Bob Ezrin. Ezrin and Wagner had become noted as a team (if Ezrin felt a performer needed a guitarist who could pull off anything, Wagner was usually his first choice.) Wagner was not only an important contributor to WELCOME TO MY NIGHTMARE, but would remain working with Alice through the next two tours and six of the next seven albums (including the live album in 1977.)

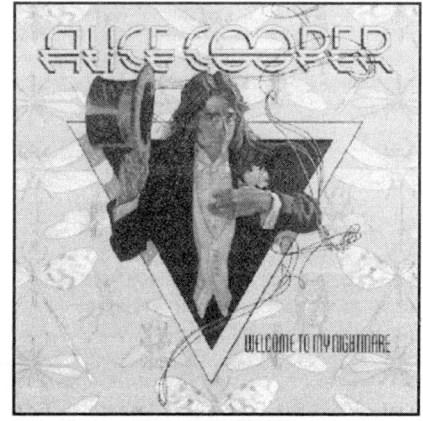

WELCOME TO MY NIGHTMARE album cover.

As a solo artist it was never Alice's intention to fill the album with guest performers (as was attempted with BILLION DOLLAR BABIES and MUSCLE OF LOVE.) However, that didn't stop the publicity machine from making it seem to be the intention during the early days of the album's production. CIRCUS magazine reported in October 1974 that the Beatles were to write the songs for the album and Marvin Hamlisch was to arrange the music. Of course, this was merely sensational hype. The only prediction that came to pass was Bob Ezrin as the album's producer.

The album was recorded with a group of musicians — Steve Hunter, Prakash John and Pentti "Whitey" Glan — who had already worked with Ezrin and Wagner (on the Lou Reed albums.) They also made up the band that toured with Alice after the album's release. It was an important factor in the album's success that Alice didn't have to experiment with new band members hoping to find a group that could work together. Time and energy were saved by merely dropping Alice into a polished band that already pretty much existed.

Featured on the album, with a small spoken role, was actor Vincent Price. Famous for his horror movies, Price made a career out of playing debonair, and sometimes over-the-top, roles, but it was his work in the early- to mid-1960's in films based on stories and poems by Edgar Allen Poe (directed by Roger Corman for American International Pictures) that cemented his claim in the horror genre (although the majority of his movies are not horror related.) Price appeared on the album at the beginning of The Black Widow, where he gives a description of the Black Widow spider that turns into a sinister rant against mankind. Price is listed as "the Curator" on the album credits, and, according to one album document, the role was original called "Jolly MacAmbre, Tour Guide at the Pasadena Palace of Insects." (One could point out that spiders aren't insects, but never mind.)

Vincent Price repeated his role in the television special made for the album called THE NIGHTMARE, which was shown on American TV in April 1975 (for details see Part 4), and even played the role in person at a show in December 1974 at the Sahara Tahoe in Las Vegas, Nevada. Price also recorded a variation of the Curator's rant for use during the WELCOME TO MY NIGHTMARE concert, and some additional narratives for the MAD HOUSE ROCK tour of 1979.

Welcome to My Nightmare was written by Alice and Dick Wagner in the middle of a mini-hurricane while vacationing in the Bahamas. As Wagner worked on the music, Alice started commenting on the weather conditions by singing the line "welcome to my nightmare" and the song took off from there.

Only Women Bleed was a track that Wagner that had done back in 1968 while in a band called The Frost. Neither Wagner nor Alice was very happy with the song's original lyrics when considering it for use on WELCOME TO MY NIGHTMARE. Alice had been contemplating lyrics for another song after mistaking a comment overheard on television as having been "Only Women Bleed." Using these as a start point, the song was developed and became the first Alice Cooper ballad to break the top 40 singles in the US. Alice continued to include ballads on later albums, and Only Women Bleed was certainly not the first ballad that Alice ever recorded (unless one thinks of "ballads" only in terms of "love songs" and you can hardly call Only Women Bleed a love song.)

Alice co-wrote Escape with Kim Fowley and Marc Anthony. Fowley is known for his work as a solo artist, and also for helping shape the early careers of bands such as Slade and The Runaways. Later, Fowley and Anthony would sue Randy Bachman of Bachman Turner Overdrive for a song written by Bachman called Down The Line which sounded too much like Escape. Bachman eventually added both of their names to the song credits. Fowley also worked with Anthony on a track for the Ezrin produced DESTROYER album by the rock band KISS in 1976.

As WELCOME TO MY NIGHTMARE began production, the idea for a television special (through Alive Enterprises) based around the album emerged. This was, in part, the reason why Atlantic, a subsidiary of Warner, was the record company to release the first Alice Cooper solo album. Other reasons involved politics inside Warner, most probably because of contractual issues pertaining to Alice Cooper the solo artist as opposed to Alice Cooper the band. Having the album issued on Atlantic (with a blurb on the back cover stating that Alice "appears by special arrangement with Warner Bros. Records") was a way to avoid contractual problems.

WELCOME TO MY NIGHTMARE was the last Alice Cooper album until FROM THE INSIDE to list Pacific Eye & Ear as the people behind the album graphics. Drew Struzan (who also worked on the GREATEST HITS album) of Pacific Eye & Ear, illustrated the front and back covers of the album. As with his previous work, the covers have a three-dimensional feel to them, and are incredible work. The painting for the album cover can be spotted in the background of a scene from the television special. The photo of Alice on the inner sleeve was done by Bret Lopez.

WELCOME TO MY NIGHTMARE was also the first album to list exactly who played what on each track, something that earlier albums didn't do.

WELCOME TO MY NIGHTMARE featured three songs that would become standards in concert throughout Alice's solo career — Welcome to My Nightmare, Only Women Bleed and Cold Ethyl. Only Women Bleed was later performed by many other artists, including Tina Turner, John Farnam and Lita Ford.

WELCOME TO MY NIGHTMARE rose in the charts to No. 5 in the US No. 19 in the UK (better than MUSCLE OF LOVE, but not as good as some of the albums previous to MUSCLE OF LOVE.) The album was certified Gold on May 30, 1975.

A special half speed vinyl re-mastering of the album was done in 1980 and released through Mobile Fidelity (see the entry later this chapter.)

Album Title: **WELCOME TO MY NIGHTMARE**
Released: February 1975 by Atlantic Records, a subsidiary of Warner Brothers.
Catalog No.: SD 18130
Media: Vinyl, Cassette and 8-Track.

Packaging for this album was not as complex as on earlier albums, so the differences between the various later reissues and the original are not as pronounced. This album came in the standard cover with a glossy paper inner sleeve that had lyrics printed on it. No other inserts or extras were included with the album. The Atlantic label used was the (at the time) standard green, white and red used for many of their releases.

Album Title: **WELCOME TO MY NIGHTMARE**
Released: March 15, 1975 by Anchor, UK.
Catalog No.: ANCL 2011
Media: Vinyl and Cassette.

Same as the US release. Anchor was the record company that released the album in the UK, Australia and most of Europe (since it wasn't on the main Warner Brothers label.)

Album Title: **WELCOME TO MY NIGHTMARE**
Released: March 1975 by Anchor, Argentina.
Catalog No.: 8121
Media: Vinyl.

Another Anchor release.

Album Title: **WELCOME TO MY NIGHTMARE**
Released: March 1975 by Anchor, Australia.
Catalog No.: ANCH 2011
Media: Vinyl and Cassette.

Same as the US release. The album reached No. 5 on the Australian charts.

Album Title: **WELCOME TO MY NIGHTMARE**
Released: March 1975 by Anchor, Belgium.
Catalog No.: 4C062-96350
Media: Vinyl.

Very similar to the UK version of album.

Album Title: **WELCOME TO MY NIGHTMARE**
Released: March 1975 by Anchor, France.
Catalog No.: 68051
Media: Vinyl.

Released by Anchor in a gatefold sleeve, which is an oddity since Anchor didn't do this for WELCOME TO MY NIGHTMARE anywhere else.

Album Title: **WELCOME TO MY NIGHTMARE**
Released: March 1975 by Anchor, Germany.
Catalog No.: 1C062-96350
Media: Vinyl.

Same as the UK release.

Album Title: **WELCOME TO MY NIGHTMARE**
Released: January 17, 1988 by Atlantic Records, Germany.
Catalog No.: ATLA 781542-2, ATLA 781542-4
Media: CD and Cassette.

First French / German reissue of the album on CD.

Album Title: **WELCOME TO MY NIGHTMARE**
Released: October 24, 1990 by Atlantic Records.
Catalog No.: ATL 19157.2 (CD) and ATL 19157.4 (cassette)
Media: CD and Cassette.

This was the first CD pressing of the album in the US, released a week after another reissue on cassette on October 17, 1990.

Album Title: **WELCOME TO MY NIGHTMARE**
Released: October 24, 1990 by Atlantic Records.
Catalog No.: ATL 19157.2 (CD) and ATL 19157.4 (cassette)
Media: CD and Cassette.

Album Title: **WELCOME TO MY NIGHTMARE**
Released: 1990 by Warner Brothers, Australia.
Catalog No.: WAR 7815422
Media: CD.

This was the first CD reissue of the album in Australia and one of the few times that the album was released on the Warner Brothers label.

Album Title: **WELCOME TO MY NIGHTMARE**
Released: October 3, 1997 by Warner Brothers, Canada.
Catalog No.: WARN CD 19157 (CD) and WARN AC 18130 (cassette)
Media: CD and Cassette.

This is the latest reissue of the album, part of mass reissuing of the Alice Cooper catalog in Canada. Released on the Warner Brothers label.

Single Title: **Department of Youth / The Secrets We Keep (by MUD)**
Released: February 1975 by Anchor.
Catalog No.: 1C006-96379
Media: 7" promotional Vinyl.

This was a promotional 7" for the first single off of the WELCOME TO MY NIGHTMARE album. On the B-side is a promotional single from the band MUD titled The Secrets We Keep. The B-side is marked as a Columbia single and has the catalog number of 96249 70041.

Single Title: **Department of Youth** (stereo) / **Department of Youth** (mono)
Released: February 1975 by Atlantic Records.
Catalog No.: 45-3280
Media: 7" promotional Vinyl.

Even though the label isn't given as Warner Brothers, that didn't stop the WB promotional gear from go into motion. This is a radio-only promotional single released to correspond with the commercial single.

Single Title: **Department of Youth / Some Folks**
Released: February 1975 by Atlantic Records.
Catalog No.: 45-3280
Media: 7" Vinyl.

Released without a picture sleeve, Department of Youth reached No. 67 on the US charts. It was the first US single to feature a B-side different from the one used for the single in other parts of the world.

Single Title: **Department of Youth / Cold Ethyl**
Released: February 1975 by Anchor, UK.
Catalog No.: Anchor 1012
Media: 7" Vinyl.

Released with a picture sleeve and with the black Anchor label. This single didn't chart in the UK.

Single Title: **Department of Youth / Cold Ethyl**
Released: February 1975 by Anchor, Australia.
Catalog No.: ANC-10731
Media: 7" Vinyl.

Department of Youth reached No. 7 on the Australian charts.

Single Title: **Department of Youth / Cold Ethyl**
Released: February 1975 by Anchor, Belgium.
Catalog No.: 4C006-93679
Media: 7" Vinyl.

This was the same as UK release, but without a picture sleeve.

Single Title: **Department of Youth / Cold Ethyl**
Released: February 1975 by Anchor, France.
Catalog No.: 2C004-96379
Media: 7" Vinyl.

Single Title: **Department of Youth / Cold Ethyl**
Released: February 1975 by Anchor, Germany.
Catalog No.: 1C006-96379
Media: 7" Vinyl.

Picture sleeve.

Single Title: **Department of Youth / Cold Ethyl**
Released: February 1975 by Anchor, Holland.
Catalog No.: 5C006-96379
Media: 7" Vinyl.

Single Title: **Department of Youth / Cold Ethyl**
Released: February 1975 by Anchor, Italy.
Catalog No.: 3C006-96379
Media: 7" Vinyl.

Single Title: **Department of Youth / Cold Ethyl**
Released: February 1975 by Anchor, Japan.
Catalog No.: IPR-10732
Media: 7" Vinyl.

Single Title: **Department of Youth / Cold Ethyl**
Released: February 1975 by Anchor, Portugal.
Catalog No.: 006-96379
Media: 7" Vinyl.

Single Title: **Department of Youth / Cold Ethyl**
Released: February 1975 by Anchor, Yugoslavia.
Catalog No.: SANC 88851
Media: 7" Vinyl.

Single Title: **Only Women Bleed** (stereo) / **Only Women Bleed** (mono)
Released: May 1975 by Atlantic Records.
Catalog No.: 45-3245
Media: 7" promotional Vinyl.

A radio-only promotional single released to correspond with the commercial single.

Single Title: **Only Women Bleed / Devil's Food**
Released: May 3, 1975 by Atlantic Records.
Catalog No.: AT 3245
Media: 7" Vinyl.

This second single from the WELCOME TO MY NIGHTMARE album reached No. 12 on the US charts.

Single Title: **Only Women Bleed / Devil's Food**
Released: July 1975 by Anchor, UK.
Catalog No.: Anchor 1018

Media: 7" Vinyl.

The single didn't chart in the UK.

Single Title: **Only Women Bleed / Devil's Food**
Released: July 1975 by Anchor, Australia.
Catalog No.: ANC-10821
Media: 7" Vinyl.

Only Women Bleed reached No. 50 on the Australian charts.

Single Title: **Only Women / Cold Ethyl**
Released: Atlantic Records, Canada.
Catalog No.: AT 3254
Media: 7" Vinyl.

Released on the standard red and black Atlantic label. As can be seen, Only Women Bleed is listed as merely Only Women. One of the few examples of Cold Ethyl being used as a B-side for Only Women Bleed.

Single Title: **Only Women Bleed / Devil's Food**
Released: July 1975 by Anchor, France.
Catalog No.: 2C004-96650
Media: 7" Vinyl.

Single Title: **Only Women Bleed / Devil's Food**
Released: July 1975 by Anchor, Germany.
Catalog No.: 1C006-95650
Media: 7" Vinyl.

Single Title: **Welcome to My Nightmare** (stereo) / **Welcome to My Nightmare** (mono)
Released: September 1975 by Atlantic Records.
Catalog No.: 45-3298
Media: 7" Vinyl.

A radio-only promotional single released to correspond with the commercial single.

Single Title: **Welcome to My Nightmare / Cold Ethyl**
Released: September 1975 by Atlantic Records.
Catalog No.: 45-3298
Media: 7" Vinyl.

As with the other two singles from the WELCOME TO MY NIGHTMARE album, this one came in a normal Atlantic 7" paper sleeve and had the normal red and black Atlantic label. Welcome to My Nightmare reached No. 45 on the US charts.

Single Title: **Welcome to My Nightmare / The Black Widow**
Released: November 1975 by Anchor, UK.
Catalog No.: Anchor 1025
Media: 7" Vinyl.

Welcome to My Nightmare didn't chart in the UK.

Single Title: **Welcome to My Nightmare / The Black Widow**
Released: November 1975 by Anchor, Germany.
Catalog No.: 16537 AT
Media: 7" Vinyl.

Single Title: **Welcome to My Nightmare / Only Women Bleed**
Released: Late 1980's by Atlantic Records.
Catalog No.: OS-13195
Media: 7" Vinyl.

Part of the "Atlantic Oldies Series", this single lists Only Women Bleed on the label as Only Women. This single was released in two variations of the Atlantic labels: a black and green label with the normal Atlantic logo, and a grey label with the label's name inside a black triangle.

Single Title: **Welcome to My Nightmare / Only Women Bleed**
Released: Late 1980's by Anchor, Australia.
Catalog No.: AN-102731
Media: 7" Vinyl.

This was a reissue in the late 1980's much like the Atlantic Records reissue above.

Single Title: **Some Folks / Some Folks**
Released: 1975 by Hit Pop, Brazil.
Catalog No.: 2805 007
Media: 7" Vinyl.

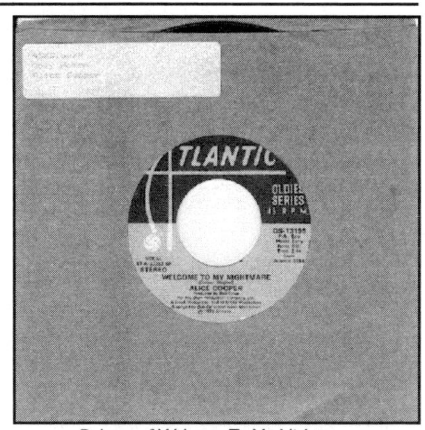

Reissue of Welcome To My Nightmare on the Atlantic Oldies Series label.

An odd release, as most countries did not consider this song as an A-side single. The B-side may not be Some Folks.

EP Title: **FOUR TRACKS FROM ALICE COOPER EP**
Released: December 1978 by Anchor Records.
Catalog No.: ANE 12001 (12" vinyl) and ANE 7001 (7" vinyl)
Media: 12" Vinyl and 7" Vinyl .
Song List: Welcome to My Nightmare / Department of Youth / Black Widow / Only Women Bleed

The cover of this EP is a photo of Alice wearing a top hat and resting his head on this fists. Unlike EPs from earlier albums, the front cover doesn't state the album from which the tracks are taken. Instead, the front cover merely states that it's "four tracks from Alice Cooper" with the song titles below it in the upper right-hand corner, while a banner stating "+ Fours 99p" is placed in the upper left-hand corner.

The back cover does give some additional information pertaining to the album, with a small photo of the WELCOME TO MY NIGHTMARE cover appearing as well. In describing the four tracks, the text manages to misspell Department of Youth and spelled Steven as "Stephen". It also describes the Black Widow spider as an "insect" and suggest that "womens-libbers" took Only Women Bleed as their anthem, which was certainly NOT the case.

FOUR TRACKS FROM ALICE COOPER EP.

Anchor released the EP as the first in a new (at the time) series of EP collections under the "Four Plus" title. Four track EPs were previously released by Warner Brothers for SCHOOL'S OUT in 1972, BILLION DOLLAR BABIES in 1973, and MUSCLE OF LOVE in 1974. Somewhat harder to find is the 7" vinyl variation of this EP with all tracks intact. It was issued with the white Anchor label.

Album Title: **WELCOME TO MY NIGHTMARE**
Released: Re-mastered, half-speed reissue released 1980 by Mobile Fidelity.
Catalog No.: 1-063
Media: Vinyl.

In the late 1970's, Mobile Fidelity began reissuing rock albums from the 1960's and 1970's (mainly the 70's) in a series called the "Original Master Recording". These albums were aimed directly at collectors, who already had the albums for a particular artist, but also had state-of-the-art stereo equipment (because just sticking a disk on Mom's dusty, old basement record player wasn't good enough.)

Mobile Fidelity's concept was a re-mastering of the album at half-speed onto a new plate, then pressing it onto high-definition (and, normally, virgin) vinyl. This resulted in better sound quality. The albums were then repackaged in a heavy-duty cardboard sleeve with the original artwork of the album's cover framed inside a larger mat stating that it was an "Original Master Recording". This re-mastering was done for several rock albums on a limited edition basis. The WELCOME TO MY NIGHTMARE album is one of the harder ones to find.

Although released in 1980 (so it really belongs in Chapter 3), it's given here in reference to the original album.

Album Title: **STAR-COLLECTION**
Released: 1975 by Warner Brothers, Germany
Catalog No.: MID 26033F
Media: Vinyl.

This was a German reissue of the LOVE IT TO DEATH album. An attempt was made to make the album look like a more recent release by discarding the original band cover for a photo of Alice with a snake (although the photo is from the right time period of 1971.) Really only an album for the collector who has everything or is missing LOVE IT TO DEATH.

Album Title: **STAR-COLLECTION**
Released: 1975 by Charter Line, Italy.
Catalog No.: CTR 46 177
Media: Vinyl.

Official German reissue of LOVE IT TO DEATH.

This was an Italian variation of the German STAR COLLECTION album, which is nothing more than a reissue of the LOVE IT TO DEATH album. As with the German variation, this is really an album for the collector who has everything or is missing LOVE IT TO DEATH.

Album Title: **ALICE COOPER GOES TO HELL**
Recorded: Recorded March - April 1976 at Soundstage, Toronto, Canada; Record Plant East, New York City, NY; and RCA Studios, Los Angeles, CA.
Production: Produced by Bob Ezrin for Migration Records Inc. A Black Widow / KRU Production. Engineered by Ringo Hrycyna, Corky Stasiak, Jim Frank and Brian Christian with John Jansen. Mastered by George Graves and Brian Christian at JAMF in Toronto, Canada. Music arranged by Bob Ezrin, Dick Wagner, Al MacMillan, John Tropea and The Hollywood Vampires (see the notes below for details.)
Additional credits: A credit is given for "Created By" in the liner notes. The thinking was most probably to give the album a Broadway-show type of feel by posting such a note in the album credits. The album was "created by" Alice Cooper, Bob Ezrin and Dick Wagner.
Personnel: Alice Cooper (vocals.) Dick Wagner (lead guitar on Go to Hell, Guilty, Wake Me Gently, Wish You Were Here and I'm Always Chasing Rainbows; guitar on You Gotta Dance, I'm The Coolest, Didn't We Meet and Give The Kid a Break; acoustic guitar on Didn't We Meet; classical guitar on Wake Me Gently; and additional vocals.) Steve Hunter (lead guitar on Go to Hell, You Gotta Dance, Didn't We Meet and Give The Kid a Break; guitar on Guilty, Wish You Were Here, I'm Always Chasing Rainbows and Going Home; acoustic guitars on I Never Cry and 12-string guitar on Wake Me Gently.) John Tropea (guitar on Go to Hell, You Gotta Dance and Give the Kid a Break; hi-string guitar on Wake Me Gently and wa-wa guitar on Wish You Were Here.) Jim Gordon (drums on I'm the Coolest, I'm Always Chasing Rainbows and Going Home.) Allan Schwartzberg (drums on all tracks not featuring Jim Gordon.) Babbitt (bass on Go to Hell.) Tony Levin (bass on all songs except Go to Hell.) Jim Maelan (percussion on all songs; soft show on I'm the Coolest and bluebird on I'm Always Chasing Rainbows.) Bob Ezrin (piano on You Gotta Dance, I'm The Coolest, Didn't We Meet, Give the Kid a Break, Wake Me Gently, I'm Always Chasing Rainbows and Going Home; Fender Rhodes on I Never Cry and synthesizer on I'm Always Chasing Rainbows.) Dick Berg (french horn on I Never Cry.) Additional vocals by Michael Sherman, Shawn Jackson, Colina Phillips, Joe Gannon, Shep Gordon, Denny Voxburgh,

Song List: Bill Misener, Laurel Ward, Sharon-Lee Williams, and Bob Ezrin. Al MacMillan is listed as playing piano on the album, but none of the individual song credits list him.

Go to Hell (Cooper, Wagner and Ezrin) / You Gotta Dance (Cooper, Wagner and Ezrin) / I'm The Coolest (Cooper, Wagner and Ezrin) / Didn't We Meet (Cooper, Wagner and Ezrin) / I Never Cry (Cooper and Wagner) / Give The Kid a Break (Cooper, Wagner and Ezrin) / Guilty (Cooper, Wagner and Ezrin) / Wake Me Gently (Cooper, Wagner and Ezrin) / Wish You Were Here (Cooper, Wagner and Ezrin) / I'm Always Chasing Rainbows (J. McCarthy and H. Carroll) / Going Home (Cooper, Wagner and Ezrin)

A quasi-sequel to WELCOME TO MY NIGHTMARE, ALICE COOPER GOES TO HELL finds Alice's story now being told to a youngster as a bedtime story. (One change in the continuation is that Steven is the main character dealt with during WTMN, while Steven becomes the youngster to whom the story is being told in ALICE COOPER GOES TO HELL.) Conceptually, the songs deal with Alice going to Hell and fighting the Devil (or, rather, fighting with the Devil over who is the coolest), while a subplot of the album (and what would have been the tour, if it had occurred) was that Hell was a disco and Alice needed to escape. As Alice reported in an interview for CIRCUS (#138, August 24, 1976, page 24), he finds that the only way to leave Hell is to sing a "pretty" song, which the Devil just can't stand. Thus, the 1918 song I'm Always Chasing Rainbows (made famous by Judy Garland, although original done by Charles Harrison) appears on the album as the tune that drives Alice out of Hell. As the album ends, Alice begins his journey home . . . or is this all still just part of the nightmare?

ALICE COOPER GOES TO HELL album.

Originally titled HELL, Alice continued the thread of concept albums with ALICE COOPER GOES TO HELL and can be congratulated for sticking very closely to the story line (I Never Cry could be argued as being a bit out of whack, but, even there, Alice found a way in interviews to suggest how it would fit in.) It would have been interesting to see how a third album in the series would have completed Alice's Inferno, but by that time Alice was ready to leave behind the horror character, and did so, as we'll see, with the release of LACE AND WHISKEY.

Working on ALICE COOPER GOES TO HELL was a group listed as "The Hollywood Vampires". The Hollywood Vampires was also a nickname given at that time to a group of famous people in the Los Angeles area who were known for their amazing drinking abilities. Alice was a member of that group, which also included John Lennon and Micky Dolenz (formerly of the Monkees), and Alice describes the group in detail in the documentary video PRIME CUTS. It was also the name of Alice's softball team at the time, which included many of the same people.

Featured in The Hollywood Vampires band were people who had by now become Cooper standards such as Dick Wagner, Steve Hunter and Bob Ezrin. Tony Levin, who played on WELCOME TO MY NIGHTMARE and the following year on LACE AND WHISKEY, also returned, as did Michael Sherman from WELCOME TO MY NIGHTMARE to sing backup vocals for the album. Several of the people listed on the album would have also played on the tour as The Hollywood Vampires if plans for the tour had not fallen through (see Part 3.) Instead, only Steve Hunter and Dick Wagner returned to tour when Alice finally hit the road again in 1977 for LACE AND WHISKEY.

Brian Christian, who had worked on the LOVE IT TO DEATH and KILLER albums, returned to co-engineer and co-master ALICE COOPER GOES TO HELL. Robert "Ringo" Hrycyna returned to work on the next album, LACE AND WHISKEY, and in 1983 on the DADA album.

It's interesting to note that the album was produced by Bob Ezrin for Migration Records Inc. instead of My Own Production Co. Ltd. as was the case on WELCOME TO MY NIGHTMARE, and then again on the next album, LACE AND WHISKEY.

I'm The Coolest was originally intended as a duet. In CRAWDADDY (August 1976), Alice suggested that he had wanted someone like Hitchcock or Orson Welles for the role of the Devil, but his third suggestion of

Henry Winkler (who played the Fonz on the television series HAPPY DAYS) developed to the point where Winkler was officially asked to play the role. Winkler turned it down, feeling that it would perpetuate his image as the Fonz and typecast him (typecasting which was already occurring thanks to the popularity of the HAPPY DAYS character.)

I Never Cry, another ballad from Alice, was the first and only single released from the album — a rarity for Alice. It was is most likely the cancellation of the tour that resulted in no other singles from GOES TO HELL being released. I Never Cry was another big hit for Alice, reaching No. 12 on the US. It also became a standard in concert for the next several tours and a million selling Gold single.

Wish You Were Here and Guilty also made the tour circuit in years to come, as did Go to Hell. A song called Menagerie, written by Alice and Alan Lee Gordon, made it to the demo stage before being rejected for the album.

Compared to other albums released by Alice over the years, ALICE COOPER GOES TO HELL is a bit disappointing design-wise. Put together by Rod Dyer and Brian Hagiwara, the front cover is merely a blown up photo of Alice from the inner sleeve of BILLION DOLLAR BABIES, with the color faded out and tinted green. While the cover does look sinister in its own right, it's hardly in the same class as the majority of the Cooper album covers before it or after. The back cover shows Alice, dressed in black, walking down a flight of steps and looking at the camera. Bret Lopez is listed as doing the "liner photography" on the album.

The single sleeve packaging contained a white paper inner sleeve with all lyrics and additional liner notes printed in red. A narration is also given at the beginning and ending of the lyrics to further suggest the conceptual nature of the album. It's here that we see the album as a bedtime story being told. As with previous studio albums, ALICE COOPER GOES TO HELL was reissued on cassette with LACE AND WHISKEY, only this time as a DOUBLE PLAY cassette (catalog number 23850-4.)

ALICE COOPER GOES TO HELL reached No. 27 on the US charts and No. 23 on the UK charts. It was certified as Gold on November 23, 1976.

Album Title: **ALICE COOPER GOES TO HELL**
Released: July 1976 by Warner Brothers.
Catalog No.: BS 2896 (vinyl) and M5 2896 (cassette)
Media: Vinyl, Cassette and 8-Track.

The packaging for this album was not as nifty as on earlier albums. The album came in a standard cover with a white paper inner sleeve with printed lyrics. The "Palm Tree" WB label was used, and no other inserts or extras were included.

Album Title: **ALICE COOPER GOES TO HELL**
Released: July 24, 1976 by Warner Brothers, UK.
Catalog No.: K 56171
Media: Vinyl and Cassette.

Same as the US release.

Album Title: **ALICE COOPER GOES TO HELL**
Released: July 1976 by Warner Brothers, Argentina.
Catalog No.: MH 5014261
Media: Vinyl.

Album Title: **ALICE COOPER GOES TO HELL**
Released: July 1976 by Warner Brothers, Australia.
Catalog No.: BS-2896
Media: Vinyl.

The album reached No. 4 on the Australian charts.

Album Title: **ALICE COOPER GOES TO HELL**
Released: July 1976 by Warner Brothers, Brazil.
Catalog No.: Unknown.

Media: Vinyl.

Album Title: **ALICE COOPER GOES TO HELL**
Released: July 1976 by Warner Brothers, France.
Catalog No.: 56171
Media: Vinyl.

Album Title: **ALICE COOPER GOES TO HELL**
Released: July 1976 by Warner Brothers, Germany.
Catalog No.: WB 56171
Media: Vinyl.

Album Title: **ALICE COOPER GOES TO HELL**
Released: July 1976 by Warner Brothers, Japan.
Catalog No.: P-10206W
Media: Vinyl.

A white-label sampler album with a 4-page booklet was also released at this time in Japan.

Album Title: **ALICE COOPER GOES TO HELL**
Released: July 1976 by Warner Brothers, South Africa.
Catalog No.: WBC 1313
Media: Vinyl.

Album Title: **ALICE COOPER GOES TO HELL**
Released: January 1, 1991 by Warner Brothers, Germany.
Catalog No.: WEA 927299-2, WEA 927299-4
Media: CD and Cassette.

This was the first French / German reissue of the album on CD.

Album Title: **ALICE COOPER GOES TO HELL**
Released: October 24, 1990 by Warner Brothers.
Catalog No.: WB2896.2 (CD) and WB2896.4 (cassette)
Media: CD and Cassette.

This was the first CD pressing of the album in the US. Released a week after another reissue of the album on cassette on October 17, 1990.

Album Title: **ALICE COOPER GOES TO HELL**
Released: 1990 by Warner Brothers, Australia.
Catalog No.: WAR 9272992
Media: CD.

This was the first CD pressing of the album in Australia.

Album Title: **ALICE COOPER GOES TO HELL**
Released: September 30, 1990 by Warner Brothers, Japan.
Catalog No.: WPCP 3493
Media: CD.

Part of the special "Forever Young Series" that WB released in Japan. The album came with an obi that listed the album's title and additional albums available in the series.

Album Title: **ALICE COOPER GOES TO HELL**
Released: October 3, 1997 by Warner Brothers, Canada.
Catalog No.: WARN CD 02896 (CD) and WARN AC 02896 (cassette)
Media: CD and Cassette.

The latest reissue of the album, part of a mass reissuing of the Alice Cooper catalog in Canada.

Single Title: **I Never Cry** (stereo) / **I Never Cry** (mono)
Released: June 1976 by Warner Brothers.
Catalog No.: WBS 8228
Media: 7" Vinyl.

A radio-only promotional single released to correspond with the commercial single. Released on the promo-only white WB label.

Single Title: **I Never Cry / Go to Hell**
Released: June 1976 by Warner Brothers.
Catalog No.: WBS 8228
Media: 7" Vinyl.

Released on the "Palm Tree" WB label, I Never Cry reached No. 12 on the US charts and went Gold on April 5, 1977. Some misprints of this single can be found with Go To Hell as the A-side and I Never Cry as the B-side.

Single Title: **I Never Cry / Go to Hell**
Released: June 1976 by Warner Brothers, UK.
Catalog No.: K 16792
Media: 7" Vinyl.

This single came in a picture sleeve (the picture of Alice is from the front cover of the ALICE COOPER GOES TO HELL album cover.) I Never Cry didn't chart in the UK.

Single Title: **I Never Cry / Go to Hell**
Released: June 1976 by Warner Brothers, Australia.
Catalog No.: WBS-8228
Media: 7" Vinyl.

I Never Cry reached No. 23 on the Australian charts.

UK single for I Never Cry.

Single Title: **I Never Cry / Go to Hell**
Released: June 1976 by Warner Brothers, Brazil.
Catalog No.: WB 16.010
Media: 7" Vinyl.

EP Title: **I Never Cry / Didn't We Meet / Wake Me Gently / You Gotta Dance**
Released: July 1976 by Warner Brothers, Brazil.
Catalog No.: 96.011
Media: 12" vinyl.

This EP was released in Brazil with songs from the ALICE COOPER GOES TO HELL album.

Single Title: **I Never Cry / Go to Hell**
Released: June 1976 by Warner Brothers, France.
Catalog No.: 16792
Media: 7" Vinyl.

The French release came in a picture sleeve.

Single Title: **I Never Cry / Wish You Were Here**
Released: June 1976 by Warner Brothers, Germany.
Catalog No.: 16802
Media: 7" Vinyl.

The picture sleeve used is the same as the album cover. One of the few countries to not use Go to Hell as the

B-side.

Single Title: **I Never Cry / Go to Hell**
Released: June 1976 by Warner Brothers, Japan.
Catalog No.: P-46W
Media: 7" Vinyl.

Came in a picture sleeve.

Single Title: **I Never Cry / Go to Hell**
Released: June 1976 by Warner Brothers, Portugal.
Catalog No.: N-S-63-107
Media: 7" Vinyl.

Came in a picture sleeve.

Single Title: **I Never Cry / You and Me**
Released: Mid-1980's by Warner Brothers.
Catalog No.: GWB 0347
Media: 7" Vinyl.

This was a reissue of two Alice hits by on one single under Warner's "Back to Back Hits" series collection.

Warner Brothers reissue of I Never Cry with You and Me on the B-side.

Album Title: **LACE AND WHISKEY**
Recorded: Recorded January - February 1977 at Soundstage, Toronto, Canada; Cherokee Studios, Los Angeles, CA; Record Plant, New York City, NY; RCA, Los Angeles, CA; and Producer's Workshop, Los Angeles, CA.
Production: Produced by Bob Ezrin for My Own Production Co. Ltd. A Black Widow / KRU Production. Engineered by Brian Christian with John Jansen, Robert Hrycyna, Jim Frank, Tony D'amico, Corky Stasiak, Galen Senegles, Rick Hart and Colonel Tubby. Mixed by John Stephens at Producer's Workshop. Production Assistance by Fundador Roman, Scott Anderson, Kris Bennett and Donna Dobbs. Music arranged by Bob Ezrin and Al MacMillan.
Additional credits: In keeping with the "tough-guy, hard-drinking" attitude of the album, Joe Gannon is listed as "Alcoholic Advisor" and Shep Gordon is listed as the star of Alive Enterprises under the credit for "Total misdirection." Alice is not even listed as the vocalist, and only one credit appears with his full name — "Alice Cooper plays himself."
Personnel: Alice Cooper (vocals.) Dick Wagner (guitar and back-up vocals on all tracks, no breakdown on guitars is given.) Steve Hunter (guitar on all tracks, no other breakdown of type of guitars is given.) Jim Gordon (drums on **Road Rats, Damned If You Do** and **My God**.) Allan Schwartzberg (drums on all tracks not featuring Jim Gordon.) Tony Levin (bass on **Lace and Whiskey, Damned If You Do** and **Ubangi Stomp**.) Prakash John (bass on **Road Rats**.) Babbitt (bass on all other tracks not featuring Tony Levin or Prakash John.) Jim Maelen (percussion and back-up vocals on all tracks.) Jozef Chirowski (keyboards, no breakdown of tracks given.) Bob Ezrin (keyboard and vocals on all tracks.) Al MacMillan (piano on **I Never Wrote Those Songs**.) Al Kooper (piano on **Damned If You Do**.) Ernie Watts (tenor sax and clarinet, no breakdown of songs given.)
Additional vocals: Venetta Fields, Julia Tillman and Lorna Willard (all on **[No More] Love at Your Convenience**) and Douglas Neslund and the California Boys' Choir.
Song List: It's Hot Tonight (Cooper, Wagner and Ezrin) / Lace and Whiskey (Cooper, Wagner and Ezrin) / Road Rats (Cooper and Wagner) / Damned If You Do (Cooper, Wagner and Ezrin) / You and Me (Cooper and Wagner) / King of the Silver Screen (Cooper, Wagner and Ezrin) / Ubangi Stomp (Chas. Underwood) / (No More) Love at Your Convenience (Cooper, Wagner and Ezrin) / I Never Wrote Those Songs (Cooper and Wagner) / My God (Cooper, Wagner and Ezrin)

By 1977, Alice was ready to expand his stage persona beyond the "Killer Alice" image that he had portrayed for several years. While WELCOME TO MY NIGHTMARE and ALICE COOPER GOES TO HELL were certainly new steps in the evolution of the character, it was still a perpetuation of Alice as the dark side of the human mind.

LACE AND WHISKEY was a step in a different direction with the invention of "Maurice Escargot, the toughest detective in town." With Escargot, Alice was able to create a concept album around the tough guy image of detective films of the 1940's and 1950's (the film noir era.) The perpetuation of a new stage persona appears to have had its effects on the conceptual nature of the album. Whereas with WELCOME TO MY NIGHTMARE and ALICE COOPER GOES TO HELL the album's concept was obvious and cleanly executed, LACE AND WHISKEY seems a bit more scatter-shot when considered as a whole.

While some of the tracks do fulfill the concept of a detective on a case (or several cases), there are songs that don't fall within that idea (such as Road Rats, Ubangi Stomp and I Never Wrote Those Songs.) Yet the theme that runs consistently through the album is "I'm tough, I don't give a damn, give me a drink to drown my sorrow as you walk out the door, because I've got my job to do" — typical of the tough guy detective. Every song, whether or not intentionally, also seems to have a personal edge to it. In fact, the album is probably one of the angriest lyrically of any of Alice's albums. Certainly, it's one of the more testosterone-driven of his albums — and not on a sexual level either. Even King of the Silver Screen, which ends up being a comical song, has the singer determined to be tough when he dresses up in front of his fellow construction workers.

LACE AND WHISKY album cover.

But perhaps such an analysis of the album is too far reaching. No doubt some fans would suggest that songs such as I Never Wrote Those Songs and My God seem to be saying more about Alice's own personal struggles at the time, but that's merely coincidental. In fact, Alice himself reflected on LACE AND WHISKEY in the liner notes of the Metal Blade CD reissue of the album in 1989 and said that he really had no clear memories of it besides having fun recording it. Perhaps that's all that it should be taken as — a side step by Alice on the journey into the dark world of the detective. Still, while it's a change of pace from earlier albums, it makes for a dark journey.

You and Me became the first single from the album and another hit for Alice. The song was included on several tours after its release. King of the Silver Screen went on to become the name of the tour to promote the album, while Road Rats went on to inspire an entire movie — ROADIE in 1980 — which co-starred Alice in a small role.

The album was recorded mainly at the Soundstage in Toronto, Canada with a mixture of performers from both WELCOME TO MY NIGHTMARE and ALICE COOPER GOES TO HELL. Most important in the mix was the expected return to the studio of Bob Ezrin, Dick Wagner and Steve Hunter. Unlike earlier albums, however, the liner notes do not differentiate who played what on each track, so Wagner and Hunter are listed only as playing guitar throughout the album. This extends to other performers as well, with Jim Maelen, Bob Ezrin, Jozef Chironwki and Ernie Watts listed in such a way as to suggest that they played on every track on the album.

Prakash John, who played on WELCOME TO MY NIGHTMARE and on the tour for that album, played bass on one track, and Tony Levin who also played on WELCOME TO MY NIGHTMARE, as well as ALICE COOPER GOES TO HELL, also plays bass. Jim Gordon, who played on ALICE COOPER GOES TO HELL, returns to play drums on three tracks. Brian Christian once again engineers the album.

Four of the musicians listed on this album also worked the same year on the Bob Ezrin-produced PETER GABRIEL album. These four were Dick Wagner, Steve Hunter, Jozef Chirowski and Tony Levin, and the album was even recorded in the same studio, Soundstage in Toronto, Canada. Considering how theatrical Gabriel himself was with Genesis and as a solo performer, it's not surprising that these musicians could fit in so readily.

Getting back to LACE AND WHISKEY, the album's cover design and photography were by Richard Seireeni of Rod Dyer, Inc., with the photos of Alice on the back cover and on the black and white paper inner sleeve taken by Terry O'Neill. Many of the props used on the cover also appear as part of the book cover, including the gun, the rosary, the whiskey bottle and the shot glass. The book is opened to appear on both the front and back cover, with the track listing for the album appearing as part of the text on the back cover. The tracks are listed in the wrong order, but this was most probably done to make the cover more appealing to the eye. (Lace and Whiskey is not listed, presumably because it's the title of the book.) The paper inner sleeve had a black and white photo of Alice as Maurice Escargot in his detective's office on one side and a proper track listing with liner notes on the other side. Some of the liner notes are written in a humorous vein to play off of the dime store detective novel persona of the album's character.

Among the promotional items released for LACE AND WHISKEY — which included a pop gun, a shot glass and a bullet-ridden T-shirt — was a paperback book which looked exactly like the one on the album cover. This book contained: a brief history of Alice Cooper albums; a track listing, with a brief story for each song; a who's who history of gangland slayings; and, at the end, a monthly planner for 1977. It's a neat little gimmick and one sought after by collectors. Promotional music clips (or videos, if you prefer) were done for You and Me and (No More) Love at Your Convenience (see Part 4 for details.)

The album was once again produced by Bob Ezrin for My Own Production Co. Ltd. (instead of Migration as for ALICE COOPER GOES TO HELL.) Alice went immediately from recording this album to rehearsing for the Australian NIGHTMARE 1977 tour with Dick Wagner, Prakash John, Whitey Glan, Bob Kulick and Mark Stein.

LACE AND WHISKEY reached No. 42 on the US charts and No. 33 on the UK charts. It was later reissued as a two-vinyl set with MUSCLE OF LOVE under the title A MAN CALLED ALICE (see Chapter 4, Part 2.) As with previous studio albums, LACE AND WHISKEY was reissued on cassette with ALICE COOPER GOES TO HELL, only this time as a DOUBLE PLAY cassette (catalog number 23850-4.)

The LACE AND WHISKY paperback, which was given away as a promotional item for the album.

Album Title: **LACE AND WHISKEY**
Released: May 1977 by Warner Brothers.
Catalog No.: BSK 3027
Media: Vinyl, Cassette and 8-Track.

The first release of the album came with a red sticker on the shrink wrap stating "Contains the hit You & Me", and came with a black and white flyer insert. The insert showed all of the Alice Cooper album covers up to and including LACE AND WHISKEY and the legend "JOIN OR DIE" to the right of the covers. The back of the flyer gave information on how to join the Alice Cooper Fan Club and how to order an Alice Cooper T-shirt. This was the only addition to the album besides the inner sleeve, details of which are listed with the main entries for the album below.

The original pressing of LACE AND WHISKEY came with a custom label on the vinyl that was similar to the book cover with the whiskey bottle. It was later reissued with the "Palm Tree" WB label. If you look closely, scratched into the inner groove of the vinyl are birds flying on one side and a flower blooming on the other.

Album Title: **LACE AND WHISKEY**
Released: May 28, 1977 by Warner Brothers, UK.
Catalog No.: K 56365
Media: Vinyl and Cassette.

Same as the US release.

Album Title: **LACE AND WHISKEY**
Released: June 1977 by Warner Brothers, Australia.
Catalog No.: BSK-3027

Media: Vinyl.

The album reached No. 3 on the Australian charts.

Album Title: **LACE AND WHISKEY**
Released: June 1977 by Warner Brothers, Brazil.
Catalog No.: Unknown.
Media: Vinyl.

Album Title: **LACE AND WHISKEY**
Released: June 1977 by Warner Brothers, France.
Catalog No.: 56345
Media: Vinyl.

Album Title: **LACE AND WHISKEY**
Released: June 1977 by Warner Brothers, Japan.
Catalog No.: Unknown.
Media: Vinyl.

Album Title: **LACE AND WHISKEY**
Released: 1989 by Metal Blade.
Catalog No.: 9 26447-2 (CD) and 9 26447-4 (cassette)
Media: CD and Cassette.

One of three Alice Cooper albums to be reissued on CD by Metal Blade in 1989. Alice himself wrote a page of liner notes explaining his thoughts and experience on the album. Alice's comments are philosophical in nature and he mentions quite clearly that the making of the album is a bit of a haze to him after all those years.

Album Title: **LACE AND WHISKEY**
Released: November 23, 1990 by Warner Brothers, Germany.
Catalog No.: WEA 926227-2, WEA 926227-4
Media: CD and Cassette.

The first French / German reissue of the album on CD.

Album Title: **LACE AND WHISKEY**
Released: September 30, 1990 by Warner Brothers, Japan.
Catalog No.: WPCP 3494
Media: CD.

Part of the special "Forever Young Series" that WB released in Japan. The album came with an obi that listed the album's title and additional albums available in the series.

Album Title: **LACE AND WHISKEY**
Released: 1990 by Warner Brothers, Australia.
Catalog No.: WAR 9262272
Media: CD.

The first reissue of this album on CD in Australia.

Single Title: **You and Me** (stereo) / **You and Me** (mono)
Released: April 1977 by Warner Brothers.
Catalog No.: WBS 8349
Media: 7" Vinyl.

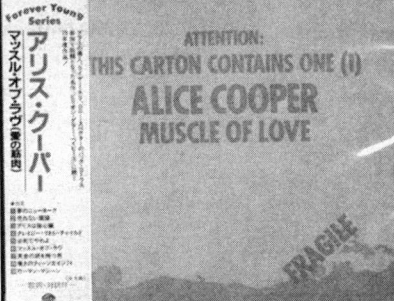

1990 Japanese "Forever Young" reissues.

A radio-only promotional single released to correspond

with the commercial single. Released on the promo-only white WB label.

Single Title: **You and Me / It's Hot Tonight**
Released: April 1977 by Warner Brothers.
Catalog No.: WBS 8349
Media: 7" Vinyl.

The first photo sleeve for an Alice single in the US for many years. What's interesting about this photo, which was used on several foreign editions of this single, is that Alice is without makeup or costume. You and Me reached No. 9 on the US charts.

Single Title: **You and Me / It's Hot Tonight**
Released: April 1977 by Warner Brothers, UK.
Catalog No.: K 16935
Media: 7" Vinyl.

Photo sleeve of Alice, same photo as the US edition. You and Me reached No. 44 on the UK charts.

Single Title: **You and Me / My God**
Released: August 1977 by Warner Brother, UK.
Catalog No.: K16984
Media: 7" Vinyl.

Reissue of the You and Me single soon after the release of (No More) Love at Your Convenience in July 1977.

Single Title: **You and Me / It's Hot Tonight**
Released: April 1977 by Warner Brothers, Australia.
Catalog No.: WBS-8349
Media: 7" Vinyl.

You and Me became Alice's biggest single in Australia, reaching No. 3 on the charts.

Single Title: **You and Me / It's Hot Tonight**
Released: April 1977 by Warner Brothers, Brazil.
Catalog No.: 16.032
Media: 7" Vinyl.

EP Title: **You and Me / I Never Wrote Those Songs / (No More) Love at Your Convenience / Lace and Whiskey**
Released: April 1977 by Warner Brothers, Brazil.
Catalog No.: 96.029
Media: 12" Vinyl.

This EP was released in support of the LACE AND WHISKEY album.

Single Title: **You and Me / It's Hot Tonight**
Released: April 1977 by Warner Brothers, France.
Catalog No.: 16914
Media: 7" Vinyl.

Came in a picture sleeve with the same photo as on US and UK releases.

Single Title: **You and Me / It's Hot Tonight**
Released: April 1977 by Warner Brothers, Germany.
Catalog No.: WB 16914
Media: 7" Vinyl.

Came in a picture sleeve with the same photo as on US and UK releases.

French single for You and Me. Note that no "in character" photo is used.

Part 2: Recordings

Single Title: **You and Me / It's Hot Tonight**
Released: April 1977 by Warner Brothers, Japan.
Catalog No.: P-180W
Media: 7" Vinyl.

Came in a picture sleeve.

EP Title: **Caught In a Dream / Be My Lover / School's Out / Elected**
Released: Spring 1977 by Warner Brothers, Australia.
Catalog No.: EPW-177
Media: 12" Vinyl.

This four song EP was released in Australia to coincide with the Australian NIGHTMARE tour that was supposed to have taken place back in 1975, but had to be delayed for numerous reasons. The EP came in a picture sleeve.

Single Title: **(No More) Love at Your Convenience / I Never Wrote Those Songs**
Released: July 1977 by Warner Brothers.
Catalog No.: WBS 8448
Media: 7" Vinyl.

The single didn't chart in the US. A promo of this single was released, but it's not clear if the single was ever released commercially in the US.

Single Title: **(No More) Love at Your Convenience / It's Hot Tonight**
Released: July 1977 by Warner Brothers, UK.
Catalog No.: K 16935
Media: 7" Vinyl.

Came in a picture sleeve with gothic writing on it and on the record label. The photo is the same as on the inner sleeve of the LACE AND WHISKEY album. (No More) Love at Your Convenience reached No. 44 on the UK charts.

Single Title: **(No More) Love at Your Convenience / My God**
Released: July 1977 by Warner Brothers, Australia.
Catalog No.: WB-6770
Media: 7" Vinyl.

UK single for (No More) Love At Your Concenience.

(No More) Love at Your Convenience reached No. 54 on the Australian charts.

Album Title: **THE ALICE COOPER SHOW**
Recorded: August 19 and 20, 1977 at the Aladin Hotel, Las Vegas, Nevada (two shows recorded.)
Production: Produced by Brian Christian and Bob Ezrin. Executive produced by Shep Gordon. A Black Widow / KRU Production. Engineered by Brian Christian. Musical Director was Dick Wagner.
Personnel: Alice Cooper (vocals.) Dick Wagner (guitar and back-up vocals.) Steve Hunter (guitar on all tracks.) Pentti (Whitey) Glan (drums.) Prakash John (bass.) Fred Mandel (keyboards.)
Song List: Under My Wheels / I'm Eighteen / Only Women Bleed / Sick Things / Is It My Body / I Never Cry / Billion Dollar Babies / Devil's Food / The Black Widow / You and Me / I Love The Dead / Go to Hell / Wish You Were Here / School's Out

The first official live Alice Cooper album was recorded during a tour that Alice considered to be one of his worst. Alice's drinking habits were beginning to affect his on-stage performance and, while the shows were still very imaginative, Alice's failing health due to the alcohol contributed greatly to his lack of energy during some, but not all, of these shows (look no further than the television special ALICE COOPER & FRIENDS for proof of this.) The KING OF THE SILVER SCREEN tour was nearing it's end in August 1977 when Alice began to consider taking steps to try and deal with his drinking habit.

Although the tour was essentially wrapped up, and Alice was ready to take some time off to get his personal affairs in order, he was contractually signed to provide Warner Brothers with another album as soon as possible. The label, wanting to put out a live album, requested that Alice fulfill the requirement by performing two shows at the Aladin Hotel in Las Vegas, Nevada. Alice was reluctant, but decided to go ahead with the shows in order to have more free time afterwards before being required to complete another album.

He agreed to the two shows, but his spirit wasn't in it, and you can tell it when you listen to the resulting recordings. Alice himself has stated that the shows were not reflective of the energy that he normally put into his concerts, and that the recordings could have been ten times better.

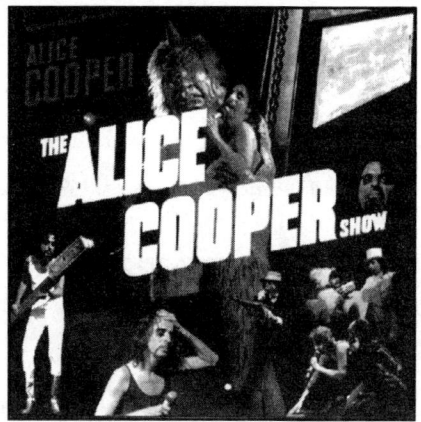

THE ALICE COOPER SHOW album.

On the positive side, you couldn't have hoped for a better band to perform with Alice at these two shows. Not only where the three standard people there to help with the production — Bob Ezrin, Steve Hunter and Dick Wagner — but there were also Prakash John, Fred Mandel and Pentti Glan, who had worked with Alice for quite a while by this time. Brian Christian also returned to help with the production of the album.

The album cover is about as lackluster as Alice's performance, with simple snapshots of Alice in concert scattered over the front and back. The inner sleeve isn't much to see either, being a black paper sleeve with two black and white photos of Alice and some information pertaining to joining the fan club. The photos were by Ken Ballard.

The album was re-mastered in 1990 for CD reissue by Lee Hershberg. THE ALICE COOPER SHOW reached No. 131 on the US charts.

Album Title: **THE ALICE COOPER SHOW**
Released: December 1977 by Warner Brothers.
Catalog No.: BSK 3138
Media: Vinyl, Cassette and 8-Track.

As mentioned above, the album came with a black paper inner sleeve that displayed two additional photos of Alice in concert.

Album Title: **THE ALICE COOPER SHOW**
Released: December 1977 by Warner Brothers, UK.
Catalog No.: K 56439
Media: Vinyl and Cassette.

Same as the US release.

Album Title: **THE ALICE COOPER SHOW**
Released: December 1977 by Warner Brothers, Australia.
Catalog No.: BSK-3138
Media: Vinyl.

The album reached No. 29 on the Australian charts.

Album Title: **THE ALICE COOPER SHOW**
Released: December 1977 by Warner Brothers, Brazil.
Catalog No.: 6709152
Media: Vinyl.

Album Title: **THE ALICE COOPER SHOW**
Released: December 1977 by Warner Brothers, France.
Catalog No.: WB 56439

Media: Vinyl.

Album Title: THE ALICE COOPER SHOW
Released: December 1977 by Warner Brothers, Germany.
Catalog No.: WB 56439 (vinyl) and K 456 439 Germany X (cassette)
Media: Vinyl and Cassette.

The original German pressing has a star on the cover stating that the album was "Recorded live on the 1977 Tour."

Album Title: THE ALICE COOPER SHOW
Released: December 1977 by Warner Brothers, Italy.
Catalog No.: W56439
Media: Vinyl.

Album Title: THE ALICE COOPER SHOW
Released: December 1977 by Warner Brothers, Japan.
Catalog No.: Unknown.
Media: Vinyl.

Album Title: THE ALICE COOPER SHOW
Released: March 7, 1988 by Warner Brothers, Germany.
Catalog No.: WEA 927342-2, WEA 927342-4
Media: CD and Cassette.

The first French / German reissue of the album on CD.

Album Title: THE ALICE COOPER SHOW
Released: September 30, 1990 by Warner Brothers, Japan.
Catalog No.: WPCP 3495
Media: CD.

Part of the special "Forever Young Series" WB released in Japan. The album came with an obi that listed the album's title and additional albums available in the series.

Album Title: THE ALICE COOPER SHOW
Released: October 24, 1990 by Warner Brothers.
Catalog No.: WB 3138.2 (CD) and WB 3138.4 (cassette)
Media: CD and Cassette.

The first CD pressing of the album in the US. Released a week after another reissue of the album on cassette on October 17, 1990. The CD came with an eight page booklet that included a brief biographical sketch of Alice's career up to and including THE ALICE COOPER SHOW album and the two photos that appear on the inner sleeve of the original vinyl release.

Album Title: THE ALICE COOPER SHOW
Released: 1990 by Warner Brothers, Australia.
Catalog No.: WAR 256439
Media: CD.

The first reissue of the album on CD in Australia.

Album Title: THE ALICE COOPER SHOW
Released: October 3, 1997 by Warner Brothers, Canada.
Catalog No.: WARN CD 03138 (CD) and WARN AC 03138 (cassette)
Media: CD and Cassette.

The latest reissue of the album, part of mass reissuing of the Alice Cooper catalog in Canada, released on the Warner Brothers label.

Single Title:	**School's Out / School's Out** (live)
Released:	December 1977 by Warner Brothers.
Catalog No.:	WBS 8607
Media:	7" Vinyl.

This single includes the original studio recording and the live version from THE ALICE COOPER SHOW.

Album Title:	**FROM THE INSIDE**
Recorded:	Recorded Fall 1978 at Davien Sound Studios, Cherokee Recording Studios, Hollywood Sound Recorders Inc., Sunset Sound and Crystal Sound-Hollywood. All, as one can guess, are in Hollywood, California.
Production:	Produced by David Foster. Executive Produced by Shep Gordon. Engineered by Humberto Gatica, Keith Olsen, David De Vore, Tom Knox and Howard Steele. Synthesizer programming by Jay Graydon and Steve Porcaro. Strings conducted by Frank DeCaro.
Personnel:	Alice Cooper (vocals.) Dick Wagner (guitars.) Davey Johnstone, Jefferson Kewley, Jay "Wah Wah" Graydon (additional guitars.) Kenny Passarelli, David Hungate, John Pierce, Dee Murray, Lee Skiar (all played bass on the album.) Rick Schlosser, Dennis Conway, Michael Ricciardella (all played drums on the album.) Jim Keltner (percussion.) David Foster, Fred Mandel and Robbie King (keyboards on the album.) Kiki Dee, Bill Champlin, Flo and Eddie, Tom Kelly, Davey Johnstone, Bobby Kimball, Marcy Levy Sheryl Cooper and "The Totally Committed Choir" (backing vocals.) Additional performers: Marcy Levy ("Millie" on Millie and Billie), Steve Lukather (guitar on one track.) Rick Nielsen (guitar on **Serious**.)
Song List:	From the Inside (Cooper, Taupin, Wagner and Foster) / Wish I Were Born in Beverly Hills (Cooper, Taupin and Wagner) / The Quiet Room (Cooper, Taupin and Wagner) / Nurse Rozetta (Cooper, Taupin, Foster and Lukather) / Millie and Billie (Cooper, Taupin and Roberts) / Serious (Cooper, Taupin, Foster and Lukather) / How You Gonna See Me Now (Cooper, Taupin and Wagner) / For Veronica's Sake (Cooper, Taupin and Wagner) / Jackknife Johnny (Cooper, Taupin and Wagner) / Inmates (We're All Crazy) (Cooper, Taupin and Wagner)

After resigning himself to the fact that he needed help to overcome his addiction to alcohol, Alice voluntarily went into treatment at the New York State Hospital in White Plains, NY. He was in the hospital from October until just before Christmas 1977 (with a brief interlude where he was allowed to return to California to film his cameo in SGT. PEPPER'S LONELY HEARTS CLUB BAND.) In the months that followed, Alice began work on the next album, an album that was to be somewhat of a reflection of his time in the hospital called FROM THE INSIDE.

Ironically, for an album that seems so conceptual that only Ezrin could have done it, Bob Ezrin was nowhere to be found. Instead the album was produced by David Foster. In fact, although there were several returning musicians for this album (and even the return of Pacific Eye and Ear to design the album cover), new production people and many new musicians were added to the mix — a departure from the pattern of Alice's first four solo albums. This shake-up in the ranks would continue even further in 1980 with the making of FLUSH THE FASHION, but more about that in Chapter 3.

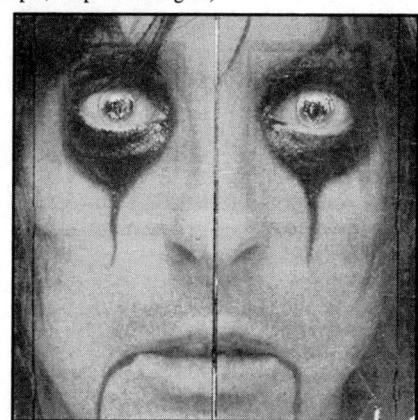

Original vinyl version of FROM THE INSIDE.

Returning were Dick Wagner (who also co-wrote seven of the ten songs) on guitar, and Fred Mandel on keyboards, but only for selected tracks on the album. Many other individuals were brought in for one or two tracks, including Cheap Trick's Rick Nielsen (on guitar for **Serious**) and Toto's Steve Lukather (who also co-wrote several tracks.) A couple of contributors to the album have names that die-hard fans may recognize — Kenny Passarelli (who is mentioned in the lyrics on Mr. and Misdemeanors on the EASY ACTION album) on bass and Jefferson Kewley (who portrayed the Operatic banjo player in the film GOOD TO SEE YOU AGAIN, ALICE COOPER and also toured with Alice during the 1978 SCHOOL'S OUT tour) on guitar. Providing backing vocals were some names well known to the public, Kiki Dee and Flo & Eddie, along with another name name well known to Alice fans, Sheryl Cooper. Marcy Levy, who sang on Millie and Billie had been a backup singer on Eric Clapton's Lay Down Sally and later changed her name to Marcella Detroit when she joined the group Shakespear's Sister, and had a hit in 1990 with the song Stay.

A connection to Elton John occurred with the arrival of Bernie Taupin to work with Alice on the songs for the album. Taupin had become quite well known for working the past few years with Elton John on his many hits and albums, and was also a drinking buddy of Alice's during their off time. Just as Alice was dealing with alcoholism, so was Taupin, and since the two had talked in the past about working together, it was deemed fit to do so on this album. In working on the song writing, Taupin ended up with credit on all ten songs on the album. FROM THE INSIDE is the only album the two have work on together.

The Elton John connection continued with the arrival of Davey Johnstone. Johnstone had played guitar with Elton John and was married to Kiki Dee, who had sung with Elton the smash hit Don't Go Breaking My Heart (and, as mentioned above, sang backup on FROM THE INSIDE.) Johnstone toured with Alice on the MAD HOUSE ROCK tour that was done in support of FROM THE INSIDE, and later played on the FLUSH THE FASHION album.

The packaging by Pacific Eye and Ear was a refreshing throwback to their work from the Alice Cooper Group days, which made the opening of the new album into a variation of opening a Christmas present — you never knew what to expect inside. The front cover, which used a photograph of Alice taken by Lauren Kinde, folded out in the middle to reveal another photo of the "inmates" from the hospital. The people in the staged photo by Alan Dockery are made up to look like the characters sung about on the album. This part of the packaging is actually a sleeve that holds the record and the inner sleeve in place, with slits on the left and right side to pull the inner sleeve out. In the upper left-hand corner of the picture on the outer sleeve is a door that's marked "The Quiet Room." The sleeve is perforated around the edges of the door, and if it's opened, you can see the inner sleeve below. When the inner sleeve is in place, you can see Alice waiting in a corner of the "quiet room." The back of the album shows two doors leading into a building. These doors are also perforated and, when opened, displayed the inner sleeve once again — this time showing Alice and the other characters from the outer sleeve running out of the hospital with their releases held in their hands.

CD cover for the FROM THE INSIDE album.

FROM THE INSIDE reached No. 68 on the US charts and No. 61 on the UK charts.

Album Title: **FROM THE INSIDE**
Released: December 1978 by Warner Brothers.
Catalog No.: BSK 3263
Media: Vinyl, Cassette and 8-Track.

Album Title: **FROM THE INSIDE**
Released: December 23, 1978 by Warner Brothers, UK.
Catalog No.: K 56577 (vinyl) and K456577 (cassette)
Media: Vinyl and Cassette.

Same as the US release.

Album Title: **FROM THE INSIDE**
Released: December 1977 by Warner Brothers, Australia.
Catalog No.: BSK-3263
Media: Vinyl.

The album reached No. 12 on the Australian charts.

Album Title: **FROM THE INSIDE**
Released: December 1978 by Warner Brothers, France.
Catalog No.: WB 56577
Media: Vinyl.

Album Title: **FROM THE INSIDE**
Released: December 1978 by Warner Brothers, Germany.
Catalog No.: WB 56577
Media: Vinyl.

Album Title: **FROM THE INSIDE**
Released: December 1978 by Warner Brothers, Italy.
Catalog No.: W 56577
Media: Vinyl.

Album Title: **FROM THE INSIDE**
Released: December 1978 by Warner Brothers, Japan.
Catalog No.: Unknown.
Media: Vinyl.

An album-sized sampler album was also released (catalog number P-10661-1.)

Album Title: **FROM THE INSIDE**
Released: December 3, 1990 by Warner Brothers, Germany.
Catalog No.: WEA 926064-2, WEA 926064-4
Media: CD and Cassette.

First French / German reissue of the album on CD.

Album Title: **FROM THE INSIDE**
Released: September 30, 1997 by Warner Brothers, Japan.
Catalog No.: WPCP 3496
Media: CD.

Part of the special "Forever Young Series" WB released in Japan. The album came with an obi that listed the album's title and additional albums available in the series.

Album Title: **FROM THE INSIDE**
Released: 1990 by Warner Brothers, Australia.
Catalog No.: WAR 9260642
Media: CD.

1997 Japanese album reissues.

First reissue of the album on CD in Australia.

Single Title: **How You Gonna See Me Now** (stereo) / **How You Gonna See Me Now** (mono)
Released: December 11, 1978 by Warner Brothers.
Catalog No.: WBS 8695
Media: 7" Vinyl.

A radio-only promotional single released to correspond with the commercial single. Released on the promo-only white WB label.

Single Title: **How You Gonna See Me Now / No Tricks**
Released: December 11, 1978 by Warner Brothers.
Catalog No.: WBS 8695
Media: 7" Vinyl.

Released in a promo version as well, with No Tricks as the B-side, this is the first single in the Alice's Warner Brothers catalog to feature a track not found on any of the albums. No Tricks featured Betty Wright on vocals, and was recorded at the time of the FROM THE INSIDE album. How You Gonna See Me Now reached No. 12 on the US charts.

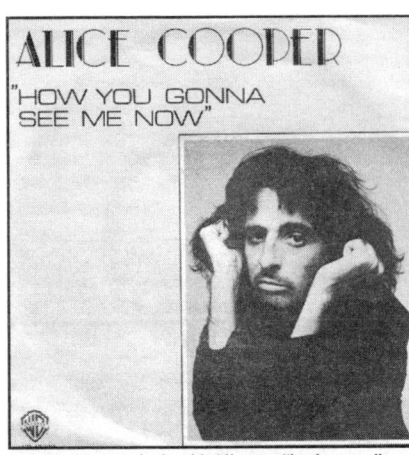

Single Title:	**How You Gonna See Me Now / No Tricks**
Released:	December 1978 by Warner Brothers, UK.
Catalog No.:	K 17270
Media:	7" Vinyl.

How You Gonna See Me Now reached No. 61 on the UK charts.

Single Title:	**How You Gonna See Me Now / School's Out** (live)
Released:	December 1978 by Warner Brothers, Australia.
Catalog No.:	WBA-4099
Media:	7" Vinyl.

A rarity for the foreign releases of this single, a live version of School's Out from THE ALICE COOPER SHOW album replaced No Tricks. How You Gonna See Me Now reached No. 9 on the Australian charts.

Another rare single with Alice not "in character."

Single Title:	**How You Gonna See Me Now / No Tricks**
Released:	December 1978 by Warner Brothers, Belgium.
Catalog No.:	WB 17270
Media:	7" Vinyl.

Single Title:	**How You Gonna See Me Now / No Tricks**
Released:	December 1978 by Warner Brothers, Brazil.
Catalog No.:	16.106
Media:	7" Vinyl.

Single Title:	**How You Gonna See Me Now / No Tricks**
Released:	December 1978 by Warner Brothers, France.
Catalog No.:	WB 17270
Media:	7" Vinyl.

The picture sleeve for this single shows Alice in dark clothes, with his hands up to the side of his head. This photo was from a session that used a photo to promote "family planning" in the Los Angeles area that same year.

Educational poster for birth control with Alice's photo. Similar to the photo used on the foreign edition of the How You Gonna See Me Now single.

Single Title:	**How You Gonna See Me Now / No Tricks**
Released:	December 1978 by Warner Brothers, Germany.
Catalog No.:	WB 17270
Media:	7" Vinyl.

Picture sleeve of Alice in the "Quiet Room" writing a letter. This is in the same vein as the musical film clip produced at the same time for the single (see Part 4.)

Single Title:	**How You Gonna See Me Now / No Tricks**
Released:	December 1978 by Warner Brothers, Holland.
Catalog No.:	WB 17 270
Media:	7" Vinyl.

Picture sleeve of Alice, same as on French release.

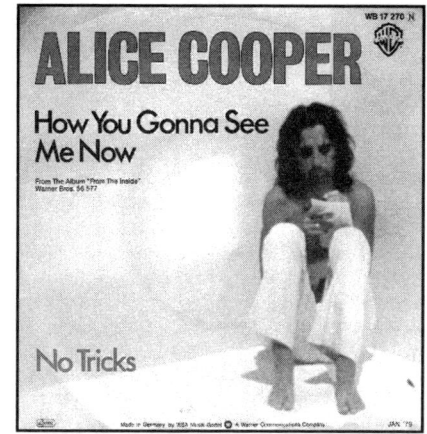

German single for How You Gonna See Me Now.

Single Title:	**How You Gonna See Me Now / No Tricks**
Released:	December 1978 by Warner Brothers, Italy.
Catalog No.:	W 17270
Media:	7" Vinyl.

Picture sleeve of Alice in the "Quiet Room." Different from the German release photo as Alice seems to be picking at his hand in the photo and grinning.

Single Title:	**How You Gonna See Me Now / No Tricks**
Released:	December 1978 by Warner Brothers, Japan.
Catalog No.:	P 352 W
Media:	7" Vinyl.

Single Title:	**From the Inside** (stereo) **/ From the Inside** (mono)
Released:	March 1979 by Warner Brothers.
Catalog No.:	WBS 8760
Media:	7" Vinyl.

Italian single for How You Gonna See Me Now.

A radio-only promotional single released to correspond with the commercial single. Released on the promo-only white WB label.

Single Title:	**From the Inside / Nurse Rozetta**
Released:	March 1979 by Warner Brothers.
Catalog No.:	WBS 8760
Media:	7" vinyl.

This single was released only in the US and there are no known foreign counterparts to it.

Part 3 — Tours 1975 - 1979

No doubt, when Alice decided to book a tour in support of his first solo album WELCOME TO MY NIGHTMARE in late 1974, there was cause for concern on the part of fans who wondered what type of band would be put together for the tour. As it turned out, there was little to worry about. Thanks to the assistance of Bob Ezrin and Dick Wagner, a band was already in place that had not only worked together in the studios during the past two years, but had also toured together with Lou Reed.

The band members were professional musicians who knew that they were on stage to support the main attraction. It was a perfect fit for Alice, and the WELCOME TO MY NIGHTMARE shows came off without a hitch — except when Alice made himself a physical wreck. But, more about that when we discuss the actual tours below.

While going out on his own did motivate Alice to put more enthusiasm back into the shows, by 1977 it was beginning to become a bit of a grind for him, and it was noticeable from the stage. The ALICE COOPER GOES TO HELL tour was never realized because of Alice's health problems, and the KING OF THE SILVER SCREEN saw a physically drained Alice still putting on a good show, but obviously struggling at times to do so.

Promotional ad used to promote the WELCOME TO MY NIGHTMARE tour in the US.

The tours between and including WELCOME TO MY NIGHTMARE and FROM THE INSIDE saw Alice trying to strengthen the conceptual nature of the show, although never to the extent of not doing older songs in concert. Having said that however, the WELCOME TO MY NIGHTMARE tour included only four songs from earlier albums.

Tour Name: **WELCOME TO MY NIGHTMARE**
Tour Period: March 1975 through September 1975. Additional dates in December 1975 in Las Vegas, Nevada.
Performers: Alice Cooper (vocals), Dick Wagner and Steve Hunter (guitars), Prakash John (bass), Pentti "Whitey" Glan (drums) and Jozef Chirowski (keyboards.) Additional performers: Sheryl G. Goddard, Robin Blythe, Uchi Sugiyzmi and Eugene Montoya (dancers). Danny Weiss replaced either Wagner or Hunter (probably Wagner) during the Las Vegas shows in December 1975.
Opening Act: Opening Band on tour: Suzi Quatro (US leg of tour); Heavy Metal Kids (European leg of tour); Rex (Evansville, Indiana show only; the band featured Rex Smith of soap opera fame.)
Set List: Welcome to My Nightmare / No More Mr. Nice Guy / Billion Dollar Babies / I'm Eighteen / Some Folks / Cold Ethyl / Only Women Bleed / Devil's Food / The Black Widow / Steven / Welcome to My Nightmare (reprise) / The Awakening / Escape / School's Out / Department of Youth

After the finish of filming for a television special based on the album, Alice began rehearsing (and staying in hotel rooms, if what Alice said in CIRCUS magazine in May 1975 is to be believed) for the tour that would take up half a year and find Alice on stage for the first time without his original band mates. The tour was the first to really expand upon the idea of additional performers beyond the "dancing tooth" and the Dentist from BILLION DOLLAR BABIES days, bringing in monsters and dancers along with the band. One of the dancers added was Sheryl Goddard, who would not only return in later tours, but would also become Alice's wife in real life.

The cyclops used would return for later tours, and even turns up as the announcer at the beginning of the video THE STRANGE CASE OF ALICE COOPER.

This was the first tour in quite a while that didn't feature Alice being executed in some form, and was the first to feature a movie screen on stage. The screen used can be seen in the WELCOME TO MY NIGHTMARE concert film where it plays a film of Alice being chased through a graveyard. At certain points in the film, Alice and the dancers emerged from behind the screen through slits, giving the appearance of people actually emerging from the movie itself. Timing was everything to make this work, and Alice and the dancers must be commended for doing an excellent job of it day in and day out. The screen would return with different film footage for the KING OF THE SILVER SCREEN tour, the MADHOUSE ROCK tour and the HEY STOOPID tour.

A giant toy box was used on stage during the show that one night caused Alice to end up in hospital. The toy box tipped over on him during the June 24, 1975 show in Vancouver, Canada and he fell into the security barriers at the front of the stage. The accident put Alice in the hospital with a concussion and broken ribs, shortening this show and canceling the next show on June 26.

Also on stage was a bed used during Cold Ethyl and Only Women Bleed. The bed had a life-size rag doll on it which, during the show, was replaced by Sheryl Goddard (the future Mr. Cooper.) This was also later used on THE NIGHTMARE RETURNS Tour for the CONSTRICTOR album in 1986.

A final week of shows was done in December 1975 at the Sahara Tahoe in Las Vegas, Nevada (the first rock performer to play at the hotel.) The first show featured Vincent Price in person doing the narration for the beginning of The Black Widow. After the first show of the tour, his voice was played on the PA system from a pre-recorded taped. This rendition of the rant is not the same as on the WELCOME TO MY NIGHTMARE album.

Years Ago is performed in concert as well, but only in bits and pieces used to tie together three songs from the Alice Cooper Group days (No More Mr. Nice Guy, Billion Dollar Babies and I'm Eighteen) early in the show. Years Ago then leads into an instrumental intro for Some Folks which allowed Alice to change from his torn red tights in the first part of the show to a white tuxedo, and provided a chance for the dancers to perform.

The tour went through Europe and the US, but a planned leg for Australia was canceled because of political problems and Alice wouldn't play in that country until Spring 1977 as part of the NIGHTMARE TOUR 1977.

March 25, 1975 - Brown County Arena, Green Bay, WI
April 4, 1975 - Richfield Coliseum, Cleveland, OH
April 8, 1975 - The Olympia, Detroit, MI
    The show was recorded from the audience.
April 26, 1975 - Boston Garden, Boston, MA
May 14, 1975 - Kiel Auditorium, St. Louis, MO
May 15, 1975 - Kiel Auditorium, St. Louis, MO
May 16, 1975 - Crosby-Kemper, Kansas City, MO
May 17, 1975 - Assembly Center, Tulsa, OK
May 18, 1975 - Sam Houston Coliseum, Houston, TX
May 21, 1975 - Civic Auditorium, Knoxville, TN
May 22, 1975 - Municipal Auditorium, Louisville, KY
May 23, 1975 - Mid-South Coliseum, Memphis, TN
May 24, 1975 - Municipal Auditorium, Mobile, AL
May 25, 1975 - Municipal Auditorium, Nashville, TN
May 27, 1975 - Freedom Hall Civic Center, Johnson City, TN
May 28, 1975 - Von Braun Civic Center, Huntsville, AL
May 29, 1975 - Barton Coliseum, Little Rock, AR
May 30, 1975 - Hirsh Memorial Coliseum, Shreveport, LA
May 31, 1975 - Fairgrounds Arena, Oklahoma City, OK
June 1, 1975 - Civic Center, Amarillo, TX
June 5, 1975 - Monroe Civic Center, Monroe, LA
June 6, 1975 - Mississippi coliseum, Jackson, MS
June 7, 1975 - City Park Stadium, New Orleans, LA
    The show was recorded from the audience.
June 8, 1975 - Moody Coliseum, Dallas, TX
June 13, 1975 - Community Center, Tucson, AZ
June 14, 1975 - Veterans Memorial Coliseum, Phoenix, AZ
June 15, 1975 - Sports Arena, San Diego, CA
June 17, 1975 - LA Forum, Los Angeles, CA
June 18, 1975 - LA Forum, Los Angeles, CA
June 20, 1975 - Portland Memorial Coliseum, Portland, OR
June 21, 1975 - Seattle Center, Seattle, WA
June 22, 1975 - Coliseum, Spokane, WA

June 24, 1975 - Vancouver, Canada
    This was the show during which the toy box used on stage fell over on top of Alice, pushing him headfirst into the security barriers in front of the stage. Alice returned to the stage and performed a few more songs before ending the show and going to hospital to get fifteen stitches to his head. He was diagnosed as having a concussion and several broken ribs.
June 26, 1975 - Coliseum, Edmonton, Alberta, Canada.
    Alice collapsed on stage after 35 minutes because of problems breathing. The show was canceled and ticket refunds were offered.
June 28, 1975 - Metropolitan Sports Arena, Minneapolis, MN
    Although pessimistic about how well Alice would do since he was still recovering from the head injury of five days before, the show went ahead as schedule and Alice played the full show.
June 29, 1975 - Civic Center, Omaha, NE
July 2, 1975 - Veledrome Arena, Winnipeg, Canada
    The show was recorded from the audience.
July 3, 1975 - Arena Auditorium, Duluth, MN
July 4, 1975 - Veterans Memorial Auditorium, Des Moines, IA
July 6, 1975 - Charleston Civic Center Auditorium, Charleston, WV
July 9, 1975 - Capitol Center, Largo, MD
July 10, 1975 - Farm Show Arena, Harrisburg, PA
July 11, 1975 - Civic Center, Pittsburgh, PA
July 12, 1975 - Roosevelt Stadium, Jersey City, NJ
July 13, 1975 - Forum, Montreal, Canada
July 16, 1975 - Civic Center, Providence, RI
    The show recorded from the audience.
July 27, 1975 - L. A. Forum, Los Angeles, CA
    The show was recorded from a mobile unit for the KING BISCUIT FLOWER HOUR radio program.
August 31, 1975 - Gruna Lund, Stockholm, Sweden
September 1, 1975 - Scandinavium, Gothenburg, Sweden
September 3, 1975 - Falkoner Theater., Copenhagen, Denmark
    The show recorded from the audience.
September 4, 1975 - Stadhalle, Bremen, Germany
September 5, 1975 - Sporthalle, Bublingen, Stuttgart, Germany
September 6, 1975 - Open Air Festival, Radstadium, Ludwigshaven, German
    Part of the show was recorded from the audience.
September 7, 1975 - Stadthalle, Vienna, Austria
    The show was recorded from the audience.
September 8, 1975 - Cirkus Krone, Munchen, Germany
September 11, 1975 - Wembley Pool, London, England.
September 12, 1975 - Wembley Pool, London, England.
    Both Wembley Pool shows were filmed for use in the WELCOME TO MY NIGHTMARE concert film released November 1975.
September 14, 1975 - Empire Pool, Liverpool, England
    The show was recorded from the audience.
September 16, 1975 - Paris, France
    The show was recorded from the audience.
September 17, 1975 - Sportspalatz, Antwerp, Belgium
September 19, 1975 - Ernst Menk, Hamburg, Germany
September 20, 1975 - Westhaller, Bortmund, Germany
December 13 - 18, 1975 - Sahara Tahoe, Lake Tahoe, NV
    A week-long series of shows at the hotel in Lake Tahoe, NV. This was actually after the tour was officially over.

Tour Name: **ALICE COOPER GOES TO HELL**
Tour Period: Tour planned for the Summer and Fall of 1976. Canceled.
Performers: Alice Cooper (vocals.) Other performers unknown, although posters that were printed for the tour list most of the same band members that appeared with Alice on the WELCOME TO MY NIGHTMARE tour, including Dick Wagner and Steve Hunter.
Opening Act: None.
Set List: Unknown, although as with the WELCOME TO MY NIGHTMARE tour, the set list would have centered around the songs from ALICE COOPER GOES TO HELL, with a few older songs dropped in here and there.

The tour was planned to begin in August after the release of the album in July of 1976. Details are sketchy about what the tour would have been like, but Alice did drop a few hints in interviews for the album done at the time. The show would have centered around a stage built on several levels and would have featured a disco as the main setting (since Disco music was considered Hell.) The show would have followed Alice's adventures in Hell, just as the WELCOME TO MY NIGHTMARE tour followed Alice's nightmare.

Although concert dates where tentatively set up (CIRCUS listed at least four dates in Canada and the US in their August 1976 issue), Alice stated that the tour itself would be taken at a more leisurely pace than previous tour. You can't get much more leisurely than canceled, which is what happened when Alice came down with Anemia and his doctor told him not to tour. Alice didn't tour again until March 1977.

Tour Name: **AUSTRALIAN NIGHTMARE TOUR 1977**
Tour Period: March 14, 1977 through April 4, 1977.
Performers: Alice Cooper (vocals), Dick Wagner and Bob Kulick (guitars), Prakash John (bass), Pentti "Whitey" Glan (drums) and Mark Stein (keyboards.) Additional performers: Sheryl G. Goddard (dancer.)
Opening Act: Unknown.
Set List: Welcome to My Nightmare / No More Mr. Nice Guy / Billion Dollar Babies / I'm Eighteen / Some Folks / Cold Ethyl / Only Women Bleed / Devil's Food / The Black Widow / Steven / Welcome to My Nightmare (reprise) / The Awakening / Escape / School's Out / Department of Youth (I Never Cry was also included in the show.)

As mentioned above in the WELCOME TO MY NIGHTMARE tour entry, Alice was to have visited Australia for a tour in late 1975. This never happened, primarily for political reasons. In April 1975, the Australian Labor and Immigration Minister, Clyde Cameron, attempted to ban Alice from touring the country, fearing that Alice would "powerfully influence the young and weak minded" (TIME magazine, April 7, 1975.)

In 1976, plans were briefly discussed for Alice to tour Australia in support of ALICE COOPER GOES TO HELL, but, due to health problems, all touring was canceled that year. Instead, it was after recording LACE AND WHISKEY in early 1977 that Alice was finally able to tour Australia. The tour brought together many of the standard performers once again, although Steve Hunter was working on other projects at the time, and was unable join the tour. Bob Kulick, a studio musician who later worked with many of the same people as Dick Wagner, joined the band for the Australian tour. It was the first time Kulick played with either Wagner or Alice, and the first "superstar" tour he was ever involved with. Kulick is the person behind an Alice Cooper tribute album set to be released in early 1999.

Six locations were played during the three weeks that Alice and the gang were "down under." Five of these were in Australia and the last was in New Zealand. A major European or American act playing in Australia is normally looked upon as a big deal, since the costs and the travel involved for a concert by a major performer are staggering, not just because of the logistics involved with getting equipment and personnel into to the country, but also because the major cities are so far apart (certainly adding New Zealand into the deal adds to the cost, especially in light of going there for only one show.) So, when a major act does make it down to Australia, it's an event. Alice Cooper appearing was no less of an event, and he justified the anticipation by breaking attendance records at shows on the tour.

The show itself was the same as the 1975 tour, although I Never Cry was thrown in since the single was just being released at the time.

March 14, 1977 - Perth Entertainment Centre, Perth, Australia
March 15, 1977 - Perth Entertainment Centre, Perth, Australia
March 18, 1977 - Adelaide Westlakes Football Stadium, Adelaide, Australia
March 21, 1977 - Melbourne Festival Hall, Melbourne, Australia
March 22, 1977 - Melbourne Festival Hall, Melbourne, Australia
  The show was recorded from the audience.
March 23, 1977 - Melbourne Festival Hall, Melbourne, Australia.
March 24, 1977 - Melbourne Festival Hall, Melbourne, Australia.
March 26, 1977 - Sydney Showground, Sydney, Australia
March 29, 1977 - Brisbane Festival Hall, Brisbane, Australia
March 30, 1977 - Brisbane Festival Hall, Brisbane, Australia
April 4, 1977 - Western Springs Stadium, Auckland, New Zealand

Tour Name:	**KING OF THE SILVER SCREEN (a.k.a. THE LACE AND WHISKEY TOUR)**
Tour Period:	June 19, 1977 through August 1977.
Performers:	Alice Cooper (vocals), Dick Wagner and Steve Hunter (guitars), Prakash John (bass), Pentti "Whitey" Glan (drums) and Fred Mandel (keyboards.) Additional performers: Sheryl G. Goddard (dancer), and unknown others.
Opening Act:	Nazareth, Sha Na Na, The Tubes and The Kinks (opening show only.) Atlanta Rhythm Section and Clover. Burton Cummings also opened several shows.
Set List:	Under My Wheels / Billion Dollar Babies / I'm Eighteen / Sick Things / Is It My Body / Devil's Food / The Black Widow / You and Me / Only Women Bleed / Unfinished Sweet / Escape / I Love the Dead / Go to Hell / Wish You Were Here / I Never Cry / It's Hot Tonight / Lace and Whiskey / King of the Silver Screen / School's Out

Alice came back from the Australian NIGHTMARE tour in April only to begin preparations for the American tour in support of the LACE AND WHISKEY album.

This tour was his first chance to really break out of the "Alice Cooper" persona with his detective character from the LACE AND WHISKEY album (the character Maurice Escargot appeared prominently in both music clips done for the album, and was front and center in the show during the Lace and Whiskey number.) The stage — once again conceived by Joe Gannon, with input from Alice — was amazing. An immense television set with lights and knobs, it either showed the band (as if from inside it) or was covered by a huge slit screen. The screen was an important part of the show, playing films that linked the various components of the show together (as was done on the WELCOME TO MY NIGHTMARE tour) and, at times, almost dominating the stage (as when it played fake television commercials during costume changes.) The band was strong, and included many of the old gang from the WELCOME TO MY NIGHTMARE tour.

The timing of the tour, however, wasn't good for Alice physically. The amount of work that he'd been doing — a steady stream of albums and tours over several years — had dwindled his reserves, and the increase in his drinking left him looking very ill (which, in reality, he was considering having had to cancel the previous year's tour due to a bout with Anemia.) His declining health was quite evident in the ALICE COOPER & FRIENDS television special, as it was on the live album THE ALICE COOPER SHOW (ironically, the only full-length live album from Alice until A FISTFUL OF ALICE in 1996.)

Nevertheless, while there may have been moments when his health problems showed, that wasn't certainly the case for most (or nearly all) of the concerts. Alice still gave the audience a show to remember, and put all his energy into it. Fans probably didn't notice anything unusual in Alice's performance, and it was a surprise to some when, after three months of touring, he checked himself into hospital for treatment of his drinking problem, and stayed the final months of 1977.

Although the chance was there for Alice to completely change his stage persona, Maurice Escargot only appeared during the middle portion of the show, doing Lace and Whiskey and a couple other songs from the album. The tour also featured some new creatures — these being four giant chickens with machines guns (because, after Escargot, "the rest are all chickens") — along with gangsters and showgirls. The chicken costumes (and the "dancing teeth") also appeared during the performance that Alice made on THE TONIGHT SHOW earlier in the year.

The show retained a lot of elements from earlier times, including the films, the execution of Alice by guillotine, Sheryl as the Black Widow that Alice kills and as the dancer for Only Women Bleed, the money sword for Billion Dollar Babies, and others. The snake used during Is It My Body was obtained only days before the first show at Anaheim Stadium in California. The snake, Angel, was chosen at a snake audition at the stadium with Alice and Flo & Eddie picking the winner.

By the Spring of 1978, Alice was rested and ready to tour again, this time not only in support of the LACE AND WHISKEY album, but also to work on songs for a new album (FROM THE INSIDE, released in December 1978.)

June 19, 1977 - Anaheim Stadium, Anaheim, CA
    The first concert of the tour was a special, day long festival with Nazareth, Sha Na Na, the Tubes and the Kinks opening the show for Alice. Parts of this show were seen on the ALICE COOPER & FRIENDS special.
June 23, 1977 - Vancouver, British Columbia
June 25, 1977 - Alberta, Edmonton, Canada
June 26, 1977 - McMahon Stadium, Calgary, Canada

Burton Cummings opened for this show.
July 1, 1977 - Tulsa, OK
July 2, 1977 - Houston, TX
July 3, 1977 - Fort Worth, TX
July 7, 1977 - Phoenix, AZ
July 8, 1977 - Jackson, MS
July 9, 1977 - Albuquerque, NM
July 10, 1977 - Macon, GA
July 12, 1977 - Mobile, AL
July 21, 1977 - Nassau Coliseum, Uniondale, NY
The show was recorded from the audience.
July 23, 1977 - Boston, MA
July 24, 1977 - Providence, RI
July 27, 1977 - Madison, WI
July 29, 1977 - Omaha, NE
July 30, 1977 - Kansas City, MO
July 31, 1977 - Wichita, KS
August 6, 1977 - Nashville, TN
August 7, 1977 - Louisville, KY
August 8, 1977 - Cobo Hall, Detroit MI
August 9, 1977 - Cobo Hall, Detroit MI
August 10, 1977 - Cobo Hall, Detroit MI
August 19, 1977 - Aladin Hotel, Las Vegas, NV
August 20, 1997 - Aladin Hotel, Las Vegas, NV
Both Aladin shows were recorded for use on THE ALICE COOPER SHOW album.
August 21, 1977 - L. A. Sports Arena, Los Angeles, CA
Dr. Hook was the opening act for this show.
August 22, 1977 - San Diego, CA
August 25, 1977 - St. Paul, MN
August 26, 1977 - Hullman Centre, Indiana State University, Indiana
Burton Cummings opened this show and several others at around this time.
August 27, 1977 - Chicago, IL
August 28, 1977 - Cedar Falls, IA
August 30, 1977 - Denver, CO

Tour Name: **SCHOOL'S OUT SUMMER TOUR 1978**
Tour Period: April 1978 through September 1978.
Performers: Alice Cooper (vocals), Steve Hunter (guitars), Jefferson Kewley (guitar), Dee Murray (bass), Dennis Conway (drums) and Fred Mandel (keyboards.) Additional performers: Sheryl G. Goddard (dancer), other unknown others.
Opening Act: AC / DC (some shows), and The Babys.
Set List: Under My Wheels / Billion Dollar Babies / I'm Eighteen / Sick Things / Is It My Body / Devil's Food / The Black Widow / You and Me / Only Women Bleed / Unfinished Sweet / Escape / I Love The Dead / Go to Hell / Wish You Were Here / I Never Cry / It's Hot Tonight / Lace and Whiskey / King of the Silver Screen / School's Out

This tour, in the late of Summer 1978, was to promote the upcoming album (FROM THE INSIDE) and to get Alice back in front of an audience again after his recent self-imposed rest for alcohol abuse.

This tour was a lot like the earlier KING OF THE SILVER SCREEN tour and was considered by most to be the second leg of that tour under a different name. Steve Hunter and Fred Mandel were with Alice once again, but other members of the band were off working on other projects and couldn't be involved. All of the band members from this tour would go on to appear on FROM THE INSIDE as well. Long time fans will recognize the name Jefferson Kewley on guitar. Kewley played an extensive role in the original version the movie GOOD TO SEE YOU AGAIN, ALICE COOPER (although he was cut from the re-edited version, he was now back working with Alice again.

The tour began in Buffalo, New York on April 27, with a special pre-tour dress rehearsal the night before for reporters and some contest winners. The main motive behind the concert was to promote Alice's return to the stage and his first show after he had stopped drinking.

The tour ended in September giving Alice time to prepare for and record FROM THE INSIDE, which was released in December 1978.

April 27, 1978 - Vet. Auditorium, Des Moines, Iowa
April 28, 1978 - St. Paul Civic Centre, Minneapolis, MN
   The show was recorded from the audience.
April 29, 1978 - New Field House, Fargo, ME
April 30, 1978 - Winnipeg, Canada
May 2, 1978 - Checker dome, St. Louis, MO
May 4, 1978 - Hara Arena, Dayton, OH
May 5, 1978 - Richfield Coliseum, Cleveland, OH
May 10, 1978 - Wendler Arena, Saginaw, MI
   This is the show recorded by Westwood One for the KING BISCUIT FLOWER HOUR. The show aired nationally in America on October 31, 1978 (one of the reasons why the date for this show has always been confused by fans.) This show has been bootlegged numerous times over the years. (See Chapter 6 for details about bootlegs.)
June 20, 1978 - War Memorial, Buffalo, NY
June 21, 1978 - Civic Center, Baltimore, MD
June 23, 1978 - Philadelphia, PA
June 24, 1978 - The Scope, Norfolk, VA
June 25, 1978 - Rupp Arena, Lexington, KY
June 26, 1978 - Civic Center, Birmingham, AL
June 28, 1978 - Knoxville, TN
June 29, 1978 - Coliseum, British Columbia
June 30, 1978 - Coliseum, Greensboro
July 2, 1978 - Alpine Valley Music Theater, Easy Troy, WI
July 4, 1978 - Gulf Coast Arena, Biloxi, MS
July 7, 1978 - Florida Sportatorium, Hollywood, Florida
   The show was recorded from the audience.
July 8, 1978 - Civic Center, Lakeland, FL
July 9, 1978 - Memorial Coliseum, Jackson, FL

Promotion certificate for the FROM THE INSIDE album.

July 28, 1978 - Coliseum, Madison, WI
August 25, 1978 - Milwaukee, WI
August 27, 1978 - Chicago, IL
September 2, 1978 - UND Field House, Grand Fork, ND
　　The Michael Stanley Band opened this show.

Tour Name: **MAD HOUSE ROCK**
Tour Period: February 1979 through April 1979.
Performers: Alice Cooper (vocals), Steve Hunter (guitar), Davey Johnstone (guitar), Prakash John (bass), Pentti "Whitey" Glan (drums) and Fred Mandel (keyboards.) Additional performers: Sheryl Cooper, Rosa Aragon, Uchi Sugiyami, Eugene Montoya and Clifford Allen (dancers); Wendy Haas and Joe Pazutto (backing vocals.)
Opening Act: Eddie Money and Blondie (for part of the tour.)
Set List: From the Inside / Serious / Nurse Rozetta / The Quiet Room / I Never Cry / Devil's Food (intro only) / Welcome to My Nightmare / Billion Dollar Babies / Only Women Bleed / No More Mr. Nice Guy / I'm Eighteen / The Black Widow (instrumental) / Wish I Was Born in Beverly Hills / Dead Babies / Ballad of Dwight Fry / All Strapped Up / It's Hot Tonight (instrumental) / Go to Hell / Wish You Were Here / How You Gonna See Me Now / Inmates (We're All) / School's Out

Only five months after the end of the previous tour, Alice was on stage again in support of the album FROM THE INSIDE. There was certainly nothing stale about the show, the set list, or the performers — they were fresh and ready to go.

Only Steve Hunter and Fred Mandel returned from the previous tour, but holes were quickly filled by Prakash John and Pentti Glan — both of whom had appeared with Alice on earlier solo tours — and Davey Johnstone, who was one of the musicians on FROM THE INSIDE. In the video THE STRANGE CASE OF ALICE COOPER, Alice jokingly introduced the band as Ultra Latex, and Prakash John as Johnny Stiletto.

New things were added to the show and the dancers, particularly Sheryl Cooper and Eugene Montoya, had a lot more to do on stage. Wish I Was Born in Beverly Hills featured a great recreation of the story, and included a prop car that, with the help of Alice, stretched out across the stage. The electric chair returned to the stage for the first time since the LOVE IT TO DEATH tour in 1970. The giant split screen projector was retained, with new footage adapted to the new tour's content, including the song All Strapped Up that was performed in concert, but never officially released. This song was performed almost completely on the screen and involved a prop long fuse bomb. The screen was also used to introduce Alice, with footage of bottles being pushed along an assembly line. One bottle tips over and Alice comes crawling out of it and onto the stage.

The set list for this show was definitely built around the FROM THE INSIDE album, with seven of the ten songs from the album being performed at every show. Additionally, attempts were made to incorporate both Jackknife Johnny and For Veronica's Sake into the concert early on in the tour, but were later dropped.

The April 9, 1979 San Diego show was filmed for home video release and was broadcast in the fall of 1979 in American syndication under the title THE STRANGE CASE OF ALICE COOPER (see entry below.) This tour was the last with the band members and additional performers that had been with Alice off and on since 1975. After this tour ended, Alice once again began experimenting with his stage character and with the musical direction for his albums and tours. And that dancing poodle costume still kills me every time I see it in STRANGE CASE.

February 11, 1979 - Field House, Grand Forks, ND
February 13, 1979 - Civic Auditorium, Omaha, NE
February 14, 1979 - Dane County Arena, Madison WI
February 16, 1979 - Cobo Hall, Detroit, MI
February 17, 1979 - Cobo Hall, Detroit, MI
February 18, 1979 - Roberts Municipal Auditorium, Evansville, IN
February 19, 1979 - Kemper Arena, Kansas City, MO
February 21, 1979 - Richfield Coliseum, Cleveland, OH
February 23, 1979 - Bet Center, Minneapolis, MN
February 25, 1979 - Unidome, Cedar Falls, IA
February 26, 1979 - Veteran's Memorial Coliseum, Green Bay, WI
February 27, 1979 - Market Square Arena, Indianapolis, IN
　　The show was recorded from the audience.

Ad for Louisville, Kentucky MAD HOUSE ROCK concert.

February 28, 1979 - Checkerdome, St. Louis, MO
March 2, 1979 - Riverfront Coliseum, Cincinnati, OH
March 3, 1979 - Freedom Hall, Louisville, KY
    The band The Babys opened this show.
March 4, 1979 - International Amphitheater, Chicago
March 6, 1979 - Milwaukee Arena, Milwaukee, WI
    The show was recorded from the audience.
March 31, 1979 - Oakland Coliseum, Oakland, CA
    The show was recorded from the audience.
April 1, 1979 - LA Forum, Los Angeles, CA
April 3, 1979 - Washington Center Coliseum, Seattle
    The show was recorded from the audience.
April 9, 1979 - San Diego Sports Arena, San Diego, CA
    This show was filmed for THE STRANGE CASE OF ALICE COOPER television special.
April 13, 1979 - Fort Worth, TX
    The show recorded from the audience.
April 14, 1979 - Norman Center, Oklahoma City, OK
    The show was recorded from the audience.
April 17, 1979 - Centroplex, Baton Rouge, LA
    The show was recorded from the audience.
April 29, 1979 - Civic Center, Rapid City, SD

Part 4 — Films and Television 1975 - 1979

Even before the Alice Cooper Group was ready to take a break, Alice was already making solo excursions into television. It started with his appearances on HOLLYWOOD SQUARES and with a brief cameo on the short lived television series THE SNOOP SISTERS, but his career in television and films really took off during the promotion of the WELCOME TO MY NIGHTMARE album.

Along with a concert film and a network television special, Alice began appearing on nationally seen interview programs, and the rock star was being transformed into a media superstar. He soon expanded his horizons by appearing in films (although he did nothing that was truly noteworthy outside fan circles.) Even during the 1977 and 1978 period, when he took a break for personal reasons, Alice was still in the minds of the public through television and films.

In addition to the few major appearances listed below, there were plenty of interviews during this period. There also exists a significant amount of 8 mm film footage of different tours shot by fans, including at least ten minutes from the KING OF THE SILVER SCREEN tour, from what is otherwise a sparsely documented period (even the ALICE COOPER & FRIENDS special was dismal in terms of displaying any of the stage set or live performances.) Collectors may also want to look for a local news clip from 1979 which shows Alice performing a bit of All Strapped Up during a concert on the MAD HOUSE ROCK tour. This is the only known film of this lost song from that tour (it's never appeared on an album or in a concert film.) The clip also shows Alice in an interview segment wearing the leather jacket covered with pins that became a standard costume for Alice during the FLUSH THE FASHION and SPECIAL FORCES years.

Film Title:	**THE SNOOP SISTERS**
Film Type:	Television.
Created:	Filmed 1973 and broadcast on March 5, 1974 on the NBC television network, US.
Music:	I Love the Dead

Alice made a brief appearance in this detective series as a warlock named Prince. He wore his traditional makeup for the program and performed I Love the Dead. The episode is known in some quarters as "The Devil Made Me Do It."

Film Title:	**HOLLYWOOD SQUARES**
Film Type:	Television game show.
Created:	Filmed in March 1974 and broadcast in April 9 through 16, 1974 on the NBC television network, US.

While performing his final shows with the Alice Cooper Group in South America, Alice appeared on this game show over the course of a few days. The program featured (normally) television stars in individual squares, which were set up to look like a huge tic-tac-toe board. Contestants were asked to "pick a square" and the host, Peter Marshall, would then ask the celebrity in the square a question. The celebrity would then either answer truthfully or make up an answer and the contestant would have to decide if the answer given was true or false. Seemed like a show right up Alice's alley.

Film Title:	**GRAMMY AWARDS**
Film Type:	Television.
Created:	Filmed May 1974 and broadcast May 1974 on the CBS television network.
Music:	None.

Alice appeared briefly on this award show to co-present an award with Helen Reddy.

Film Title:	**THE SMOTHERS BROTHERS SHOW**
Film Type:	Television variety show.
Created:	Filmed December 1974 and broadcast January 13, 1975 on the NBC television network.
Music:	Unfinished Sweet

Although Alice had already completed most of the WELCOME TO MY NIGHTMARE album, during his appearance on THE SMOTHERS BROTHERS SHOW he performed in a production number for the earlier Alice Cooper Group song Unfinished Sweet.

The Smothers Brothers, who were always entertaining, were sometimes a bit too serious when it came to music. They felt a need to explain what Alice's production number was all about, and, introducing it as "drama rock", Tommy Smothers spent time explaining the story behind the song's lyrics. While today this would seem a bit much, at that time Alice was still seen by the general public as a deviant and was normally only seen on late-night television. The number featured Alice, without makeup, sitting in a dentist's office. He sings the song while waiting for and then seeing the dentist. As the dentist looks into his mouth and Alice sings "the teeth are OK, but the gums got to go," the scene switches to a stage built like the inside of a giant mouth, with dancers dressed up as teeth. As Alice grabs a huge pair of pliers and pulls Tommy Smothers, dressed as a tooth, out of the mouth, and then Alice suddenly returns to the dentist's office and finds that everything is all right.

Film Title:	**DEPARTMENT OF YOUTH**
Film Type:	Promotional film clip.
Created:	Filmed February 1975 and shown on television to promote the single.
Music:	Department Of Youth

A promotional film for the first single off of the WELCOME TO MY NIGHTMARE album, this short shows Alice in concert with fans getting up on stage with him, much like in the WELCOME TO MY NIGHTMARE concert film. Some people have confused this clip with merely being an excerpt from the film, but it's a separate entity entirely.

Film Title:	**THE NIGHTMARE** (a.k.a. **WELCOME TO MY NIGHTMARE**)
Film Type:	Full length movie.
Created:	Filmed March 1975.
	Broadcast April 25, 1975, 11:30 p.m., EST on the ABC televisions network as part of the WIDE WORLD IN CONCERT series.
	Released on video in 1984 by Warner Brothers (catalog number 34056), it also appeared numerous times back in 1982 and 1983 on the cable channel, USA, during its NIGHT FLIGHT program.
Production:	An Alive Enterprise, Inc. Production in association with Valhalla Corporation. Executive producer was Shep Gordon. Produced by Carolyn Pfeiffer and Jorn Winther. Associate producers were Don Clark and Wendy Riche. Directed by Jorn Winther. Written by Alan Rudolph and Tony Hudz. Musical Directions by Bob Ezrin. Choreography by Don Gillies with additional choreography by David Winters. Song Recordings provided by Jeff Smith at Sounds Interchange in Toronto, Canada.
Personnel:	Alice Cooper (as Steven) and Vincent Price (as "The Spirit of the Nightmare".)
	Additional performers: Linda Googh (as Cold Ethyl); Robyn Blythe, Eugene Montoya, Uchi Sugiyama and Sheryl Goddard (dancers.)
Music:	Steven (part only) / Welcome to My Nightmare / Devil's Food / Some Folks / Only Women Bleed

/ Cold Ethyl / The Black Widow / Years Ago / Department of Youth / Years Ago (reprise) / Steven / Awakening / Ballad of Dwight Fry / Escape / Awakening (reprise) / Welcome to My Nightmare (instrumental reprise)

Run Time: One hour, six minutes and seven seconds.

The plot surrounds Steven being visited by the Spirit of the Nightmare while sleeping and being offered the chance to have a thrilling nightmare on the condition that he doesn't try to escape. Upon agreeing, Steven goes through many different phases of the nightmare until he finally cracks and decides he needs to escape. He awakens in his bed, but the nightmare is never really over.

Filmed after the completion of the WELCOME TO MY NIGHTMARE album, this television special was a showcase for the album, featuring all of its tracks plus a remake of Ballad of Dwight Fry.

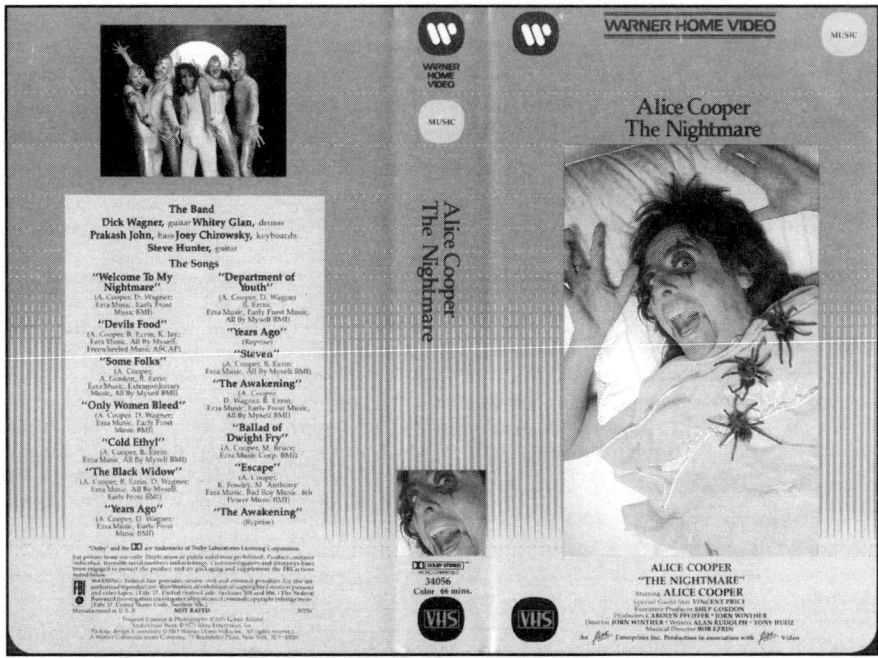

Video cassette case for THE NIGHTMARE.

In line with the television standards of the time, several songs had to be reworded to stay within language guidelines. Many of the songs used in the special also had lyrics changed and/or music rewritten so as to more closely match the actions that the audience saw, or to allow an action sequence to be extended.

Vincent Price, whose voice was heard on the album and on taped introductions in concert, appears as the narrator of Steven's story. He was a lot of fun to see, although his rendition of the rant opening The Black Widow wasn't quite as fiery as on the album.

Many elements of the special found their way into the concert tour, including the Black Widow spider costumes, the dancing "Cold Ethyl", the cyclops, the bed, and the dancing skeletons during Some Folks. David Winters, who did choreography for the program, went on to direct the theatrical film WELCOME TO MY NIGHTMARE which was filmed the same year (see the entry below for details.) Incidentally, Carolyn Pfeiffer — who worked as Alice's publicist in the early days — was later associated with Vincent Price on his last film, THE WHALES OF AUGUST, and continued her association with Alice by co-producing the film ROADIE (see Chapter 3, Part 4 for details.)

The TV special was aired on IN CONCERT, the same program that Alice with the original band had appeared on (the debut episode of the series in September 1972.) By this time, the show had changed hands from Don Kirshner to Dick Clark and had become know as WIDE WORLD IN CONCERT instead of just IN CONCERT, and Alice's appearance was on the very last episode of the series. TV GUIDE wrote a good synopsis in their program listings and also mentioned the show in a preview section near the front of the magazine issue. Ads for the album that appeared in March 1975 issues of many publications also made mention of the special and when it was to be aired.

The special resulted in an Emmy award in 1976 for Nick V. Giordano for "Outstanding Achievement in Video Tape Editing for a Special." It was also nominated for "Best Video Album" when it was released on home video in 1984 by Warner Brothers. The video has not been reissued since, and has never been released outside the US. The video is now considered a collectors' item.

Rare TV listing cover and insert for the 1975 television special THE NIGHTMARE.

Film Title:	**WELCOME TO MY NIGHTMARE**
Film Type:	Full length movie.
Created:	Concert footage filmed September 11 and 12, 1975 at Wembley Pool, London, England. Cemetery footage filmed September 1975 at Sheperton Studios, London, England.
Production:	A Dabill Production (listed in the film) / A Tommy J. Production (listed in print ads and on the video cassette.) A David Winters Film. Executive producer was William Silberkleith. Produced by David Winters. Associate producers were Larry Pizer (listed in the film) and Aaron Magidow (listed in print ads.) Directed by David Winters. Choreographed by David Winters. Stage production presented by Harvey Goldsmith for John Smith Enterprises. Show conceived by Alice Cooper, Shep Gordon, Joe Gannon and David Winters Released theatrically by Key Pictures. Inc., November 28, 1975. Released on video 1989 by Rhino Video (catalog number RNVD 1913.) Re-released by Rhino Video 1998.
Personnel:	Alice Cooper (vocals.) Dick Wagner (guitar.) Steve Hunter (guitar.) Whitey Glan (drums.) Jozef Chirowski (keyboards.) Additional performers: Robyn Blythe, Eugene Montoya, Uchi Sugiyama and Sheryl Goddard (dancers.) Vincent Price (as "The Spider's voice".)
Music:	Steven (intro only) / Awakening / Welcome to My Nightmare / Years Ago (part only) / No More Mr. Nice Guy / Years Ago (part only) / I'm Eighteen / Years Ago (part only) / Some Folks / Cold Ethyl / Only Women Bleed / Steven (part only) / Years Ago (part only) / Billion Dollar Babies / Devil's Food (instrumental for dual guitar solo) / Black Widow / Steven / Welcome to My Nightmare (reprise) / Escape / School's Out / Department of Youth / Only Women Bleed (shown again under credits.)
Run Time:	One hour, twenty-four minutes and twelve seconds.

After the quick disappearance of GOOD TO SEE YOU AGAIN, ALICE COOPER in 1974, another attempt was made to bring Alice's show to the big screen with this concert film from the Wembley Pool show in London (for the WELCOME TO MY NIGHTMARE album.) This film, unlike GOOD TO SEE YOU AGAIN, enjoyed major distribution in the US and played in hundreds of mainstream theaters.

The film is a great presentation of Alice's stage presence and shows how the WELCOME TO MY NIGHTMARE stage show worked, although filming is generally too "close-up" to give the viewer the perspective from the audience's point of view.

Performing in the movie with Alice was an almost quintessential group of people. The band members included those who had performed on the album, and would continue to perform with Alice for future albums and tours. Also included were dancers who would be with Alice up through the MADHOUSE ROCK tour in 1979, including Sheryl Goddard, who would later become Alice's wife. Vincent Price's voice can be heard introducing

Early video release of the WELCOME TO MY NIGHTMARE movie.

Video cassette case for the WELCOME TO MY NIGHTMARE movie.

Rhino release of WELCOME TO MY NIGHTMARE.

The Black Widow (in a variation of the monologue / rant that he performed on the WELCOME TO MY NIGHTMARE album.) Greatly involved was David Winters, who not only produced and directed the film, but did the choreography as well. Winters was well experienced in bringing a musical theme to life on film, having played one of the gang members, Action (as in Easy Action), in WEST SIDE STORY, and through working on Elvis films such as VIVA LAS VEGAS and EASY COME, EASY GO, and even directing episodes of THE MONKEES television series.

The film was edited by Stuart Baird and released to theaters in late 1975. The movie poster for the film states that it's "The JAWS of Rock" (playing off the recent hit movie JAWS) and features the cover art from the WELCOME TO MY NIGHTMARE album. The poster lists the songs performed, although it mistakenly leaves out both Some Folks and Awakening and adds Hello, Hooray, (which doesn't appear in the film.) It's also odd to see contradictions between the film and the poster (and print ads) which give different names for the associate producer and the production company. The poster also lists the title as THE ALICE COOPER SHOW - WELCOME TO MY NIGHTMARE, while the film gives the title as simply WELCOME TO MY NIGHTMARE (and does so twice for some reason.) Incidentally, some of the cemetery scene footage was taken from GOOD TO SEE YOU AGAIN, ALICE COOPER.

Other credits worth mentioning are: Alice listed as playing "Steven / Alice", and a general credit for "Music conceived by Alice Cooper, Dick Wagner and Bob Ezrin," which was sure to put off members of the original band who co-wrote some of the older songs (although they are listed properly with the songs in the ending credits.)

Rhino released the video in 1989 with a cover showing Alice from the STRANGE CASE OF ALICE COOPER movie on the front and three photos on the back, of which one is also from the STRANGE CASE film. For some reason, one of the four song titles listed on the back of the box to entice buyers with The Awakening.

In the UK, the film has been released several times with different covers. The first had the cover of the WELCOME TO MY NIGHTMARE album, and after that, the cover has been photos of Alice from the film itself.

Film Title:	**TONIGHT SHOW**
Film Type:	Interview.
Created:	Filmed and broadcast November 24, 1975 on the NBC television network, US.

Alice appeared on the famous talk show for the first time with McLean Stevenson as the guest host (instead of Johnny Carson.) Alice appeared to promote the November 26, 1975 release of the WELCOME TO MY NIGHTMARE concert film to theaters, and to discuss the Lake Tahoe shows that he would perform in December 1975.

Alice was not listed as a guest on the program in TV GUIDE that week. Since guest host episodes of THE TONIGHT SHOW were never repeated, this clip is a real rarity, and only audio copies of the interview appear to be circulating among fans.

Film Title:	**DINAH**
Film Type:	Interview.
Created:	Filmed January 1976; broadcast January 6, 1976 in syndication on American television.
Music:	None.

Alice appeared with host Dinah Shore and co-host Vincent Price to discuss the tour for WELCOME TO MY NIGHTMARE, and to give Price a Gold Album award for the album. Other guests on the program were Frank Sinatra Jr., Millie Jackson and Larry Storch. While Alice doesn't sing on the program, Vincent Price does a medley of songs about food with Dinah. This episode is sometimes listed as having been aired the following week, which, in fact, it was in some parts of the country.

Film Title:	**MIDNIGHT SPECIAL**
Film Type:	Interview, with additional concert clips.
Created:	Filmed August 5, 1976 and broadcast August 7, 1976 at 1:00 a.m. EST on the NBC television network.
Music:	Various.

This was a sit down interview between Alice and audience members on the MIDNIGHT SPECIAL stage in Burbank, California. In between interview segments, clips are show from the GOOD TO SEE YOU AGAIN, ALICE COOPER movie and the Elected promotional film. This interview was shown during the fourth anniversary of the program and repeated a few years later on another anniversary special.

Film Title:	**ROCK MUSIC AWARDS**
Film Type:	Award show.
Created:	Broadcast live on September 18, 1976 on the ABC television network.
Music:	Go to Hell, Wish You Were Here and I Never Cry.

Alice co-hosted this award show and did three songs from ALICE COOPER GOES TO HELL.

Film Title:	**TONY ORLANDO & DAWN RAINBOW HOUR**
Film Type:	TV variety show.
Created:	Filmed August 1976; broadcast September 21, 1976 at 8:00 p.m. EST on the CBS television network, US.
Music:	I Never Cry and Give the Kid a Break.

Alice appeared as a guest on the third season opener of this variety show, one of the many such shows that were cranked out during the 1970's. Alice performed two songs — I Never Cry (incorrectly listed in TV GUIDE as "I'll Never Cry") and **Give the Kid a Break**. He also appeared in a sketch as himself in a TO TELL THE TRUTH spoof.

Film Title: **You and Me**
Film Type: Promotional Music Clip.
Created: Filmed April 1977 and shown on musical programs.

Unlike the WELCOME TO MY NIGHTMARE album, which had a whole music special made in conjunction with it, LACE AND WHISKEY had only two promotional films made to support the singles off the album. The first was You and Me, which featured Alice in his Maurice Escargot character. The plot line has the detective Escargot returning to his office and turning on the television to see Alice performing the song in his traditional makeup. As the song plays out, Maurice gets himself comfortable and decides to get some sleep. In a dream, a group of shadowy and shady figures appear to look upon the sleeping Escargot.

The clip was used on many of the rock shows being produced at the time and is really just an early version of what would now be called a music video. A portion of this promo was also broadcast during Alice's appearance on THE TONIGHT SHOW in May 1977.

Film Title: **THE TONIGHT SHOW**
Film Type: Interview and song.
Created: Filmed and broadcast May 1977 on the NBC television network, US.
Music: **Lace and Whiskey** and **You and Me**.

In support of the just released LACE AND WHISKEY album, Alice appeared to perform the song **Lace and Whiskey** (with the dancing chickens) and to show a bit of the **You and Me** promotional clip.

Film Title: **THE GONG SHOW**
Film Type: Television variety/game show.
Created: Filmed and broadcast May 1977 on the NBC television network, US.

On this unique game show, contestants tried to perform songs, comedy, dance or other oddball things without being "gonged" (rejected) by the panel of celebrity judges. The show was tremendously popular for a few years (it even spawned a theatrical motion picture), and many famous people graced the stage of THE GONG SHOW as surprise "joke" appearances.

The show was so popular that special hour long prime time episodes were done. Alice appeared on one of these specials with his head in a miniature guillotine, singing **Think I'm Going Out Of My Head**. After a few seconds, Chuck Barris (creator and host of THE GONG SHOW) pushed the blade down on the guillotine and ended the song.

Film Title: **DINAH**
Film Type: Interview.
Created: Filmed and broadcast May 1977 in American syndication.
Music: None.

In support of LACE AND WHISKEY, Alice talked to Dinah Shore and co-host Paul Williams about the album and the tour. Performers are brought out for a bit of a fashion show to display some of the costumes used during the tour.

Film Title: **(No More) Love at Your Convenience**
Film Type: Promotional Music Clip.
Created: Filmed June 1977.

This was the second promotional film made in support of a single from the LACE AND WHISKEY album. This is the rarer of the two clips, and was hard to find until 1997 when an Australian program called RAGE featured an Alice retrospective that showed the promo clip in full. The clip shows Alice once again as Maurice Escargot, only this time with an angry, pregnant woman in his bed (played by Sheryl Cooper), and a steady stream of visitors that sing the title track.

Film Title:	**ALICE COOPER AND FRIENDS**
Film Type:	Full-length concert movie.
Created:	Filmed June 19, 1977 at Anaheim Stadium, Los Angeles, CA. Broadcast September 1977 in syndication by K-Pay Entertainment with Drew Cummings Productions / Funtelevision Productions. Executive producer was Shep Gordon. Creative Consultants were Mark Volman and Howard Kaylan. Produced by David Forest. Directed by Martin Morris, with Rob Iscove directing the Alice Cooper segments of the program. Written by Eddie Rodrigue and Bobby Muraco. The announcer was Eddie Rodrigue. Released on video in 1982.
Music:	School's Out (beginning of program) / Is It My Body (part only) / Under My Wheels / Billion Dollar Babies (part only) / You and Me / Only Women Bleed / Lace and Whiskey / I Love The Dead (part only)

Coming two years after the preceding television special, ALICE COOPER AND FRIENDS was produced for television syndication. It was aired around the US, but usually appeared in time slots reserved for bad horror movies and repeats of the local newscast (in other words, after 1:00 am on a Saturday or Sunday morning.) Perhaps that was just as well, since it's a dismal program to watch.

Filmed at the first show of the KING OF THE SILVER SCREEN tour in support of the LACE AND WHISKEY album, this concert was a special all day event with Sha Na Na, Nazareth, The Tubes and The Kinks appearing before the headliner, which was Alice. Songs from each of these performers, with the exception of The Kinks, appear in the special. One segment from Alice's performance is shown at the beginning of the program, and the rest is in the last twenty minutes of the show.

Video box for the only official US release of ALICE COOPER AND FRIENDS.

The performances of the other acts are terrific — which comes as no surprise. The Tubes were well on their way to becoming known for their theatrics and colorful performances, Nazareth was just coming off of their hit Love Hurts (which they perform in the program), and Sha Na Na was still a year away from becoming too much of a parody (instead of a homage to the music of the 1950's.) Each is given multiple songs in the film, with Sha Na Na doing four, Nazareth doing three and The Tubes doing only two (both of which are cover songs, although their frantic version of Love Will Keep Us Together is worth seeing.)

However, their performances are not enough to combat the weaknesses of the program — the filming and editing of the show, and Alice's performance. Although this was only the start of the American tour, Alice, as report-

Original US release of ALICE COOPER AND FRIENDS.

ed elsewhere, was in no shape to take on another tour. Instead of the usually lively Alice who is master of the stage, his performance is incredibly lethargic. The stadium atmosphere doesn't help either, since Alice's usual ability to interact with the crowd is unavailable because of the distance between the stage and the audience. This is obvious during **Billion Dollar Babies** when Alice picks up his sword prop then quickly discards it again when he sees there's no use for the prop without audience participation.

What might have been a redeeming feature, at least from an historical perspective, was showing fans what the KING OF THE SILVER SCREEN stage set looked like. It was also a chance to have seen Alice performing in his Maurice Escargot character. Unfortunately, the program is shot and edited in such a fashion that you never get a good look at the stage set up. And while **Lace and Whiskey** does feature Maurice, it's too little too late to be of much interest. In fact, if you didn't know that the stage was supposed to represent a giant television screen, you'd never guess it from seeing this program.

The show further loses momentum by including songs that have been performed on previous films (and on television specials) in much more exciting ways than seen here. If more songs from the newest album had been included, the show might have had some use for fans in an historical nature. As it is, the program ends with the last song cut off before completion, a fitting end to a special that feels less than complete anyway.

A missed opportunity, and really only for fans who want to see something from the LACE AND WHISKEY period. Incidentally, Mark Volman and Howard Kaylan (the film's creative consultants) are perhaps better known as Flo and Eddie.

Film Title:	**SGT. PEPPER'S LONELY HEARTS CLUB BAND**
Film Type:	Full-length movie.
Created:	Filmed October 1977 through December 1977 in Culver City, California. Released on video 1987 and 1997 by MCA Home Video. Released 1978 by Universal Studios. An RSO production.
Music:	Because

Alice appears two-thirds of the way into the film as a villain by the name of Father Sun. While brainwashing kids to become servants of the Future Villain Band (played by Aerosmith) through audio-video programming, Father Sun is also keeping one of the magical musical instruments that belong to Sgt. Pepper's Lonely Hearts Club Band (played by Peter Frampton and the Bee Gees.) Frampton and the boys show up during a programming session to steal the instrument back. Alice plays two sides of the same character in the scene — one as the demonic teacher in the audio-video programming singing **Because**, and the other as a normal Joe in a T-shirt who makes sure the programming is running okay between eating his dinner and watching sports on a little television set. While Alice ends up the scene with pie on his face, his character does inadvertently help in the electrocution of Peter Frampton's character (so, one could say it's a win-win situation.)

Although in the hospital the time to deal with his drinking problem, Alice got an okay from the doctors to return to California to film his scene in the movie. Once the scene was completed, Alice returned to the hospital to complete his stay.

Some fans may have felt it better if Alice had stayed in the hospital (avoiding the movie) in view of the damage it did to the careers of some other performers. However, the film does have a strange kitsch charm to it (it was certainly a film that could only have been made in the 1970's.) Alice certainly does fine with his small role and doesn't embarrass himself. It's also one of the very few times that Alice appeared publicly with a mustache (grown during his stay in the hospital.)

Video cassette for
SGT. PEPPER'S LONELY HEARTS CLUB BAND.

This film was available on video several years ago, but was hard to find until 1997 when MCA re-mastered the soundtrack album for its CD release and then decided to reissue the video as well (to play off the CD.) When the movie was issued on video, the song mixes were replaced with those from the soundtrack album. This is significant because Alice's vocals in the film mix were stronger than on the soundtrack album, and also because the video mix is different than the original film released in 1978. The Bee Gees provided backing vocals for Alice, and George Martin produced the song.

Film Title:	SEXETTE
Film Type:	Full-length movie.
Created:	Filmed December 1977 through January 1978 in Hollywood, California. Released 1979 by Crown-International Pictures, Inc. Released 1982 on video by Media and re-released 1997 on video by Rhino. Catalog number: M188 (Media release) and 2310 (Rhino).
Music:	Next Next

The plot (Is it really necessary? Well, all right, here's the part readers will want to know) includes Alice appearing briefly near the end of the film as a hotel porter. As Mae West finishes reading a "Dear Jane" letter, Alice arrives to console her by singing the upbeat tune Next Next (sometimes referred to in some Mae West biographies as "The Next Time [Next, Next]".) As he sings, other hotel personnel arrive to pack West's things and dance along.

This movie was the final film for Mae West, who was a legendary comedic actress, best known for her scandalous movies and plays (In fact, SEXTETTE is based on a play West had written for herself.) No doubt, for a movie buff such as Alice, appearing with Mae West in a film was something that could hardly be passed up. It was certainly enough to bring other well known performers to the film including Ringo Starr, Tony Curtis, Keith Moon, (pre-Bond) Timothy Dalton and Dom DeLuise.

Originally, the script called for West's character to be upset about the letter she receives and Alice was to sing a song entitled No Time for Tears. West, however, felt it was uncharacteristic for her or her character to be crying "over a man" and refused to participate until the song was rewritten (with some input from Alice himself, according to the West biography by Maurice Lenoardi, MAE WEST: EMPRESS OF SEX.)

Video box for Rhino reissue of the Mae West movie.

The song is bubbly and cute, and Alice is fine in a movie that was looked upon as a real turkey when it was released. As it was, Mae West tried to revive her seductress character in a movie that was made, unfortunately, much too late in her career for it to come off as anything other than a bit, well, creepy. She was also having problems and resorted to using an ear-piece to assist her with the dialogue and stage movements. Ultimately, the script was not very good. The movie was filmed in December 1977 and was ready for release in March 1978, but after initial interest from Warner Brothers and Universal, no distributor was found for the film until Crown-International took interest. Even then, the film was not released nationally until June 1979.

A cute final highlight is when Alice finishes the song and is leaving the hotel room. As he walks away from the camera, Dom DeLuise enters and, in passing, says (breaking character) "Oh, hello, Alice!"

The film was originally released on video in the US in 1982 by Media (an early movies-on-video company), and quickly forgotten. It was not until 1997 that the film was finally re-released by Rhino Video.

Film Title:	**THE MUPPET SHOW**
Film Type:	Comedy television show with songs.
Created:	Filmed July 1978 in London, England for the ITC network. Broadcast in syndication on American television the week of November 3, 1978. Released on video 1996 (catalog number 2597.)
Music:	Welcome to My Nightmare, You and Me and School's Out

During the popular TV series' second year, Alice appeared as the special guest star. Each episode of the series featured at least one human guest star, and the show often featured people who didn't normally make this type of appearance, so having Alice on the program was nothing unusual.

Alice sang special arrangements of three songs, Welcome to My Nightmare, You and Me and School's Out. He also appeared in numerous sketches dealing with Alice trying to get one of the Muppets to sign up with the devil (it was a special Halloween episode.) A cute show, it later turned up in syndication with the rest of the episodes and was rebroadcast in the mid-1980's and again on the TNT cable channel in the early 1990's.

The episode can also be found on video as the second half of a cassette entitled MONSTER LAUGHS WITH VINCENT PRICE (the first half being an episode of the program with Price as the guest star.) Two songs from the show (Welcome to My Nightmare and School's Out) can also be fond on the videocassette called JIM HENSON'S MUPPET VIDEO: ROCK MUSIC WITH THE MUPPETS. Included on the tape besides Alice are Debbie Harry, Helen Reddy, Linda Ronstadt, Leo Sayer, Paul Simon and Loretta Swit.

Video box for THE MUPPETS SHOW.

Film Title:	**How You Gonna See Me Now**
Film Type:	Promotional Music Clip.
Created:	Filmed November 1978 in Los Angeles, California.
Music:	How You Gonna See Me Now

A promotional music clip for the single from FROM THE INSIDE, this was the last conceptual promotional film made for an Alice Cooper single until the release of He's Back in 1986. The film's plot deals with Alice writing to his wife from the hospital, expressing his thoughts of their upcoming reunion. It counterpoints Alice's writing with a look at his awaiting home life, which includes two bratty kids and a wife who's drinking heavily. After a flashback showing Alice running into his girl's arms, and a sequence showing him being released from the hospital after shock therapy, he runs home only to arrive in time to see his wife and kids — all with Alice-type makeup on their faces — being packed away and on route to the hospital. Confused, Alice watches as the ambulance pulls away and then goes into the house. A great film that captured the essence of the album in one short clip. Worth having in any fan's collection.

Film Title:	**THE SOUPY SALES SHOW**
Film Type:	Television comedy.
Created:	Filmed and broadcast 1979 in American syndication.

Alice appears in a brief bit where Soupy offers to help him audition a new spider for the stage show. While the winner is being decided, Fang arrives and squashes the spider. To finish it all off, Alice then gets hit in the face with a pie (a Soupy Sales staple in the series), continuing the grand tradition of Alice ending up with pie or cake on his face.

Film Title:	**MIDNIGHT SPECIAL**
Film Type:	Television rock performances.
Created:	Filmed February 16, 1979 and broadcast February 18, 1979 at 1:00 a.m. EST on the NBC television network, USA.
Music:	From the Inside, Serious, I'm Eighteen, Only Women Bleed, Billion Dollar Babies and Inmates (We're All Crazy)

Alice performs for the majority of this program in support of the FROM THE INSIDE album. There is also a sequence in the show where Alice is being tormented by doctors in a cell. This sequence has no music from Alice in it, instead an instrumental track from the movie MIDNIGHT EXPRESS is heard.

Film Title:	**STRANGE CASE OF ALICE COOPER**
Film Type:	Concert film.
Created:	Filmed April 9, 1979 at the San Diego Sports Arena, San Diego, California. A Jaybar Industries, Inc. Production for Twentieth Century Fox Telecommunications, Inc. Executive producers were Shep Gordon, Allan Strahl and Denny Vosburgh. Produced by Jackie Barnett Stage production conceived by Joe Gannon, Shep Gordon and Rob Iscove. Broadcast in syndication on American television 1979 as part of the LEVI BLUE JEAN specials. Released on video 1979 by Magnetic Video Corporation (catalog number 1064.) No director is listed in the credits.
Personnel:	Alice Cooper (vocals.) Steve Hunter (guitar.) Davey Johnstone (guitar.) Pentti "Whitey" Glan (drums.) Prakash John (bass.) Fred Mandel (keyboards.) Additional performers: Sheryl Cooper, Rosa Aragon, Uchi Sugiyami, Clifford Allen and Eugene Montoya (dancers.) Vincent Price (pre-recorded monologue before Devil's Food.)
Music:	Short interview with Alice / Cyclops in doctor's outfit introduces the show / film played of bottles going through an assembly line and as one bottle tips over, Alice emerges from the screen to begin with From the Inside / Serious / Nurse Rozetta / The Quiet Room / I Never Cry / Devil's Food (intro only) / Welcome to My Nightmare / Billion Dollar Babies / Only Women Bleed / No More Mr. Nice Guy / I'm Eighteen / The Black Widow (instrumental) / Wish I Was Born in Beverly Hills / Ballad of Dwight Fry / It's Hot Tonight (instrumental) / Go to Hell / Wish You Were Here / How You Gonna See Me Now / Inmates (We're All Crazy) / School's Out / some additional interview bits with Alice.
Run Time:	One hour, fourteen minutes and twenty-three seconds.

Contrary to what the film may look like to fans who have viewed it on videotape, this was a special made specifically for the home video and television market. While some fans may be disappointed that this concert film was never seen on the big screen, it's an excellent special and is probably the best documentary of an Alice Cooper show until THE NIGHTMARE RETURNS in 1986. The film also allows fans to see Alice coming back strong with a show based around the FROM THE INSIDE album, a band that couldn't be beat, a stage set and props that were new (or at least improved variations of former props), dancers that really seem to be enjoying the show, and Alice himself, whose performance is just plain perfect.

This film was first shown on television in 1979, and was then released on video (the first official pre-recorded videotape featuring Alice) from Magnetic Video, one of the first companies to release TV specials and movies on videotape. It was available for sale and rental in 1979. The film hasn't been reissued on video since that time and is now considered a collectors' item, not only by Cooper fans, but by videocassette collectors as well. Copies of the film have circulated in fan circles for years, but the one that seems to float around the most has a huge black, distorted horizontal line going through the picture throughout the film. Most speculation points to this being an early "copyguard" protection used on the cassette to dissuade people from making copies. If so, it's an early attempt that's effective, but quite different from the more recent and better known Macrovision production used today on many tapes and DVDs.

Two of the songs performed during the concert didn't make it into the special — Dead Babies and All Strapped Up. All Strapped Up was a song done only in concert and it was never officially released on any Alice Cooper albums. The concert performance of the song involved the split screen on stage (seen briefly as Alice emerges at the beginning of the program) and a previously filmed segment of Alice and others. Little is known definitively as to why this song was cut (especially considering that the song is not to be found anywhere else), but it's been suggested that the filmed segment just didn't look right when seen on video. Most likely, both it and **Dead Babies** were cut in order to fit the program into the 90 minute time slot available for the television program.

During the performance, Vincent Price's voice can be heard demanding that Alice go back through time before the intro for **Devil's Food**, which was a nice flashback to the WELCOME TO MY NIGHTMARE days. Nurse Rozetta is cut short in the performance. While introducing the performers during the final segment of the show, Alice makes up a couple of names, calling Prakash John "Johnny Stiletto" and introducing Eugene Montoya as "Martin Luther Queen." Alice also fun with his growing disgust for disco during the final segment.

An excellent special and it is a shame that it has yet to be reissued on cassette.

Part 5 — Books and Comics 1975 - 1979

Publicity for Alice was plentiful between WELCOME TO MY NIGHTMARE and FLUSH THE FASHION, comprising numerous magazine and newspaper articles. There were, however, far fewer books about Alice than we saw earlier in his career.

This isn't too surprising since the books that came out before late 1974 were still available for sale and Bob Greene's book certainly satisfied a lot of readers curious about Alice. In fact, there was only one major book to come out during this period, and that was Alice's autobiography, ME, ALICE. After his autobiography, there was no serious discussion of Alice's career (aside from scattered references and/or brief biographies in rock music encyclopedias) until the mid-1990's with the release of Michael Bruce's book NO MORE MR. NICE GUY (discussed in Chapter 5.)

It was in 1979 that the first comic book pertaining to Alice was published. It was directly related to an album (like the THE LAST TEMPTATION comics of the 1990's), and was co-plotted by Alice himself.

Cover of Alice's official autobiography ME ALICE.

Book Title: **ME, ALICE**
Published: Released in hardback 1976 by G. P. Putnam's Sons, New York, NY. ISBN 399-11535-8. Published simultaneously in Canada by Longman, Canada Limited, Toronto, Canada.
Author: Written by Alice Cooper and Steven Gaines (see notes below.)
Content: A biography of Alice "told in his own words", which goes from his years growing up through to the breakup of the Alice Cooper Group.

With the success of Alice Cooper in the original band and as a solo performer, his autobiography was sure to find a wide audience. Bob Greene's book BILLION DOLLAR BABY, released the year before, had been quite successful. The new book also provided a chance for Alice to reflect on some things touched on in Greene's book that Alice wanted to get off of his chest.

Steven Gaines, a writer who had worked as an editor at CIRCUS magazine and had written many articles about the band during the early 1970's, had asked Alice about working together on his biography. Gaines wrote most of the book on his own during 1974-75, with Cooper later working on changes and corrections. Gaines went on to write other rock books such as THE LOVE YOU MAKE (about the Beatles) and HEROES AND VILLAINS: THE TRUE STORY OF THE BEACH BOYS. Alice's father wrote the introduction to the book.

Although the book is very entertaining, it's a bit light on facts and relevant information that die-hard fans were probably searching for about Alice's life. Instead of dealing with how albums were recorded and how the stage shows were created, Alice spends a lot of time discussing motels, sex, meeting celebrities and being a celebrity. The book reads on a polite conversational level and doesn't dig very deeply into the details (unlike

Greene's book from the previous year.)

The book, unfortunately, contains inaccuracies because of the lack of information available to Gaines (and Alice) at the time of its writing. Alice's memory was clouded by his growing use of alcohol, and Gaines had only limited resources beyond his own past articles about the band. So, even though the book was reviewed by Alice and his manager before going to press, pieces of inaccurate information still made it into the book.

ME, ALICE is an interesting read and it's certainly entertaining, if you make allowance for the inconsistencies. The book was never reprinted after it's hard cover release, and has become a collector's item in Cooper fan circles.

Book Title: MARVEL PREMIERE #50 (title unknown)
Published: Released August 3, 1979 by Marvel Comics (the cover says October 1979.)
Author: Plot: Alice Cooper, Jim Saucrup and Roger Stern. Writer: Ed Hanigan. Artists: Tom Sutton (penciller) and Terry Austin (inker.) Colorist: Marie Severin. Editor: Jim Saucrup.
Content: 17 pages of artwork, with a one page article about the comic.

While waiting to enter a clinic to calm his nerves, Alice is mistaken for an insane person known as Alex Cooper and taken to an asylum. Once there, he meets up with many of the characters from the FROM THE INSIDE album. Wanting to get away from the people there, he finally breaks out with the help of his snake, Veronica. Walking the streets the next day, Alice comes across a thunderous political rally for Alex Cooper. In trying to warn the people there about Alex, Alice is once again picked up by the police and taken back to the asylum. Once there, he has a breakdown and realizes that he's better off in the asylum after all.

This excellent first comic book about Alice was one in a series from Marvel Comics that spotlighted new characters that had the potential for a continuing series of their own. Marvel first considered an Alice Cooper comic book in the 1970's (for WELCOME TO MY NIGHTMARE), but nothing panned out until 1979 and the release of the FROM THE INSIDE album. The plot was developed by Alice, Jim Saucrup and Roger Stern (an excellent writer at Marvel who was just starting to work on some of his best material), with artist / writer Ed Hanigan writing the script. Important to comic book fans is the addition of Terry Austin as the inker. He was well known for putting in additional jokes in the background of comics that he worked on (he was also becoming quite well-known for his inking on THE UNCANNY X-MEN at the time.) It was heartening to see Marie Severin's work in the Alice comic book. She was involved with MAD back in its comic book days in the 1950's and the Marvel Comic certainly has many MAD-like moments (such as Archie from ARCHIE COMICS strapped up in a straitjacket shouting for Veronica, or the cops looking like Officers Toody and Muldoon from CAR 54, etc.)

Marvel Preimere #50

It's a very funny book and certainly one of the best rock music-related comics to be produced over the years. While it's a shame that there was never a series (which was highly unlikely anyway), it's understandable in light of the story. Copies of the comic book tend to go for high prices in rock music circles, but it's average price in comic book circles the is still around $10.

~~~ Chapter 3: 1980 - 1982 ~~~

Part 1 — "Six Is Having Problems . . ."

The 1970's began with most of popular music following one genre — rock music. It may have been folk rock or funk rock, but it was still rock. As the 70's progressed, rock music began to diversify, splitting into groups such as disco, pop and rock. By the beginning of 1980, there were only three ways to go: disco, punk / new wave or pop.

Alice fell into the center of things. He was too heavy for pop fans to want him, and too commercial for the punkers to identify with him. Other rock performers, like KISS and Aerosmith, were confused and uncertain about what to play and found themselves producing albums that were unsatisfying for their fan base and received only lukewarm interest outside of their fans.

For Alice, it was a different matter altogether. Instead of scrounging to find a niche, Alice instead embraced the new decade with a passion. He'd been wanting to advance his "Alice" character past the well known "killer" mode, and 1978's FROM THE INSIDE album helped him to develop another side to the character and show more of its inner workings. The punk and new wave movements helped propel the character into a new area, into an area that dealt more with psychological ideas and nightmares, with world problems and personal struggles. The world saw a post-nuclear Alice — an "Apocalypse Alice."

Alice dropped much of the excess baggage of the 1970's tours and scaled the performance back to just the band and a few special effects. His makeup and costume also changed (which it had been doing since as early as the end of the FROM THE INSIDE tour and the ROADIE movie), and an even more dangerous Alice emerged to face the world in 1980 with the FLUSH THE FASHION album and tour.

While some fans were a bit uncertain about the new side of Alice appearing on the album, FLUSH THE FASHION did have a minor hit with Clones (We're All) and the tour was certainly successful. After this, Alice dove even further into the militant look of his new "Alice" with the SPECIAL FORCES album that arrived in 1981. Yet this time, the hits didn't come in the US, although the album and singles did fine in the UK and Europe. It was beginning to look like the character wasn't going over quite as well as expected.

A further problem developed with Alice's return to the bottle. The drinking again took over aspects of his life and it slowed the progression of his music. During this time came the two more experimental albums, ZIPPER CATCHES SKIN and DADA. Neither album was accompanied by a tour, nor saw much promotion. The albums fared poorly and by 1983 Warner had decided to drop Alice Cooper. He became a free agent again for the first time in fifteen years.

Part 2 — Recordings 1980 - 1982

Alice began the new decade with the decision to revise his stage character, to not only bring it up to date, but to even go beyond what was currently happening in music in 1980. What was happening was punk and new wave.

The appearance and attitude of neither of these movements — the ratty, destroyed clothes of the punkers, nor the clean, crisp jacket and tie look of the new wavers — was a direction that Alice embraced at the outset of the 1980's (although the years following FLUSH THE FASHION saw Alice going in both these directions — the ratty, military clothes for SPECIAL FORCES and the rolled up jacket look for the Talk Talk single.) Instead it was the addition of more keyboard instruments and computerized enhancements that characterized his music between 1980 and 1983. That's not to say that these were completely new to Alice's music. Keyboards had always been apart of his music, even in the days of the original Alice Cooper Group, with a keyboard instrument occasionally providing the focus for a track, rather than guitar or drums. Nor did 1983 signal the end of Alice using keyboards, as material from CONSTRICTOR shows, still, it was a development that enhanced his music to a greater extent than during any other period. 1980 to 1982 produced some of the most experimental music of Alice's career since his work with the original band back in the late 1960's.

Song lyrics, especially with the first three albums of the new decade, were also somewhat more political in nature than they had been in the past — something that was also typical of the new wave and punk movements.

On the production side, it was during these years was that the final demise of the 8-track tape was seen, and FLUSH THE FASHION was the last of Alice's albums to be released in this format. Compact Discs, however, didn't really emerge until 1984. So most albums produced between 1981 and 1984 were available on vinyl and cassette only.

Another demise was the "extras" in the packaging of Alice Cooper albums. FLUSH THE FASHION was the only album from this period to have an inner sleeve that listed additional album information. Until CONSTRICTOR, each album was released in a clear plastic inner sleeve inside a cardboard cover, and nothing more.

FLUSH THE FASHION produced a hit single with Clones (We're All), but the follow up album, SPECIAL FORCES, didn't do at all well in the charts. The two albums released after that, ZIPPER CATCHES SKIN and DADA, didn't even chart in the US, and led to Alice and Warner Brothers going their separate ways after nearly fifteen years together.

Things were ripe for a change in direction in 1980, however, and the time had come to put up the hair and show the new kids how it was done.

Album Title: **FLUSH THE FASHION**
Recorded: February - March 1980 at Cherokee Recording Studios, Los Angeles, California.
Production: Produced by Roy Thomas Baker. Executive Produced by Shep Gordon. Associate producer was Ron Volz Musical arrangements by Alice Cooper, Fred Mandel and Davey Johnstone.
Personnel: Alice Cooper (vocals), Davey Johnstone (lead guitar), Fred Mandel (guitar and keyboards), Dennis Conway (drums), "Cooker" John LoPresti (bass.) Backing vocals by Joe Pizzul, Fred Mandel, Ricky "Rat" Tierney, Keith Allison and Flo & Eddie.
Song List: Talk Talk (Sean Bonniwell) / Clones (We're All) (Carron) / Pain (Alice Cooper, Davey Johnstone and Fred Mandel) / Leather Boots (Wester) / Aspirin Damage (Cooper, Johnstone, Mandel) / Nuclear Infected (Cooper, Johnstone, Mandel) / Grim Facts (Cooper, Johnstone and Mandel) / Model Citizen (Cooper, Johnstone Mandel) / Dance Yourself to Death (Cooper and Crandall) / Headlines (Cooper, Johnstone and Mandel)

The FROM THE INSIDE tour ended during the final days of April 1979, and Alice took some time off before beginning work on his short role in the movie ROADIE during the fall of 1979 (ROADIE was released in the Spring of 1980. See Part 4 for details.) During his work on the film, Alice had already begun reevaluating his on-stage character. This included both changing the look of the character (pulling his hair up into a bun, changing his makeup to exaggerate the sullen cheeks and mascara eyebrows, and allowing his costume to become less uniform from tour to tour and even show to show), and a change in musical direction as well.

With the growing emphasis in pop music on keyboards and synthesizers, although keyboards had always been an element in Alice's music, they now became more so. Fred Mandel, Alice's keyboard player from several previous albums and tours, became a vital part of the evolution of Alice's music. Mandel co-wrote six of the ten songs, and played both guitar and keyboards on the tour that followed. He was listed as creating the musical arrangements with Alice and Davey Johnstone.

The FLUSH THE FASHION album cover.

Davey Johnstone returned after the success of FROM THE INSIDE to play guitar on the new album and also co-wrote six songs with Mandel and Alice. Johnstone didn't join Alice on the subsequent tour, however.

New to the mix were Dennis Conway on drums and John LoPresti on bass. While both performed on the entire album — making FLUSH THE FASHION the first album since the Alice Cooper Group days to feature the same musicians on every track — they didn't join the subsequent tour. Aside from a select few, the people on this album were not the ones that Alice had worked consistently over the past few years. He wasn't unhappy with those people, but merely felt the need for new blood on the new album. Even the people singing backing vocals were different, with only Fred Mandel and Flo & Eddie coming back.

Brought in to produce the album was the Cars' and Queen's designated producer Roy Thomas Baker, who created a stripped-down feel for the album that went well with the "punk-like" feel of the music. A change from the preceding four studio albums, FLUSH THE FASHION was intentionally not conceptual in nature. Instead, the music is somewhat more political and confrontational in nature — directly in keeping with the direction that some New Wave and Punk bands were simultaneously exploring in the late 1970's and early 1980's (before they become midstream and commercialized.)

Alice once explained that song ideas and titles had come from headlines in the National Enquirer (a story that's actually true.) This album, however, included songs written by people other than Alice and / or his bandmates. Talk Talk was a song originally recorded by the Los Angeles band Music Machine back in the late 1960's, and Clones and Leather Boots were both written by outsiders.

Clones, the first single from the album, has fascinating lyrics relating to old science fiction television programs. The most obvious was a late-1970's movie called CLONES, but there were others as well. THE PRISONER television series (that had long been one of Alice's favorites) featured Patrick McGoohan as a character going by the name of "Number 6", who had problems adjusting to being part of the self-contained society of people who were all the same (". . . 6 is having problems adjusting to his clone status . . . "), and "the Doctor" from DOCTOR WHO occasionally fought an alien race of clones called the Sontarens ("You're through, Doctor, we don't need your kind . . . ") Coincidental? Deliberate? Maybe a little of both — either way, it is certainly fascinating to think about.

As was the feel of the music, the packaging for the album was stripped down. The cover art was conceived by Alice and Peter Whorf. The front cover (by Fred Valentine) has the album title in a scrawled-out fashion on a wall. Alice's name appears at the top in block letters with "'80" after his name to reinforce the new Alice persona on record and in concert. The back cover is a photo by Jonathan Exley of a steadfast Alice, dressed in black and holding a riding crop. The inner sleeve contained another photo of Alice by Johnathan Exley, along with liner notes and lyrics for the songs.

A three month North American tour followed the album, with six out of the ten songs from the album making it into the show. FLUSH THE FASHION reached No. 44 on the US charts, and No. 96 on the UK charts. The album was later reissued with SPECIAL FORCES on a DOUBLE PLAY 2 ON 1 cassette (catalog number 23855-4.)

Album Title: **FLUSH THE FASHION**
Released: May 1980 by Warner Brothers.
Catalog No.: BSK 3436
Media: Vinyl, Cassette and 8-Track.

The US release also came with a small flyer advertising a Warner Brothers promotional sampler album called A LA CARTE.

Album Title: **FLUSH THE FASHION**
Released: May 17, 1980 by Warner Brothers, UK.
Catalog No.: K 56805
Media: Vinyl and Cassette.

Album Title: **FLUSH THE FASHION**
Released: May 1980 by Warner Brothers, Argentina.
Catalog No.: BSK 3436
Media: Vinyl.

Album Title: **FLUSH THE FASHION**
Released: May 1980 by Warner Brothers, Australia.
Catalog No.: BSK-3436
Media: Vinyl.

The album reached No. 32 on the Australian charts.

Album Title: **FLUSH THE FASHION**
Released: May 1980 by Warner Brothers, Brazil.
Catalog No.: 36157
Media: Vinyl.

Album Title: **FLUSH THE FASHION**
Released: May 1980 by Warner Brothers, France.
Catalog No.: K456805; France WE451 Germany U
Media: Vinyl.

Album Title: **FLUSH THE FASHION**
Released: May 1980 by Warner Brothers, Germany.
Catalog No.: K456805: France WE 451 Germany U
Media: Vinyl.

Album Title: **FLUSH THE FASHION**
Released: May 1980 by Warner Brothers, Holland.
Catalog No.: 56805
Media: Vinyl.

Album Title: **FLUSH THE FASHION**
Released: May 1980 by Warner Brothers, Italy.
Catalog No.: W 56805
Media: Vinyl.

Album Title: **FLUSH THE FASHION**
Released: May 1980 by Warner Brothers, Japan.
Catalog No.: P-10823W
Media: Vinyl.

Album Title: **FLUSH THE FASHION**
Released: May 1980 by Warner Brothers, Portugal.
Catalog No.: WAR 456805
Media: Vinyl.

Album Title: **FLUSH THE FASHION**
Released: May 1980 by Warner Brothers, South Africa.
Catalog No.: WBC 1472
Media: Vinyl.

Album Title: **FLUSH THE FASHION**
Released: December 3, 1990 by Warner Brothers, Australia.
Catalog No.: WAR 9262292
Media: CD.

First Australian reissue of the album on CD.

Album Title: **FLUSH THE FASHION**
Released: December 3, 1990 by Warner Brothers, Germany.
Catalog No.: WEA 926229-2, WEA 926229-4
Media: CD and Cassette.

First French / German reissue of the album on CD.

Album Title: **FLUSH THE FASHION**
Released: 1997 by EMI, Australia.
Catalog No.: EMI 8140302
Media: CD.

Second Australian reissue of the album on CD, this time on EMI instead of Warner Brothers.

Album Title: **FLUSH THE FASHION**
Released: September 30, 1997 by Warner Brothers, Japan.
Catalog No.: WPCP 3497
Media: CD.

Part of the special "Forever Young Series" that WB released in Japan. The album came with an obi that listed the album's title and additional albums available in the series.

Single Title: **Clones (We're All)** (stereo) /
Clones (We're All) (mono)
Released: June 1980 by Warner Brothers.
Catalog No.: WBS 49204
Media: 7" Vinyl.

1997 Japanese reissue of the album.

A radio-only promotional single released to correspond with the commercial single. Released on the promo-only white WB label.

US single for Clones (We're All).

Single Title: **Clones (We're All) / Model Citizen**
Released: June 1980 by Warner Brothers.
Catalog No.: WBS 42904
Media: 7" Vinyl.

Picture sleeve, with a photo of Alice holding a riding crop as seen on the FLUSH THE FASHION album. This photo was used for the majority of the foreign picture sleeves for this single. Clones reached No. 40 on the US charts. It was the last US Top 40 hit for Alice until Poison in 1989.

Single Title: **Clones (We're All) / Model Citizen**
Released: August 1980 by Warner Brothers, UK.
Catalog No.: K 17598
Media: 7" Vinyl.

Clones charted briefly in the UK, but exact chart ranking is unknown. The follow-up single from FLUSH THE FASHION, Talk Talk, wasn't released at all in the UK.

Single Title: **Clones (We're All) / Model Citizen**
Released: August 1980 by Warner Brothers, Australia.
Catalog No.: WBS-49204
Media: 7" Vinyl.

Clones reached No. 36 on the Australian charts. The follow-up single, Talk Talk, wasn't released in Australia.

Single Title: **Clones (We're All) / Model Citizen**
Released: July 1980 by Warner Brothers, Brazil.
Catalog No.: 16.162
Media: 7" Vinyl.

Single Title: **Clones (We're All) / Model Citizen**
Released: August 1980 by Warner Brothers, France.
Catalog No.: 17598

Media: 7" Vinyl.

Picture sleeve.

Single Title: **Clones (We're All) / Model Citizen**
Released: August 1980 by Warner Brothers, Germany.
Catalog No.: WB 17598
Media: 7" Vinyl.

Picture sleeve.

Single Title: **Clones (We're All) / Model Citizen**
Released: August 1980 by Warner Brothers, Holland.
Catalog No.: 17598
Media: 7" Vinyl.

Picture sleeve.

Single Title: **Clones (We're All)** (stereo) /
Clones (We're All) (mono)
Released: August 1980 by Warner Brothers, Italy.
Catalog No.: PROMO 112
Media: 7" promotional Vinyl.

Single Title: **Clones (We're All) / Model Citizen**
Released: December 1978 by Warner Brothers, Italy.
Catalog No.: W 17598
Media: 7" Vinyl.

Picture sleeve, with the same photo of Alice that appears on the FLUSH THE FASHION album.

Single Title: **Clones (We're All) / Model Citizen**
Released: August 1980 by Warner Brothers, Japan.
Catalog No.: P-570W
Media: 7" Vinyl.

Italian single for Clones (We're All).

Picture sleeve.

Single Title: **Clones (We're All) / Model Citizen**
Released: August 1980 by Warner Brothers, Portugal.
Catalog No.: WAR 17598
Media: 7" Vinyl.

Same picture sleeve as on the US release.

Single Title: **Talk Talk** (stereo) / **Talk Talk** (mono)
Released: September 1980 by Warner Brothers.
Catalog No.: WBS 49526
Media: 7" Vinyl.

A radio-only promotional single released to correspond with the commercial single. Released on the promo-only white WB label.

Single Title: **Talk Talk / Dance Yourself to Death**
Released: September 1980 by Warner Brothers.
Catalog No.: WBS 49526
Media: 7" Vinyl.

Single Title: **Talk Talk / Dance Yourself to Death**
Released: September 1980 by Warner Brothers, France.

Catalog No.: 17697
Media: 7" Vinyl.

Picture sleeve.

Single Title: **Talk Talk / Dance Yourself to Death**
Released: September 1980 by Warner Brothers, Germany.
Catalog No.: WB 17697
Media: 7" Vinyl.

Picture sleeve of Alice with his hair pulled back and wearing jeans, T-shirt and a stripped jacket with the sleeves rolled up. The lower right-hand corner says that the songs came from the FLUSH THE FASHION album.

Single Title: **Talk Talk / Dance Yourself to Death**
Released: September 1980 by Warner Brothers, Holland.
Catalog No.: WB 17697
Media: 7" Vinyl.

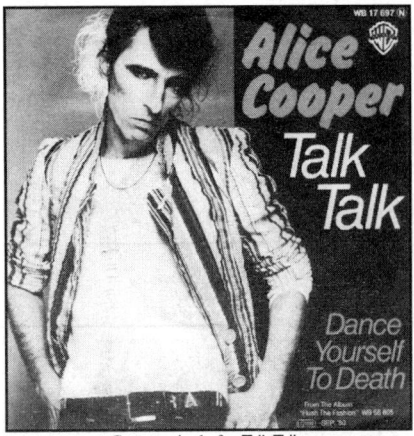

German single for Talk Talk.

Picture sleeve.

Album Title: **SPECIAL FORCES**
Recorded: Recorded May 1981 at American Recording Company, Los Angeles, California.
Production: Produced by Richard Podolor. Executive Produced by Shep Gordon. Engineered by Bill Cooper. Mixed by Richard Podolor and Bill Cooper.
Personnel: Alice Cooper (vocals), Danny Johnson (guitar), Mike Pinera (guitar), Craig Kampf (drums), Erik Scott (bass), Duane Hitchings (keyboards).
Song List: Who Do You Think We Are (Cooper and Hitchings) / Seven and Seven Is (Albert Lee) / Prettiest Cop on the Block (Cooper, Johnstone and Mandel) / Don't Talk Old to Me (Cooper, Johnstone and Mandel) / Generation Landslide '81 (Live) (Cooper, Bruce, Dunaway, Smith, Buxton) / Skeletons in the Closet (Cooper and Hitchings) / You Want it, You Got it (Cooper, Scott, Kampf, Steele and Kaz) / You Look Good in Rags (Cooper and Hitchings) / You're a Movie (Cooper and Hitchings) / Vicious Rumours (Cooper, Hitchings, Scott and Pinera)

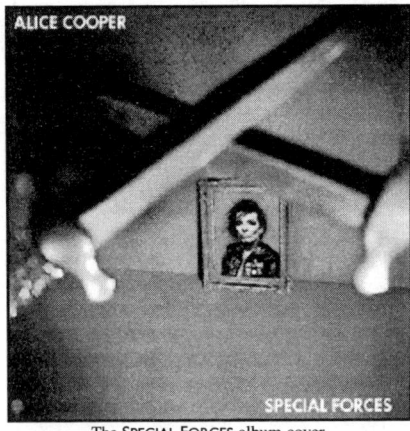

The SPECIAL FORCES album cover.

For the first time since WELCOME TO MY NIGHTMARE in 1974, this album included songs developed from possibilities that were explored in concert before making it to the studio. Who Do You Think We Are became a vital part of the SPECIAL FORCES tour, and Seven and Seven Is was part of the show once the tour hit Europe at the beginning of 1982. None of the other songs from this album made it to the show — a sharp contrast with albums before this one.

This album is almost an extension of the back-to-basics style of FLUSH THE FASHION, and the two tracks from Cooper, Johnstone and Mandel would have worked just as well on FLUSH as they do on SPECIAL FORCES. The album's musicians were people who had worked with Alice on the FLUSH THE FASHION tour (Hitchings, Pinera and Scott), along with Craig Kampf on drums and Danny Johnson on guitar. Hitchings co-wrote half the songs on the album, and sometimes sneaked a bit of Vicious Rumours into the keyboard solo of School's Out on the tour.

This album was produced rather quickly in May 1981, right before the North American tour that began in June, and the rush led to the album packaging listing a song that never got past the demo stage. The song, Look at You Over There, Ripping the Sawdust From My Teddy Bear was to have appeared on the album, but was dropped at the last minute because it didn't fit in musically with the other tracks. The song remains a mystery and fans have been anxious to it hear for years (especially after being teased with such a great title.) Fortunately, the track will be part of the planned boxed set due out in early 1999.

Although the remake of Generation Landslide is listed as a live cut, it was actually re-recorded in the studio during the making of SPECIAL FORCES and not in front of an audience. It was, however, part of the set during the European portion of the tour. Seven and Seven Is was a cover of a song done back in the 1960's by the band Love.

The stripped down album packaging is quite bland, with a picture of Alice (by Jonathan Exley) framed against a wall with two swords in the foreground. Art direction for the album was provided by Alice and Richard Seireeni, and the cover photos were done by Eric Blum.

SPECIAL FORCES reached No. 125 in the US charts and No. 96 in the UK. The album was later reissued with FLUSH THE FASHION on a DOUBLE PLAY 2 ON 1 cassette (catalog number 23855-4.)

Album Title: **SPECIAL FORCES**
Released: September 12, 1981 by Warner Brothers.
Catalog No.: BSK 3581
Media: Vinyl, Cassette and 8-Track.

Came in a plastic inner sleeve.

Album Title: **SPECIAL FORCES**
Released: September 12, 1981 by Warner Brothers, UK.
Catalog No.: K 56927
Media: Vinyl and Cassette.

Album Title: **SPECIAL FORCES**
Released: September 1981 by Warner Brothers, Argentina.
Catalog No.: 26052
Media: Vinyl.

Album Title: **SPECIAL FORCES**
Released: September 1981 by Warner Brothers, Australia.
Catalog No.: BSK-3581
Media: Vinyl.

The album reached No. 76 on the Australian charts. It was the last Alice album to reach the charts until CONSTRICTOR in 1986.

Album Title: **SPECIAL FORCES**
Released: September 1981 by Warner Brothers, Brazil.
Catalog No.: Unknown.
Media: Vinyl.

Album Title: **SPECIAL FORCES**
Released: September 1981 by Warner Brothers, Canada.
Catalog No.: XBS 3581
Media: Vinyl.

Album Title: **SPECIAL FORCES**
Released: September 1981 by Warner Brothers, France.
Catalog No.: WB 56927
Media: Vinyl.

Album Title: **SPECIAL FORCES**
Released: September 1981 by Warner Brothers, Germany.
Catalog No.: WB 56927
Media: Vinyl.

Album Title: **SPECIAL FORCES**
Released: September 1981 by Warner Brothers, Holland.
Catalog No.: 56927
Media: Vinyl.

Album Title: **SPECIAL FORCES**
Released: May 1980 by Warner Brothers, Italy.
Catalog No.: W 56927
Media: Vinyl.

Album Title: **SPECIAL FORCES**
Released: December 3, 1990 by Warner Brothers, Germany.
Catalog No.: WEA 926230-2, WEA 926230-4
Media: CD and Cassette.

First French / German reissue of the album on CD.

Album Title: **SPECIAL FORCES**
Released: December 3, 1990 by Warner Brothers, Australia.
Catalog No.: WAR 9262302
Media: CD.

First CD pressing of the album in Australia.

Album Title: **SPECIAL FORCES**
Released: September 30, 1997 by Warner Brothers, Japan.
Catalog No.: WPCP 3498
Media: CD.

Part of the special "Forever Young Series" that WB released in Japan. The album came with an obi that listed the album's title and additional albums available in the series. Look at You... is listed on the CD packaging, although the song does not appear.

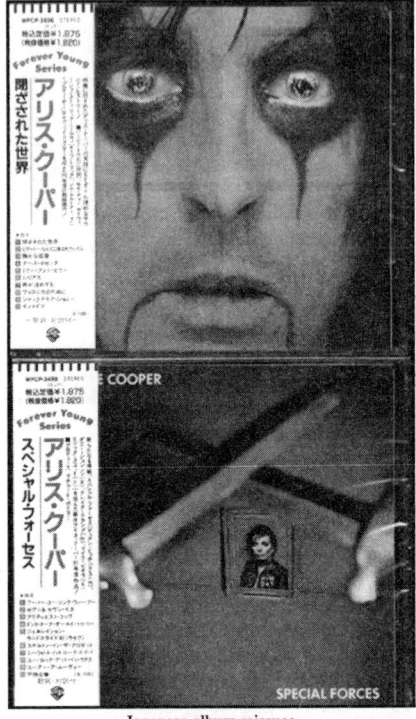

Japanese album reissues.

Single Title: **You Want It, You Got It** (stereo) / **You Want It, You Got It** (mono)
Released: September 1981 by Warner Brothers.
Catalog No.: WBS 49780
Media: 7" Vinyl.

A radio-only promotional single released to correspond with the commercial single. Released on the promo-only white WB label.

Single Title: **You Want It, You Got It / Who Do You Think We Are**
Released: September 1981 by Warner Brothers.
Catalog No.: PRO-A-971
Media: 12" promotional Vinyl.

Single Title: **You Want It, You Got It / Who Do You Think We Are**
Released: September 1981 by Warner Brothers.
Catalog No.: WBS 49780
Media: 7" Vinyl.

You Want It, You Got It didn't chart in the US.

Single Title: **You Want It, You Got It / Who Do You Think We Are**
Released: September 1981 by Warner Brothers, Australia.
Catalog No.: WBS-49780

Media: 7" Vinyl.

You Want It, You Got It reached No. 74 on the Australian charts. It was the last Alice single for Warner Brothers to hit the charts in Australia.

Single Title: **You Want It, You Got It / Who Do You Think We Are**
Released: September 1981 by Warner Brothers, Brazil.
Catalog No.: 16.203
Media: 7" Vinyl.

Single Title: **You Want It, You Got It / Who Do You Think We Are**
Released: September 1981 by Warner Brothers, France.
Catalog No.: 17903
Media: 7" Vinyl.

Picture sleeve.

Single Title: **You Want It, You Got It / Who Do You Think We Are**
Released: September 1981 by Warner Brothers, Germany.
Catalog No.: WB 17846
Media: 7" Vinyl.

Picture sleeve.

Single Title: **You Want It, You Got It / Who Do You Think We Are**
Released: September 1981 by Warner Brothers, Holland.
Catalog No.: 17846
Media: 7" Vinyl.

Picture sleeve.

Holland single for You Want It.

Single Title: **You Want It, You Got It / Who Do You Think We Are**
Released: September 1981 by Warner Brothers, Italy.
Catalog No.: W 17846
Media: 7" Vinyl.

Picture sleeve, very similar to the album cover.

Single Title: **Seven and Seven Is** (stereo) / **Seven and Seven Is** (mono)
Released: February 1981 by Warner Brothers.
Catalog No.: WBS 49848
Media: 7" Vinyl.

A radio-only promotional single released to correspond with the commercial single. Released on the promo-only white WB label.

Italian single for You Want It.

Single Title: **Seven and Seven Is / Generation Landslide '81** (live)
Released: February 1981 by Warner Brothers.
Catalog No.: WBS 49848
Media: 7" Vinyl.

Seven and Seven Is didn't chart in the US.

Single Title: **(No More) Love at Your Convenience / Generation Landslide '81** (live)
Released: February 1982 by Warner Brothers, UK.
Catalog No.: K17914
Media: 7" Vinyl.

Released in support of Alice's tour of the UK in February 1982, this was quickly pulled when it was realized that the A-side wasn't a song from SPECIAL FORCES, but instead a secondary A-side from the 1977 album, LACE AND WHISKEY.

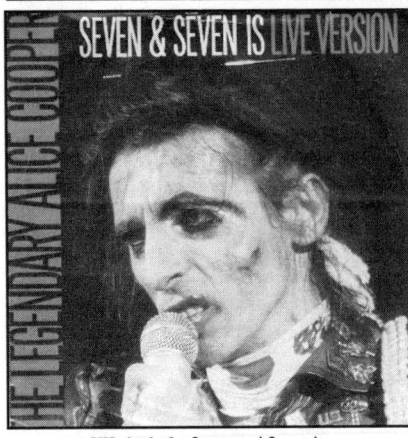

UK single for Seven and Seven Is.

Single Title: **Seven and Seven Is / Generation Landslide '81** (live)
Released: February 1982 by Warner Brothers, UK.
Catalog No.: K 17924
Media: 7" Vinyl.

Released the same month as the pulled (No More) Love at Your Convenience single (above), Seven and Seven Is reached No. 62 on the UK charts.

Single Title: **Seven and Seven Is / Generation Landslide '81** (live)
Released: February 1982 by Warner Brothers, UK.
Catalog No.: K 17924
Media: 7" Vinyl.

Same as on the other UK single with these two tracks, except that the 7" vinyl single comes in a gatefold cover. The back of the cover advertises the ALICE COOPER GREATEST HITS album.

Single Title: **Seven and Seven Is / Generation Landslide '81** (live)
Released: February 1981 by Warner Brothers, Germany.
Catalog No.: WB 17924
Media: 7" Vinyl.

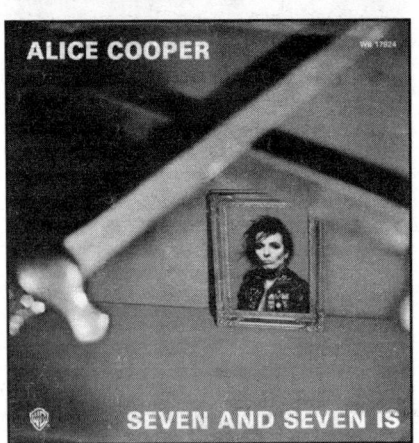

Picture sleeve.

> Second part of gatefold for special addition of UK Seven and Seven Is (center).
> German single for Seven and Seven Is (bottom).

Single Title: **Seven and Seven Is** (stereo) / **Seven and Seven Is** (mono)
Released: February 1981 by Warner Brothers, Holland.
Catalog No.: 17924
Media: 7" Vinyl.

A radio-only promotional single released on the promo-only white WB label to correspond with the commercial single.

Single Title: **Seven and Seven Is / Generation Landslide '81** (live)
Released: February 1981 by Warner Brothers, Holland.
Catalog No.: 17924
Media: 7" Vinyl.

The picture sleeve is of the cover of the SPECIAL FORCES album. It's quite possible that this same single was released in Germany, Belgium and France as a way to save on costs. **Generation Landslide '81 (live)** is listed as simply **Generation Landslide**.

EP Title: **FOR BRITAIN ONLY**
Recorded: April 1982 by Warner Brothers, UK.
Production: K 17940 T
Song List: Who Do You Think We Are (live) / Model Citizen (live) / For Britain Only / Under My Wheels (live)

A special single released in both 7" (see below) and 12" vinyl versions to thank fans in the UK for their support during the SPECIAL FORCES tour in early 1982. Alice recorded For Britain Only at the Air Studios in London, England during the first few days of March 1982.

Included with this track were three live songs recorded February 19, 1982 at the Apollo Theatre in Glasgow, Scotland. These three songs were also part of a radio broadcast of the concert that night, which has turned up on a few bootlegs over the past several years (see Chapter 6 for more details.)

There were rumors of a picture disc version of this release (either in the 12" or 7" version) with the catalog number K17940 M mentioned in a magazine article. Unfortunately, the rumors are nothing more than that and no such picture disc exists. FOR BRITAIN ONLY reached No. 66 on the UK charts.

Single Title: **FOR BRITAIN ONLY**
Recorded: April 1982 by Warner Brothers, UK.
Production: K 17940
Song List: For Britain Only / Under My Wheels (live)

See the entry above for more details about the recording of this special single. The 7" version came in both a normal picture sleeve and a gatefold picture sleeve. All versions of this release have the same cover design with photos of Alice in action on stage.

For Britain Only 7" single.

Album Title: **ALICE COOPER COLLECTION**
Recorded: Released Summer 1982 by Warner Brothers, Germany.
Catalog No.: 26241
Song List: School's Out / Elected / Billion Dollar Babies / Who Do You Think We Are / Teenage Lament '74 / Hello Hooray / Hallowed Be My Name / No More Mr. Nice Guy / I'm Eighteen / You Want It, You Got It / How You Gonna See Me Now / Killer

Another "greatest hits" package, released only in Germany.

Album Title: **ZIPPER CATCHES SKIN**
Recorded: May - June 1982 at Cherokee Studios, Los Angeles, CA.
Production: Produced by Alice Cooper and Erik Scott. Executive producer was Shep Gordon. Recorded and mixed by Dee Robb. Musical arrangements by Alice Cooper and Erik Scott. "I Am the Future" produced by Steve Tyrell and recorded by Ed Barton at Jennifudy Studios, Los Angeles, CA.
Personnel: Alice Cooper (vocals and synthesizer.) Mike Pinera (guitar.) Dick Wagner (guitar.) John Nitzinger (guitar.) Billy Steele (guitar.) Jan Uvena (drums and percussion.) Craig Kampf (percussion.) Erik Scott (bass.) Duane Hitchings (synthesizer.) Additional performers: Frannie Golde, Joanne Harris and Flo and Eddie (backing vocals.) Patty Donahue on additional vocals and "sarcasm."
Song List: Zorro's Ascent (Cooper, Nitzinger, Scott and Steele) / Make That Money (Cooper and Wagner) /

I Am the Future (Lalo Schifrin and Osborne) / No Baloney Homo Sapiens (Cooper and Wagner) / Adaptable (Anything for You) (Cooper, Scott and Steele) / I Like Girls (Cooper, Nitzinger and Scott) / Remarkably Insincere (Cooper, Nitzinger and Scott) / Tag,You're It (Cooper, Nitzinger and Scott) / I Better Be Good (Cooper, Scott and Wagner) / I'm Alive (That Was the Day My Dead Pet Returned to Save My Life) (Cooper, Scott and Wagner)

The time was Summer 1982 and it was time for another Alice Cooper album to hit the record store racks, as had FLUSH THE FASHION in early Summer 1980, and SPECIAL FORCES in late Summer 1981. The packaging trend was also continued with this album — cut to the bare essentials with a single cardboard sleeve and a plastic inner sleeve, and no additional materials. The album cover (conceived by Alice with Jonathan Exley and designed by Jimmy Wachtel) was innovative. The album lyrics were inventively displayed on the front cover, and the back cover was a photo by Jonathan Exley of Alice in dress pants, and shirt and tie with a very painful expression on this face (as the album's title would lead you to expect.)

After an absence of two albums, Dick Wagner returned to work with Alice again. He played guitar on the album and co-write four of the ten songs. One of the songs that he co-wrote, Make That Money, was based on a song that Alice had worked on in the late 1970's (as part of a never completed concept album based on Scrooge from Dickens' A CHRISTMAS CAROL.) Wagner also co-wrote the song with the best title — I'm Alive (That Was the Day My Dead Pet Returned to Save My Life).

The ZIPPER CATCHES SKIN album cover.

Returning from the SPECIAL FORCES tour of earlier in 1982 to work on ZIPPER CATCHES SKIN was Erik Scott (co-producing and co-arranging the music) along with Mike Pinera and Duane Hitchings. Craig Kampf from the SPECIAL FORCES album played some percussion on the new album. Flo & Eddie again appeared to sing some backing vocals. The late Patty Donahue, who sang on the album, is probably best remembered as the lead singer of the Rock / New Wave band The Waitresses, who had an early 1980's hit with I Know What Boys Want.

Most of the album was recorded at Cherokee Studios in Los Angeles, but Alice recorded I Am the Future at Jennifudy Studios in Los Angeles as part of a commitment to do a track for the movie CLASS OF 1984. The film was released the same month as ZIPPER CATCHES SKIN, and the song was released in August 1982 in a remixed version as a single for both the movie and the album. Lalo Schifrin, who co-wrote the song, was the composer for the film and also composed the music for the films MISSION: IMPOSSIBLE, THE AMITYVILLE HORROR, MAGNUM FORCE, ENTER THE DRAGON and the theme from the STARSKY AND HUTCH TV series.

There was no tour to support this album and none of the songs became standards for any later tours. ZIPPER CATCHES SKIN didn't reach the charts in either the US or the UK.

Album Title: **ZIPPER CATCHES SKIN**
Released: August 1982 by Warner Brothers.
Catalog No.: 923719-1
Media: Vinyl and Cassette.

Came with a plastic inner sleeve.

Album Title: **ZIPPER CATCHES SKIN**
Released: August 1982 by Warner Brothers, UK.
Catalog No.: K 57021
Media: Vinyl and Cassette.

Album Title: **ZIPPER CATCHES SKIN**
Released: August 1982 by Warner Brothers, Australia.
Catalog No.: BSK-3581

Media: Vinyl.

The album didn't chart in Australia.

Album Title: **ZIPPER CATCHES SKIN**
Released: August 1982 by Warner Brothers, Brazil.
Catalog No.: 26.080
Media: Vinyl.

Album Title: **ZIPPER CATCHES SKIN**
Released: August 1982 by Warner Brothers, France.
Catalog No.: 57021
Media: Vinyl.

Album Title: **ZIPPER CATCHES SKIN**
Released: August 1982 by Warner Brothers, Germany.
Catalog No.: WB 57021
Media: Vinyl.

Album Title: **ZIPPER CATCHES SKIN**
Released: August 1982 by Warner Brothers, Holland.
Catalog No.: 57021
Media: Vinyl.

Album Title: **ZIPPER CATCHES SKIN**
Released: August 1982 by Warner Brothers, Italy.
Catalog No.: W 57021
Media: Vinyl.

Album Title: **ZIPPER CATCHES SKIN**
Released: December 3, 1990 by Warner Brothers, Germany.
Catalog No.: WEA 923719-2, WEA 9223719-4
Media: CD and Cassette.

First French / German reissue of the album on CD.

Album Title: **ZIPPER CATCHES SKIN**
Released: 1990 by Warner Brothers, Australia.
Catalog No.: WMI 9237192
Media: CD.

First Australian reissue of the album on CD

Album Title: **ZIPPER CATCHES SKIN**
Released: September 30, 1997 by Warner Brothers, Japan.
Catalog No.: WPCP 3499
Media: CD.

Part of the special "Forever Young Series" that WB released in Japan. The album came with an obi that listed the album's title and additional albums available in the series.

Single Title: **I Am the Future** (stereo) / **I Am the Future** (mono)
Released: August 1982 by Warner Brothers.
Catalog No.: 7-29828
Media: 7" promotional Vinyl.

A radio-only promotional single, released on the promo-only white WB label, to correspond with the commercial single.

Single Title: **I Am the Future / Tag, You're It**
Released: August 1981 by Warner Brothers.

Catalog No.: 7-29828
Media: 7" Vinyl

No picture sleeve. The B-side of this single changed depending on the country of origin. It was released in each country in conjunction with the film CLASS OF 1984. The US single is the only one with Tag,You're It as the B-side.

Single Title: **I Am the Future** (remix) / **Zorro's Ascent**
Released: March 1983 by Warner Brothers, UK.
Catalog No.: K 15004
Media: 7" Vinyl

This single featured the remixed version of I Am the Future that appeared in the film CLASS OF 1984. The remix was paired with Zorro's Ascent in many foreign countries and was released at different times to correspond with the release date of the movie in each country.

Single Title: **I Am the Future** (remix) / **Zorro's Ascent**
Released: October 1982 by Warner Brothers, Australia.
Catalog No.: WB-0706
Media: 7" Vinyl

Picture sleeve.

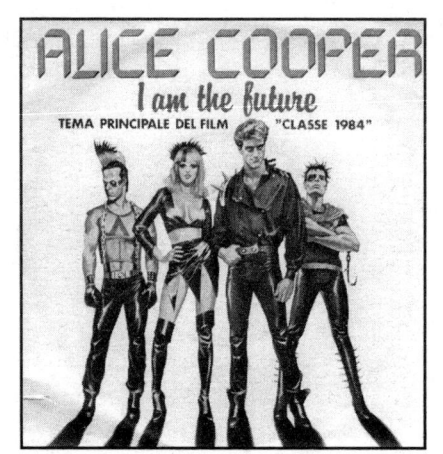

Italian single for I Am The Future.

Single Title: **I Am the Future / I Like Girls**
Released: September 1982 by Warner Brothers, France.
Catalog No.: 92 9868-7
Media: 7" Vinyl

Picture sleeve.

Single Title: **I Am the Future / Zorro's Ascent**
Released: March 1982 by Warner Brothers, Italy.
Catalog No.: W 15004
Media: 7" Vinyl

There are two variations of this single in Italy, one where the picture sleeve states that I Am the Future is remixed, and the other where there is no mention of a remix.

Portugal single for I Am The Future.

Single Title: **I Am the Future** (remix) / **Zorro's Ascent**
Released: October 1982 by Warner Brothers, Portugal.
Catalog No.: WAR 15004
Media: 7" Vinyl

Picture sleeve with a portrait of Alice in a black leather top with his hair pulled back. In the lower left-hand corner is a mention of the CLASS OF 1984 film.

Single Title: **I Like Girls / Zorro's Ascent**
Released: 1982 by Warner Brothers.
Catalog No.: 7-29928
Media: 7" Vinyl.

It's unknown if this was a US release (it follows the typical catalog numbering system of Warner Brothers in the US), but it's a rare case of the two B-sides of I Am the Future being released together.

Album Title: **DADA**
Recorded: Spring 1983 at Phase One Studios, Toronto, Canada and ESP Studios, Buttonville.
Production: Produced by Bob Ezrin. Executive Produced by Shep Gordon. Assistant producers were Richard Wagner and Robert (Ringo) Hryeyna. Engineered by Bob Ezrin, Robert Hrycyna and Lenny DeRose. Arranged by Alice Cooper, Richard Wagner and Bob Ezrin.
Personnel: Alice Cooper (vocals.) Dick Wagner (guitars, bass and vocals.) Graham Shaw (OBX-8, Roland Jupiter and vocals.) Bob Ezrin (C.M.J. Fairlight computer, keyboards, drums, percussion and vocals.) Additional performers: Richard Kolinda (drums on Former Lee Warmer, Scarlet and Sheba and Pass the Gun Around.) John Anderson (drums on Fresh Blood.) Prakash John (bass on Fresh Blood) Karen Hendricks and Lisa DalBello (additional backing vocals.) Sarah Ezrin (as DaDa.)
Song List: Da Da (Ezrin) / Enough's Enough (Cooper, Wagner, Shaw and Ezrin) / Former Lee Warmer (Cooper, Wagner and Ezrin) / No Man's Land (Cooper, Wagner and Ezrin) / Dyslexia (Cooper, Wagner, Shaw and Ezrin) / Scarlet and Sheba (Cooper, Wagner and Ezrin) / I Love America (Cooper and Shaw) / Fresh Blood (Cooper, Wagner and Ezrin) / Pass the Gun Around (Cooper and Wagner)

Spring 1983 saw Alice working again on a new album for Warner Brothers. This time, however, he took a step back by inviting the help of both Dick Wagner (who had helped on the previous album, ZIPPER CATCHES SKIN) and Bob Ezrin (who Alice hadn't worked with since THE ALICE COOPER SHOW back in 1977.) When finished, DADA proved to be almost a sister album to the last Ezrin produced studio album, LACE AND WHISKEY, not only because Alice was once again working under the storm of alcoholism (although he quit for good after DADA was released), but also because the songs written for DADA are filled with the same type of "film noir" self-angst that made up the LACE AND WHISKEY album. Certainly tracks such as Fresh Blood, No Man's Land and Pass the Gun Around could have been placed on the earlier album with only minor alterations.

The DADA Album cover.

What was different about DADA was Alice's experimentation (with the wholehearted cooperation of Ezrin) with electronics and computer generated music. To this end, Ezrin used the C.M.J. Fairlight computer to program several drum tracks (only four of the nine tracks feature a live drummer, mostly Richard Kolinda.) While Alice continued his use of keyboards on later albums, DADA was the pinnacle of his fascination with the field of electronics.

Returning from the 1970's was Prakash John, who played bass on Fresh Blood. John had last played with Alice on the KING OF THE SILVER SCREEN tour and was also featured on the previous Ezrin produced album, THE ALICE COOPER SHOW. Robert Hrycyna was another Alice veteran, having helped engineer both ALICE COOPER GOES TO HELL and LACE AND WHISKEY.

Ezrin continued the tradition of featuring his children on the albums that he produced by including his daughter Sarah Ezrin as the voice of Da Da.

The album cover, as for many past albums, was designed by Pacific Eye & Ear. The front cover was done by Glen McKenzie and is a takeoff on the Salvador Dali painting "Slave Market with the Disappearing Bust of Voltaire." In McKenzie's painting, only part of the original painting is parodied — a segment featuring two people in black and white who, when the viewer steps away from the painting, look like a human face (thus, the "disappearing bust" part of the painting.) In McKenzie's takeoff, Alice's face replaces those in the original painting. The back cover featured the lyrics to the songs (with calligraphy by Ingrid Haenke) and a small, opened locket in the upper right-hand corner with a picture of Alice from his youth holding a puppy, and a picture of an odd old man. Album credits are listed on the back as well, with a "special thanks" to Judge Joseph A. Wapner (the star of the television series THE PEOPLE'S COURT, a favorite show of Alice's at the time.) Pacific Eye & Ear contributed nothing to the packaging beyond the artwork on the cover. The inner sleeve is a plain, clear, plastic sleeve. Al in all, one of the weakest packages for an Alice album before or since.

DADA didn't hit the Top 200 in the US, but reached No. 93 on the UK charts. It was the last original studio album from Alice for Warner Brothers. After DADA, Warner Brothers and Alice went their separate ways and Alice was looking for a record label for the first time since 1968.

Album Title: **DADA**
Released: October 1983 by Warner Brothers.
Catalog No.: 7599-23969-1 / 9 23969-1
Media: Vinyl and Cassette.

The label on the vinyl states the album's catalog number as "1-23969" instead of "23969-1."

Album Title: **DADA**
Released: November 12, 1983 by Warner Brothers, UK.
Catalog No.: 92-3696-1
Media: Vinyl.

Album Title: **DADA**
Released: November 1983 by Warner Brothers, Australia.
Catalog No.: 23969-1
Media: Vinyl.

DADA didn't chart in Australia.

Album Title: **DADA**
Released: 1990 by Warner Brothers, Australia.
Catalog No.: WMI 9239692
Media: CD.

First CD reissue of the album in Australia.

Album Title: **DADA**
Released: September 3, 1990 by Warner Brothers, Germany
Catalog No.: WEA 923969-2, WEA 923969-4
Media: CD and Cassette.

First French / German reissue of the album on CD.

Single Title: **I Love America / Fresh Blood / Pass the Gun Around**
Released: November 1983 by Warner Brothers, UK.
Catalog No.: ALICE 1T
Media: 12" Vinyl single.

Came in a picture sleeve of Alice in concert. This 12" single was the only single released in the world from the DADA album. I Love America, while a great song, didn't chart in the UK. It was the last single released from a new studio album from Alice for Warner Brothers.

Part 3 — Tours 1980 - 1982

Taking time off from touring to work on other projects, Alice ironically ended up back on a concert stage for part of his performance in the film ROADIE. After this, and then working on FLUSH THE FASHION between February and March of 1980, Alice once again went out on tour in June 1980. While it was a return to the stage, it was not a return to the same old Alice on stage.

The Illustrated Collector's Guide To *Alice Cooper* 157

Tour Name: **FLUSH THE FASHION**
Tour Period: June through August 1980, with additional shows in October and November.
Performers: Alice Cooper (vocals), Mike Pinera (guitar), Fred Mandel (guitar), Duane Hitchings (keyboards and guitar), Erik Scott (bass) and Ross Salomone (drums.) Additional performers: unknown.
Opening Act: Billy Squier and Triumph
Set List: Model Citizen / Grim Facts / Go to Hell / Guilty / Pain / I Never Cry / Talk Talk / I'm Eighteen / Gutter Cat Vs. the Jets / Only Women Bleed / Clones (We're All) / Under My Wheels / Dance Yourself to Death / Road Rats / Elected / School's Out

Just as the album featured a stripped down, punked-up Alice for the 1980's, the tour was a slimed down, bare essentials Alice Cooper show. Gone were the executions and several other pieces of theatrics that had become standards. Some new effects took their places, but the majority of the program concentrated more on the music than on trying to make the show into a coherent story line (as the WELCOME TO MY NIGHTMARE and KING OF THE SILVER SCREEN tours had done.)

Fred Mandel was the only returning tour member. Some of the new members, Mike Pinera, Duane Hitchings and Erik Scott, also went on to work with Alice on the next two studio albums and on the tour for SPECIAL FORCES in 1981. Pinera and Hitchings both co-wrote songs for the SPECIAL FORCES album.

The set list for the tour remained relatively stable, but the sequencing of songs was sometimes revised. Nuclear Infected from FLUSH THE FASHION was occasionally included in the show (at the expense of another song.) Changes to the set list had rarely been made in the past (because of the restrictions of a more theatrical production), but were now more common, and added a comfortable looseness to the show.

The show scheduled for Toronto on August 19, 1980 was one of the few times that Alice was unable to perform because of his health. When the show was canceled, the crowd began to riot. Film footage of the destruction caused by the riot has been circulating in fan circles for years.

The FLUSH THE FASHION tour book.

While FLUSH THE FASHION didn't do as well in the charts as previous albums, Alice was still considered a major concert attraction and did very well at the box office.

June 4, 1980 - Coliseum, El Paso, TX
This show was recorded by Westwood One for broadcast on the radio program SUPERSTARS IN CONCERT. It later turned up on bootleg in several forms including the album THE (EL PASO) SHOW.

June 7, 1980 - Las Vegas, NV
June 11, 1980 - Amphitheater, San Diego, CA
  The show was recorded from the audience.
June 13, 1980 - San Francisco, CA
June 17, 1980 - Greek Theatre, Los Angeles, CA
  The show was recorded from the audience.
June 18, 1980 - Greek Theatre, Los Angeles, CA
  The show was recorded from the audience.
June 20, 1980 - San Antonio, TX
June 21, 1980 - Will Rogers Auditorium, Fort Worth, TX
  The show was recorded from the audience.
June 22, 1980 - Houston, TX
June 26, 1980 - New Orleans, LA
June 29, 1980 - Baton Rouge, LA

Part 3: Tours

July 2, 1980 - Biloxi, MS
July 3, 1980 - Birmingham, AL
July 4, 1980 - Nashville, TN
July 6, 1980 - Atlanta, GA
July 9, 1980 - Palladium, New York, NY
July 11, 1980 - Will Rogers Auditorium, Fort Worth, TX
   The show was recorded from the audience.
July 12, 1980 - Providence, RI
July 13, 1980 - Springfield, MO
July 16, 1980 - Sunrise Theatre, Miami, FL
   The show was recorded from the audience.
July 17, 1980 - Jacksonville, FL
July 18, 1980 - St. Petersburg, FL
July 20, 1980 - Miami, FL
July 24, 1980 - Cincinnati, OH
July 25, 1980 - Indianapolis, IN
July 26, 1980 - Castle Farms, Charlesvoix, MI
   The show was recorded from the audience.
July 27, 1980 - Richfield Coliseum, Cleveland, OH
July 31, 1980 - Green Bay, WI
August 1, 1980 - State Fair Park, West Allis, WI
   The show was recorded from the audience.
August 2, 1980 - Chicago, IL
August 3, 1980 - Kansas City, MO
   The show was recorded from the audience.
August 7, 1980 - Louisville, KY
August 8, 1980 - Cobo Arena, Detroit, MI
August 12, 1980 - Petersburgh, MI
August 14, 1980 - Saginaw, MI
August 15, 1980 - Kalamazoo, MI
August 17, 1980 - Omaha, NE
August 19, 1980 - C.N.E. Stadium, Toronto, Canada
   The show was canceled, after doors were opened, because Alice had an attack of Bronchial Asthma. Fans rioted when the cancellation was announced.

Tour Name: **SPECIAL FORCES TOUR**
Tour Period: The North American tour ran from June through August 1981, with scattered dates in September, October and November. The UK and European tour ran from January to February 1982.
Performers: Alice Cooper (vocals), Mike Pinera (guitar), Fred Mandel (guitar), Duane Hitchings (keyboards and guitar - first half of tour only), Wayne Cook (keyboards - second half of tour only), Erik Scott (bass) and Jan Uvena (drums.) No additional performers.
Opening Act: Spider (with a pre-David Letterman Anton Fig on drums) opened some shows on the North American tour. Big Country opened some shows in the UK early on and were later replaced by Sapphire.
Set List: Who Do You Think We Are / Model Citizen / Go to Hell / Guilty / I'm Eighteen / Cold Ethyl / Only Women Bleed / No More Mr. Nice Guy / Clones (We're All) / Under My Wheels / I Never Cry / Grim Facts / Pain / Billion Dollar Babies / Generation Landslide / Who Do You Think We Are (reprise) / School's Out

As with the FLUSH THE FASHION tour from the previous year, the SPECIAL FORCES tour featured a scaled back theatrical show for the new decade.

In keeping with its name, the SPECIAL FORCES show had a military tinged atmosphere to it, with the band in camouflage clothes and a beret-wearing skull as a backdrop to the set. During the tour, Alice pushed the punk look a bit further than previously, including the addition of a leather jacket with large metal pins attached to it that slowly (over 2-3 years) grew in number. This jacket was seen briefly in the latter part of the MAD HOUSE ROCK tour in 1979, and was last seen during the Twisted Sister music video for Be Crool to Your Scuel.

Again, as with the FLUSH THE FASHION tour, there was no execution of Alice during the show, but the sword and the snake remained. In fact, it was during this tour that Alice had an accident with the sword and stabbed himself through the leg. It wasn't too serious and he was able to continue the show without much further ado.

The tour began at the end of June, even though the album wasn't to be released until September 1981. This led to a situation that hadn't arisen for years — Alice was touring in support of an album that hadn't yet been released. The North American portion of the tour included only Who Do You Think We Are from the album, although Seven and Seven Is sometimes replaced No More Mr. Nice Guy or Grim Facts as the album's September release date approached. After the album's release, Seven and Seven Is became a full time part of the set list.

After spending part of December 1981 and most of January 1982 recording a French television special (commonly referred to at THE PARIS SPECIAL or 16 TRACKS), the tour began its Europe leg in late January. Seven and Seven Is became a regular part of the show, normally appearing after I Never Cry. In France, both Guilty and Grim Facts were discarded from the set list, while Vicious Rumors sometimes got a brief airing during School's Out. Vicious Rumors was co-written by lead guitarist Mike Pinera, and he would normally try to sneak in a few bars of the song during his guitar solo in School's Out (during the normal "introduction of the band" portion of the song.) When this happened, Alice would sing a couple of verses from Vicious Rumors, but the song was never played completely and it wasn't officially a part of the show.

Another song played on the tour was Generation Landslide. Because the album and the Seven and Seven Is single feature a live version of Generation Landslide, it was assumed that the song was performed during the tour on a regular basis. Actually, this wasn't the case. As discussed in Part 2 above, the track isn't a "live concert" recording at all, and was recorded in the studio specifically for the album. This song was, however, performed on the European leg of the tour.

Before the European tour, guitarist / keyboardist Duane Hitchings left the band for other pursuits and was replaced by Wayne Cook. Hitchings returned briefly to work on the next album, ZIPPER CATCHES SKIN.

The Glasgow, Scotland show was recorded for radio broadcast and some of the tracks from this recording showed up on the FOR BRITAIN ONLY special EP released in the spring of 1982. SPECIAL FORCES was the last North American tour Alice did until THE NIGHTMARE RETURNS tour of 1986.

June 20, 1981 - Concord Pavilion, Concord, CA
   Y&T opened the show.
June 21, 1981 - Memorial Auditorium, Sacramento, CA
June 30, 1981 - Greek Theatre, Los Angeles, CA
   The show was recorded from the audience.
July 1981 - Five Seasons Center, Cedar Rapids, IA
July 10, 1981 - Joe Louis Arena, Detroit, MI
   The show was recorded from the audience.
July 21, 1981 - Front Row Theater, Cleveland, OH
July 22, 1981 - Front Row Theater, Cleveland, OH
   The show was recorded from the audience.
July 24, 1981 - Sunrise Theater, Miami, FL
   The show was recorded from the audience.
August 4, 1981 - Jackson Sports Arena, Jackson, MI
August 5, 1981 - Jackson Sports Arena, Jackson, MI
August 6, 1981 - Uptown Theater, Chicago, IL
   The show was recorded from the audience.
August 8, 1981 - Uptown, Theater, Kansas City, MO
August 1981 - The Palace, Albany, NY
August 13, 1981 - Melody Fair, North Tonawanda, NY
August 14, 1981 - Savoy Cabaret, New York, NY
   The show was recorded from the audience.
August 15, 1981 - Savoy Cabaret, New York, NY
   The show was recorded from the audience.
August 16, 1981 - Savoy Cabaret, New York, NY
   The show was recorded from the audience.
August 18, 1981 - Mid-Hudson Civic, Poughkeepsie, NY
August 19, 1981 - Wallace Civic Center, Fitchburg, MA
August 20, 1981 - Providence, RI
August 21, 1981 - Portland, ME
August 22, 1981 - Cap Cod Arena, Cape Cod, MA
August 24, 1981 - Foutain Casino, Mantawan, NJ

August 25, 1981 - Painter's Mill, Baltimore, MD
August 28, 1981 - Emerald City, Cherry Hill, NJ
August 30, 1981 - St. George's Theater, Staten Island, NY
   The show was recorded from the audience.
September 23, 1981 - Tennessee State Fairgrounds, Nashville, TN
October 6, 1981 - The Agora, Cleveland, OH
October 10, 1981 - Capitol Theatre, Passaic, NJ
   The show was recorded from the audience.
October 1981 - Portland, ME
   The show was recorded from the audience.
November 28, 1981 - Maple Leaf Gardens, Toronto, Canada
January 26, 1982 - Midem Festival, Cannes, France
   The show was recorded from the audience.
January 27, 1982 - Palais d'Hivers, Lyon, France
   The show was recorded from the audience.
January 28, 1982 - Alpes Expo, Grenoble, Grenoble, France
   The show was recorded from the audience.
January 29, 1982 - Palais des Sports, Montpellier, France
January 30, 1982 - Halle Aux Grains, Toulouse, France
February 1, 1982 - Palais Des Sports, Barcelona, Spain
February 2, 1982 - Foire Des Manse, Marseilles, France
February 4, 1982 - Palais Saint Sauveur, Lille, France
February 5, 1982 - Palace des Sports, Dijon, France
   The show was recorded from the audience.
February 6, 1982 - L'Hippodrome, Paris, France
February 8, 1982 - Palais des Sports, Caen, France
February 9, 1982 - Parc des expositions Grigy, Metz, France
February 11, 1982 - Brighton Center, Brighton, England
   The show was recorded from the audience.
February 12, 1982 - Birmingham Odeon, Birmingham, England
   The show was recorded from the audience.
February 14, 1982 - Hammersmith Odeon, London, England
   The show was recorded from the audience.
February 15, 1982 - Hammersmith Odeon, London, England
   The show was recorded from the audience.
February 16, 1982 - Hammersmith Odeon, London, England
   The show was recorded and filmed from the audience.
February 17, 1982 - Apollo Theatre, Manchester, England
   The show was recorded from the audience.
February 18, 1982 - Apollo Theatre, Manchester, England
   The show was recorded from the audience.
February 19, 1982 - Apollo Theatre, Glasgow, Scotland
   This show was recorded for radio broadcast. Several tracks from the recording eventually turned up on official singles, including the FOR BRITAIN ONLY singles released in April 1982. The broadcast has also been reproduced on a number of bootleg albums (see Chapter 6 for details.) A recording of the show from the audience has also appeared in fan circles.
February 27, 1982 - Hall Rhein, Strasbourg, Germany

Part 4 — Films and Television 1980 - 1982

In contrast to his many film and television projects of the 1970's, the first half of the 1980's saw only one film appearance, one television special and one major television interview, plus a scattering of minor appearances on other programs.

This lack of visual material is disappointing, since it was a period in his career that saw many changes to Alice's stage character — from "Killer" Alice to "Apocalypse" Alice, from the "demented clown" look to the exaggerated eyebrows and sunken cheekbones makeup; from the latex-leather bondage look to the militarist, punker clothes, from the exaggerated theatrics to bare bones sleekness. By the time Alice began once again appearing in videos, movies and in concert (1985-86), he had returned to the "Killer" Alice that everyone knew and loved. So, a whole cycle of Alice's character and career occurred almost without visual documentation. Still, there is some material from these years, including a movie that gave fans a chance to see the beginnings of the transition in Alice's character.

Film Title:	**ROADIE**
Film Type:	Full-length movie.
Created:	Filmed Fall 1979 in Los Angeles, California and in various locations in Texas. An Alive Enterprise Production. An Alan Rudolph Film. Produced by Zalman King and Carolyn Pfeiffer. Associate producer was John Pommer. Directed by Alan Rudolph. Choreographed by David Myers. Story by Big Boy Medlin, Michael Ventura, Zalman King and Alan Rudolph. Written by Big Boy Medlin and Michael Ventura. Released theatrically by Transamerica, Spring 1980. Released on video in mid-1980's and reissued 1996 by MGM.
Music:	Pain, Road Rats and Only Women Bleed.
Plot:	Meatloaf stars as Travis W. Redfish, a simpleton who becomes known as the master roadie for rock bands. Alice appears periodically in the film as himself (as do other performers like Blondie, Roy Orbison, Hank Williams, Jr. and Asleep at the Wheel.)

Video box for the original release of ROADIE on video cassette. This artwork was also used for the film's posters when it appeared in theaters.

Reissue of the ROADIE video cassette, this time specifically pointing out Meat Loaf, Debbie Harry and Alice Cooper.

The story line for this film was sparked by the song **Road Rats** from Alice's LACE AND WHISKEY album (released a couple of years before film production began.) The song dealt with the people in the road crews that set up concert halls for rock bands. These people are normally called "roadies."

Alice appears in the movie as himself and performs portions of three songs — **Pain**, **Road Rats** and **Only Women Bleed**. With him in these scenes are Fred Mandel and Davey Johnstone (members of his band at the time) along with three members of the rock band Utopia (Kasim Sultan, John "Willie" Wilcox and Roger Powell.) The fourth member of Utopia, Todd Rundgren, produced Alice's songs in the movie and contributed some guitar work to the tracks as well (for details about the soundtrack album, see Chapter 6.)

The movie didn't do well when released and was only issued on video when Meat Loaf made a strong comeback in 1993/94 with the BAT OUT OF HELL II album. Alice being involved was a plus for Meat Loaf, as was a growing interest in the group Blondie. In fact, Meat Loaf, Alice Cooper and Debbie Harry of Blondie are prominently featured on the box for the video cassette (they were featured in the artwork for the original movie poster.)

Although the movie didn't do well, it's a good time waster and a nice look back to a time when rock and roll still had some innocence to it. Alice Cooper fans seeing the film will get a look at the first stages of his changing the Killer Alice character into Apocalypse Alice — a change was essentially complete by the time FLUSH THE FASHION was released in late Spring 1980.

Alice's wife, Sheryl Cooper, has in a bit part in the movie (listed as playing "herself" in the credits), and long-time stage production associate, Joe Gannon, appears as the stage manager during the Alice sound check scene. Well worth checking out on a slow movie night.

Film Title: **PINK LADY AND JEFF**
Film Type: Television series episode.
Created: Filmed March 1980, location unknown. Aired April 4, 1980 on the NBC television network, USA.
Music: Clones (We're All)

A television series still remembered as a low point in television history — and a leading factor in the demise of network president Fred Silverman — which Alice can perhaps look at as a saving grace considering his appearance on the program. He did the program as a favor to the program's producers Sid and Marty Kroft, who were friends of his. Alice's appearance was separate from the rest of the program, and was really a video for the single that was out at the time (from FLUSH THE FASHION.) The military aspects of Alice's character during this period can be seen in the video, of which a snippet appears in the PRIME CUT video documentary.

Film Title: **THE TOMORROW SHOW**
Film Type: Interview and performance.
Created: Filmed October 13, 1981 in New York City, NY. Aired October 13, 1981 on the NBC television network, USA.
Music: Who Do You Think We Are / Seven and Seven Is / Under My Wheels

One of the rare times that Alice both performed live and was interviewed on a network television program. THE TOMORROW SHOW was hosted by Tom Snyder, and ran successfully for years seen after Johnny Carson's THE TONIGHT SHOW.

The show was in its final days in 1981 (in February 1982 it was replaced by LATE NIGHT WITH DAVID LETTERMAN), and, in an attempt to beef up ratings, a studio audience and performances by famous artists were added. The show's crew, and Snyder himself, were still getting used to the new format which may explain the stilted camera work and some of Snyder's questions.

Alice seems to have been in good spirit, although he was a bit off in responding to questions — perhaps because it was one of the few serious TV interviews that he did in full makeup and costume. Overall, a good clip from the SPECIAL FORCES time period.

Film Title: **ROCK AND ROLL THE FIRST 25 YEARS**
Film Type: Television documentary series.
Created: Filmed September 1981, location unknown. Aired September 1981 in American television syndication.
Music: Who Do You Think We Are / Seven and Seven Is / Go to Hell

This began as a series of documentaries about the first 25 years of rock music. As the series progressed, they attempted to attract more viewers by adding new performances into the shows. Alice is listed as the host of this episode, but his contribution is mainly through performance footage, doing material from the SPECIAL FORCES tour.

Film Title: **THE OLD GREY WHISTLE TEST**
Film Type: Brief interview and film clips.
Created: Aired February 11, 1982 on British television.

Music: Under My Wheels, Is It My Body and Seven and Seven Is.

As Alice was beginning the UK portion of his SPECIAL FORCES tour, this well known rock program did a brief interview with Alice, and showed clips of Under My Wheels, Is It My Body and Seven and Seven Is.

Film Title: **RIVERSIDE**
Film Type: Interview and film clips.
Created: Aired February 22, 1982 on British television.
Music: Under My Wheels and Seven and Seven Is.

Alice did a short interview for this BBC program while touring for the SPECIAL FORCES album in the UK. A clip of Under My Wheels from the 1972 OLD GREY WHISTLE TEST program and a new clip of Seven and Seven Is were shown between interview segments.

Film Title: **ALICE IN PARIS** (a.k.a. THE PARIS SPECIAL, a.k.a. 16 TRACKS)
Film Type: Television special.
Created: Filmed December 1981 through January 1982 in Paris, France. Aired February 1982 in France on the TRL Television network. Produced by unknown. Directed by unknown.
Performers: Alice Cooper, Mike Pinera, John Nitzinger, Wayne Cook, Erik Scott and Jan Uvena. Additional performer: Sheryl Cooper.
Run Time: 55 minutes.
Music: You and Me / Generation Landslide '81 / Under My Wheels / Clones (We're All) / Pain / Seven and Seven Is / Prettiest Cop on the Block / Model Citizen / Cold Ethyl / Only Women Bleed (new recording) / Go to Hell / Who Do You Think We Are (new recording) / You're a Movie (new recording) / Vicious Rumours / I'm Eighteen (new recording) / Billion Dollar Babies (new recording) / School's Out (new recording) / Who Do You Think We Are (Reprise) (new recording)

Filmed as a special for French television, this is a perplexing viewing experience for fans since there is little background information about the program. The show consists of eleven "MTV-style" videos to go with the music, while the final seven are recorded in a television sound stage. There is also a brief comedy bit between Go to Hell and Who Do You Think We Are, which features Alice in a dual role as both himself and a radio interviewer speaking in French.

The majority of the music is from original recordings, although seven songs (mainly from the "stage" portion of the program) were recorded specifically for the special (listed above as "new recording".) Three of these tracks later turned up as B-sides of singles released for the CONSTRICTOR album — Billion Dollar Babies, School's Out and Only Women Bleed. Crowd noise was added when the tracks were remixed as B-sides to give them more of an "in concert" feel, even though they were recorded live.

Most fan copies of this special are missing the opening and closing credits, so many have been calling it THE PARIS SPECIAL. The show is also known as 16 TRACKS (although if you counted the "reprise" of Who Do You Think We Are and the inclusion of You and Me, the total is actually be 18 tracks.) However, the official title of the program is ALICE IN PARIS.

Film Title: **ZIPPER CATCHES SKIN**
Film Type: Promotional short film.
Created: Filmed Summer 1982.

This was an in-house promotional film made to advertise the new album (released in August 1982.) It was only shown to people in the record business. The clip is cute, with Alice stepping up to a urinal in a men's room only to have an increasing number of people recognize him and want to interview him.

Part 5 — Books and Comics 1980 - 1982

There had been quite a variety of printed material about Alice through the preceding years (both as part of the Alice Cooper Group and as a solo artist) — books, printed interviews, reviews and articles were plentiful, and even comic books dealing with Alice had appeared since the 1968 release of the first Cooper album. The years between 1980 and 1984, however, saw very little printed material published about Alice, and certainly nothing in the same league as ME, ALICE or BILLION DOLLAR BABY. Articles that did see print during this period were brief (sometimes nothing more than a two sentence "Where are they now"-type filler), and interviews were nearly nonexistent.

Instead of printed media, Alice was concentrating most of his energy on radio and television interviews and performances to generate publicity. Even so, after the SPECIAL FORCES tour, Alice slipped further from public view, concentrating instead on the two albums that he recorded over the following two years, ZIPPER CATCHES SKIN and DADA.

No doubt, a combination of factors contributed to Alice's disappearing act — slowing sales of new studio releases (thanks in part to erratic promotion), Alice's problem with alcohol (which had resurfaced in 1981), and reduced touring for the preceding two albums. The lack of publicity found Alice in a situation that would have eroded away the career of a lesser performer: Lack of promotion caused little interest in publicity for the media, and, with no publicity, there was little incentive for promoting new material. It had killed many another's career, but for Alice it was more of a state of hibernation. With 1985 in view, Alice emerged once again — this time with both guns blazing.

Chapter 3: 1980 - 1982

~~~ Chapter 4: 1984 - 1990 ~~~

Part 1 — "He's Back!"

With the poor performance of DADA, Alice decided to take a step back and look at where he was. In doing so, he realized that the drinking had become a problem again, and decided that there was no chance of being able to continue if alcohol was going to be a part of his life. In turning his back on drink, Alice decided to spend some time away from the spotlight and with his family.

By 1984, however, Alice was again feeling the need to be creatively involved in something and first dipped his feet back in by appearing in the film MONSTER DOG. Following that, he was asked to participate in a recording for the new Twisted Sister song, Be Chrool to Your Scuel. It was this chance meeting that brought to Alice's attention the new heavy metal movement that was emerging in 1984/85. He saw that bands such as Twisted Sister, W.A.S.P., and others, were doing the same type, or variations of, the show that he used to do himself. Reflecting on this, Alice began working in earnest on his comeback album CONSTRICTOR, which was released in 1986.

With the album, appearances on MTV, and a new tour, Alice brought his personal form of mayhem to a new generation with a return to the "Killer Alice" of old. CONSTRICTOR did well for Alice, and his new label, MCA, was more than happy to release the follow-up album, RAISE YOUR FIST AND YELL, in 1987. A tour followed the album, which did well, but MCA began to lose interest. Alice saw a chance to jump to Epic Records and did so in 1989 with the release of his next album, TRASH.

TRASH was a mega-success for Alice, and was accompanied by a world tour that lasted almost till the end of 1990. The first single from the album, Poison, was one of Alice's biggest hits ever. With the success of TRASH, Alice had beaten the odds. He'd become a successful solo artist, had hits in the 1970's, and would still be a driving force in new music at the end of the 1980's.

Abandoning his attempts to change the Alice character into "Apocalypse Alice" on SPECIAL FORCES and FLUSH THE FASHION, or the clean-shaven Alice of ZIPPER CATCHES SKIN and DADA, Alice returned to the "Killer" for CONSTRICTOR and onward. The big difference this time around, was that instead of trying to move beyond "Killer Alice," he would find ways to extend "Killer" into the themes that he wanted to pursue — from violence (CONSTRICTOR and RAISE YOUR FIST AND YELL) to sex (TRASH) to life (HEY STOOPID) to redemption (THE LAST TEMPTATION.) Within the next few years, Alice expanded his character from Little Steven in the nightmare to the nightmare's ringmaster. In doing so, he was no longer subjected to the whims of "Killer Alice" as he had been previously — Alice the performer now had control of the show.

CONSTRICTOR was a "back to square one" step, after which Alice slowly transformed his relationship with the "Killer." By the time of THE LAST TEMPTATION, the transformation was complete. No longer was it "Alice, the killer" controlling the show. Finally, it was Alice, the man.

Part 2 — Recordings 1984 - 1989

Alice's didn't immediately return to recording. He realized that he needed to get off alcohol for good. In fact, he took a year off at the end of 1983 and through most of 1984 to spend some time with his family and consider what direction he wanted his music to take.

To some fans, a year is a long time. It probably seemed especially so to Alice Cooper fans. After all, the longest period that he'd ever before gone without a new album was roughly a year. It was nearly three years after the release of DADA 1983 before a new studio album from Alice appeared. Yet, unlike other artists, some of whom normally spent three years and more between projects, Alice had rarely taken more than a few months off at a time since 1968.

By 1985 fans had become aware of two projects that Alice had been working on: first as co-lead vocalist on the Twisted Sister track Be Chrool to Your Scuel (see Chapter 6 for details.); and then in the film MONSTER DOG (see Part 4 in this chapter.) MONSTER DOG featured new music from Alice, Identity Crises and See Me in the Mirror, both to be featured in the boxed set due for release in early 1999.

MONSTER DOG was also the starting point of a collaboration between Alice and Aerosmith lead guitarist Joe Perry. The initial idea was for the two to work on material for the movie, and about three songs were written during their time together. There was also talk between them of Perry working on a more regular basis with Alice, but he soon rejoined Aerosmith, and, except for playing on the TRASH album — along with Steve Tyler and two other members of Aerosmith — nothing further came of the collaboration. While the recordings from the two of them together do exist, it's probably safe to assume that they were unsatisfied with the results, otherwise these songs would have appeared on subsequent releases.

News also hit fans in late 1985 that Alice was heading back to the studio to work on a new album under a contract with MCA — the first new company that Alice had recorded with (after Warner Brothers) since 1971 (or 1968 if you include Straight as a Warner-related label.) Alice stayed with MCA for two albums, CONSTRICTOR and RAISE YOUR FIST AND YELL, before signing with Epic Records in 1988.

Unlike Warner Brothers and Epic, MCA encoded the media type (vinyl, cassette or CD) of each release into its catalog number. The catalog number for a vinyl release was the letters "MCA" followed by a unique set of numbers. The cassette release of the same title was "MCAC" followed by the same number set, and the CD release was "MCAD" followed, again, by the same number set (so catalog numbers for CONSTRICTOR are MCA 5761, MCAC-5761 and MCAD-5761 for vinyl, cassette and CD respectively.) This is the general scheme for catalog numbers only, and there are many exceptions. For simplicity, only the vinyl catalog numbers are listed in the entries below.

Epic used the same type of numbering system that Warner used starting in the late 1970's, with a series of numbers followed by a final dashed digit to designate the media type (the catalog number for the TRASH CD is 7464-45137-2, while the TRASH cassette is 7464-45137-4.) However, this "last digit" designation normally only appeared on the Universal Price Code on the back of the album, not elsewhere on the packaging, or on the disc / vinyl / cassette itself. On the recording surface, only the middle set of numbers was used, with an "EK" (for vinyl or CD) or "ET" (for audio-tape) preceding it (the TRASH CD is EK 45137, while the TRASH cassette is ET 45137.)

An example of a cassette release in long box packaging.

By 1986, Compact Discs had become the norm for the recording industry, and the first Alice Cooper CD released in the US was CONSTRICTOR on January 5, 1987, nearly three months after its release on vinyl and cassette. From that point forward, CDs were released for new Alice Cooper albums. Reissues of earlier albums also began popping up on CD by 1988, with Warner Brothers in Germany and France leading the pack and Japan and the US following by 1990. The upswing in CD sales didn't immediately signal the end of the vinyl market, but it was dwindling as the 1990's approached. Yet, there was still interest in the good old black wax during the late 1980's, and it wasn't until THE LAST TEMPTATION in 1994 that a new Alice Cooper album was released in the US without a vinyl edition.

The 1980's produced a change in the way singles were packaged in the UK. Although the simple 7" vinyl single, perhaps with a picture sleeve, was still available, there would also be a "special edition" 7" vinyl single with a poster, or a picture disc 12" single, or a 12" black vinyl single with an Alice patch to put on your clothes, etc. This became a standard offering in the UK in the early 1980's, being seen with the FOR BRITAIN ONLY single released in 1982, and becoming most evident during the MCA and Epic Alice Cooper days. This is significant for collectors of the singles and "special editions."

During Alice's years with Warner Brothers, records released in Australia were based on the North American releases. With the move to MCA (known as BMG in Australia), the albums and singles for CONSTRICTOR reflected the UK releases in catalog numbers and packaging. However, for RAISE YOUR FIST AND YELL, the cataloging reverted to North American numbers.

Examples of the many Alice Cooper picture CD's.

Single Title: **He's Back (The Man Behind the Mask) / He's Back (The Man Behind the Mask)**
Released: September 1986 by MCA.
Catalog No.: MCA-52904 (7") and MCAL-3317177 (12")
Media: 7" and 12" promotional Vinyl singles.

This was a special promotional single released simultaneously on 7" and 12" vinyl. Both versions came in a simple sleeve.

Single Title: **He's Back (The Man Behind the Mask) / Billion Dollar Babies** (live)
Released: September 1986 by MCA.
Catalog No.: MCA-52904
Media: 7" Vinyl.

See the CONSTRICTOR album entry for details on the making of this song. The US edition of this single came in a picture sleeve of Alice with Jason's hockey mask from the FRIDAY THE 13TH movie.

Although the B-side is listed as a live track from 1976, it was actually recorded in January 1982 as part of the French television special ALICE IN PARIS (a.k.a. THE PARIS SPECIAL.) The song was recorded live on the program, but without an audience. Crowd noises were added to the mix later for use here. "He's Back reached No. 56 on the US charts. It was the only commercial single released from the CONSTRICTOR album in North America.

Single Title: **He's Back (The Man Behind the Mask) / Billion Dollar Babies** (live)
Released: October 1986 by MCA, UK.
Catalog No.: MCA 1090
Media: 7" Vinyl.

There are two variations of this single with the same catalog number, one in a regular picture sleeve, and another in a sleeve wrapped around a folded poster of Alice. The picture sleeve is again Alice holding Jason's hockey mask from the FRIDAY THE 13TH movie. The photo is framed inside a drawing of theater seats full of people, as if Alice were appearing on a movie screen. He's Back reached No. 61 on the UK charts.

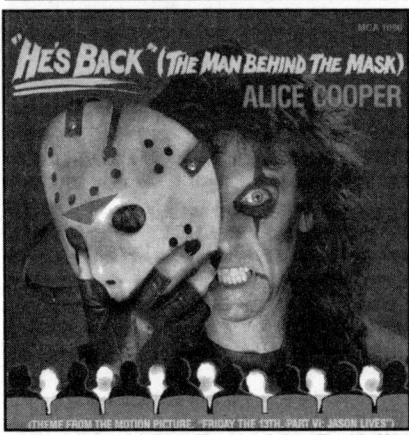

UK single for He's Back (The Man Behind The Mask).

Single Title: He's Back (The Man Behind the Mask) / Billion Dollar Babies (live) / I'm Eighteen (live)
Released: October 1986 by MCA, UK.
Catalog No.: MCAT 1090
Media: 12" Vinyl.

Released with the same artwork as the 7" vinyl single, this 12" edition of the single included one additional live track from the 1982 French television special. As with Billion Dollar Babies, it was remixed to give the appearance of an audience present.

Single Title: He's Back (The Man Behind the Mask) / Billion Dollar Babies (live)
Released: October 1986 by MCA (BMG), Australia.
Catalog No.: MCA 7-52904
Media: 7" Vinyl.

Came with the same picture sleeve as on the US and UK releases.

Single Title: He's Back (The Man Behind the Mask) / Billion Dollar Babies (live)
Released: October 1986 by MCA, France.
Catalog No.: 258574-7
Media: 7" Vinyl.

Same picture sleeve of Alice as other releases of this single.

Single Title: He's Back (The Man Behind the Mask) / Billion Dollar Babies (live)
Released: October 1986 by MCA, Germany.
Catalog No.: 258574-7
Media: 7" Vinyl.

Same picture sleeve of Alice as other releases of this single.

Single Title: He's Back (The Man Behind the Mask) / Billion Dollar Babies (live) / I'm Eighteen (live)
Released: October 1986 by MCA, Germany.
Catalog No.: 2585530
Media: 12" Vinyl.

Similar to the UK 12" single listed above, including the same artwork on the sleeve.

Single Title: He's Back (The Man Behind the Mask) / Billion Dollar Babies (live)
Released: October 1986 by MCA, Japan.
Catalog No.: P-2178
Media: 7" Vinyl.

Released with a variation of the same picture sleeve of Alice.

Japanese single for He's Back (The Man Behind The Mask).

Chapter 4: 1984 - 1990

Album Title: **CONSTRICTOR**
Recorded: All tracks but **He's Back** recorded January - February 1986 at Atlantic Studios, New York, NY. **He's Back (The Man Behind the Mask)** recorded Summer 1986 at Amigo Studios, Los Angeles, CA.
Production: Produced by Beau Hill, except for **He's Back**. Production Coordinator was Anita Bourne. Engineered by Stephen Benben, with assistance by Ira McLaughlin. **He's Back** produced by Michael Wagener, with assistance by Garth Richardson. Mixed by Michael Wagener for Double Trouble Productions, Inc. at Amigo Studios, Los Angeles, CA. Assistance on the mix by Garth Richardson. Mastered at the Mastering Lab, Los Angeles, CA by Mike Reese.
Personnel: Alice Cooper (vocals.) Kane Roberts (lead guitar, guitar, bass, keyboards, vocals and drums.) David Rosenburg (drums.) Donnie Kisselbach (bass.) Kip Winger (bass.) Paul Delph (keyboards and backing vocals on **He's Back**.) Tom Kelly (backing vocals on **He's Back**.) Beau Hill (additional backing vocals.)
Song List: **Teenage Frankenstein** (Cooper and Roberts) / **Give It Up** (Cooper and Roberts) / **Thrill My Gorilla** (Cooper and Roberts) / **Life and Death of the Party** (Cooper and Roberts) / **Simple Disobedience** (Cooper and Roberts) / **The World Needs Guts** (Cooper and Roberts) / **Trick Bag** (Cooper, Roberts and Wagener) / **Crawlin'** (Cooper and Roberts) / **Great American Success Story** (Cooper, Roberts and Hill) / **He's Back (The Man Behind the Mask)** (Cooper, Roberts and Kelly)

In 1985, as Alice began emerging from his self-imposed exile, rumors began spreading about Alice working on a new album. While there was initially talk of the album being a return to the WELCOME TO MY NIGHTMARE days (and rumored to be called WELCOME TO MY NIGHTMARE II), there was little of actual evidence in the press as to what Alice was, in fact, planning for his next recording project.

Photos turned up that year of Alice spending time with Andy McCoy of the Swedish rock band Hanoi Rocks, and while rumor was that the two were working together on material for the next album, nothing has ever appeared to suggest that this was the case. Another project mentioned in 1985 came by way of BILLION DOLLAR BABY author Bob Greene in an article about Alice in ESQUIRE magazine. This project had Alice working on an hour-long video featuring himself and several other heavy metal performers in a sort of hard rock version of the classic western THE MAGNIFICENT SEVEN, with Alice in the Yul Bryner role. However, it was obvious from Alice's discussions of the project in the article that it was still very much on the drawing board, and wouldn't appear within the year. Several of the songs on the CONSTRICTOR album were actually written for this project.

Instead, Alice went into the studio in January 1986 with RATT producer Beau Hill to work out material for the new album. Joining Alice was someone new to the Cooper world, Kane Roberts, who co-wrote all of the songs on both CONSTRICTOR and the following album RAISE YOUR FIST AND YELL. Roberts was a signature performer for the two tours in support of these two albums, and no wonder — with his body builder, Rambo-like presence (including a guitar shaped like an M-16 rifle), Roberts was the complete antithesis of the "pretty-boy" stereotype heavy metal guitarist. His appearance was a shocking rebellion against the heavy metal norm, and perfect for the Cooper stage. Roberts later left Alice after recording a solo album during the time of the RAISE YOUR FIST AND YELL tour, but would continue to be associated with Alice on projects such as the SHOCKER album, among others.

Another musician who joined Alice for this album, its tour, and the RAISE YOUR FIST AND YELL album was Kip Winger. Kip later left Alice to form his own group, Winger, which had several hit songs including She's Only 17. The band lasted for a few years and included fellow Alice alumni Paul Horowitz (a.k.a. Paul Taylor), on keyboards. Kip Winger has since gone solo and has had a few albums out since the Winger days. Incidentally, the back cover of the CONSTRICTOR album misspells Winger's name as "Kip Wringer."

During an early album session, Alice and Roberts were joined by Neal Smith and Dennis Dunaway (of the original Alice Copper Group) for an afternoon. Perhaps to the disappointment of longtime fans, though they had fun with the session, the material recorded wasn't released.

As the album was nearing completion, Alice was asked to contribute to the soundtrack for the upcoming film FRIDAY THE 13th, PART VI: JASON LIVES. Eagerly accepting the invitation, Alice provided three songs for use in the film — Teenage Frankenstein, Hard Rock Summer and He's Back. Teenage Frankenstein and Hard Rock Summer were accepted for brief use in the film, but Paramount Studios and the film's producers initially turned down He's Back since it was felt to be "too heavy metal-like" for their tastes. Alice returned to the studio — this time, the Amigo Studios in Los Angeles — in the summer of 1986 to rewrite and re-record He's Back. Beau Hill wasn't available, so Michael Wagener was recruited to produce the track, which was given a more keyboard oriented style, and new lyrics. The original music also had new lyrics added and became the song Trick Bag on the CONSTRICTOR album. He's Back was the first single released from the album, appearing about a month before the album's release, to help promote the film that was being released in early September 1986. The music video done for He's Back was the first video produced for an Alice Cooper single since How You Gonna See Me Now in 1978. An extended "dance mix" of this track is known to exist, but it wasn't officially released and is not considered a part of the official Alice catalog. Also in the film world, the song The All-American Success Story had been considered for a Rodney Dangerfield movie called BACK TO SCHOOL, but was dropped before the film was released.

Four additional songs were written for CONSTRICTOR that didn't make the final cut. Three of these four songs — Don't Blame It on Me, Drain the Vain (both written by Alice and Robert William Athis) and If You Don't Like It (written by Alice and Kane Roberts) — made it to the demo stage before being rejected. The final song, Nobody Move (written by Alice and Beau Hill), made it as far as the test pressing of the album before it was also removed.

The album packaging was a standard single sleeve cardboard cover including a trick photo with a snake emerging from Alice's mouth and wrapped around his throat. The cover was censored in the UK and was released instead with the snake only circling over Alice's mouth. An American import for the UK also displayed the censored cover. The photo was taken by Kevin Schill, based on a concept by David Hale Associates. Lyrics were printed on the back of the album cover (most of his albums had contained lyric sheets since the days of BILLION DOLLAR BABIES.) This time, however, it was done at the request of the P.M.R.C., which also requested that a "warning" sticker be put on the front of the album advising parents that the album could contain material that was too strong for children. Alice welcomed the extra requirement since it only served to draw more attention to the album. The album also came with a pullout, album-sized insert with additional album credits and another photo of Alice with the snake. For the record (so to speak), the legs photographed on the back of the album cover are not Alice's, but those of his personal assistant Brian "Renfield" Nelson.

This was the first of two studio albums that Alice recorded for MCA, and the first full studio album after leaving Warner Brothers. Alice moved to Epic Records starting with the TRASH album in 1989.

Along with reissues, CONSTRICTOR also appeared as part of a two vinyl and two CD set with the MCA companion album RAISE YOUR FIST AND YELL (see below.) Many of the tracks these on two albums also ended up on a variety of "best of" albums from MCA over the years after Alice left the company — some as early as 1989. Epic followed suit with their own "best of" collections from the three studio albums recorded there between 1989 and 1994 (see Chapter 6 for details).

CONSTRICTOR reached No. 59 in the US and No. 41 on the UK charts. It was also the first Alice Cooper album to be produced on CD near the time of its original release, although it was not available on the market until three months after the vinyl and cassette versions of the album were released.

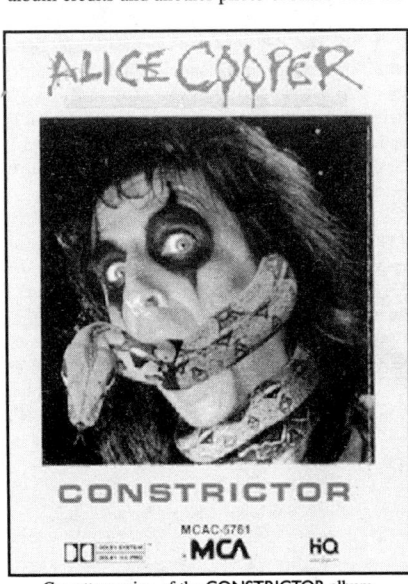

Cassette version of the CONSTRICTOR album.

Album Title: **CONSTRICTOR**
Released: Vinyl and cassette released October 1986 by MCA. CD released January 5, 1987.
Catalog No.: MCA-5761 / 76732-5761-1
Media: Vinyl, CD and Cassette.

Originally released on vinyl with an additional album-size insert (see the main entry above for details.)

Album Title: **CONSTRICTOR**
Released: October 1986 by MCA, UK.
Catalog No.: MCF 3341 (vinyl) and MCFC 3341 (cassette)

Media: Vinyl and Cassette.

Came with the same insert as with US release.

Album Title: **CONSTRICTOR**
Released: November 1, 1986 by MCA, UK.
Catalog No.: MCFP 3341
Media: 12" picture disc Vinyl.

Picture disc version of the full album with the front cover photo on the vinyl itself.

Album Title: **CONSTRICTOR**
Released: November 1, 1986 by MCA (BMG), Australia.
Catalog No.: MCA 5761-1
Media: Vinyl and Cassette.

CONSTRICTOR reached No. 94 on the Australian charts.

Album Title: **CONSTRICTOR**
Released: November 1986 by MCA, Japan.
Catalog No.: P-13405
Media: Vinyl and Cassette.

As for other foreign markets, the album came with the same insert as with the US release. The obi strip with the album showed several other Alice Cooper album covers. A lyric sheet was also enclosed.

Album Title: **CONSTRICTOR**
Released: 1987 by MCA, Japan.
Catalog No.: MVCM 21028
Media: CD.

Later reissue of the album on CD in Japan.

Album Title: **CONSTRICTOR**
Released: July 1, 1991 by MCA, Germany.
Catalog No.: MCA 03341 / 7599-54253-2 (CD release) and 7599-54253-4 (cassette release.)
Media: CD and Cassette.

First French / German reissue of the album on CD.

Album Title: **CONSTRICTOR**
Released: January 1, 1995 by MCA.
Catalog No.: MSP 5761
Media: CD.

US reissue of the album.

Album Title: **CONSTRICTOR**
Released: 1995 by BMG, Australia.
Catalog No.: MCD 03341
Media: CD.

First Australian pressing of the album on CD.

Album Title: **CONSTRICTOR**
Released: October 3, 1997 by MCA, Canada.
Catalog No.: MCBBD 5761
Media: CD.

Most recent reissue of the album in Canada.

Single Title: **Give It Up**
Released: December 1986 by MCA.
Catalog No.: L33-17205
Media: 12" promotional single.

Promotional single for a track from the CONSTRICTOR album. There was no commercial single released for this song.

Single Title: **Teenage Frankenstein / School's Out** (live)
Released: March 1987 by MCA, UK.
Catalog No.: MCA 1113
Media: 7" Vinyl single.

In typical UK fashion, two variations of the 7" single exist — one with a standard picture sleeve, and the other with a folded poster of Alice wrapped around the standard sleeve. Both sleeves featured the same cover of Alice in white tux jacket and top hat on stage. School's Out is from the 1982 French television special ALICE IN PARIS (a.k.a. THE PARIS SPECIAL), with crowd noises added to the mix.

Single Title: **Teenage Frankenstein / School's Out** (live) / **Only Women Bleed** (live)
Released: March 1987 by MCA, UK.
Catalog No.: MCAT 1113
Media: 12" Vinyl single.

UK single for Teenage Frankenstein.

This record came in a picture sleeve with the same photo that appeared on the 7" vinyl single sleeve. Only Women Bleed is another track taken from the ALICE IN PARIS television program, with crowd noises mixed in.

Single Title: **Teenage Frankenstein / School's Out** (live)
Released: March 1987 by MCA (BMG), Australia.
Catalog No.: MCA 7-13824
Media: 7" Vinyl single.

This came in a sleeve similar to the UK issue, with the same photo of Alice on the sleeve.

Single Title: **Teenage Frankenstein / School's Out** (live) / **Only Women Bleed** (live)
Released: March 1987 by MCA (BMG), Australia.
Catalog No.: 655061-3 (CD-single) and 0-13825 (12" vinyl single.)
Media: CD-single and 12" Vinyl.

The first official Australian CD release was this single from the CONSTRICTOR album (TRASH would be the first full studio album to be released on CD in Australia.) These two releases were packaged in much the same manner as the UK 12" Vinyl single, and was the last MCA single released in Australia.

Album Title: **RAISE YOUR FIST AND YELL**
Recorded: Recorded Summer 1987, location not given on the album.
Production: Produced engineered and mixed by Michael Wagener for Double Trouble Productions, Inc. Additional engineering by Garth Richardson. Mastered by Stephen Maarcussen at Precision Laquer, Los Angeles, CA.
Personnel: Alice Cooper (vocals.) Kane Roberts (lead guitar, guitar, and vocals.) Ken K. Mary (drums.) Kip Winger (bass and vocals, also played keyboards on Gail.) Paul Horowitz (keyboards.)
Song List: Freedom (Cooper and Roberts) / Lock Me Up (Cooper and Roberts) / Give the Radio Back (Cooper and Roberts) / Step on You (Cooper and Roberts) / Not That Kind of Love (Cooper and Roberts) / Prince of Darkness (Cooper and Roberts) / Time to Kill (Cooper and Roberts) / Chop,

Chop, Chop (Cooper and Roberts) / Gail (Cooper, Roberts and Winger) / Roses on White Lace (Cooper and Roberts)

Alice has always had an unconscious preoccupation with writing albums in pairs, and the latest pair was no exception. Just as ALICE COOPER GOES TO HELL has a direct connection to WELCOME TO MY NIGHTMARE, SPECIAL FORCES is a companion to FLUSH THE FASHION, and DADA and ZIPPER CATCHES SKIN are a pair, RAISE YOUR FIST AND YELL is a companion to the previous album, CONSTRICTOR. Perhaps that's why seeing MCA pair the two albums as a double vinyl release (and later a double CD) wasn't at all surprising.

RAISE YOUR FIST AND YELL continued the theme of violence and rebellion that drove the CONSTRICTOR album, and stayed with the 1980's heavy metal crunch sound that was so much apart of the earlier album. Kane Roberts and Kip Winger returned to work on the album (with Roberts co-writing every song with Alice, and Winger co-writing one song), and two other members of THE NIGHTMARE RETURNS touring band joined Alice in the studio for the first time, Ken Mary and Paul Horowitz.

The RAISE YOUR FIST AND YELL album cover.

The album cover included unsettling artwork by Jim Warren on the front, and, once again, lyrics on the back, along with additional artwork by Kevin L. Spinney. As with CONSTRICTOR, the album sized paper insert that enclosed the vinyl contained additional information about the album, and also a black and white print of a drawing by Airic Brumitt. The drawing is the same one appearing on the T-shirt that Alice wears on the cover of the TRASH album.

Original copies of the album came with a sticker on the cover that read "Featuring Freedom, Step on You, Give the Radio Back." Promotional cassettes of the album were also released before the album packaging was completed and had only the MCA logo and the song titles typed on the card contained with the cassette.

The song Prince of Darkness was used as the closing theme to the John Carpenter film of the same name released in 1987. Alice also makes a brief appearance in the film, along with Kane Roberts who was under so much makeup in his role that he is unrecognizable (see Part 4 for details about the movie.)

Freedom was the sole single released from the album. A music video was also produced for the single, which aired on MTV a few times before disappearing completely.

With early working titles of "SUMMER BLOOD" and "SEX, DEATH AND MONEY" (which is what's conveyed by Airic Brumitt's artwork on the album insert), RAISE YOUR FIST AND YELL reached No. 73 on the US charts and No. 48 on the UK charts. It was the last album that Alice recorded for MCA.

Album Title: **RAISE YOUR FIST AND YELL**
Released: October 5, 1987 by MCA.
Catalog No.: MCA-42091 / 7674-22091-1
Media: Vinyl, CD and Cassette.

The album came with a clear plastic inner sleeve and an additional paper insert that listed information about the album.

Album Title: **RAISE YOUR FIST AND YELL**
Released: November 7, 1987 by MCA, UK.
Catalog No.: MCF 3392 (vinyl), DMCF 3392 (CD)
Media: Vinyl, CD and Cassette.

Came with insert, as with US release.

Album Title: **RAISE YOUR FIST AND YELL**
Released: November 1987 by MCA, UK.

Catalog No.: MCFP 3392
Media: Picture disc Vinyl.

Picture disc vinyl release of the new album. This was released under the same catalog number for two different editions — one with just the picture disc for RAISE YOUR FIST AND YELL, and the other with both the new album and a pressing of CONSTRICTOR on picture disc vinyl.

Album Title: **RAISE YOUR FIST AND YELL**
Released: November 1987 by MCA, UK.
Catalog No.: MCFP 3392
Media: Double Picture-disc Vinyl.

This was released under the same catalog number for two different editions — one with just the picture disc for RAISE YOUR FIST AND YELL, and the other with both the new album and a pressing of CONSTRICTOR on picture disc vinyl. The two albums were reissued as a double CD in 1996 by MCA Germany (see TAKE 2 below.)

Album Title: **RAISE YOUR FIST AND YELL**
Released: November 1987 by MCA, Australia.
Catalog No.: MCA-42091-1
Media: Vinyl and Cassette.

The album didn't chart in Australia and no singles were issued from the album.

Album Title: **RAISE YOUR FIST AND YELL**
Released: November 1987 by MCA, Brazil.
Catalog No.: WEA 6704100
Media: Vinyl.

Album Title: **RAISE YOUR FIST AND YELL**
Released: November 1987 by MCA, France.
Catalog No.: 255074-1
Media: Vinyl and CD.

German pressing released domestically in France under the same catalog numbers.

Album Title: **RAISE YOUR FIST AND YELL**
Released: November 1987 by MCA, Germany.
Catalog No.: 255074-1
Media: Vinyl and CD.

Album Title: **RAISE YOUR FIST AND YELL**
Released: November 1987 by MCA, Japan.
Catalog No.: P-13588 (vinyl) and 32XD-866 (CD)
Media: Vinyl, CD and Cassette.

Album Title: **RAISE YOUR FIST AND YELL**
Released: October 25, 1990 by MCA.
Catalog No.: MCA 42091
Media: CD.

CD reissue.

Album Title: **RAISE YOUR FIST AND YELL**
Released: July 1, 1991 by MCA, Germany.
Catalog No.: MCA 03392
Media: CD.

CD reissue of the album.

Album Title: **RAISE YOUR FIST AND YELL**
Released: 1995 by BMG, Australia.
Catalog No.: MCD 03392
Media: CD.

First Australian pressing of the album on CD.

Album Title: **RAISE YOUR FIST AND YELL**
Released: September 1997 by MCA, Japan.
Catalog No.: MVCM 21029
Media: CD.

CD reissue of album.

Single Title: **Freedom / Freedom**
Released: October 1987 by MCA.
Catalog No.: MCA-53212 (7") and MCAL-3317416 (12")
Media: 7" and 12" promotional Vinyl single.

Simultaneous special promotional single releases. Both came in a simple sleeve.

Single Title: **Freedom / Time to Kill**
Released: October 1987 by MCA.
Catalog No.: MCA-53212 (7") and MCA-53212 (cassette)
Media: 7" Vinyl and Cassette.

Came in a picture sleeve of the cover with additional hands added to the painting.

Single Title: **Freedom / Time to Kill**
Released: March 1988 by MCA, UK.
Catalog No.: MCA 1241
Media: 7" Vinyl.

Released in March ahead of the April 1988 RAISE YOUR FIST AND YELL tour, this single came in a picture sleeve of Alice sitting in what appears to be an electric chair. On the back of the picture sleeve is a listing of dates that Alice was to play when in the UK. Freedom reached No. 50 on the UK charts.

Single Title: **Freedom / Time to Kill / School's Out** (live)
Released: March 1988 by MCA, UK.
Catalog No.: MCAX 1241
Media: 12" Vinyl.

Picture sleeve for the Freedom single.

UK single for Freedom.

Released with the same artwork as the 7" vinyl single, this 12" edition of the single included one additional live track from the 1987 Cincinnati Gardens concert that was broadcast on American radio stations. As with the 7" single, it was released in March 1988 to coincide with Alice's UK tour of April 1988. The single came in two variations — both came with a normal 12" single picture sleeve, displaying the same photo of Alice in the chair as was seen on the 7" single and UK tour dates on the back, but one came in a limited edition plastic "snakeskin" sleeve. Both had the same catalog numbers.

Single Title: **Freedom / Time to Kill**
Released: March 1988 by MCA, Germany.
Catalog No.: 258 138-7
Media: 7" Vinyl.

Picture sleeve of the RAISE YOUR FIST album cover.

Album Title: TAKE 2
Released: 1996 by MCA, Germany.
Catalog No.: MCD 33004
Media: Double CD.

This was a reissue of the two MCA studio albums, CONSTRICTOR and RAISE YOUR FIST AND YELL, in one double CD package. As with other German releases, this was also released in France and was a common import in the UK and the US at the time.

Album Title: A MAN CALLED ALICE
Released: 1987 by Pair, a Warner Special Products release.
Catalog No.: PDL2-1163
Media: Double Vinyl.

This double album was a repackaging of the 1973 MUSCLE OF LOVE album and the 1977 LACE AND WHISKEY album. It came with a front cover photo by Rick Dunham of Alice holding a doll's head.

Single Title: I Got a Line on You
See Chapter 6, Part 3 for details of this one off recording for the IRON EAGLE II movie soundtrack.

Album Title: TRASH
Recorded: Recorded May - June 1989 at Bearsville Studios, Power Station, Sigma Studios and Right Track Recording, all in New York City, NY; Village Recorder, The Complex and Record Plant, all in Los Angeles, CA; Blue Jay Studios in Boston, MA; and the Sanctuary Sound Studios in New Jersey.
Production: Produced by Desmond Child. Executive producer was Bob Pfeifer. Production manager was Michael Anthony. Recorded by Sir Arthur Payson. Mixed by Steve Thompson and Michael Barbiero. Mastered by George Marino at Sterling Sound.
Personnel: Alice Cooper (vocals.) John McCurry (guitar.) Hugh McDonald (bass.) Bobby Chouinard (drums.) Alan St. John (keyboards.) Additional performers: Steven Tyler (additional vocals on Only My Heart Talkin'.) Jon Bon Jovi (additional vocals on Trash.) Kip Winger (additional vocals on I'm Your Gun.) Joe Perry (additional guitar on House of Fire.) Richie Sambora and Steve Lukather (additional guitars on Hell is Living Without You.) Kane Roberts (additional guitar on Bed of Nails.) Guy Mann-Dude (additional guitar on Why Trust You, Spark in the Dark and This Maniac's in Love With You.) Tom Hamilton (bass on Trash.) Joe Kramer (drums on Trash.) Mark Frazier and Jack Johnson (guitars on Trash.) Paul Chiten (additional keyboards.) Steve Deutsch (synth programming.) Gregg Mangiafico (additional keyboards and special effects.)
Additional backing vocals: Myriam Valle, Maria Vidal, Diana Graselli, Desmond Child, Bernie Shanahan, Louie Merlino, Alan St. John, Tom Teeley, Michael Anthony, Stiv Bator, Hugh McDonald, Jango, Jamie Sever and Joe Turano.
Song List: Poison (Cooper, Child and McCurry) / Spark in the Dark (Cooper and Child) / House of Fire (Cooper, Joan Jett and Child) / Why Trust You (Cooper and Child) / Only My Heart Talkin' (Bruce Roberts and Andy Goldmark, with additional lyrics by Alice) / Bed of Nails (Cooper, Diane Warren and Child) / This Maniac's in Love With You (Cooper, Tom Teeley, Bob Held and Child) / Trash (Cooper, Mark Frazier, Jamie Sever and Child) / Hell Is Living Without You (Cooper, John Bon Jovi, Richie Sambora and Child) / I'm Your Gun (Cooper, McCurry and Child)

After deciding to leave MCA in 1988, Alice was offered a chance to work for Epic Records, a division of Sony. Having been given free reign on the album, as long as he brought them another hit, Alice decided to move away from the heavy metal crunch of CONSTRICTOR and RAISE YOUR FIST AND YELL, and away from the theme of violence, and work on material built more around lyrics and song writing.

The first step was recruiting Desmond Child, who was known not only as a songwriter of hit material, but as a producer with successful albums behind him. It was with Child that Alice decided to make the next album's themes sex, love, and sexual attitudes in the 1980's. TRASH became one of Alice's biggest sellers, and the first album since GOES TO HELL to reach the Top 40 in the US, and it also reached No. 2 on the UK charts. TRASH also produced Alice's first Top 10 single (Poison) since You and Me back in 1977.

Along with Child came a variety of additional performers who would also work with Alice on future projects, (mainly the SHOCKER soundtrack album, also produced by Desmond Child later that same year), and guest appearances for artists such as Guy Mann-Dude. Many well known performers worked with Alice on the album including members of Aerosmith, Jon Bon Jovi and Richie Sambora of Bon Jovi, and Alice alumni Kip Winger and Kane Roberts.

Several songs written for the album didn't make the final cut, including Low Class Reunion (written by Alice and Child), Bad Angel, Good Girl Gone Bad, and a song by Jon Bon Jovi called The Ballad of Alice Cooper. The Bon Jovi song was again considered when recording HEY STOOPID in 1991, but Alice felt awkward singing a song about himself and dropped it.

Music videos were made for the four singles from the album that were released in most parts of the world, Poison, Bed of Nails, House of Fire and Only My Heart Talkin'. The first three videos were combined and released on videocassette as ALICE COOPER - VIDEO TRASH in 1990. A concert video was released featuring the TRASH album called ALICE COOPER TRASHES THE WORLD (see Part 4 for more details on the videos and cassettes.)

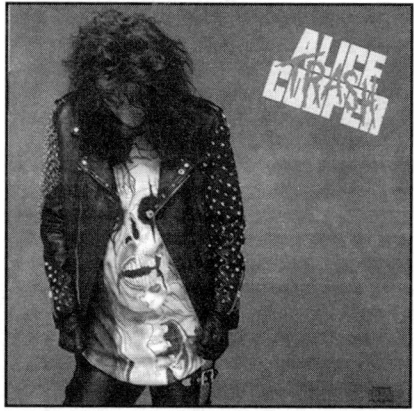

The TRASH album.

The album came with an inner sleeve containing lyrics and additional information about the album. Alice is wearing a T-shirt on the album cover (based on the artwork on the RAISE YOUR FIST AND YELL insert) with makeup on it (so TRASH doesn't completely abandon Alice's makeup.) The two photos used on TRASH were taken by Glen LaFerman, and the logo design used on the cover was created by David Coleman.

TRASH had an original working title of "LOW CLASS REUNION", and reached No. 20 on the US charts and No. 2 on the UK charts.

Album Title: **TRASH**
Released: July 12, 1989 by Epic Records.
Catalog No.: OE 45137 / 7464-45137-1
Media: Vinyl, CD and Cassette.

Originally released on vinyl with a paper inner sleeve containing lyrics and additional album information.

Album Title: **TRASH**
Released: August 26, 1989 by Epic Records, UK.
Catalog No.: 465130-1
Media: Vinyl, CD and Cassette.

This came with the same paper inner sleeve with additional info as the US release.

Album Title: **TRASH**
Released: August 1989 by Epic Records, Argentina.
Catalog No.: 70089
Media: Vinyl.

Album Title: **TRASH**
Released: August 1989 by Epic Records, Australia.
Catalog No.: 465130-1
Media: Vinyl, CD and Cassette.

This was the first new album by Alice to be released simultaneously on vinyl, cassette and CD in Australia.

Album Title: **TRASH**
Released: August 1989 by Epic Records, Australia.
Catalog No.: 465130-5
Media: Vinyl release with a limited edition poster.

Album Title: **TRASH**
Released: August 1989 by Epic Records, Australia.
Catalog No.: 465130-0
Media: Picture-disc Vinyl.

Limited edition repressing of the TRASH album on picture disc vinyl.

Album Title: **TRASH**
Released: April 1990 by Epic Records, Australia
Catalog No.: 465130-9
Media: CD.

Special limited edition repackaging of the album in connection with Alice touring Australia during April 1990 — the first such trip to Australia since 1977.

Album Title: **TRASH**
Released: August 1989 by Epic Records, Czechoslovakian.
Catalog No.: 210040-1 311
Media: Vinyl.

Australian picture disc pressing of the TRASH album.

This particular edition of the TRASH album was released on green vinyl.

Album Title: **TRASH**
Released: August 1989 by Epic Records, Holland.
Catalog No.: 465130-1
Media: Vinyl and CD.

The same catalog number was used for both France and Germany.

Album Title: **TRASH**
Released: August 1989 by Sony, Japan.
Catalog No.: 25.8 5278
Media: CD.

Album Title: **TRASH**
Released: October 3, 1997 by Epic Records, Canada.
Catalog No.: WEK 45137
Media: CD.

Most recent reissue of the album in Canada.

Single Title: **Poison / Poison**
Released: July 1989 by Epic Records.
Catalog No.: 34-68958 (7"), EAS 1663 (12") and ESK 1665 (CD single)
Media: 7" Vinyl, 12" Vinyl and CD promotional single.

Came in a plain white sleeve with a red sticker stating that the artist was Alice Cooper and the track was Poison.

Single Title: **Poison / Trash**
Released: July 1989 by Epic Records.
Catalog No.: 34-68958 (7") and 34T-68958 (cassette)
Media: 7" Vinyl and Cassette single.

The 7" vinyl came in a picture sleeve showing the cover

US single for Poison.

of the TRASH album. The cassette single came with a different cover, however. Poison reached No. 7 on the US charts.

Single Title: **Poison / Trash**
Released: July 1989 by Epic Records, UK.
Catalog No.: 655061 7
Media: 7" Vinyl.

This came in a picture sleeve showing the back cover of the TRASH album. Poison reached No. 2 on the UK charts.

Single Title: **Poison / Trash /**
Ballad of Dwight Fry (live)
Released: July 1989 by Epic Records, UK.
Catalog No.: 655061 8
Media: 12" Vinyl single.

This 12" single came in a picture sleeve of the same photo that appeared on the 7" vinyl single sleeve. Ballad of Dwight Fry was taken from the 1987 Cincinnati Gardens show that was broadcast on American radio as part of the Superstars in Concert series.

US cassette single for Poison.

UK single for Poison.

Single Title: **Poison / Trash / Cold Ethyl** (live) **/**
I Got a Line on You
Released: July 1989 by Epic Records, UK.
Catalog No.: 655061 9
Media: 12" Vinyl single.

Released at the same time as another 12" single in the UK, this contains a different live track from the Cincinnati Gardens show of 1987, plus the song that Alice recorded for the IRON EAGLE II soundtrack album. The lettering on the cover is written in blue instead of a cream color as on the other UK singles for Trash.

Single Title: **Poison / Trash / Ballad of Dwight Fry** (live) **/ I Got a Line on You**
Released: July 1989 by Epic Records, UK.
Catalog No.: 655061 2 and 655165 2 (both 5" CD single); and 655061 3 (3" maxi-single CD)
Media: CD single (three variations.)

This CD has the same music as found on the first 12" single released in connection with the TRASH album. The first variation of the CD comes in the standard picture sleeve cover, while the second comes in a limited edition, bottle shaped sleeve. The third and final CD is actually a mini-CD with the same tracks on it. the 3" mini-CDs are relatively scarce other than in Japan, and are a valuable collectible to those fans interested in variations of singles.

Single Title: **Poison / Trash**
Released: July 1989 by Epic Records, Australia.
Catalog No.: 655061-7
Media: 7" Vinyl single.

Comes in a picture sleeve of the TRASH cover. Poison reached No. 3 on the Australian charts.

Single Title: **Poison / Ballad of Dwight Fry** (live) /
                Cold Ethyl (live)
Released: July 1989 by Epic Records, Australia.
Catalog No.:   655061-1
Media: CD single.

This single claims that both live tracks were from 1989, but they're actually from the 1987 Cincinnati Gardens show that was broadcast on American radio as part of the Superstars in Concert series.

Single Title: **Poison / Ballad of Dwight Fry** (live) /
                Cold Ethyl (live)
Released: July 1989 by Epic Records, Austria.
Catalog No.:   655061 3
Media: 3" maxi-single CD.

This is a 3" mini-CD, which are relatively scarce in markets other than Japan and are a bit of a valuable collectible to fans who collect variations of singles. Once again, the live tracks are from the 1987 Cincinnati Garden show that was broadcast on American radio stations as part of the Superstars in Concert series. The cover of the single is the same as the TRASH album front cover, with the name of the single and Alice's name in a yellow splodge on the top right-hand corner.

UK special CD single for Poison.

Single Title: **Poison / Ballad of Dwight Fry** (live) / **Cold Ethyl** (live)
Released: August 1989 by Epic Records, Germany.
Catalog No.:   655061 6 (12") and 655061 3 (CD)
Media: 12" Vinyl and CD.

Same as the Australian release above.

Single Title: **Poison / Trash**
Released: July 1989 by Epic Records, Holland.
Catalog No.:   655061-7
Media: 7" Vinyl single.

Picture sleeve of TRASH cover.

Single Title: **I'm Your Gun**
Released: Summer 1989 by Epic Records.
Catalog No.:   EAS 1890
Media: 12" Vinyl promotional single.

Promotional single released in the US, although a commercial single was never released. Came in a white sleeve with the artist and track title printed on it.

Single Title: **Trash**
Released: September 1989 by Epic Records.
Catalog No.:   EAS 1686
Media: 12" Vinyl promotional single.

Promotional single released in the US. Came in a white sleeve with the artist and track title printed on it.

Single Title: **Trash / Bed of Nails**
Released: September 1989 by Epic Records.
Catalog No.:   OE 45137
Media: Audio Cassette single release.

Hard to find single release of Trash.

Single Title: **Bed of Nails / I'm Your Gun**
Released: September 25, 1989 by Epic Records, UK.
Catalog No.: ALICE 3, ALICE R3, ALICE G3 and ALICE B3; also ALICE M3
Media: 7" Vinyl released in a multitude of colors; and the Cassette single with the same tracks.

Released with a picture sleeve of Alice holding his dance cane. The singles came in a standard black vinyl edition (ALICE 3), and three variations of colored vinyl (ALICE R3 for red vinyl, G3 for green and B3 for blue.) Bed of Nails reached No. 38 in the UK.

Single Title: **Bed of Nails / I'm Your Gun / Go to Hell** (live)
Released: September 25, 1989 by Epic Records, UK.
Catalog No.: ALICE T3 (12" black vinyl) and ALICE P3 (picture disc vinyl.)
Media: 12" black and picture disc Vinyl.

Two variations of the same 12" single, one done as a picture disc of the single's cover. Go to Hell is another track from the 1987 Cincinnati Gardens concert.

Single Title: **Bed of Nails / I'm Your Gun / Go to Hell** (live) / **Only Women Bleed** (live)
Released: September 25, 1989 by Epic Records, UK.
Catalog No.: ALICE C3
Media: CD single.

UK single for Bed Of Nails.

CD single with an additional live track from the 1987 Cincinnati Gardens concert. The cover of the CD is the same as the sleeve for the other Bed of Nails single.

Single Title: **Bed of Nails / I'm Your Gun**
Released: September 1989 by Epic Records, Australia.
Catalog No.: 655318-7, 655318-0, 655318-0 / 4 and 655318-1
Media: 7" Vinyl, Cassette and CD single, respectively.

There was one CD single (655318-1) and three variations of the 7" vinyl single available in Australia. All have the same sleeve, but the 7" variations are as followed: 655318-7 is a standard picture sleeve of Alice with the dance cane, 655318-0 is a standard picture sleeve that came with a poster of Alice enclosed, and 655318-0 / 4 is a standard picture sleeve that came with a poster of Alice and a cassette single of Bed of Nails / I'm Your Gun shrink wrapped to the vinyl single. Bed of Nails reached No. 15 on the Australian charts.

Single Title: **Bed of Nails / I'm Your Gun / Go to Hell** (live)
Released: September 1989 by Epic Records, Germany.
Catalog No.: 655318 6
Media: 12" Vinyl.

Came in a standard picture sleeve of Alice with his dance cane. See the entry for UK 12" vinyl of these same tracks for details.

Single Title: **Bed of Nails / I'm Your Gun / Go to Hell** (live) / **Only Women Bleed** (live)
Released: September 1989 by Epic Records, Germany.
Catalog No.: 655318 3
Media: CD single.

Came in a standard picture sleeve of Alice with his dance cane. See the entry for UK variation of the same single for details.

Single Title: **House of Fire**
Released: November 1989 by Epic Records.
Catalog No.: ESK 73085

Media: CD promotional single.

This promotional single was red on top (of the disc itself.)

Single Title: **House of Fire / Ballad of Dwight Fry** (live)
Released: November 1989 by Epic Records.
Catalog No.: 34-73085 (7") and 34T-73085 (cassette)
Media: 7" Vinyl and Cassette single.

Came in a picture sleeve of Alice. The live track comes from the 1987 Cincinnati Gardens concert. House of Fire reached No. 56 on the US charts.

Single Title: **House of Fire / This Maniac's in Love With You**
Released: November 1989 by Epic Records, UK.
Catalog No.: ALICE 4, ALICE R4, ALICE Y4, and two variations of ALICE P4.
Media: 7" black Vinyl, color Vinyl and picture-disc Vinyl.

UK black vinyl single for **House of Fire**.

The UK did it again with so many different variations of singles that it makes the eyes hurt. All have the same picture sleeve of Alice, with his body facing to the left and his head turned towards the camera. The background is a solid gold. ALICE 4 is a normal 7" black vinyl edition of the single. ALICE R4 is orange vinyl. ALICE Y4 is yellow vinyl. ALICE P4 comes in two picture disc editions, one that's cut to the shape of a close-up photo of Alice's face with information about the album and single on the back, and the other on a normal picture disc of the same photo not cut to size. House of Fire reached No. 65 on the UK charts.

Single Title: **House of Fire / Poison** (live)
Released: November 1989 by Epic Records, UK.
Catalog No.: ALICE X4
Media: 7" Vinyl.

A variation of the 7" single with a live track from the December 14, 1989 concert at the NEC in Birmingham, England. The cover has a silver background instead of gold as on the other UK versions of the **House of Fire** single.

Special edition of the UK single for House of Fire with a live version of Poison on the B-side.

Single Title: **House of Fire / This Maniac's in Love With You / Billion Dollar Babies** (live) **/ Under My Wheels** (live)
Released: November 1989 by Epic Records, UK.
Catalog No.: ALICE T4 (12"), ALICE S4 (12" with a patch), ALICE C4 (CD) and ALICE M4 (cassette)
Media: 12" Vinyl, CD and Cassette single.

Same cover as the other singles in this series, with ALICE S4 being enclosed with a small Alice Cooper patch (saying "Trashes the U.K. 1989".) The two live tracks are from the 1987 Cincinnati Gardens concert.

Single Title: **House of Fire / Poison** (live) **/ Spark in the Dark** (live) **/ Under My Wheels** (live)
Released: November 1989 by Epic Records, UK.
Catalog No.: ALICE Q4 and ALICE L4.
Media: 12" Vinyl.

Same cover as the others, only these two with the silver background instead of gold. ALICE S4 comes with a poster. Poison and Spark in the Dark come from the December 14, 1989 Birmingham, England concert, while Under My Wheels comes from the 1987 Cincinnati Gardens concert.

Single Title: **House of Fire /
This Maniac's in Love With You**
Released: November 1989 by Epic Records, Australia.
Catalog No.: 655472-7
Media: 7" Vinyl.

Came in a standard sleeve of Alice. House of Fire reached No. 72 on the Australian charts.

UK singles ALICE Q4 and L4 for House of Fire.

Single Title: **House of Fire / Under My Wheels** (live) **/ This Maniac's in Love With You / Billion Dollar Babies** (live)
Released: November 1989 by Epic Records, Australia.
Catalog No.: 655472-6 (12") and 655472-3 (CD)
Media: 12" Vinyl and CD single.

Came in a standard sleeve of Alice. Billion Dollar Babies and Under My Wheels are from the 1987 Cincinnati Gardens concert.

Single Title: **House of Fire / Under My Wheels** (live) **/ This Maniac's in Love With You / Billion Dollar Babies** (live)
Released: November 1989 by Epic Records, Germany.
Catalog No.: 654472 6
Media: 12" Vinyl.

Came in a standard sleeve of Alice. Billion Dollar Babies and Under My Wheels are from the 1987 Cincinnati Gardens concert.

Single Title: **House of Fire / Poison** (live)
Released: November 1989 by Epic Records, Japan.
Catalog No.: ESDA 7013
Media: 3" CD single.

Came in a picture sleeve and some type of gimmick packaging. Poison is from the December 14, 1989 Birmingham, England concert. The 3" CD single was a novelty item that was quite popular at the time.

Single Title: **Only My Heart Talkin' / Only My Heart Talkin'** (edit)
Released: January 1990 by Epic Records.
Catalog No.: ESK 73268
Media: CD promotional single.

Promotional single.

Single Title: **Only My Heart Talkin' /
Only Women Bleed** (live)
Released: January 1990 by Epic Records.
Catalog No.: 34-73268 (7") and 34T-73268 (cassette)
Media: 7" Vinyl and Cassette single.

Contrary to what may seem to be the case, the single for Only My Heart Talkin' was released in the US. It reached No. 99 on the US charts.

Back of the promotional CD single for Only My Heart Talkin'.

Single Title: **Only My Heart Talkin' / Only Women Bleed** (live)
Released: January 1990 by Epic Records, Australia.
Catalog No.: 655758-7, 655758-0, 655758-7 / 4
Media: 7" Vinyl.

Came in a picture sleeve of Alice in concert in front of a skull and crossbones. 655758-0 came with a poster enclosed, while 655758-7 / 4 came with the poster and a cassette single shrink wrapped with the 7" vinyl single. Only Women Bleed is another track from the 1987 Cincinnati Gardens concert. Only My Heart Talkin' reached No. 72 on the Australian charts.

Single Title: **Only My Heart Talkin' / Only Women Bleed** (live) / **Cold Ethyl** (live)
Released: January 1990 by Epic Records, Australia.
Catalog No.: 655758-6 (12") and 655758-3 (CD)
Media: 12" Vinyl and CD single.

Came in the same sleeve as the 7" version. Only Women Bleed and Cold Ethyl are both from the 1987 Cincinnati Gardens concert.

Single Title: **Only My Heart Talkin' / Only Women Bleed** (live)
Released: January 1990 by Epic Records, Germany.
Catalog No.: 655758 7
Media: 7" Vinyl.

Came in a standard sleeve of Alice in front of skull and crossbones.

Single Title: **Only My Heart Talkin' / Only Women Bleed** (live) / **Cold Ethyl** (live)
Released: January 1990 by Epic Records, Germany.
Catalog No.: 655758 6
Media: 12" Vinyl.

Came in the same sleeve as the 7" version. Only Women Bleed is from the 1987 Cincinnati Gardens concert, while Cold Ethyl is from the 1989 Birmingham, England concert.

Single Title: **Only My Heart Talkin' / Under My Wheels**
Released: January 1990 by Epic Records, Japan.
Catalog No.: ESDA 7034
Media: CD single.

Came in a standard picture sleeve of Alice with skull and crossbones. Under My Wheels is from the 1987 Cincinnati Gardens concert.

Single Title: **THE ALICE COOPER SINGLES**
Released: November 1989 by Epic Records, Australia.
Catalog No.: SAMP 1416
Media: CD promotional single.
Song List: Poison / House of Fire / Only My Heart Talkin' / Bed of Nails

Promotional-only CD single that contained all of the singles released from the album TRASH. The CD came in a standard plain white cardboard sleeve with information printed on a sticker on the sleeve.

Single Title: **ALICE COOPER**
Released: 1989 by Warner Brothers, Germany.
Catalog No.: 921 132-2
Media: 3" CD single.
Song List: Hello Hooray / School's Out / Billion Dollar Babies / Elected

With the renewed success of Alice thanks to TRASH,

3" CD single from Germany released in 1989 from Warner Brothers.

Warner Brothers released this "best of" CD single in Germany. The release is on the 3" maxi-CD format that had limited success during the late 1980's / early 1990's. Because of the limited interest in the item, it is now difficult to find in the collector's market. The cover shows the song titles with a picture of Alice inside a star.

Part 3 — Tours 1984 - 1990

By the end of 1985, Alice was reevaluating the "Killer Alice" character, contemplating what could be done with him for the next album and tour. What emerged was a chance to reintroduce (and introduce, period, to younger fans) "Killer" who hadn't been seen since the days of the MAD HOUSE ROCK tour (he really hadn't been seen in full form since the WELCOME TO MY NIGHTMARE days.) What he saw was a chance to start fresh at "Square One" for the next tour, correctly entitled THE NIGHTMARE RETURNS tour, and then redevelop the character on stage over the next several albums. This allowed Alice to redefine the character for each tour (from crazed killer once again of the NIGHTMARE RETURNS tour, to the elder statesman of the nightmare in THE LAST TEMPTATION and afterward), and to continue using "Killer Alice" in the concert, while still being able to develop new material not constrained by a fixed character. As time passed, Alice even abandoned the makeup until the latter part of the show, but that didn't come about until the time of the TRASH album and the tours that followed it.

In concert, the execution (or, at least, torture) of the Alice character — last seen during the MAD HOUSE ROCK tour — returned for all of the tours in between CONSTRICTOR and HEY STOOPID. Executions were a staple of the old shows, and it was an obvious move to include them on the tour that reintroduced Alice to the new crowds awaiting him in 1986, and fans were not disappointed. The guillotine was used for the CONSTRICTOR and TRASH tours, while a hanging was used for the RAISE YOUR FIST AND YELL album tour in between.

And, once again, performers into the show were not limited to musicians. From nurses, dancers and executioners (sometimes all by the same performer) to clowns, the concerts again consisted of several performance pieces and sometimes complicated effects. The years between THE NIGHTMARE RETURNS tour and the TRASHES THE WORLD tour also saw an increase in the venues that Alice played, especially after the success of TRASH and the single Poison.

As time passed, the shows included more diversified material and even (once in a while) cover songs. Alice was obviously having more fun on stage than in the past, and this made the concerts even more enjoyable. The years since THE NIGHTMARE RETURNS tour have produced concerts that have never been anything less than excellent, and fans knew that an Alice Cooper concert would always mean a good time.

Tour Name: **THE NIGHTMARE RETURNS (CONSTRICTOR Tour)**
Tour Period: October - November 1986 in California and the East Coast of the US. November through the beginning of December 1986 in the UK. December 1986 - March 1987 in North America. With one additional show at the Reading Festival in Reading, England on August 30, 1987.
Performers: Alice Cooper (vocals), Kane Roberts (guitar), Devlin 7 (guitar), Ken Mary (drums), Kip Winger (bass), Paul Horowitz (keyboards.) Additional performers: Linda Albertano (nurse and executioner), Sylvia Dohi (dancer), Tracy Dea (photographer.) Brian "Renfield" Nelson appeared in the Detroit show as a cameraman who steps on stage and gets speared by Alice with a microphone stand.
Opening Act: Vinnie Vincent Invasion, Faster Pussycat, Megadeth and Guns 'N Roses (each during a different segment of the American tour.) Zodiac Mindwarp was to open on the UK tour, but due to illness was replaced by Dr. and the Medics in London and Alien Sex Fiend for the rest of the tour.
Set List: Welcome to My Nightmare / Billion Dollar Babies / No More Mr. Nice Guy / Be My Lover / I'm Eighteen / The World Needs Guts / Give It Up / Cold Ethyl / Only Women Bleed / Go to Hell / Ballad of Dwight Fry / Teenage Frankenstein / Sick Things / I Love the Dead / School's Out / Elected / Under My Wheels

Alice's return to the stage for the first time since February 1982 found him a strong, confident Alice, doing a show that featured many old favorites, both music and set pieces, along with some new songs and special effects.

He donned again the leather outfit from the MAD HOUSE ROCK tour (including the red cup and lettering on the pants), although this time it was a jacket with tails and a skull on the back. Alice wore this outfit for the first couple of songs in the show. He also returned to the "demented clown" makeup of the 1970's, which he hadn't worn since the MAD HOUSE ROCK tour. The stage, by Joe Gannon, was reminiscent of the WELCOME

THE NIGHTMARE RETURNS tour book.

TO MY NIGHTMARE stage without looking like a copy.

Continuing this theme of similar-yet-different, there were slight variations in some of the old standards in the show. Cold Ethyl begins as a full-sized doll with black hair instead of the regular reddish hair (which makes sense as the dancer for the tour has dark hair), and at the end of **Only Women Bleed**, Ethyl has her revenge on Alice by rising up and strangling him. The executioner was a woman this time, who not only pulls Alice's bloody head from the basket at the foot of the guillotine, but kisses it and then gets blood spat in her face by the decapitated head. The giant balloons sent into the audience during the encore also returned, only this time with a mixture of confetti and stage blood.

Chapter 4: 1984 - 1990

New to most fans were the trick sword that made it appear as if Alice was cutting himself during **The World Needs Guts** (it had been used during the SPECIAL FORCES tour), the already mentioned microphone stand trick, and the animation of the Teenage Frankenstein monster during the song of the same name. Another new effect was given to Kane Roberts — his guitar / rifle shot a flare when the trigger was pulled.

On hand from the recording of the CONSTRICTOR album were Kip Winger and Kane Roberts. All of the other tour musicians were new to working with Alice. However, except for Kip Winger, they all returned for the following tour for the RAISE YOUR FIST AND YELL album, and Roberts, Winger, Horowitz and Mary performed on the next album.

Hired for the tour was Randy Piper, formally of W.A.S.P., but he was replaced after the first rehearsal for performance reasons. A couple of the musicians went under stage names during the tour, Devlin 7, also know as Johnny Dime on the RAISE YOUR FIST AND YELL tour, was actually Arthur Funaro, and Paul Horowitz was renamed Paul Horrors, since Horowitz isn't the most "rockin'" of stage names. Horowitz later changed his name to Paul Taylor and joined Kip Winger in the band Winger before working for some time with former Journey lead vocalist, Steve Perry.

Vinnie Vincent Invasion opened the show for a month in the US, with Guns 'N Roses opening a few shows on the West Coast. Zodiac Mindwarp was scheduled to open for Alice during the UK portion of the tour, but was replaced by Alien Sex Fiend for most of the tour because of illness. After returning to the US, Megadeth opened for Alice Cooper.

One surprise on the tour was the absence of **He's Back** from the set list. Although the song hadn't been a huge hit in the US or UK, it was still well known by fans, who were a bit disappointed at not being able to hear it live. No doubt about it, the tour was a success, and led to Alice revisiting many of the same venues (in the same order) on the next tour.

October 1986 - Arlington Theater, Santa Barbara, CA
    This was Alice's first concert performance since February 1982.
October 24, 1986 - National Orange Showgrounds, San Bernadino, CA
    Guns 'N Roses opened the show.
October 28, 1986 - Civic Center, Lansing, MI
October 29, 1986 - Saginaw, MI
October 30, 1986 - Joe Louis Arena, Detroit, MI
    An additional show added when the Halloween show on October 31 sold out. The show was recorded from the audience.
October 31, 1986 - Jose Louis Arena, Detroit, MI
    This concert was broadcast live on MTV, and was later released as the video THE NIGHTMARE RETURNS.
November 1, 1986 - Toledo, OH
November 2, 1986 - Kalamazoo, MI
November 4, 1986 - Fort Wayne, IN
    The show was recorded from the audience.
November 6, 1986 - Vet's Memorial, Columbus, OH
November 7, 1986 - Hara Arena, Dayton, OH
November 8, 1986 - Cleveland Music Hall, Cleveland, OH
    The show was recorded from the audience.
November 9, 1986 - Erie, PA
    The show was recorded from the audience.
November 11, 1986 - Syria Mosque, Pittsburgh, PA
    The show was recorded from the audience.
November 12, 1986 - Wilkes Barre, PA
November 13, 1986 - George Washington University Patriot Center, Fairfax, VA
    The show was recorded from the audience.
November 14, 1986 - Philadelphia, PA
November 15, 1986 - Binghampton, NY
    The show was recorded from the audience.
November 16, 1986 - Rochester, NY
November 19, 1986 - Centrum, Worcester, MA
    The show was recorded from the audience.
November 23, 1986 - Wembley Arena, London, England
    The show was recorded from the audience.

November 25, 1986 - Edinburgh Playhouse, Edinburgh, Scotland
The show was recorded from the audience.
November 26, 1986 - Edinburgh Playhouse, Edinburgh, Scotland
The show was recorded from the audience.
November 28, 1986 - Apollo Theater, Manchester, England
The show was recorded from the audience.
November 29, 1986 - Apollo Theater, Manchester, England
The show was recorded from the audience.
November 30, 1986 - Apollo Theater, Manchester, England
The show was recorded from the audience.
December 1, 1986 - City Hall, Newcastle, England
The show was recorded from the audience.
December 3, 1986 - Odeon, Birmingham, England
The show was recorded from the audience.
December 4, 1986 - Odeon, Birmingham, England
The show was recorded from the audience.
December 5, 1986 - Odeon, Birmingham, England
The show was recorded from the audience.
December 12, 1986 - Tower Theater, Philadelphia, PA
December 13, 1986 - Public Hall, Cleveland, OH
The show was recorded from the audience.
December 14, 1986 - Auditorium, Utica, NY
December 15, 1986 - Landmark Theater, Syracuse, NY
December 18, 1986 - Civic Center, Baltimore, MD
December 19, 1986 - Coliseum, Charlotte, NC
December 20, 1986 - Cumberland Civic Center, Fayetteville, NC
December 22, 1986 - Galliard Auditorium, Charleston, SC
December 26, 1986 - Fox Theater, Atlanta, GA
December 27, 1986 - Sun Dome, Tampa, FL
The show was recorded from the audience.
December 28, 1986 - Auditorium, West Palm Beach, FL
December 29, 1986 - Ocean Center, Daytona, FL
December 31, 1986 - James L. Knight Center, Miami, FL
January 2, 1987 - Municipal Auditorium, Nashville, TN
January 3, 1987 - Convention Center, Memphis, TN
January 4, 1987 - Gardens, Louisville, KY
January 6, 1987 - Charleston, WV
The show was recorded from the audience.
January 9, 1987 - New Orleans Done, New Orleans, LA
January 10, 1987 - Municipal Auditorium, Mobile, AL
January 11, 1987 - University of New Orleans Lakefront, New Orleans, LA
January 18, 1987 - Memorial Coliseum, Corpus Christi, TX
January 22, 1987 - Opera House, Spokane, WA
January 23, 1987 - Civic Center, Portland, OR
January 24, 1987 - Arena, Seattle, WA
January 27, 1987 - Kaiser Convention Center, Oakland, CA
The show was recorded from the audience.
January 28, 1987 - Civic Center, Bakersfield, CA
January 29, 1987 - Thomas and Mack Center, Las Vegas, NV
January 31, 1987 - Coliseum, Phoenix, AZ
February 4, 1987 - Tulsa, OK
The show and sound check were recorded from the audience.
February 6, 1987 - Veteran's Coliseum, Des Moines, IA
The show was recorded and filmed from the audience.
February 7, 1987 - Roy Wilkins Auditorium, St. Paul, MN
The show was recorded from the audience.
February 10, 1987 - Mecca Arena, Milwaukee, WI
The show was recorded from the audience.
February 12, 1987 - UIC Pavilion, Chicago, IL
The show was recorded from the audience.
February 13, 1987 - Joe Louis Arena, Detroit, MI

The show was recorded from the audience.
February 14, 1987 - La Crosse Centre, La Crosse, WI
   The show was recorded from the audience.
February 16, 1987 - Syria Mosque, Pittsburgh, PA
February 20, 1987 - Mid-Hudson Civic Center, Poughkeepsie, NY
February 21, 1987 - Aitken Centre, Frederickton, Canada
   Sword opened for this show and all the subsequent Canadian shows.
February 26, 1987 - Maple Leaf Gardens, Toronto, Canada
   The show was recorded from the audience.
February 28, 1987 - Verdun Arena, Montreal, Canada
   The show was recorded from the audience.
March 4, 1987 - Victor J. Copps Coliseum, Hamilton, Ontario, Canada
   The show was recorded from the audience.
March 5, 1987 - Civic Auditorium, La Porte, IN
   Tesla opened this show.
March 6, 1987 - Cincinnati Gardens, Cincinnati, OH
   This show was recorded for radio broadcast as a SUPERSTAR CONCERT SERIES program. Several tracks from this recording were later used as B-sides for singles. The recording also appeared on a few bootlegs (see Chapter 6 for details.)
March 21, 1987 - Long Beach Convention Center, Long Beach, CA
   The show was recorded from the audience.
March 28, 1987 - Winnipeg, Manitoba, Canada
   The show was recorded from the audience.
March 31, 1987 - Olympic Saddledome, Calgary, Alberta, Canada
August 30, 1987 - Reading Festival, Reading, England
   This show was on the last night of the three day festival. It was also the 25th anniversary of the festival. The show was recorded from the audience.

Tour Name: **LIVE IN THE FLESH TOUR (the RAISE YOUR FIST AND YELL tour)**
Tour Period: North American tour, October 1987 - February 1988. UK tour, April 1988. European tour, April - May 1988.
Performers: Alice Cooper (vocals), Kane Roberts (guitar), Johnny Dime (guitar), Ken Mary (drums), Steve Steele (bass), Paul Horowitz (keyboards.) Additional performers: Karen Russel and Lisa Oakley.
Opening Act: Frehley's Comet opened for Alice during the first month of the tour, after which Faster Pussycat continued with the remainder of the North American tour. Motorhead also performed as the opener for some of the shows, and Chrome Molly opened for most of the shows during the UK and European portion of the tour.
Set List: Teenage Frankenstein / No More Mr. Nice Guy / Billion Dollar Babies / Is It My Body / I'm Eighteen / Go to Hell / Prince of Darkness / Chop, Chop, Chop / Gail / Roses on White Lace / Only Women Bleed / Devil's Food / The Black Widow / Dead Babies / Killer / School's Out / Freedom / Under My Wheels

This tour continued in the manner of THE NIGHTMARE RETURNS tour of combining bits and pieces from the past shows with new elements. With the previous tour having been such a success, there was no desire to tempt the fates, and so this tour included many similarities, right down to some of the tour dates being incredibly similar to those from the year before.

The new tour featured the gallows and Alice's execution, along with the Teenage Frankenstein monster from THE NIGHTMARE RETURNS tour. The same musicians were used as on the previous tour, with the exception of Kip Winger, who was beginning to work on his own band, Winger, which would see a good deal of success in the late 1980's and early 1990's.

The RAISE YOUR FIST AND YELL tour book.

Although **He's Back** wasn't part of the regular set list for the US and UK tours, it was performed whenever Alice played Sweden, since the song had been a huge hit there. When played during the Swedish portion of the tour, **He's Back** would normally appear before **Freedom** in the set list. The music video for **Freedom** was recorded during dress rehearsals for the tour.

Frehley's Comet, led by former KISS member Ace Frehley, provided the second former KISS member to open for Alice — Vinnie Vincent had opened for Alice during the 1986 tour with his Vinnie Vincent Invasion band.

October 22, 1987 - Wilson Theater, Fresno, CA
October 23, 1987 - Civic Auditorium, Oxnard, CA
October 24, 1987 - Orange Pavilion, San Bernadino, CA
October 28, 1987 - Wendler Arena, Saginaw, MI
 The show was recorded from the audience.
October 29, 1987 - Wings Stadium, Kalamazoo, MI
 The show was filmed from the audience.
October 30, 1987 - Toledo Arena, Toledo, OH
October 31, 1987 - Joe Louise Arena, Detroit, MI
November 3, 1987 - Hara Arena, Dayton, OH
November 4, 1987 - Vet's Memorial Coliseum, Columbus, OH
November 5, 1987 - Memorial Coliseum, Fort Wayne, IN
November 6, 1987 - Market Square Arena, Indianapolis, IN
 The show was recorded from the audience.
November 7, 1987 - Civic Center, Erie, PA
November 8, 1987 - Broome County Arena, Binghampton, NY
 The show was recorded from the audience.
November 10, 1987 - Mid-Hudson Arena, Poughkeepsie, NY
 The show was recorded from the audience.
November 12, 1987 - Memorial Auditorium, Buffalo, NY
 The show was recorded from the audience.
November 13, 1987 - RPI Field House, Albany, NY
November 14, 1987 - Public Hall, Cleveland, OH
November 17, 1987 - Garden, Boston, MA
 The show was recorded from the audience.
November 18, 1987 - Coliseum, New Haven, CT
November 19, 1987 - Cumberland Civic Center, Portland, ME
November 20, 1987 - Tower Theatre, Philadelphia, PA
November 21, 1987 - Tower Theatre, Philadelphia, PA
November 22, 1987 - Tower Theatre, Philadelphia, PA
November 25, 1987 - Municipal Auditorium, Nashville, TN
November 27, 1987 - UNO Lakefront, New Orleans, LA
November 28, 1987 - Hirsch Memorial Auditorium, Shreveport, AL
November 29, 1987 - Mississippi Coliseum, Biloxi, MS
December 17, 1987 - Civic Centre, St. Paul, MN
 The show was recorded from the audience.
December 18, 1987 - Centrum, Worcester, MA
 The show was recorded from the audience.
December 24, 1987 - Atlanta, GA
December 27, 1987 - Victoria, British Columbia
 The show was recorded from the audience.
December 28, 1987 - Vancouver, British Columbia
 The show was recorded from the audience.
December 30, 1987 - Portland, OR
 The show was recorded from the audience.
December 31, 1987 - Seattle Coliseum, Seattle, WA
 The show was recorded from the audience.
January 5, 1988 - Salt Palace Center, Salt Lake City, UT
January 8, 1988 - Memorial Auditorium, (city unknown), KS
January 12, 1988 - Roberts Stadium, Evansville, IN
 Although Motorhead was announced as the opening act, Armored Saint opened instead.
February 6, 1988 - Halifax, Nova Scotia
 The show was filmed from the audience.

February 10, 1988 - Forum, Montreal, Canada
The show was recorded from the audience.
February 12, 1988 - Maple Leaf Gardens, Toronto, Canada
The show was filmed from the audience.
February 13, 1988 - London Gardens, London, Ontario
February 14, 1987 - Ottawa Civic Center, Ottawa, Canada
The show was recorded from the audience.
February 26, 1988 - Long Beach Arena, Long Beach, CA
The encore was recorded from the audience. This was the show where members of Guns 'N Roses appeared on stage to sing Under My Wheels.
February 1988 - L. A. Forum, Los Angeles, CA
April 1, 1988 - Edinburgh Playhouse, Edinburgh, Scotland
The show was recorded from the audience.
April 2, 1988 - Edinburgh Playhouse, Edinburgh, Scotland
April 4, 1988 - City Hall, Sheffield, England
The show was recorded from the audience.
April 5, 1988 - National Exhibition Center, Birmingham, England
The show was recorded from the audience.
April 7, 1988 - Wembley Arena, London, England
The show was recorded from the audience.
April 8, 1988 - City Hall, Newcastle, England
The show was recorded from the audience.
April 9, 1988 - City Hall, Newcastle, England
April 10, 1988 - Apollo Theater, Manchester, England
Part of the concert was filmed from the audience. The show was recorded from the audience.
April 11, 1988 - Apollo Theater, Manchester, England
The show was recorded from the audience.
April 12, 1988 - Apollo Theater, Manchester, England
The show was recorded from the audience.
April 15, 1988 - K. B. Halle, Copenhagen, Denmark
The show was recorded from the audience.
April 16, 1988 - Ice Stadium, Stockholm, Sweden
The show was recorded from the audience.
April 18, 1988 - Stadthalle, Osnabruck, Germany
The show was recorded from the audience.
April 20, 1988 - Sporthalle, Boblingen, West Germany
The show was recorded from the audience.
April 21, 1988 - Stadthalle, Furth, Germany
The show was recorded from the audience.
April 22, 1988 - Gruga Halle, Essen, Germany
The show was filmed and recorded from the audience.
April 23, 1988 - Le Zenith, Paris, France
The show was recorded from the audience.
April 24, 1988 - Eberthalle, Ludwigshafen, Germany
The show was filmed and recorded from the audience.
April 26, 1988 - Stadthalle, Offenbach, Germany
The show was recorded from the audience.
April 27, 1988 - Eullachalle, Winterthur, Switzerland
The show was recorded from the audience.
April 28, 1988 - Kurhalle Oberlaa, Vienna, Austria
The show was recorded from the audience.
April 30, 1988 - Pallouer, Rome, Italy
May 2, 1988 - Pallazo Della Sport, Florence, Italy
May 3, 1988 - Palatrussardi, Milan, Italy
The show was recorded from the audience.
May 5, 1988 - Rijnhal, Arnhem, The Netherlands
The show was recorded from the audience.
May 6, 1988 - Forest National, Brussels, Belgium
The show was recorded from the audience.

Tour Name:	**TRASHES THE WORLD (the TRASH tour)**
Tour Period:	From October 31, 1989 through August 30, 1990, with a couple of final dates in October 1990.
Performers:	Alice Cooper (vocals), Al Pitrelli (guitar), Pete Friesen (guitar), Jonathon Mover (drums, first part of tour), Tommy "T-Bone" Carradonna (bass), Derek Sherinian (keyboards) and Devon Meade (backing vocals.) Eric Singer replaced Jonathon Mover on drums starting with the US portion of the tour.
Opening Act:	Great White opened for the European and Canadian portions of the tour, and Danger Danger opened the US portion of the tour. Great White and Britney Fox played on the UK portion of the tour.
Set List:	Hello Hooray (part only, on tape) / Trash / Billion Dollar Babies / I'm Eighteen / I'm Your Gun / Desperado / House of Fire / No More Mr. Nice Guy / This Maniac's in Love With You / Steven / Welcome to My Nightmare / Ballad of Dwight Fry / Gutter Cat Vs. the Jets / Only Women Bleed / I Love the Dead / Poison / Muscle of Love / Spark in the Dark / Bed of Nails / School's Out / Under My Wheels Only My Heart Talkin' was added to the set list after it was released as a single (January / February 1990.)

After two tours with Alice in full makeup and in full "Killer Alice" persona, the TRASH tour saw another Alice emerge onto the stage. This is not to say that "Killer Alice" never appeared, because he did during these shows, and has done in tours ever since. There was, however, a new approach to the show, with Alice appearing on stage — rough, tough and ready to give the audience his all — without having to immediately resort to "Killer Alice" to get him through.

The stage set-up followed was along the same lines as the music videos done for the TRASH album, particularly the one for **Poison**. The look was an attempt to replicate a feeling similar to what the alternate dimension sets in the film HELLRAISER gave that movie, with chains, metal, and a touch of a bondage feel to it. The shows were still theatrical, including the use of the guillotine once again during I Love the Dead, but they stepped away from the blood and gore that came with the CONSTRICTOR and RAISE YOUR FIST AND YELL tours.

Initially, Alice had hoped that he could get guitar wizard Steve Vai to join up with the tour, but Vai wasn't available, having just joined Whitesnake for a tour. In his place, Vai had recommended Al Pitrelli, who played for this tour and then moved on. Meanwhile, the other guitarist for the TRASH tour, Pete Freisen, would return for the subsequent tours promoting the HEY STOOPID album.

The TRASH tour book.

After the European portion of the tour, Jonathon Mover left and was replaced by former Black Sabbath and Badland (among others) drummer, Eric Singer. Eric played out the rest of the tour and the subsequent tours up through 1991 before moving on as drummer for the rock band KISS. After leaving KISS in 1996, Eric would join Alice for part of the most recent tour during the summer of 1998.

Derek Sherinian was the new keyboardist on this tour, and would continue with Alice for the subsequent tour up through 1991. He would later tour with KISS for a while, at the recommendation of Eric Singer, during part of the 1990's.

Some replacements in the set list occurred during on this tour, including Only My Heart Talkin' replacing Muscle of Love around March 1990 (as the single was just then coming out.) The Awakening was performed at the first show in Brussels on November 21 (The Cathouse show in Los Angeles was a warm up show), but it was dropped after the one show. Additional songs were thrown into the mix in Australia and in Sweden. In Australia, the song added was Department of Youth, while in Sweden the additional song was He's Back. In both cases, it was because the respective songs were huge hits in those countries.

This was the longest tour Alice went on since the mid 1970's, taking up a full year (with some weeks off at different times.) The tour also included the performance would become the concert video ALICE COOPER TRASHES THE WORLD (see Part 4 for details.)

October 31, 1989 - The Cathouse, Los Angeles, CA
Warm up show for the tour.
November 21, 1989 - Forest National, Brussels, Belgium
The show was recorded from the audience. The Awakening was performed only at this show.
November 22, 1989 - Ahoy Stadium, Rotterdam
Britney Fox, in addition to Great White, opened the show. The show was filmed from the audience. Is It My Body and Cold Ethyl were performed in addition to the regular set list.
November 23, 1989 - The Marquee, London, England
The show was recorded from the audience (an abbreviated set.)
November 25, 1989 - Icehall, Helsinki, Finland
The show was recorded from the audience.
November 27, 1989 - Skedsmohallen, Oslo, Norway
The show was recorded from the audience.
November 29, 1989 - Olympen Hall, Lund, Sweden
The show waw recorded from the audience.
November 30, 1989 - K. B. Hallen, Copenhagen, Denmark
December 1, 1989 - Scandinavium, Gothenburg, Sweden
The show was recorded from the audience.
December 2, 1989 - Isstadion, Stockholm, Sweden
December 5, 1989 - Exhibition Centre, Glasgow, Scotland
The show was recorded from the audience.
December 6, 1989 - King's Hall, Belfast, Ireland
December 7, 1989 - Whitley Bay Ice Rink, Newcastle, England
The show was filmed from the audience.
December 10, 1989 - Wembley Arena, London, England
The show was recorded from the audience.
December 11, 1989 - Wembley Arena, London, England
The show was recorded from the audience.
December 13, 1989 - National Exhibition Center, Birmingham, England
The show was recorded from the audience.
December 14, 1989 - National Exhibition Center, Birmingham, England
The show was filmed and released as the ALICE COOPER TRASHES THE WORLD videocassette. Numerous tracks from this performance later turned up as the B-sides of official singles, and on bootlegs released over the years.
December 16, 1989 - Grugahalle, Essen Germany
The show was recorded from the audience.
December 17, 1989 - Hallenstadion, Zurich Switzerland
The show was recorded from the audience.
December 18, 1989 - Schwabenhalle, Augsburg, Germany
The show was recorded from the audience.
December 19, 1989 - Kurhalle, Vienna, Austria
The show was recorded from the audience.
December 21, 1989 - Hehenstaufhalle, Goppingen, Germany
The show was recorded from the audience.
December 22, 1989 - Stadthalle, Freiburg, Germany
December 23, 1989 - Festhalle, Frankfurt, Germany
The show was co-headlined with Bon Jovi, and recorded from the audience.
December 28, 1989 - Civic Centre, Ottawa, Ontario, Canada
The show was recorded from the audience.
December 29, 1989 - Memorial Auditorium, Peterborough, Ontario, Canada
December 30, 1989 - London Gardens, London, Ontario, Canada
December 31, 1989 - Sky Dome, Toronto, Canada
The show was recorded from the audience.
January 1, 1990 - Memorial Gardens, Sault St. Marie, Ontario, Canada
January 3, 1990 - Arena, Sudbury, Canada
January 4, 1990 - Memorial Centre, Kingston, Ontario
January 5, 1990 - Forum, Montreal, Canada
January 6, 1990 - Colisee De Quebec, Quebec City, Quebec, Canada

January 8, 1990 - Metro Centre, Halifax, NS
January 9, 1990 - Coliseum, Moncton, NB
January 10, 1990 - Centre Zoo, Sydney, NS
January 11, 1990 - Aitken University Centre, Fredericton, NB
January 15, 1990 - Saskatchewan Palace, Saskatoon, Saskatchewan
January 16, 1990 - Olympic Saddledome, Calgary, Alberta, Canada
January 18, 1990 - Pacific National Exhibition Centre, Vancouver, British Columbia
January 20, 1990 - Northland's Coliseum, Edmonton, Alberta, Canada
February 23, 1990 - Music Hall, Houston, TX
February 24, 1990 - Bronco Bowl, Dallas, TX
February 25, 1990 - Municipal Auditorium, San Antonio, TX
February 26, 1990 - City Coliseum, Austin, TX
February 28, 1990 - Fox Theatre, Atlanta, GA
March 2, 1990 - Knight Center, Miami, FL
March 3, 1990 - Orlando, FL
March 4, 1990 - Performing Arts Center, Tampa, FL
March 5, 1990 - Florida Theater, Jacksonville, FL
March 7, 1990 - Auditorium, Roanoke, VA
March 8, 1990 - Mosque, Richmond, VA
March 9, 1990 - Tower Theater, Philadelphia, PA
  The show was recorded from the audience.
March 10, 1990 - Syria Mosque, Pittsburgh, PA
March 12, 1990 - The Ritz Club, New York, NY
  The show was recorded from the audience.
March 13, 1990 - Clifton Park Arena, Albany, NY
  The show was filmed from the audience.
March 14, 1990 - Orpheum, Boston, MA
March 15, 1990 - Paramount Theater, Springfield, MA
March 17, 1990 - Music Hall, Cleveland, OH
March 18, 1990 - Fox Theater, Detroit, MI
March 19, 1990 - Fox Theater, Detroit, MI
March 20, 1990 - Fox Theater, Detroit, MI
March 21, 1990 - Fox Theater, Detroit, MI
March 23, 1990 - Riviera, Chicago, IL
March 24, 1990 - Milwaukee, WI
March 25, 1990 - St. Paul Civic Center, St. Paul, MN
  The show was recorded from the audience.
March 27, 1990 - Fox Theater, St. Louis, MO
  The show was recorded from the audience.
March 28, 1990 - Shrine Auditorium, Springfield, MO
March 29, 1990 - Memorial Hall, Kansas City, MO
  The show was filmed from the audience.
March 31, 1990 - CISC, Denver, CO
April 2, 1990 - Convention Center, Spokane, WA
April 3, 1990 - Paramount Theater, Seattle, WA
  The show was recorded from the audience.
April 4, 1990 - The Armory, Salem, OR
April 6, 1990 - Warfield Theater, San Francisco, CA
April 7, 1990 - Pantages Theater, Los Angeles, CA
April 8, 1990 - Riverside Convention Center, Riverside, CA
April 9, 1990 - Las Vegas, NV
  The show was recorded from the audience.
April 10, 1990 - Amphitheater, Mesa, AZ
April 19, 1990 - Canberra National Indoor Stadium, Canberra, Australia
  The show was recorded from the audience.
April 20, 1990 - National Tennis Centre, Melbourne, Australia
  The show was recorded from the audience.
April 21, 1990 - National Tennis Centre, Melbourne, Australia
  The show was recorded from the audience.
April 23, 1990 - Entertainment Centre, Sydney, Australia
  The show was recorded from the audience.

April 24, 1990 - Entertainment Centre, Sydney, Australia
April 26, 1990 - Entertainment Centre, Brisbane, Australia
  The show was recorded from the audience.
July 1, 1990 - Midtfna Festival, Ringe, Denmark
  The show was recorded from the audience.
July 3, 1990 - Christinehof Castle, Helsingborg, Denmark
July 5, 1990 - Karlskoga Festival, Karlskoga, Sweden
July 7, 1990 - Oulu Festival, Oulu, Finland
July 10, 1990 - Olympia, Paris, France
  The show was recorded from the audience.
July 11, 1990 - Theatre Antique de Fourvieres, Lyon, France
  The show was recorded from the audience.
July 12, 1990 - Sporthalle, Cologne, Germany
July 13, 1990 - Sporthalle, Cologne, Germany
  The show was recorded from the audience.
July 14, 1990 - Ellenfeld Stadium, Neunkirchen, Germany
  The show was recorded from the audience.
July 17, 1990 - Dom Sportova, Zagreb, Yugoslavia
July 19, 1990 - Tao Stadium, Athens, Greece
  The show was recorded from the audience.
July 21, 1990 - Sajam Hall, Belgrade, Yugoslavia
July 22, 1990 - MTK, Budapest, Hungary
August 18, 1990 - Omiya, Japan
August 20, 1990 - Tokyo, Japan
August 22, 1990 - Tokyo, Japan
August 23, 1990 - Tokyo, Japan
August 26, 1990 - Yokohama, Japan
August 27, 1990 - Kouseinenkin Hall, Osaka, Japan
  The show was recorded from the audience.
August 28, 1990 - Kouseinenkin Hall, Osaka, Japan
  The show was recorded from the audience.
August 30, 1990 - Nagoya, Japan
October 26, 1990 - Arizona State Fair Coliseum, Arizona
October 31, 1990 - Los Angeles, CA
  This was a private concert for winners of a contest sponsored by Miller Beer.

Part 4 — Films and Television 1984 - 1990

In 1985, Alice was once again in front of the camera, working on new musical projects. The first of these to hit the public was the music video for the Twisted Sister song Be Chrool to Your Scuel, a fun video that highlighted Alice in a very positive way. It was also a chance to see him in a transitional period, moving from the SPECIAL FORCES look (the leather jackets with the pins covering the lapels, and the SF shirt) back to "Killer Alice" once again (whereas the film ROADIE in late 1979 shows the opposite transition, from "Killer Alice" to his FLUSH THE FASHION style.) Since this was a guest appearance for Alice, the video and song are covered in Chapter 6.

Following the success of his album in the second half of the 1980's, Alice was being seen a lot more on television, including music videos for each album, and even a couple of videocassette for the TRASH album. This success also led to more of his earlier material reappearing on the market, including the release of the WELCOME TO MY NIGHTMARE film on video (see Chapter 2, Part 4.) It was a golden era for those who wanted to see Alice videos. He didn't disappoint his fans.

During this period, Alice also began contributing new songs to movies, some of which featured him in cameo appearances. He's Back is, of course, an obvious example, but there were also songs appearing in films that either had limited exposure on CD and vinyl (such as I Got a Line on You for the film IRON EAGLE II, and Shockdance from the SHOCKER film), or, up to 1999, had yet to be released in any format (such as the two songs in the MONSTER DOG movie.) Fortunately, there's a boxed set due out in early 1999, so that at least some of these songs will be reappearing for Alice fans. Some of these songs appeared on the soundtrack albums for their respective films, and are dealt with in Chapter 6.

Film Title:	**MONSTER DOG**
	Alternative titles: Leviatan (original Spanish release title) and The Bite and Los Perros de la Muerte. Also known in pre-production as Pierce My Heart.
Film Type:	Movie.
Created:	Filmed 1984 on location in Torrelodones, Spain. A Continental Pictures presentation. Produced by Carlos Aured. Executive producers were Helen Sarlui and Eduard Sarlui. Written and directed by Claudio Fragasso (under the pseudonym of Clyde Anderson.) Released theatrically by Continental Pictures in 1985. Released 1986 on video in the US by Trans World Entertainment (catalog number 38013)
Music:	Identity Crises and See Me in the Mirror
Plot:	Alice plays Vincent Raven, a rock star who takes a small film crew and his girlfriend to his family's estate to film his latest video. Before arriving at the estate, the group is told about a series of grisly slayings in the area, but they decide to press on. A series of incidents convince the group to abandon their stay at the estate, but a group of locals soon arrives to stop the "family curse" from continuing by killing Vincent. Hilarity ensues. (Well, no, it doesn't, but wouldn't it have been great if it had?)

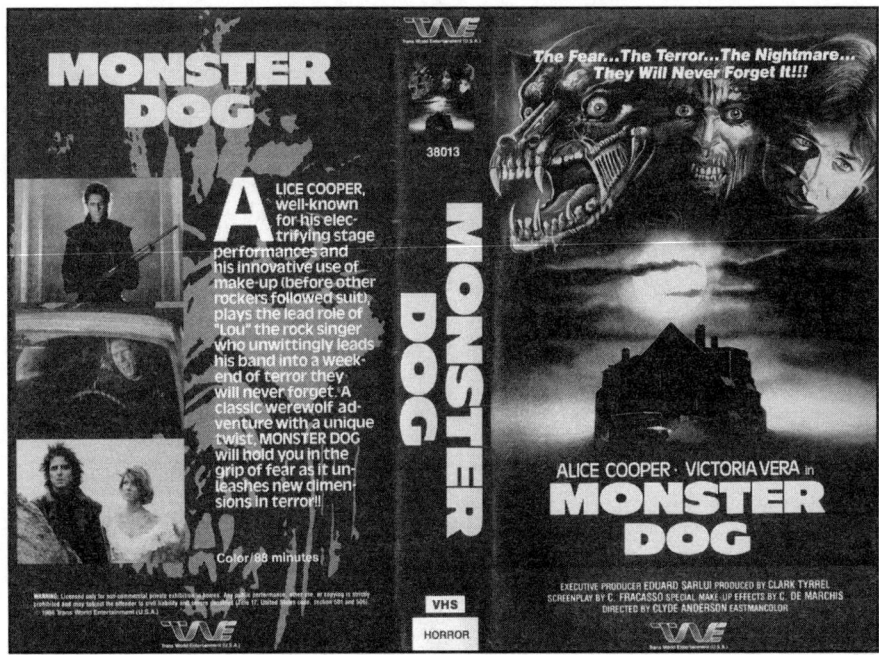

Front and back cover for the MONSTER DOG video cassette.

Have you tried the monster dogs? They're pretty tasty.

Seriously, Alice's first project after taking a year off to spend with his family not only had him acting in front of the camera, but also give him a chance to do some musical work again. Appearing in the movie are two songs that Alice co-wrote and arranged with Teddy Bautista, a well known and well respected musician and composer in Spanish rock history. The first, **Identity Crises** (listed as "Identity Chrises" in the film credits), is played after the opening credits and before the ending credits as a music video (the latter showing clips from the film itself.) It's an excellent song, and very much a transitional song, both musically and lyrically, between DADA and CONSTRICTOR. The second song, **See Me in the Mirror**, is played out in the film itself as the video being filmed at the estate. This second song is a bit of a disappointment after the first one, but it does allow fans to see Alice using a bit of the SPECIAL FORCES makeup on his face (the exaggerated eyebrows and the blue mascara on the eyelids.) Both songs were performed by Alice with a band called Dicotomia, who also recorded the music for another Spanish production that same year.

The film was a Spanish-Puerto Rican production, and was directed by an Italian director who made many horror / sci-fi B-movies after this one. Everyone in the film spoke English (some phonetically), but it was later overdubbed to with more "American" sounding voices — including Alice. This explains why people in the film appear to be saying their lines in English, but their voices and mouth movements seem a little bit off.

Alice had appeared, and would later appear, in other films, but this is the only movie to date that features him in the lead role. Although assured at the time of filming that the movie would never be seen in other countries, once Alice began to achieve some renewed popularity in 1985 / 86, the film was quickly released on video by Trans World Entertainment in the US. It was released in both Beta and VHS versions, and came in a hard shell plastic case with the poster art from the movie on the front cover (Alice turning from a "monster dog" into what is supposed to be him, but looks rather more like Jan Michael-Vincent), and three movie stills of Alice from the film on the back. The synopsis on the back of the box incorrectly names Alice's character as "Lou."

The movie is actually a good time waster, but is long out of print and increasingly hard to find. Alice would follow this project up with his work on **Be Chrool to Your Scuel** for the Twisted Sister album COME OUT AND PLAY.

Film Title: **He's Back (The Man Behind the Mask)**
Film Type: Music video.
Created: Filmed August 1986 and shown on television music programs and channels like MTV.
Music: He's Back (The Man Behind the Mask)

This is the promotional music clip for the first single from the CONSTRICTOR album and the FRIDAY THE 13TH PART VI movie. By this time, the concept of promotional music material had changed from being simply a part of the advertising for a record to being the best way to get a song on the charts at all. This was due to the success of MTV, and how it essentially became the MOR "top 40's" station of the 1980's, where songs became successful if played regularly on the network. It also changed how the clips were described, and by 1986, promotional films were normally referred to as "music videos" and nothing else.

This video is conceptual in nature, and begins with a teenage boy being lectured by his father about his date for the evening. The boy then goes with his girlfriend to the movies and ends up becoming part of the film itself, with Alice as the villain. Clips from the FRIDAY THE 13TH film are edited into the video. The video is very amusing and was a great way to let fans know that Alice was back.

Film Title: **ALICE COOPER - THE NIGHTMARE RETURNS**
Film Type: Concert movie.
Created: Filmed October 31, 1986 at the Joe Louis Arena, Detroit, MI. Broadcast October 31, 1986 on MTV cable television network. Executive producer was Shep Gordon. Produced by Radia Dockray. Produced for the stage by Joe Gannon Directed by Marty Callner. Released on video by MCA as THE NIGHTMARE RETURNS Catalog number MCA 80635 (US; 1987 and reissued July 1, 1991); CAST 63217 (UK: issued January 30, 1991) and HEN 2052D (UK issued mid-1990's.)
Performers: Alice Cooper (vocals), Kane Roberts (guitar), Devlin 7 (guitar), Ken Mary (drums), Kip Winger (bass), Paul Horowitz (keyboards.) Additional performers: Linda Albertano (nurse and executioner), Sylvia Dohi (dancer), Tracy Dea (Teenage Frankenstein and other roles.) Brian "Renfield" Nelson as the cameraman who gets speared with a microphone stage by Alice during Go to Hell. And girl in audience exposing herself (well, you do have to say she was a performer now, don't you?)
Music: Welcome to My Nightmare / Billion Dollar Babies / No More Mr. Nice Guy / Be My Lover / I'm Eighteen / The World Needs Guts / Give It Up / Cold Ethyl / Only Women Bleed / Go to Hell / Ballad of Dwight Fry / Teenage Frankenstein / Sick Things / I Love the Dead / School's Out / Elected / Under My Wheels

The tour for CONSTRICTOR (and Alice's return to the stage after an absence of about four and a half years) had started barely a week before this concert aired live on the MTV network as a Halloween special (after a four hour stint of Elvira hosting as VJ.) Although it's very early on in the tour, Alice, the musicians, and the performers are in fine form for the show and it was a treat to see what the show would be like before most of America got a chance to go to the concert (most of the US did not get to see the tour until December 1986 through March 1987.)

The program was later edited slightly (to reduce some awkward delays between songs only) and released by MCA on video in 1987 under the title THE NIGHTMARE RETURNS. Surprisingly, a shot of a teenage girl exposing herself (at the beginning of **Under My Wheels**) remained in the video when it was re-edited and released on tape (since the MTV airing was live, it was understandable that it would appear there, but one would have thought it would have been edited out of subsequent showings.)

Front and Back cover for the UK release of THE NIGHTMARE RETURNS concert.

Left: Original video box for the US release of THE NIGHTMARE RETURNS concert.

Missing from the official videotape is a brief epilogue that was broadcast right after the initial MTV airing. The film shows a janitor with his back to the camera cleaning up the concert stage (supposedly after the show.) As he cleans and mumbles to himself, he comes across a trash can that contains the CONSTRICTOR album. Looking at the album, he mutters about how sick Alice is, following which, he turns to face the camera, revealing himself to be Alice in full makeup. While staring at the camera he says, "And so are you!" The camera then fades to black.

The movie provides a chance for fans spot a few things that may have been missed in later concerts. The snake used in the program was returned to its owner only a few weeks into the tour, and replaced with a smaller snake because the original was so huge that Alice had difficulty handling it the way he wanted to during the show (you can see Alice being unable to do much with the snake but hold it in one position during the program.) The program is also a chance to see the "guest" appearances by Jason from the FRIDAY THE 13TH film in a couple of quick appearances (including in the ending epilogue for the MTV broadcast.) The cameraman who is killed during the show is portrayed (for this one appearance only) by Alice's personal assistant Brian "Renfield" Nelson (the role was normally played by

Tracey Dea as a photographer.) And Alice does a great left handed catch of a straitjacket from the crowd during Go to Hell.

Film Title: **Teenage Frankenstein**
Film Type: Music video.
Created: Filmed October 31, 1986 at Joe Louis Arena, Detroit, MI and shown on MTV.
Music: Teenage Frankenstein

This clip is from THE NIGHTMARE RETURNS television special that aired on MTV.

Film Title: **THE TUBE**
Film Type: Interview.
Created: Filmed June 1987 and broadcast on UK television on June 23, 1987.

Alice appeared to discuss his career and his return to the stage.

Film Title: **PRINCE OF DARKNESS**
Film Type: Movie.
Created: Filmed Summer 1987 and released October 23, 1987 by Paramount. Directed by John Carpenter. Written by John Carpenter. Released on video and laser disc 1988. Released on DVD April 29, 1998.
Music: Prince of Darkness

Alice appears in this dark science fiction tinged horror film as a "Zombie Tramp" who, at one point, runs in a victim with a broken bicycle much like how Alice killed the cameraman with the microphone stand during THE NIGHTMARE RETURNS tour. It's a brief role, but it's obviously Alice. The lead guitarist for Alice at the time, Kane Roberts, supposedly also appears in the film, but under so much makeup that he's hard to distinguish from the other actors.

Alice's role, which was as a homeless person who is taken over by an evil presence, was part of a controversy at the time of the film's release. As the evil presence could take over the will of animals and individuals like Alice's character, the film made the disturbing connection that homeless people were no better than animals on the streets. Although that was not the intention of the film maker, there were some pickets outside of theaters because of this line of thought.

The Alice-penned song **Prince of Darkness** can be heard in the film. It's also on the RAISE YOUR FIST AND YELL album.

Right: Video box for the original US release of PRINCE OF DARKNESS.

Film Title: **Freedom**
Film Type: Music video.
Created: Filmed October 1987 and shown on television music programs and channels like MTV.
Music: Freedom

Filmed during dress rehearsals at Birmingham NEC for the RAISE YOUR FIST AND YELL tour, the video is an "in concert" film of the band performing the song. There is no audience present, however.

Film Title: **PEPSI POWER HOUR**
Film Type: Interview.
Created: Filmed February 1988 and broadcast on Much Music, Canada on February 2, 1988.

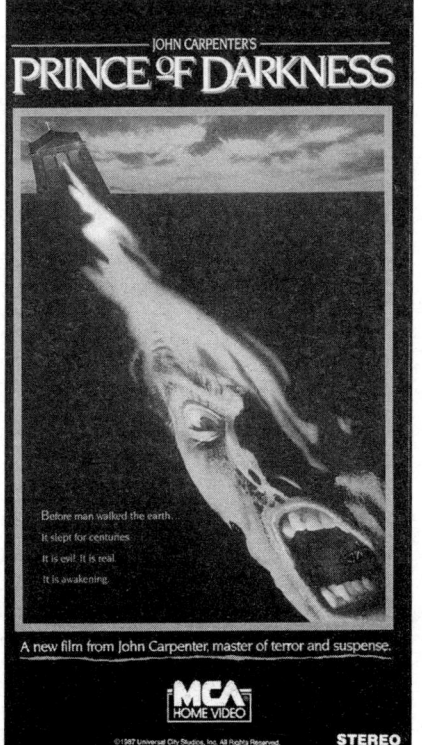

Much like MTV (only a bit looser), Much Music is a music cable TV channel in Canada. Alice and Kane Roberts are interviewed while touring in Canada with the RAISE YOUR FIST AND YELL tour.

Film Title: **I Got a Line on You**
Film Type: Music video.
Created: Filmed 1988 and shown on television music programs and channels like MTV.
Music: I Got a Line on You

This music video was filmed for the IRON EAGLE II movie soundtrack album. Alice appears with a few of the musicians from the album performing the song over footage from the film.

Film Title: **DECLINE OF WESTERN CIVILIZATION PART II: THE METAL YEARS**
Film Type: Documentary.
Created: Filmed 1988 in various locations. Released 1988 by New Line Cinema. Released on video 1990 by RCA / Columbia Video.

Alice is interviewed briefly during this documentary about heavy metal music in the 1980's. Also interviewed were Gene Simmons and Paul Stanley of KISS, Ozzy Osbourne, members of Megadeth, Lemmy of Motorhead, and several others. Alice also contributed vocals to a remake of Under My Wheels for the soundtrack (see Chapter 6 for details about the soundtrack album.)

Film Title: **INTERNATIONAL ROCK AWARDS**
Film Type: Awards ceremony.
Created: Filmed May 31, 1989 and shown on European television.

Alice presented an award during the program.

Film Title: **Poison**
Film Type: Music video.
Created: Filmed Summer 1989 and shown on television music programs and channels like MTV.
Music: Poison

This was the first music video from the TRASH album, for the song that was Alice's biggest hit in years. There are three known versions of the video in circulation: one with a little bit of female nudity and some bondage references; another featuring no nudity and just a hint of a bondage reference; and a final one that had neither nudity nor bondage. MTV normally ran the third one, while the second version can be found on the VIDEO TRASH videocassette that came out in 1990.

Film Title: **Bed of Nails**
Film Type: Music video.
Created: Filmed Summer 1989 and shown on television music programs and channels like MTV.
Music: Bed of Nails

This was the video for second single from the TRASH album, and was released in September 1989. Since the single wasn't released commercially in the US, the video wasn't seen in North America until it was released on the VIDEO TRASH videocassette. The video was seen in Australia and Europe, however. The hand seen in the video driving the hammer down is that of Alice's assistant Brian "Renfield" Nelson.

Film Title: **House of Fire**
Film Type: Music video.
Created: Filmed Summer 1989 and shown on television music programs and channels like MTV.
Music: House of Fire

This was the music video for the third single from the TRASH album. The single was released in November 1989, so that's when the video would have aired. It also can be found on the VIDEO TRASH videocassette.

Film Title: **ALICE COOPER VIDEO TRASH**
Film Type: Videocassette and laser disc.
Created: Filmed Summer 1989 (footage intercut between the music video was shot on December 14, 1989 at the Birmingham, England show that was filmed and released as the ALICE COOPER TRASHES THE WORLD videocassette.) Produced by Lisa Holingshead for The Foundry. Directed by Nigel

Dick. Released on videocassette (catalog number 2VS-49033) and laser disc (ID7292CB) early 1990 by CMV Enterprises and Sony Music Video.
Music: Poison / House of Fire / Bed of Nails

The videocassette contains all three music videos for the TRASH album, with some incidental footage shot of the TRASH stage in between them. The laser disc edition of this video came in an 8" format.

Film Title: **Only My Heart Talkin'**
Film Type: Music video.
Created: Filmed December 1989 and shown on television music programs and channels like MTV.
Music: Only My Heart Talkin'

Filmed after the VIDEO TRASH videocassette was in post-production, this was the final music video done for the TRASH album.

The video (filmed partly in color, and partly black and white, a style very much in vogue at the time) shows Alice and the band rehearsing the song, then flashing to a woman packing her things and eventually showing up at the rehearsal hall to return her backstage pass. At the end of the video, Alice realizes his mistake and goes after the woman, just in time to see her taking off in a car with a license plate reading "TYLER." After the car takes off, Alice returns to the backstage door only to find a woman waiting there for him to start all over again. Steven Tyler of Aerosmith sang backing vocals on this track, so it's an amusing touch to have Alice's girlfriend taking off in what is believed to be Tyler's car. The video did not get much air play on MTV.

Film Title: **ALICE COOPER TRASHES THE WORLD**
Film Type: Concert movie.
Created: Filmed December 14, 1989 at the National Exhibition Center, Birmingham, England. Released on video (19V-49042) and laser disc (catalog number unknown) Spring 1990. Produced by Linda Hollingshead for The Foundry. Directed by Nigel Dick.
Performers: Alice Cooper (vocals), Al Pitrelli (guitar), Pete Friesen (guitar), Jonathon Mover (drums), Tommy "T-Bone" Carradonna (bass), Derek Sherinian (keyboards) and Devon Meade (backing vocals.)
Music: Hello Hooray (part only, on tape) / Trash / Billion Dollar Babies / I'm Eighteen / I'm Your Gun / Desperado / House of Fire / No More Mr. Nice Guy / This Maniac's in Love With You / Steven / Welcome to My Nightmare / Ballad of Dwight Fry / Gutter Cat Vs. the Jets / Only Women Bleed / I Love the Dead / Poison / Muscle of Love / Spark in the Dark / Bed of Nails / School's Out / Under My Wheels

This is a complete concert from the TRASHES THE WORLD tour (the final night of the UK portion of the tour.) The tour had begun only three weeks before (with only a few shows during those three weeks) so the energy level is very high. Although not as "in your face" as THE NIGHTMARE RETURNS video is, it's excellent documentation for the TRASH tour and Alice's show at this point in time.

Film Title: **HARD -N- HEAVY Volume 1**
Film Type: Videocassette (interviews, music videos and cartoons.)
Created: Released on video cassette 1989 by MPI Home Entertainment. A production of Directors International Video. Catalog number MVP 9911833.

This was the first volume in a regular series of videos released through MPI that covered heavy metal bands.

ALICE COOPER TRASHES THE WORLD video cassette.

The videos were made up of a grab-bag of interviews, music videos and cartoons. A review of Alice in movies appears on this cassette, and a picture of Alice in a straitjacket singing appeared on the back of the video box.

Film Title: **HARD -N- HEAVY Volume 3**
Film Type: Videocassette (interviews, music videos and cartoons.)
Created: Released on video cassette 1989 by MPI Home Entertainment (MP1678.) A production of Directors International Video.

In this volume of the series, Alice appears in the "Trick Or Treat" segment. The idea behind it was to have a performer go through a bag and discuss the objects found within. It's pretty entertaining to hear Alice speak about some of the early albums and even pull out the pirated Spider Vs. The Nazz single.

Film Title: **AMERICAN MUSIC AWARDS**
Film Type: Awards presentation (performance appearance.)
Created: Broadcast live and shown on the ABC television network on January 22, 1990.
Music: **House of Fire**

Alice appeared with his band to perform **House of Fire**.

Film Title: **METAL HEAD VIDEO MAGAZINE**
Film Type: Videocassette (interview appearance.)
Created: Released 1990 by Goodtimes Home Video (8127.)

A variation of the HARD-N-HEAVY video cassettes, this production of METAL HEAD featured a short segment on the SHOCKER premiere party, and a brief interview with Alice at the party. Alice is also seen on stage throwing the switch on Dave Mustaine's electric chair.

Film Title: **HARD -N- HEAVY Volume 7**
Film Type: Videocassette (interview appearance.)
Created: Released 1990 by MPI Home Entertainment. A production of Directors International Video.

Alice appears in two segments. The first is an interview for the SHOCKER premiere party, and the second, an interview about **Only My Heart Talking**.

Film Title: **TODAY SHOW**
Film Type: Interview.
Created: Broadcast live on April 9, 1990 on the NBC television network.

Alice is interviewed about the TRASH album.

HARD-N-HEAVY Volume 7. Although Alice appeared on many volumes in this series, Volume 7 is one of the few with Alice's photo on the front cover.

Part 5 — Books and Comics 1984 - 1990

Although Alice had faced a ton of publicity by the end of the 1980's thanks to the success of all of his albums from CONSTRICTOR through TRASH, there wasn't much new in the way of printed material about Alice except in magazine and newspaper articles.

Alice did make it a priority to do interviews throughout the period, and was always willing to promote the new albums whenever an opportunity arose. However, besides being mentioned in books about rock music overall, there just wasn't much material coming out in book form about Alice. There was, however, at least one unauthorized comic that came out during this period.

Book Title: **ROCK N' ROLL COMICS #18**
Published: October 1990 by Revolutionary Comics.
Author: Writer: Spike Steffenhagen. Artists: Steven Goupil, Scott Jackson (front cover) and R. Garcia (back cover.)
Content: Story Title: "Alice Cooper." A 23 page unauthorized biography of Alice from his school days through to the release of TRASH.

Rock N' Roll Comics was a short lived comic series that attempted to tell unauthorized biographies, in comic book form, of many different rock artists. It was also known, as was its parent company, as an outfit that was constantly facing problems with artists who didn't want to be written about in this manner (including The New Kids on The Block, who went to court over the issue devoted to them.) For a time, these comics were going for higher prices than the cover prices, but the market has since dropped out (except for a few early issues) and most can now be found for for between 50 cents and $1 apiece.

The comic (as can be expected with only 23 pages to work with) is basically a Cliff notes' view of Alice's career. While it covers some of the highlights of Alice's career, there is very little there that fans wouldn't already know. The writing is all right, and the artwork could use a little more work, but at least it captures the look of the band members from time to time.

The Alice bio was later reissued in a larger format along with a bio about AC / DC. Mainly for the collectors who need to have everything, and certainly not for collectors looking only for official merchandise.

ROCK N' ROLL comic #18.

Book Title: **ROCK N' ROLL COMICS #7**
Published: April 1991 by Revolutionary Comics.
Author: Writer: Spike Steffenhagen. Artist: Steven Goupil.
Content: Story Title: "Alice Cooper." A 23 page unauthorized biography of Alice from his school days through to the release of TRASH.

This was the magazine-sized reprint of the unauthorized Alice Cooper biography from ROCK N' ROLL COMICS #18. The first part of the magazine contains a reprint of an unauthorized AC / DC biography.

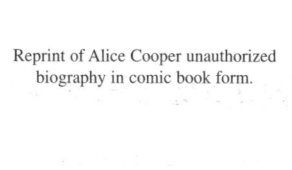

Reprint of Alice Cooper unauthorized biography in comic book form.

~~~ Chapter 5: 1991 - 1998 ~~~
Part 1 — "It's Me"

No doubt about it, TRASH had done extremely well for Alice, and for his new label, Epic. The album reached the Top 20 both in the US and in parts of Europe, and the single Poison reached the Top 10. The tour for the album went extremely well during 1989-1990, and sales of both VIDEO TRASH and ALICE COOPER TRASHES THE WORLD were nothing to sneeze at either. In fact, the only downside of the entire success of TRASH was that fans had to wait two years before getting a new album from Alice. Although the TRASH tour officially ended in August 1990, Alice made a couple more stops in October, making the end of the tour really at October 31, 1990 — a year to the day after the tour began. After that, Alice took some time off before working on his follow up album, released in July 1991, HEY STOOPID.

HEY STOOPID did well in the charts — perhaps not quite as well as TRASH in the US (reaching only No. 47), but certainly doing so in other parts of the world (in the UK, HEY STOOPID reached No. 6, while in Australia it reached No. 18) — sometimes rising within reach of TRASH's highest ranking. What may have killed the album in the long run, however, was the dismal results from a tour that Alice became apart of at the time of HEY STOOPID's release, OPERATION ROCK N' ROLL. This tour, an attempt to create a traveling hard rock festival, featured Alice co-headlining with Judas Priest. Along for the ride as opening bands were the likes of Motorhead, Metal Church and Dangerous Toys. The tour finished after only two months, leaving Alice with a hiatus of five weeks before his European tour was to start at the end of September 1991. Alice filled this time with a promotional tour for the album that included a series of mini-concerts around the East Coast of the US and Canada. After the European portion of the tour, there was then be a break of nearly four years before Alice would appear in front of an audience to perform a full show again, and close to five years before he'd do a full-fledged tour again.

Because of the tour, and the drop in the charts, people tended to see Alice's output in the 1990's as resulting in poor sales. Which is a shame since HEY STOOPID and THE LAST TEMPTATION did even better in the charts than the MCA albums CONSTRICTOR and RAISE YOUR FIST AND YELL. Looking at the numbers, Alice was clearly not only putting out music that fans enjoyed, but was doing a satisfactory job in the charts as well. Yet, the assumption is there, and is, unfortunately, a hard one to eradicate. More important, it began to effect how the record labels released Alice's material.

Alice next stepped into the studio in early 1993 to begin work on a concept album that would be released in July 1994 as THE LAST TEMPTATION. As the album was being prepared, an executive at Epic, Bob Pfeifer, left Epic to join the Disney-associated label Hollywood Records. Pfeifer had become a friend of Alice's, had been supportive of his work at Epic, was the executive producer on both TRASH and HEY STOOPID (with a "special thanks" on THE LAST TEMPTATION), and had also co-written seven tracks on the HEY STOOPID album. Wanting to stay close to a record executive who not only understood his work, but also made the effort to allow that work to be issued the way that Alice wanted, Alice requested that Epic release him from his contract so that he could join Pfeifer at Hollywood. Epic agreed to do so. This led to a problem in supporting the final Epic album just then being released. With Alice leaving the company to go elsewhere, Epic wasn't likely to help finance a concert tour to promote the album. They did, however, promote the album with two music videos and a small promotion tour in Europe and elsewhere. Still, without a major concert tour, it was a couple of years before most fans got to see how some of the new songs worked on stage.

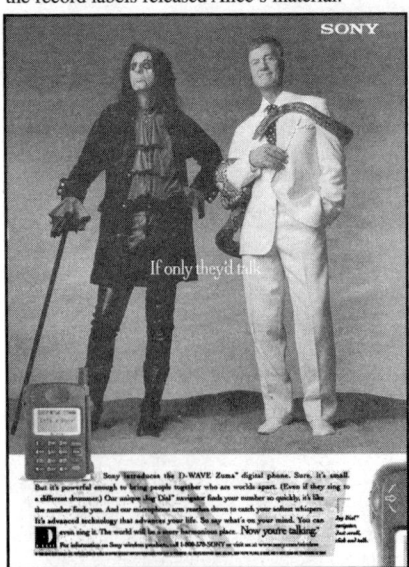

Ad for Sony featuring the pairing of Alice Cooper with Pat Boone.

Alice did a very short South American tour in 1995, which spurred him on to revisiting the touring circuit in the US in 1996 as part of an Alice Cooper / Scorpions double bill. The summer tour in 1996 went over so well, along with an annual visit to the Detroit, Michigan area at New Year's, that Alice decided to divide his year up into a summer tour and the New Year's trip in 1996, 1997 and 1998 as well.

Upon arriving at the new label, Alice recorded a live album on June 2, 1996 that became A FISTFUL OF ALICE. This album was to have been released at the end of 1996 on Hollywood Records (and, in fact, a promo copy of the album does exist on Hollywood Records), but was delayed after Bob Pfeifer decided to leave Hollywood. The album was eventually released by Guardian Records, a subsidiary of EMI (who also released some CD reissues from the Cooper catalog in other parts of the world), in July 1997.

Alice also became more involved in television and film work. Although he'd never been shy about the idea of moving onto the silver screen, it really wasn't until the 1990's that Alice began doing more film work than just an occasional guest appearance. He also took part in a special, two week long radio program in the summer of 1995 entitled ALICE'S ATTIC, which aired on the satellite hard rock station Z-Rock. The show, co-hosted by Lon Friend, was done four hours a day during the work week and featured Alice interviewing other performers and playing music, as well as giving away a ton of autographed material from himself and other performers.

After the large volume of work released in the 1970's and 80's, it's been a frustration for Alice Cooper fans that only three official albums have been released so far in the 1990's (only two of which were new studio albums.) One major reason for delays in releasing new material is the anticipated boxed set from Warner Brothers that was first announced to be released for Christmas 1993. Since then, the Warner set has been continually delayed, normally for four to six months later after each announced release date has come and gone. A boxed set for a long successful artist is certainly not unusual, and plenty of other artist's boxed sets, both before and since, have proven to be successful not only for the music, but also as historical documents.

Warner's problems with releasing the boxed set stem from having had other priorities within the company. This holds true for other boxed sets as well as Alice's set. Warner has been going through personnel changes since 1993, and boxed sets have basically been put on the back burner until the storm has settled a bit. Fans may have understood the situation, but have clearly been frustrated by the continuing cycle of announcements and delays. In fact, by mid-1998, some fans were referring to the boxed set as something that would never appear at all. It's also evident that delays in release of THE LAST TEMPTATION and A FISTFUL OF ALICE resulted from waiting for Warner to release the boxed set. After all, why compete with yourself? So, with each announced setback of the boxed set, the release of Alice's new material was pushed back.

Things changed in 1998 when Warner bought the retrospective rock label, Rhino. Rhino had been for years presenting albums and artists that were well remembered, but were being overlooked by the major labels. Rhino often reissued albums for special markets (as with the ALICE COOPER LIVE AT THE WHISKY A GO GO album from 1992), and were well known for their boxed sets. Moreover, they were quite well known for taking an historical look at rock music and treating it with more than just a nod at the dollar sign.

With Rhino under Warner's wing, the Alice Cooper boxed set was now in the hands of people who could make it happen. With release now promised for early 1999, the boxed set has grown from three CDs (as originally announced) to four, with an 80 page booklet discussing the history of Alice and his recordings included. Also included will be several tracks not released on albums, along with demos from over the years, which will no doubt make it a favorite among fans.

Some fans seem to be upset that Alice's career has settled into a series of tours and a retrospective boxed set. They not only want new material from Alice Cooper, but they want to prove to the world that Alice is still a deciding force in music. Some fans seem to look at such bands as Marilyn Manson and feel that Alice's role in the history of music is being threatened in some way (because of the new artists that take bits and pieces of Alice's persona and rework it in their own fashion.) The thing is, there's really nothing to worry about. If Alice never sang another line or played another note and retired forever today, his role in the history of rock music would be absolutely secure. Alice has been in rock music for more than 30 years, and during that time has produced a number of songs that still get regular air play on radio stations and are considered classics (I'm Eighteen, School's Out, Welcome to My Nightmare, etc.) It was Alice Cooper who first took theatrical rock music into the homes and minds of Middle-America, so that now the Marilyn Manson's of the world seem quite commonplace. More importantly, Alice has always stretched to reach for new goals in his art, and has normally achieved them. Unlike some of the performers trying to take his place, Alice's career shows the growth and development which truly indicates a performer interested in developing his craft instead of just "freaking out" the public.

Good news for fans — the announced boxed set will be merely the start of what can only be a good year for Alice. With the boxed set, a possible re-mastering of the Cooper catalog, and a new album on the agenda, no doubt Alice will once again be a name on everyone's lips.

An important aspect of Alice's development was his decision to talk about life's choices in his work, and to express ideas outside the typical topics of rock music. When THE LAST TEMPTATION was released in 1994, at least one reviewer tore the album apart because Alice dared to talk about morality — why was he not writing songs about carving people up? The reviewer just couldn't handle the idea of serious concepts being discussed on Alice's new album. The reviewer was offended. The final irony was that, even at this late stage of the game, Alice could still shock and offend. He got people to think, and that's all he ever wanted.

Part 2 — Recordings - 1991 in into the future

As described in Part 1, the 1990's saw only three official albums being released before 1999, two of which were under the Epic label, HEY STOOPID and THE LAST TEMPTATION, and the final one, the live A FISTFUL OF ALICE, originally part of a contract with Hollywood Records, released on an EMI subsidiary label, Guardian.

HEY STOOPID was the last album released in the US on vinyl. After this, only cassettes and compact discs were made available to the general public. US collectors could at least find vinyl copies of THE LAST TEMPTATION as an import from foreign markets, but the talked about vinyl edition of A FISTFUL OF ALICE never appeared.

Singles also became a relic in the US after the HEY STOOPID album, with only a handful of promotional CD singles released for tracks from THE LAST TEMPTATION album. The UK, however, continued doing at least two to four variations of each single for both HEY STOOPID and THE LAST TEMPTATION. Other parts of the world saw singles from both albums. No singles from A FISTFUL OF ALICE were released anywhere in the world.

1999 looks to be a big year for new Alice material hitting the record store shelves with the release of THE LIFE AND CRIMES OF ALICE COOPER boxed set, talk of a new studio album from Alice later in the year, and work with composer Alan Menken (of the Disney film BEAUTY AND THE BEAST and the musical version of LITTLE SHOP OF HORRORS) on a musical based on the seven deadly sins. It's looking like Alice's discography will never really end.

Album Title: **HEY STOOPID**
Recorded: January - February 1991 at Bearsville Studios, New York, NY and The Complex, Los Angeles, CA.
Production: Produced by Peter Collins for Jill Music, Ltd. Executive producer was Bob Pfeifer. Recorded by Paul Northfield. Mixed at A&M Studios, Los Angeles, CA. Mastered by Bob Ludwig at Masterdisc. Engineering assistants were George Cowan (Bearsville), and David Levy and Scott Jochim (The Complex.)
Personnel: Alice Cooper (vocals.) Stef Burns (guitar on all tracks except Dirty Dreams.) Hugh McDonald (bass on all tracks except Feed My Frankenstein.) Mickey Curry (drums.) John Webster (keyboards on all tracks except Dangerous Tonight, Might As Well Be on Mars, Hurricane Years and Dirty Dreams; B3 Organ on Dangerous Tonight.) Robert Bailey (keyboards on Love's a Loaded Gun, Dangerous Tonight, Might As Well Be on Mars, Feed My Frankenstein, Hurricane Years, Die for You and Wind-Up Toy.)
Additional performers: Slash (guitars on Hey Stoopid.) Joe Satriani (guitars on Hey Stoopid, Burning Our Bed, Feed My Frankenstein, Little by Little and Wind-Up Toy; backing vocals on Hey Stoopid.) Steve Vai (guitar on Feed My Frankenstein.) Vinnie Moore (guitar on Hurricane Years and Dirty Dreams.) Mick Mars (guitar on Die for You.) Nikki Sixx (bass on Feed My Frankenstein.) Steve Droes (Synclavier on Hey Stoopid and Die for You.) Jai Winding (keyboards on Might As Well Be on Mars.) Chris Boardman (string arrangement on Might As Well Be on Mars.)
Additional backing vocals: Ozzy Osbourne (Hey Stoopid) and Zachary Nevel (Hey Stoopid.) The East Coast Gang was Jack Ponti, Vic Pepe, Tony Palmucci, Scott Bender, Corky McClennan, Lance Bulen, Kelly Keeling and were arranged by Jack Ponti and Vic Pepe. The West Coast Gang

Song List: was Terry Wood, Shaun Murphy, Sherwood Ball, Cali, Garry Falcone, Mike Finnigan, Stan Bush and arranged by David Campbell, with Joey Carbone and David Campbell arranging Burning Our Bed. The British Gang was Ian Richardson, Nick Coler and Mick Wilson.

Song List: Hey Stoopid (Cooper, Jack Ponti, Vic Pepe and Bob Pfeifer) / Love's a Loaded Gun (Cooper, Ponti and Pepe) / Snakebite (Cooper, Ponti, Pepe, Pfeifer, Lance Bulen and Kelly Keeling) / Burning Our Bed (Cooper, Al Pitrelli, Pfeifer, and Steve West) / Dangerous Tonight (Cooper and Desmond Child) / Might As Well Be on Mars (Cooper, Dick Wagner and Child) / Feed My Frankenstein (Cooper, Zodiac Mindwarp, Nick Coler and Ian Richardson) / Hurricane Years (Cooper, Ponti, Pepe and Pfeifer) / Little by Little (Cooper, Ponti, Pepe and Pfeifer) / Die for You (Cooper, Nikki Sixx, Mick Mars and Jim Vallance) / Dirty Dreams (Cooper, Vallance and Pfeifer) / Wind-Up Toy (Cooper, Ponti, Pepe and Pfeifer)

HEY STOOPID, the first album released after the successful TRASH album and tour, saw Alice continuing with the thread of sex and love as seen on the TRASH album. With this album, Alice began a new cycle of observational lyrics that looked at life and the struggles that people have. This sort of thinking was certainly not new to Alice — you need look no further than FROM THE INSIDE to see a similar narrative thread — but the messages conveyed by the lyrics now became more directed at the listener than at a third party as previously.

Hey Stoopid was a prime example of this kind of thinking, with lyrics that go directly to the heart of the question of suicide — what is the point of doing it? It's certainly one of the more powerful statements that Alice makes, and starts the album off strongly. Hey Stoopid was the first single and music video released from the album (although it received limited air play). The only other music video done for this album was Love's a Loaded Gun, even though there were four singles released altogether (some of which, however, were not released in all countries.) Hey Stoopid, Love's a Loaded Gun, Burning Our Bed and Feed My Frankenstein were released as singles over a period of several months following the album's release.

The HEY STOOPID album.

One thing that helped the promotion of Feed My Frankenstein was it's use in the movie (and on the soundtrack album) WAYNE'S WORLD, along with Alice making a brilliant cameo appearance in the film (see Part 4 for more details.) The movie also featured footage of Alice and his band performing the song on stage in a brief clip. The song was co-written by Zodiac Mindwarp, a performer who Alice had enjoyed in concert and who was supposed to open for Alice during the CONSTRICTOR tour (THE NIGHTMARE RETURNS tour), but had to cancel due to illness.

Joining in on the writing of the tracks were two familiar names, Desmond Child and Dick Wagner, who co-wrote the track Might As Well Be on Mars with Alice, with Child also co-writing Dangerous Tonight. Five other songs were known to be written that didn't make it to the finished album, three of which were co-written by either Child or Wagner. Child co-wrote two songs with Alice, one called Take It Like a Woman, which was never recorded, and another, Your Love Is My Prison, which made it to demo form before being rejected. Wagner co-wrote with Alice, Tommy Caradonn and Derek Sherinian a song called If Fourth Street Could Talk, but this was also rejected. Additionally discussed for the album and rejected were Underground and the Jon Bon Jovi-penned song The Ballad of Alice Cooper, which had been also considered for the TRASH album.

During the recording of TRASH, Child had also worked with Alice on a demo entitled It Rained All Night, which was completed and recorded in a finished form during the HEY STOOPID sessions. This track eventually turned up as an extra track on the album when it was released in Japan, and wound up as the B-side to the Hey Stoopid single. Another song recorded during the sessions, but not included on the album, was a remake of the Jimi Hendrix classic Fire. It eventually turned up as the B-side to the Love's a Loaded Gun single.

Recording the album was another "guest-stars" extravaganza, with performers such as Steve Vai, Joe Satriani, Slash, Vinnie Moore, Mick Mars, Nikki Sixx and Ozzy Osbourne joining Alice in the studio at different times (a clip of Slash working out his part in the studio with Alice can be seen on the PRIME CUTS video documentary.) Additional backing vocals were performed by a group of people listed as either the "British," "East Coast" or "West Coast" gang. The magazine HOT METAL reported (June 1991) that Alice had hopes of getting Axl Rose, Sebastian Bach, Ozzy Osbourne and Rob Halford for the title track — considering the fact that such performers had been accused of contributing to the suicide of kids with their earlier tracks. However, only Osbourne is listed on the album as working on the track. The other backing vocalist on Hey Stoopid was Zachary Nevel, who had placed a winning bid at a charity auction on Los Angeles' rock station KNAC-FM, and was given the opportunity to meet Alice and sing backup on the song.

Of the main performers on the album, only Hugh McDonald returned from TRASH to work on HEY STOOPID. Stef Burns and Vinnie Moore joined returning touring drummer Eric Singer and returning keyboardist Derek Sherinian on the tour in support of the HEY STOOPID album.

Vinyl albums were fast disappearing from the record store shelves by this point, and HEY STOOPID was no exception — finding the vinyl edition of the disc came down to hunting from store to store. The situation was the same for the following album, THE LAST TEMPTATION.

HEY STOOPID came with artwork (or "lethal art" as the record credits state) by Mike McNeilly. The artwork depicts a skull with Alice's makeup in the center of the photo, surrounded by two mannequin arms — one with bloody money, the other with jewels. One arm has a snake, while the other has a chain, wrapped around it. Drum sticks complete the shot in the lower right-hand corner of the cover. The photo used for the artwork was actually a revised version, after the initial version (which showed hypodermic needles, pills and other forms of a slow death) was deemed to be too graphic and hardcore. The logo used on the front cover, done in the same style as the one used for TRASH, was again designed by David Coleman. The photos used on the back of the album and the inner sleeve were by Randee St. Nicholas.

The album came with a paper sleeve that had lyrics and an additional photo. The album sleeve also mentioned that TRASH was available on cassette and CD, while also promoting the VIDEO TRASH and ALICE COOPER TRASHES THE WORLD video cassettes. Most interesting for horror fans was the brief "thank you" to Cassandra Peterson in the credits. Peterson is best known as the horror movie host Elvira, and she provided one line in the track Feed My Frankenstein.

HEY STOOPID was the second Alice Cooper album released on Epic, and reached No. 47 on the US charts and No. 4 on the UK charts.

Album Title: **HEY STOOPID**
Released: Vinyl, CD and cassette released July 2, 1991 by Epic.
Catalog No.: E46786
Media: Vinyl, CD and Cassette.

Also released as a promotion CD with the catalog number ESK 4085. All other information for the promo is the same as the commercial release.

Album Title: **HEY STOOPID**
Released: July 1, 1991 by Epic, UK.
Catalog No.: 468816-1 (vinyl), 468416-2 (CD) and 468416-4 (cassette)
Media: Vinyl, CD and Cassette.

Album Title: **HEY STOOPID**
Released: July 1991 by Epic, Australia.
Catalog No.: 468416-2
Media: CD and Cassette.

HEY STOOPID reached No. 18 on the Australian charts. Same as US and UK release.

Album Title: **HEY STOOPID**
Released: July 1991 by Epic, Austrian.
Catalog No.: 468416-2
Media: CD.

Same as the US and UK release.

Album Title: **HEY STOOPID**
Released: July 1991 by Epic, Germany.
Catalog No.: 468416-2
Media: CD.

Same as the US and UK release.

Album Title: **HEY STOOPID**
Released: July 1991 by Epic, Japan.
Catalog No.: ESCA-5370
Media: CD and Cassette.

Released with the additional track It Rained All Night. A promo copy of the album was also released in Japan under the same catalog number.

Album Title: **HEY STOOPID**
Released: July 1991 by Epic, Korea.
Catalog No.: CPL-1183 / EK 46786
Media: Vinyl.

Came with a lyric sheet.

Album Title: **HEY STOOPID**
Released: October 3, 1997 by MCA, Canada.
Catalog No.: EK 46786
Media: CD.

Most recent reissue of the album in Canada.

Single Title: **Hey Stoopid** (Bebe Edit) / **Hey Stoopid**
Released: June 1991 by Epic.
Catalog No.: ESK 73845
Media: Promotional CD single.

This special digi-pak promo of the first single from the HEY STOOPID album came with the normal track and a shortened version of the song (the "Bebe Edit.")

Single Title: **Hey Stoopid / It Rained All Night**
Released: June 1991 by Epic.
Catalog No.: 34-73845
Media: 7" Vinyl.

No picture sleeve. The single came with It Rained All Night as the B-side, which was a track recorded during the HEY STOOPID sessions, but only appeared on the Japanese edition of the album. Hey Stoopid reach No. 78 on the US charts.

Single Title: **Hey Stoopid / Wind-Up Toy**
Released: June 1991 by Epic, UK.
Catalog No.: 656983-7
Media: 7" Vinyl.

Came in picture sleeve of the HEY STOOPID album cover. Hey Stoopid reached No. 21 on the UK charts.

Single Title: **Hey Stoopid / It Rained All Night / Wind-Up Toy**
Released: June 1991 by Epic, UK.
Catalog No.: 656983-6 (12"), 656983-8 (12" picture-disc), 656983-2 (CD single) and 656983-9 (CD digi-pak)

UK single for Hey Stoopid.

Media: 12" black Vinyl, 12" picture-disc and CD single.

As was typical for UK single releases, there were three variations of the Hey Stoopid single besides the 7" vinyl release. The 12" black vinyl and CD single came in a picture sleeve of the HEY STOOPID album cover, while the picture disc came in a clear plastic sleeve with the artwork from the album cover on the disc itself.

Single Title: **Hey Stoopid / It Rained All Night**
Released: June 1991 by Epic, Australia.
Catalog No.: 656983-2
Media: CD single.

Came in a picture sleeve of the album cover. Hey Stoopid reached No. 37 on the Australian charts.

Single Title: **Hey Stoopid**
Released: June 1991 by Epic, Japan.
Catalog No.: ESCA 5370
Media: Promotional CD single.

Single Title: **Hey Stoopid / Wind-Up Toy**
Released: June 1991 by Epic, Japan.
Catalog No.: ESDA-7074
Media: 3" CD single.

One of the few 3" CD singles released for Alice over the years. Such singles, while interesting, were basically a novelty that had a limited shelf life and have a limited collector's appeal. Mainly for the fan who has everything or for collectors of such novelties.

Single Title: **Hey Stoopid / Hey Stoopid**
Released: June 1991 by Epic, Mexico.
Catalog No.: 95466
Media: Promotional 12" Vinyl single.

Album Title: **OPERATION ROCK 'N' ROLL**
Released: July 1991 by Columbia / Epic.
Catalog No.: ESK 4097 (CD) and EAT 4097 (cassette)
Media: Promotional CD and Cassette.
Song List: Hey Stoopid (Side B, Track 1 on cassette)

Released as a promotional item to help support the OPERATION ROCK 'N' ROLL tour, which featured Alice and Judas Priest headlining. See Part 3 for more details about this tour.

Single Title: **Love's a Loaded Gun**
Released: September 1991 by Epic.
Catalog No.: ESK 73983
Media: Promotional CD single.

Only promotional singles were released for this track in the US. Never released commercially.

Single Title: **Love's a Loaded Gun / Fire**
Released: September 1991 by Epic, UK.
Catalog No.: 657438-7 (7" Vinyl) and
657438-4 (cassette)
Media: 7" Vinyl and Cassette.

Released in a picture sleeve of Alice. In the lower left-hand corner is an announcement about a "Meet Alice in person" contest. A competition form was enclosed with the single for fans to use in taking part in the contest. Fire is Alice's remake of the Jimi Hendrix classic. Alice recorded it while working on the HEY

UK single for Love's a Loaded Gun.

STOOPID album, but it's not included on the album. Love's a Loaded Gun reached No. 38 on the UK charts.

Single Title: **Love's a Loaded Gun /
I'm Eighteen** (live) / **Fire**
Released: September 1991 by Epic, UK.
Catalog No.: 657438-8 (12" picture-disc) and
657438-9 (CD single)
Media: 12" picture-disc and CD single.

The 12" picture disc states that it's a "1991 Souvenir Tour Picture Disc" and has tour dates listed on the back of the cardboard insert that came with the plastic sleeve. Alice's picture appears on the front of the disc, with lyrics to Love's a Loaded Gun on the back. The CD single came in a gun shaped sleeve. I'm Eighteen was recorded at the first show of the OPERATION ROCK 'N' ROLL tour (July 12, 1991 at the Irving Meadow Amphitheater, Los Angeles, CA) which was also filmed for the ABC TV series IN CONCERT.

UK picture disc 12" single for Love's a Loaded Gun.

Single Title: **Love's a Loaded Gun / Fire**
Released: September 1991 by Epic, Australia.
Catalog No.: 657438-5
Media: CD single.

Came with a standard picture sleeve. The single was sealed and came with a patch.

Single Title: **Love's a Loaded Gun / Fire**
Released: September 1991 by Epic, German.
Catalog No.: 657438-7
Media: 7" Vinyl.

Released in a picture sleeve of Alice. In the lower left-hand corner is an announcement about a "Meet Alice in person" contest. A competition form was enclosed with the single for fans to use in taking part in the contest.

Single Title: **Love's a Loaded Gun / I'm Eighteen** (live) / **Fire**
Released: September 1991 by Epic, German.
Catalog No.: 657438-2
Media: CD single.

I'm Eighteen was recorded at the first show of the OPERATION ROCK 'N' ROLL tour (July 12, 1991 at the Irving Meadow Amphitheater, Los Angeles, CA) which was also filmed for the ABC TV series IN CONCERT.

Single Title: **Love's a Loaded Gun / Fire**
Released: September 1991 by Epic, Holland.
Catalog No.: 657340-7
Media: 7" Vinyl.

Came in a standard picture sleeve of Alice.

Single Title: **Burning Our Bed / Love's a Loaded Gun** (live)
Released: January 1992 by Epic, Australia.
Catalog No.: 657698-2
Media: CD single.

Came in a picture sleeve of Alice looking into a mirror. The live track is from the September 13, 1991 Electric Ladyland performance recorded for radio broadcast. A rare occasion where a foreign single did not have an US or UK counterpart.

Single Title: **Burning Our Bed / Love's a Loaded Gun** (live)
Released: January 1992 by Epic, Holland.
Catalog No.: 657691-7
Media: 7" Vinyl.

Came in a picture sleeve of Alice looking into a mirror. The live track is from the September 13, 1991 Electric Ladyland performance recorded for radio broadcast.

Single Title: **Feed My Frankenstein / Feed My Frankenstein**
Released: February 1992 by Epic, UK.
Catalog No.: XPR 1772
Media: 12" Vinyl promotional single.

Promotional single with only the one track featured on the vinyl.

Single Title: **Feed My Frankenstein / Burning Our Bed**
Released: February 1992 by Epic, UK.
Catalog No.: 658092-7
Media: 7" Vinyl.

UK single for Feed My Frankenstein.

Released to promote both the HEY STOOPID album and the WAYNE'S WORLD movie. The single came in a picture sleeve that shows Alice in concert and from the movie. Feed My Frankenstein reached No. 38 in the UK.

Single Title: **Feed My Frankenstein / Burning Our Bed / Poison / Only My Heart Talking**
Released: February 1992 by Epic, UK.
Catalog No.: 658092-6 (12" picture disc) and 658092-2 (CD single)
Media: 12" picture disc and CD single.

A variation of the 7" single for Feed My Frankenstein that included two tracks from the POISON album. The picture disc showed Alice in concert on the front and from the movie WAYNE'S WORLD on the back. The cardboard insert with the disc also gave additional information about the movie and the HEY STOOPID and TRASH albums. The CD single came in a variation of the sleeve used for the 7" vinyl release.

Back of the UK single for Feed My Frankenstein. The photo of Alice is from the WAYNE'S WORLD movie.

Single Title: **Feed My Frankenstein / Burning Our Bed / Hey Stoopid / Bed of Nails**
Released: February 1992 by Epic, UK.
Catalog No.: 658092-9
Media: CD single digi-pak.

This was a special limited edition digi-pak (listed as a "Monster CD") for the Feed My Frankenstein single that contained two alternate tracks from the CD single and 12" picture disc released simultaneously.

Single Title: **Feed My Frankenstein / Burning Our Bed / Poison / Only My Heart Talking**
Released: July 1992 by Epic, Austria.
Catalog No.: 658092-5
Media: CD single.

Came in picture sleeve as seen with the UK version of the same material. The WAYNE'S WORLD movie was released in Austria during July 1992, which explains the delay in this single appearing commercially in that country.

Single Title: **Feed My Frankenstein / Poison / Bed of Nails**
Released: 1992 by Epic, Australia.
Catalog No.: 658155-2
Media: CD single.

A variation of the tracks used for the Feed My Frankenstein single, with both Poison and Bed of Nails coming from the TRASH album and no other tracks from the HEY STOOPID album. Came in a picture sleeve of Alice in concert (as with the other variations of this single.)

Single Title: **Unholy War**
Released: May 1994 by Epic.
Catalog No.: ESK 5995
Media: CD promotional single.

Released just before the Lost in America promotional single was issued. There was no commercial release of this track as a single in the US.

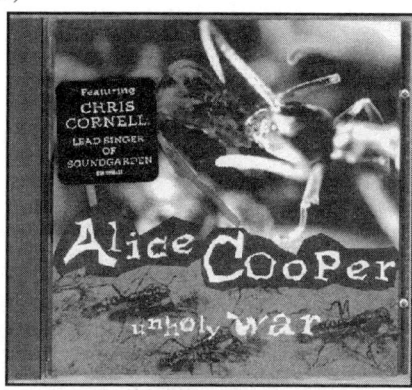

Unholy War CD single.

Single Title: **Lost in America**
Released: May 1994 by Epic.
Catalog No.: ESK 6045
Media: Promotional CD single.

Promotional single for the first single from THE LAST TEMPTATION album. While the song was released commercially in other parts of the world, only the promotional single was released in the US.

UK CD single for Lost In America.

Single Title: **Lost in America / Hey Stoopid** (live) **/ Billion Dollar Babies** (live) **/ No More Mr. Nice Guy** (live)
Released: May 16, 1994 by Epic, UK.
Catalog No.: XPR 2048 (12" promotional vinyl), 660347-6 (12" picture-disc), 660347-4 (cassette single) and 660347-2 (CD single)
Media: 12" promotional Vinyl, 12" picture-disc, Cassette and CD single.

Released for the then upcoming THE LAST TEMPTATION album, it included three tracks from the radio show that Alice recorded on September 13, 1991 for The Album Network. These tracks were also included on the LIVE AT ELECTRIC LADY bonus CD with the Japanese edition of the album, and have turned up on bootleg albums. The single came in a picture sleeve of Alice. The picture disc also came with lyrics for Lost in America. Lost in America reached No. 22 on the UK charts.

UK single for Lost In America.

Single Title:	**Lost in America / Billion Dollar Babies** (live) **/ Only Women Bleed** (live)
Released:	May 1994 by Epic, Australia.
Catalog No.:	660347-2
Media:	CD.

Came in picture sleeve of Alice in concert. **Lost in America** did not chart in Australian.

Album Title:	**THE LAST TEMPTATION**
Recorded:	January - February 1994 at various locations. Sideshow, Stolen Prayer, Unholy War and Cleansed by Fire recorded at Music Grinder, Hollywood, CA and Sony Studios, Santa Monica, CA. Produced and recorded by Andy Wallace. Segues between tracks also produced by Andy Wallace. Nothing's Free, Lost in America and Bad Place Alone recorded at Record One, Sherman Oaks, CA and Sony Studios, Santa Monica, CA. by John Agnello. Produced by Don Fleming for Instant Mayhem Productions. You're My Temptation, Lullaby and It's Me recorded by Duane Baron at Devonshire Studios, North Hollywood, CA and Music Grinder Studios, Hollywood, CA. Produced by Duane Baron and John Purdell.
Production:	As above, plus: Additional guitar track for "Lost in America" engineered by Steve Escallier at Chaton Studios, Phoenix, AZ. Mixed by Andy Wallace at Quantum Studios, Jersey City, NJ and Soundtrack Facility, New York City, NY. Mastered by Howie Weinberg at Masterdisk, New York City, NY.
Personnel:	Alice Cooper (vocals.) Stef Burns (guitar and vocals.) Greg Smith (bass and vocals.) Derek Sherinian (keyboards and vocals.) David Uosikkinen (drums.) Additional performers: Chris Cornell (vocals on Stolen Prayer and Unholy War.) Dan Wexler (guitar on Lost in America.) John Purdell (additional keyboards on You're My Temptation, Lullaby and It's Me.) Additional backing vocals by Lou Derlino, Mark Hudson, Craig Copeland and Brett Hudson.
Song List:	**Sideshow** (Cooper, Smith, Brooks, Norwood, Wexler and Saylor) / **Nothing's Free** (Cooper, Wexler and Saylor) / **Lost in America** (Cooper, Wexler and Saylor) / **Bad Place Alone** (Cooper, Wexler and Saylor) / **You're My Temptation** (Cooper, Blades and Shaw) / **Stolen Prayer** (Cornell and Cooper) / **Unholy War** (Cornell) / **Lullaby** (Cooper and Vallance) / **It's Me** (Cooper, Blades and Shaw) / **Cleansed by Fire** (Cooper, Hudson, Dudas and Saylor)

Cassette version of THE LAST TEMPTATION.

In January 1994, Alice went into the studio to begin work on an album that would be his first proper concept album since FROM THE INSIDE, and one that would reinvent the "Killer Alice" character as a more mature and sinister person than before.

With a working title of "Along Came a Spider," the concept for the album was created by Alice with the help of Neil Gaiman. Gaiman, a writer of fiction and of the study of fiction, had become quite well known by 1993 / 94 for his work on the comic book series from DC Comics called SANDMAN. Gaiman had also written a hilarious book about good and evil at the end of the world called GOOD OMEN, and seemed not only interested in the same morality issues that Alice tended to deal with, but also shared the type of warped humor that Alice would unleash in his music.

The narrative began with Alice, who wanted to work on a concept album concerning morality, and wanted to take it beyond the group of songs and into another medium. With Gaiman's help, Alice fully developed story line into a story more comprehensive than needed for just the songs themselves. Gaiman and Alice worked together for a time, then Gaiman followed through with the writing of the three part comic book series, the first of which was issued with the album when it was released (more about this aspect of the packaging below.)

In addition to Gaiman, Alice invited the help of other people to work on the album, but with a difference this time — THE LAST TEMPTATION was not to be a star-studded event like HEY STOOPID and TRASH had been. Instead, the involved people — Chris Cornell of Soundgarden, Tommy Shaw (from Styx) and Jack Blades of Damn Yankees — would help mainly with the writing of the album, and then on only a few selected tracks. As it happened, only Cornell ventured into the studio (to record some additional vocals for the two songs he had written / co-written, **Stolen Prayer** and **Unholy War**.)

Performing on the album were members of Alice's band at the time, Stef Burns, Greg Smith and Derek Sherinian. Playing drums was David Uosikkinen, probably best known as the drummer for the band The Hooters (who had a 1985 hit with **And We Dances**, among other songs.) Besides these people, only Dan Wexler (from the Phoenix band ICON, which Alice helped briefly on one album, and who would go on to play on the one studio track from A FISTFUL OF ALICE) and John Purdell were included in the recording of the album.

Included in the early stages of the writing were Bob Ezrin and Dick Wagner, who had written a track that was loosely related to the concept of the album. The song was demoed for the album, but didn't get any further. Alice also wrote a handful of songs with Tommy Shaw and Jack Blades, of which only **You're My Temptation** and **It's Me** made the final cut. Two other tracks co-written with Shaw and Blades made it to demo form before being rejected — **I Dare You** and **Invisible Strings**. Two other songs are known to have been written for the album but rejected for one reason or another — **Blood Brother** (which evolved into **Bad Place Alone**) and **Best Friend**.

The tracks for the album were written more than eight months before Alice went into the studio in January 1994. By that time, he had a clear definition of what he wanted to appear on the album and how he wanted it to sound, and even got everyone together for two weeks of rehearsals before even venturing into the studio. Most of the album was recorded at the Sony Studios in Santa Monica, California and the Music Grinder Studios in Hollywood, California, with additional work done at three other studios.

A big change that Alice made in the studio for this album was using additional producers. While this wasn't the first time (he'd done so for CONSTRICTOR), it was the first time that as many as four different producers were involved with an album. At the time of the album's release, Alice viewed the use of different producers as a way of getting the different styles that he wanted for specific tracks, reasoning that since he himself didn't fit only a single mode of music (having had hits with ballads, pop and rock), his album shouldn't be forced into a single mode either.

The album was finished in February 1994, but it was decided to wait on releasing the album until the comic book being written by Gaiman and illustrated by Mike Zulli was ready for release. When the first issue was finally ready and printed, the album was released in June in two different formats — just the album by itself, and the album with a copy of the first issue of the comic book. The album-comic combo was available as a limited edition and the comic included was printed with the same cover as on the album (the "newsstand" edition of the comic featured an alternative cover by Dave McKean.) For more information about the comic book series, see Part 5.

THE LAST TEMPTATION was the first Alice Cooper album to be released in the US on CD and cassette only, although a European edition on vinyl was available as an import in the US for a time. The cover of the album, created by Dave McKean with a photo of Alice by Dean Karr, was designed not only to showcase Alice, but also to give the cover a sense of mystery and oddity. In keeping with the "sideshow" theme that surrounds the album's concept, the cover features some Japanese slogans in the upper right-hand corner that translate as: "Honored by being viewed by the Emperor three times," "Nothing like it in the world" and (roughly) "Stupendous illusions."

The album came with a lyric sheet on the inner sleeve of the vinyl, and inside the cover on the CD and cassette. Included on the lyric sheet was some artwork from the comic book that helps to introduce the concept of the album in a more visual fashion.

Two picture discs were used for the CD version of this album, one featuring a pair of hands (which was released with the CD-only edition of the album), and the another featuring a gray and unfocused picture of Alice's face that came with the CD / comic combination edition.

Although Alice didn't do a performance tour for this album, he did do a short promotional tour, which included performances of Lost in America on TOP OF THE POPS. Two music videos were also filmed, one each for It's Me and Lost in America.

THE LAST TEMPTATION reached No. 68 on the US charts, but did very well in the UK, reaching No. 6 on the charts there. It was the last album that Alice did for Sony before moving to Hollywood Records in late 1994.

Album Title: **THE LAST TEMPTATION**
Released: July 12, 1994 by Epic.
Catalog No.: 7464-52771-2 / EK 52271 (CD) and ET 52271 (cassette)
Media: CD and Cassette.

As mentioned in the main entry, the album could be purchased at the time of its release in two formats: the album by itself, or a limited edition package of the CD or cassette with Issue #1 of THE LAST TEMPTATION comic book.

Album Title: **THE LAST TEMPTATION**
Released: June 6, 1994 by Epic, UK.
Catalog No.: 476594-1
Media: Vinyl, CD and Cassette.

Came as a single item, or packaged with Issue #1 of the comic book.

Album Title: **THE LAST TEMPTATION**
Released: July 1994 by Epic, Australia.
Catalog No.: 476594-2
Media: CD and Cassette.

Came as a single item or packaged with Issue #1 of the comic book. THE LAST TEMPTATION did not chart in Australian.

Special packaging of THE LAST TEMPTATION album with the first issue of the comic book mini-series. The audio cassette was also released in this fashion.

Album Title: **THE LAST TEMPTATION**
Released: July 1994 by Epic, Japan.
Catalog No.: ESCA 5959-5960
Media: Double CD.

The Japanese edition of THE LAST TEMPTATION was released with a bonus CD of seven tracks recorded September 13, 1991 at the Electric Lady Studios in New York City, New York. The additional CD was listed as ESCA 5960, while THE LAST TEMPTATION was catalog number ESCA 5959. The tracks included on the additional CD were Sick Things / Only Women Bleed / Wind-Up Toy / No More Mr. Nice Guy / Billion Dollar Babies / Poison and Hey Stoopid. These tracks were recorded for a radio show that aired in the US on The

Album Network at Halloween 1991. Some of the tracks also ended as B-sides for THE LAST TEMPTATION singles, while several tracks were featured on the compilation album FREEDOM FOR FRANKENSTEIN. The additional CD featured a photo cover of Alice in concert. A booklet was enclosed with the bonus CD to explain more about the recording and why it was being included with THE LAST TEMPTATION. As in other countries, there were two editions of the album, one that came with just the CDs, the other that also contained Issue #1 of the comic book.

Single Title: **It's Me**
Released: July 1994 by Epic.
Catalog No.: Unknown.
Media: CD promotional single.

Second promotional single in the US from THE LAST TEMPTATION album.

Single Title: **It's Me / School's Out** (live)
Released: July 1994 by Epic.
Catalog No.: 34T 77524
Media: Cassette single.

This was the only single released commercially in the US from THE LAST TEMPTATION. School's Out is from the September 13, 1991 Electric Lady Studio recordings.

Single Title: **It's Me**
Released: July 1994 by Epic, UK.
Catalog No.: XPCD 455
Media: CD promotional single.

Released in support of the commercial release of the second single from THE LAST TEMPTATION album.

Single Title: **It's Me / Bad Place Alone / Poison** (live) **/ Sick Things** (live)
Released: July 11, 1994 by Epic, UK.
Catalog No.: 660563-6 (12" picture disc), 660563-2 (CD single) and 660563-4 (cassette)
Media: 12" picture-disc, Cassette and CD single.

CD single released in the UK for It's Me.

Final single release in the UK from THE LAST TEMPTATION and for a new studio album from Alice. The two live tracks were (again) from the September 13, 1991 Electric Lady Studio recordings. It's Me reached No. 34 on the UK charts.

Single Title: **It's Me / Bad Place Alone**
Released: July 11, 1994 by Epic, Australia.
Catalog No.: 660563-1
Media: CD.

Final single released in Australia for a new studio album from Alice. It's Me did not chart in Australia.

Album Title: **A FISTFUL OF ALICE**
Recorded: Live tracks recorded June 2, 1996 at the Cabo Wabo Cantina, Cabo San Lucas, Mexico. Is Anyone Home? recorded October 1996 at A&M Studios and Phase Four Recording in Tempe, AZ.
Production: Live tracks produced by Thom Panunzio. Live tracks engineered by Thom Panunzio. Location recording engineered by Mark Hutchins and Brian Kingman for Effanel Music. Mixed by Phil Kaffel, with Rod Michaels, at Skip Saylor Recording. Is Anyone Home? produced by Alice Cooper. Engineered by Phil Kaffel at A&M Studios. Mixed by Chris Lord Alge at Image Recording. Mastered by Bob Ludwig at Gateway Mastering.
Personnel: Alice Cooper (vocals.) Reb Beech (guitar and vocals.) Ryan Roxie (guitar.) Paul Taylor (keyboards and guitar.) Todd Jensen (bass and vocals.) Jimmy DeGrasso (drums.) Additional performers: Slash (guitar on Lost in America, Only Women Bleed and Elected.) Rob Zombie (additional vocals on Feed My Frankenstein and Elected.) Sammy Hagar (guitar on School's Out.)

	Performers on Is Anyone Home?: Alice Cooper (vocals.) Dan Wexler (guitar.) Steve Farris (guitar.) Matt Laug (drums.) Merrit Morrison (bass.) Additional performers on Is Anyone Home?: Bennet Salvey, Peter Kent, Mario DeLeon, Darrin McCann and Erika Duke-Kirkpatrick (strings section.)
Song List:	(US edition) School's Out / I'm Eighteen / Desperado / Lost in America / Teenage Lament '74 / I Never Cry / Poison / Billion Dollar Babies / Welcome to My Nightmare / Only Women Bleed / Feed My Frankenstein / Elected / Is Anyone Home?

Fold-out cover for A FISTFUL OF ALICE.

After THE LAST TEMPTATION album, Alice requested that he be released from Epic / Sony so that he could follow Bob Pfeifer to Hollywood Records. As mentioned previously, Pfeifer was an Epic executive who enjoyed Alice's music, and was willing to let Alice work out for himself exactly what he wanted to produce for his albums. Pfeifer co-wrote seven songs on the HEY STOOPID album, surely a sign that he got along well with Alice. So, when Pfeifer left Epic, Alice thought it best to follow.

Upon arriving at Hollywood, Alice began working on other projects, including some television appearances, and even a daily four hour long radio program called ALICE'S ATTIC in 1995. Meanwhile, Alice and his fans were waiting for Warner Brothers to release the career spanning boxed set promised since 1993, now scheduled for the fall of 1994.

By 1996, Alice had agreed to a co-headlining tour with the Scorpions and was going back out on the road for what would be known as the SCHOOL'S OUT TOUR 1996. To start the tour off with a bang, Alice performed a complete show (the Scorpions tour set list was a bit shorter) in Sammy Hagar's club in Cabo San Lucas, Mexico called the Cabo Wabo Cantina. The show was filmed (portions of which were broadcast on MTV's sister channel VH1 as a half hour special), and recorded for release as a live album. The live album was to have been Alice's first release on his new label, Hollywood Records. But, it didn't quite work out that way. The album was set for a late Fall 1996 release and then pushed back. By the end of 1996, Bob Pfeifer had decided to leave Hollywood Records, and Alice soon found himself working with a company that was unsure of what to do with the live album. It continued to be pushed back by Hollywood until the EMI subsidiary, Guardian Records, requested a chance to release the album. Hollywood gladly gave them permission and the album was finally released to the public in June 1997. Several guest performers appeared with Alice at the Cabo Wabo Cantina show, and while announced guests Steve Vai, Joey Ramone and Joe Satriani couldn't make it, Slash, Rob Zombie and Sammy Hagar did.

Guardian / EMI put together a very nice package, with a picture disc CD and a booklet cover that folded out to show concert photos shot by Alex Solca and Matt Sherlock. The photo on the cover (of Alice leaning in a doorway as three kids carry the snake away) was shot by Hugh Syme and Dimo Safari. This photo is interesting not just for the cute kids, but also for graffiti scratched into the wall to the left of Alice that reads "Alice for Patron" (i.e. "Alice for President"), and a small sign to the far-left of the kids that reads "The Alice Is Here." There is also a printing mistake to the upper-left of the window, where it appears that there was a hair on the master photo when it was printed. Three additional photos by Hugh Syme and Dimo Safari appear with the album: the first being Alice walking through the streets, which can be found in the booklet; the second, a different pose of Alice leaning against the doorway that can be seen on the picture disc; and the third, Alice under a street lamp that appears on the back cover of the CD.

The album was released in three variations in different locations. The US / Canada edition featured the thirteen tracks listed above, the European edition included an alternate track and one additional track, and the Japanese edition had four additional tracks. The purpose of the differing editions wasn't to make fans buy more than copy of the album, but rather to entice people into buying the album domestically rather than as a cheaper US import. Imports were traveling freely between countries at this time and a US import of an album cost less than the domestic issue, so the record companies added additional "bonus" tracks to the domestic releases.

Is Anyone Home? was recorded after the 1996 tour was finished. The song was added as an additional incentive to check out the live album.

No singles were released from the album in most of the world, although France evidently released a single of School's Out, and there are reports of a special edition of the album that featured a second CD tray for an additional CD single that featured the one studio track. A FISTFUL OF ALICE was the last album released in the official catalog of Alice Cooper until the release of the boxed set in early 1999.

Special edition of A FISTFUL OF ALICE that included a CD single for Is Anyone Home?

Album Title: **A FISTFUL OF ALICE**
Released: June 29, 1997 by Guardian, US.
Catalog No.: 7243 8 33080 2 6
Media: CD and Cassette.

No vinyl release was made for this album in the US.

Album Title: **A FISTFUL OF ALICE**
Released: June 16, 1997 by Guardian, UK.
Catalog No.: CTMCD 331
Media: CD.

Same as the US release. A limited edition (2,000 were to be pressed) picture disc vinyl was announced but then canceled. The UK and European edition of this album included a couple of additional tracks over and above what appears on the US version — Under My Wheels and No More Mr. Nice Guy. Billion Dollar Babies, however, is missing from the UK / European edition of the album. For the most complete version of this show, your best bet is the Japanese edition of the album.

Album Title: **A FISTFUL OF ALICE**
Released: August 18, 1997 by EMI, Australia.
Catalog No.: 859657-2
Media: CD.

Released on Guardian in the US, the album was released on Guardian's parent label EMI in Australia. EMI also reissued FLUSH THE FASHION on CD in Australia.

Album Title: **A FISTFUL OF ALICE**
Released: October 8, 1997 by EMI, Japan.
Catalog No.: TOCP 50269
Media: CD.

Picture disc CD for A FISTFUL OF ALICE.

This Japanese edition of the live album included four additional tracks not issued with the US version — Under My Wheels (which appears between School's Out and I'm Eighteen), Bed of Nails, Clones (We're All) and No More Mr. Nice Guy (which appear in this order between Poison and Billion Dollar Babies.)

Album Title: **A FISTFUL OF ALICE**
Released: October 16, 1997 by EMI, Germany.
Catalog No.: ANGE 8330812
Media: CD and Cassette.

Album Title: **A FISTFUL OF ALICE**
Released: October 3, 1997 by EMI, Canada.
Catalog No.: EMI 33080 2B
Media: CD.

Part 3 — Tours 1991 - 1998

1991 saw the release of HEY STOOPID, so a tour was bound to follow. And it fit what had been the normal pattern since 1986: CONSTRICTOR was released, and THE NIGHTMARE RETURNS tour began in the Fall of 1986; RAISE YOUR FIST AND YELL came in the Fall of 1987 with the LIVE IN THE FLESH tour following soon after (sometimes playing the same arenas and theaters within days of the dates when Alice played them the previous year.) Then there was a year off, followed by the next tour in (once again) the Fall of 1989 (November to be precise) in support of the TRASH album.

The TRASH tour escaped the pattern, since it was truly a "world" tour and didn't end until the Fall of 1990. Then came a few months while Alice relaxed and worked on the HEY STOOPID album, which was finally released in July 1991. Fans sat back and wait to hear about the HEY STOOPID tour, wondering what Alice would bring to the stage this time, but something happened — OPERATION ROCK N' ROLL happened. As described in Part 1 above, the tour floundered and crashed. Alice then did a short promotional tour in the US for HEY STOOPID that included a series of mini-concerts in a variety of public places (rooftops, streets, parking lots, etc.) This was followed up by a major European tour for the album. It wasn't until 1995 that Alice performed in concert again.

A South American tour in 1995 led to Alice agreeing to appear with the Scorpions on a double bill tour in 1996. Because of the layout of the tour, Alice decided to cut back on some of the special effects in his theatrics, and also to bring back a few songs that hadn't been heard in concert for years. The summer tour of 1996 went so well that Alice continued with summer tours each year after that — the ongoing ROCK AND ROLL CARNIVAL tour, which ran in 1997 and 1998. 1996 was also the first year that Alice played a small series of concerts (normally 3-4 dates) in the Detroit, Michigan area (and the surround region) at the end of the year. These shows, the NEW YEAR'S ROTTEN EVE tour, were also done in 1997 and 1998.

As for future Alice Cooper tours, it's hard to say. No doubt, the boxed set in 1999 will be a reason to tour, but there's also talk of a new studio album, so any tour may be held up until that album is released. Either way, Alice will always have fans ready to head to the show, to see his acts of mayhem once again.

Tour Name: **OPERATION ROCK N' ROLL** (American **HEY STOOPID TOUR**)
Tour Period: July 12, 1991 through August 19, 1991. USA and Canada.
Performers: Alice Cooper (vocals), Stef Burns (guitar), Vinnie Moore (guitar), Greg Smith (bass), Eric Singer (drums), Derek Sherinian (keyboards.) Additional performers: unknown.
Opening Act: Co-headlining a festival tour with Judas Priest. Opening at several shows were Motorhead, Dangerous Toys and Metal Church.
Set List: Under My Wheels / Trash / No More Mr. Nice Guy / Billion Dollar Babies / Love's a Loaded Gun / Bed of Nails / I'm Eighteen / I Love the Dead / Devil's Food / Steven / Black Widow / Sick Things / Feed My Frankenstein / Cold Ethyl / Only Women Bleed / Poison / Snakebite / Go to Hell / School's Out / Hey Stoopid / Elected

OPERATION ROCK N' ROLL was an intriguing idea on paper, but just never jelled when it was put into action. Epic Records, looking at its roster of heavy metal and hard rock acts, had hit upon the idea of structuring a festival-type tour around a handful of their bands. To make it even more appealing to headbangers everywhere, it was decided to top the bill with two headliners. Chosen for the role were Judas Priest and Alice Cooper. The shows were opened with the likes of Motorhead, Metal Church and Dangerous Toys.

As a concept, it wasn't the worst idea in the world. Festivals had become a growing commodity for concert-goers and record labels alike, especially after the success of the Lollapalooza Festival, which was just at that time becoming popular. Traveling festivals had also been done in the past, though rarely featuring the same performers throughout the entire tour. In addition, seeing tours featuring two or even three opening metal acts for a top-of-the-line headliner wasn't at all uncommon in those lingering days of heavy metal's decline at the turn of the decade. Alice himself had done that in the late 1980's.

The problem lay with the fact that these acts never really meshed, even on the drawing board. Dangerous Toys were more from the "glam" metal persona, while both Motorhead and Metal Church were more "punk-style" metal and showed little interest in the "let's put on a show" attitude of some of the other bands on the tour. While Judas Priest was (and remain) popular, they hadn't seen any huge successes since the early- to mid-1980's with new releases. This left Alice as the anchor of the tour, and while Alice's fans were eager to see him, many were probably not willing to sit through four acts before Alice came on stage.

The tour lasted just over a month, before crashing and burning. With it came cancellations, shows where half the bands didn't perform, and a tour that did little to promote the HEY STOOPID album. The end of the tour also brought with it a five week period when Alice had no tour to promote the album (the HEY STOOPID tour was to begin in Europe at the end of September, but OPERATION ROCK N' ROLL died in mid-August.) To make up the time, and to help advertise the album, Alice did a promotional tour called the NIGHTMARE ON YOUR STREET tour (see the next entry).

While the OPERATION ROCK N' ROLL tour had problems, Alice's portions of the concerts weren't bad. In fact, they were really were the highlight of the whole program. Alice was in fine voice, and performed a variety of songs (both old and new), sometimes doing more than 20 songs in a show.

The stage set was lacking in terms of what fans got with the CONSTRICTOR and RAISE YOUR FIST AND YELL tours, but certainly consistent with the cutting back of SOME of the theatrics during the TRASH tour. The split screen made a big comeback for this tour. Used during tours in the 1970's, particularly for the LACE AND WHISKEY and the MAD HOUSE ROCK tours, the screen was a major set piece for the new show, with Alice entering the screen to be tormented by a couple of masked henchmen in a lab, and finally captured by a giant skull. The film ended with the skull emerging onto the stage so Alice could break free from it to perform the encore.

For part of the show, Alice's costume was the full black leather and metal getup that was essential to match up with the split screen film sequence. As with the TRASH tour, the "demented clown" makeup made an appearance, but normally only during the middle of the show.

From the TRASH tour, only Eric Singer and Derek Sherinian returned for the OPERATION ROCK N' ROLL tour, while Stef Burns continued with Alice following the recording of the HEY STOOPID album.

A promo CD and cassette were released by Epic in support of the tour which featured tracks from the various performers, including Alice doing **Hey Stoopid**. See Part 2 of this chapter for more info on this release. The film footage of Alice and the band performing **Feed My Frankenstein** and the backstage scenes seen in the movie WAYNE'S WORLD were shot at the end of the tour at the Universal Amphitheater, Los Angeles, California. See Part 4 for more details on the film.

June 21, 1991 - Irvine Meadows Amphitheater, Irvine, CA
   The show was recorded and **I'm Eighteen** from this show appeared as the B-side of the **Love's a Loaded Gun** single in the UK. The show was also filmed for later use on the ABC television series IN CONCERT '91.
July 13, 1991 - Shoreline Amphitheater, Mountain View, CA
   Joe Satriani made a guest appearance during this show to perform **Hey Stoopid**. The show was recorded from the audience.
July 14, 1991 - Cal Expo, Sacramento, CA
   The show was filmed from the audience.
July 16, 1991 - Red Rocks Amphitheater, Denver, CO
July 17, 1991 - Salt Palace, Salt Lake City, UT
July 18, 1991 - Five Seasons Arena, Cedar Rapids, IA
July 19, 1991 - Target Center, Minneapolis, MN
July 20, 1991 - World Amphitheater, Chicago, IL
July 21, 1991 - Starwood Amphitheater, Nashville, TN
July 23, 1991 - Lakeland Civic Center, Lakeland, FL
   The show was filmed from the audience.
July 24, 1991 - The Arena, Orlando, FL
July 25, 1991 - Lakewood Amphitheater, Atlanta, GA

July 27, 1991 - The Summit, Houston, TX
July 28, 1991 - Starplex Amphitheater, Dallas, TX
July 30, 1991 - Carrowinds, Charlotte, NC
July 31, 1991 - Walnut Creek Amphitheater, Raleigh, NC
August 2, 1991 - Starlake Amphitheater, Pittsburgh, PA
August 3, 1991 - Pine Knob, Clarkston, MI
August 4, 1991 - Val Du Lakes, Mears, MI
August 6, 1991 - Deer Creek Amphitheater, Indianapolis, IN
August 7, 1991 - Richfield Coliseum, Cleveland, OH
August 8, 1991 - Cayaga County Fairground, Syracuse, NY
   The show was filmed from the audience.
August 9, 1991 - Nassau Coliseum, Uniondale, NY
   The show was filmed from the audience.
August 10, 1991 - Spectrum, Philadelphia, PA
   The show was filmed from the audience — incomplete.
August 11, 1991 - Lake Compounce, Bristol, CT
   Canceled.
August 13, 1991 - Sea Pac, Portland, ME
August 14, 1991 - Great Woods, Mansfield, MA
August 15, 1991 - Capitol Center, Largo, MD
August 16, 1991 - Raceway, Middleton, NY
   The show was filmed from the audience.
August 17, 1991 - The Forum, Montreal, Canada
   The show was filmed from the audience.
August 19, 1991 - Maple Leaf Gardens, Toronto, Canada
   The show was filmed from the audience.

Tour Name: **NIGHTMARE ON YOUR STREET** (American **HEY STOOPID** mini-concert tour)
Tour Period: September 1991 along the East Coast of the US and Toronto, Canada.
Performers: Alice Cooper (vocals), Stef Burns (guitar), Pete Friesen (guitar), Greg Smith (bass), Eric Singer (drums), Derek Sherinian (keyboards.) Additional performers: no additional performers.
Opening Act: No opening acts.
Set List: The set list varied with each mini-concert, but was usually four to six songs. Songs normally performed (not in order) were I'm Eighteen / No More Mr. Nice Guy / School's Out / Hey Stoopid / Love's a Loaded Gun / Billion Dollar Babies. Under My Wheels and Elected were also performed occasionally.

After the demise of the dismal OPERATION ROCK N' ROLL tour in mid-August 1991, there was little Alice could do until the start of the European portion of the HEY STOOPID tour set to begin at the end of September. Not wanting to just sit around with a full band for close to six weeks — but knowing that additional tour dates couldn't be scheduled quickly — Alice instead decided to promote the new album by doing a series of "mini-concerts" along the East Coast. All of these concerts had one thing in common — previously, all concerts had been performed in a standard hall or arena, but these "mini-concerts" were held out in the open, and usually in a busy part of town. For example, Alice's appearance in Time Square occurred during the week and in midday, causing a commotion with workers in their suits and ties from around the Broadway area coming out to see Alice perform. The shows were normally only four to six songs long and sometimes included Alice doing an autograph session.

By this time, Vinnie Moore had left the band and was replaced by Pete Friesen, who had played with Alice on the TRASH tour. Friesen stayed with the band for the European HEY STOOPID tour.

September 2, 1991 - Miami Beach, FL
   Labor Day concert for radio station WSHE.
September 3, 1991 - Sound Warehouse rooftop, St. Louis, MO
September 5, 1991 - Ed Deberics parking lot, Chicago, IL
September 6, 1991 - Sound Warehouse parking lot, Sterling Heights, MI
   The show was filmed from the audience.
September 10, 1991 - County Courts Building steps, Towson, MD
   The show was filmed by two different fans from the audience. Both versions have circulated in fandom.
September 11, 1991 - Jude Lewis Quadrangle, Independence Mall, Philadelphia, PA
   The show was filmed from the audience.

September 12, 1991 - WBCN rooftop, Boston, MA
September 13, 1991 - Times Square, New York NY
  Alice recorded a performance the same day at Electric Ladyland Studio for radio broadcast on October 31, 1991. Songs from that performance later turned up on the special Japanese edition of THE LAST TEMPTATION and on bootlegs. Individual tracks were also used as B-sides for some later Alice singles and Sick Things was included on the FREEDOM FOR FRANKENSTEIN compilation album in 1998.
September 1991 - HMV rooftop, Toronto, Ontario

UK ad for the HEY STOOPID tour.

Tour Name: **HEY STOOPID TOUR** (European tour for the HEY STOOPID album.)
Tour Period: From September 28, 1991 through November 8, 1991 in the UK, France, Germany, Norway, Denmark, Finland and Sweden.
Performers: Alice Cooper (vocals), Stef Burns (guitar), Pete Friesen (guitar), Greg Smith (bass), Eric Singer (drums), Derek Sherinian (keyboards.) Jimmy DeGrasso would replace Eric Singer on drums near the end of the tour. No additional performers.
Opening Act: Wolfsbane and Almighty.
Set List: Under My Wheels / Trash / No More Mr. Nice Guy / Billion Dollar Babies / Love's a Loaded Gun / Bed of Nails / Wind-Up Toy / I'm Eighteen / I Love the Dead / Devil's Food / Steven / Black Widow / Sick Things / Feed My Frankenstein / Cold Ethyl / Only Women Bleed / Poison / Snakebite / Go to Hell / School's Out / Hey Stoopid / Elected

The European tour for the HEY STOOPID album was of a more consistent nature than the American tour that preceded it. The show itself varied little from what had been done for the OPERATION ROCK N' ROLL tour, and the set list remained the same except that **He's Back** replaced **Snakebite** when Alice played in Sweden. **Dirty Dreams** and **Ballad of Dwight Fry** were also performed occasionally during the European tour.

Nearing the end of the tour, the rock band KISS asked Eric Singer to join them as a permanent member of the band. Replacing Eric for the short remainder of the tour was Jimmy DeGrasso, who remained with Alice through all of his subsequent tours until June 1998 (when he was replaced, ironically enough, by Eric Singer.)

After the HEY STOOPID tour, it was nearly four years before Alice again performed a full show, and close to four and a half years before he did another several-month-long tour.

September 28, 1991 - Point Theatre, Dublin, Ireland
September 30, 1991 - Wembley Arena, London, England
  The show was recorded from the audience. **Dirty Dreams** was performed during this show.
October 1, 1991 - Wembley Arena, London, England
  The show was filmed from the audience.
October 3, 1991 - Coliseum, St. Austell, Cornwall, England
October 4, 1991 - Bournemouth Centre, Bournemouth, England
October 5, 1991 - Sheffield International Arena, Sheffield, England
October 7, 1991 - Whitley Bay Ice Rink, Whitley Bay, England
October 8, 1991 - Playhouse, Edinburgh, Scotland
October 9, 1991 - National Exhibition Centre, Birmingham, England
October 10, 1991 - National Exhibition Centre, Birmingham, England
October 12, 1991 - Sport Palais, Gent, Belgium
  The show was filmed from the audience.
October 13, 1991 - Ahoy Stadium, Rotterdam, Holland
  The show was filmed from the audience.
October 15, 1991 - Hallenstadion, Zurich, Switzerland
October 16, 1991 - Frankenhalle, Nuremberg, Germany
October 17, 1991 - Schleyer Hall, Stuttgart, Germany
October 18, 1991 - Stadthalle, Frieberg, Germany
  The show was filmed from the audience.
October 20, 1991 - Deutschlandhalle, Kien, Germany
  The show was filmed from the audience.
October 21, 1991 - Sporthalle, Hamburg, Germany
  The show was filmed from the audience.
October 22, 1991 - Gruga Halle, Essen, Germany
  The show was filmed from the audience.
October 23, 1991 - Le Zenith, Paris, France
  The show was filmed from the audience.
October 24, 1991 - Fest Halle, Frankfurt, Germany
October 26, 1991 - Eissport Halle, Kassell, Germany
  The show was filmed from the audience.
October 27, 1991 - Sport Halle, Cologne, Germany
  The show was filmed from the audience.
October 28, 1991 - Stadthalle, Bremen, Germany
  The show was filmed from the audience.

October 29, 1991 - Osteehalle, Kiel, Norway
The show was filmed from the audience.
November 1, 1991 - Spectrum, Oslo, Norway
November 2, 1991 - K. B. Halle, Copenhagen, Denmark
November 3, 1991 - Olympen, Lund, Sweden
The show was filmed from the audience.
November 5, 1991 - Ice Rink, Helsinki, Finland
November 6, 1991 - Typhoon, Turkuu, Finland
November 8, 1991 - Globen, Stockholm, Sweden
The show was filmed from the audience.
November 10, 1991 - Scandinavium, Gothenburg, Sweden
The show was filmed from the audience.

Tour Name: **SOUTH AMERICA 1995**
Tour Period: September 2, 1995 through September 9, 1995 in Brazil, Chile and Venezuela.
Performers: Alice Cooper (vocals), Stef Burns (guitar), Paul Taylor (guitar), Greg Smith (bass), Jimmy DeGrasso (drums), Derek Sherinian (keyboards.) Additional performers: Sheryl Cooper (dancer) and Brian Nelson.
Opening Act: Local acts, except for the September 4, 1995 concert.
Set List: Under My Wheels / Billion Dollar Babies / I'm Eighteen / No More Mr. Nice Guy / Desperado / Lost in America / It's Me / Cleansed by Fire / Go to Hell / Devil's Food / Steven / Black Widow / Gutter Cat Vs. the Jets / Feed My Frankenstein / Only Women Bleed / Welcome to My Nightmare / Ballad of Dwight Fry / School's Out / Hey Stoopid / Elected

Alice did this short tour in 1995 while waiting for developments in his transition to Hollywood Records. The tour featured the same performers that finished his 1991 HEY STOOPID tour, and saw the return of Sheryl Cooper performing in the show (along with Alice's assistant, Brian Nelson, performing once again.)

The show was a stripped down event, with little in the way of theatrics other than a few set pieces. This meant no execution for Alice during the show, but there were new variations on some old tricks. What at first looked to be the old electric chair execution actually turned out to be a bizarre shock therapy device that Alice is strapped into during the end of **Welcome to My Nightmare**. Sheryl Cooper also did a variation on her "Cold Ethyl" character, first as a punk in the gang that opposes Alice during **Gutter Cat**, and then being turned into the mannequin version of Cold Ethyl during a magic trick portion of **Feed My Frankenstein**. Alice hadn't yet reached the point of turning himself into "Killer Alice" on stage in front of the audience, and would leave the stage to do so during the instrumental medley of **Devil's Food**, **Steven** and **Black Widow**.

The set list for this tour was somewhat flexible, and the songs changed from night to night. **Sideshow** was dropped after the first show in Sao Paulo, Brazil.

The final concert on September 9 was a festival organized as a Monsters of Rock performance with Ozzy Osborne and Faith No More. Alice would return to the touring circuit in June 1996 for a tour co-headlining with the Scorpions.

September 2, 1995 - Sao Paulo, Brazil
A bit of **Jumping Jack Flash** was throw into **Sideshow** when the song was performed during this concert. The show was filmed professionally.
September 4, 1995 - Rio De Janero, Brazil
The show was filmed professionally, although only four songs are circulating presently in fan circles.
September 7, 1995 - Santiago, Chile
This concert was filmed and broadcast as part of a MONSTERS OF ROCK special on South American television. The concert was then released on bootleg as ALICE COOPER GOES TO CHILE.
September 9, 1995 - Ferrocarril Oeste Stadium, Buenos Aires, Venezuela
MONSTERS OF ROCK festival with Ozzy Osbourne and Faith No More.

Tour Name: **SCHOOL'S OUT SUMMER 1996**
Tour Period: June through August 1996 in North America.
Performers: Alice Cooper (vocals), Reb Beach (guitar), Ryan Roxie (guitar), Todd Jensen (bass), Jimmy DeGrasso (drums), Paul Taylor (keyboards and guitar.) Additional performers: Brian Nelson.
Opening Act: Local acts were normally used, if at all. Alice co-headlined this tour with the Scorpions.
Set List: Under My Wheels / Billion Dollar Babies / I'm Eighteen / Desperado / No More Mr. Nice Guy /

Lost in America / Feed My Frankenstein / Poison / Welcome to My Nightmare / Only Women Bleed / Gutter Cat Vs. the Jets / Street Fight / Steven (instrumental) / Ballad of Dwight Fry / School's Out / Elected

After moving to Hollywood Records, Alice was asked by the hard rock German group, the Scorpions, to join him on a co-headlining tour of the US. With equal billing and a chance to tour across the country again, Alice agreed, giving him his first chance to work on a live album since THE ALICE COOPER SHOW back in 1977.

Alice put together a new band for this tour, with only Paul Taylor and Jimmy DeGrasso remaining from the 1995 South American tour. This version of Alice's band remained with him (with the exception of Derek Sherinian playing keyboards during the New Year's shows in 1996) up to and including a portion of the ROCK AND ROLL CARNIVAL 1998 tour, and a more impressive group of musicians couldn't have been hoped for.

Because of the arrangements of the co-headlining, Alice normally appeared first, with the Scorpions closing. This was pretty much a necessity and not a slight on Alice, since Alice had decided to scale back his show to give it a more raw and in-your-face type feel than what the Scorpions did for their segment of the program. Alice's stage set was a throwback to the "street punk" days of the early Alice Cooper Group, with a graffiti-covered fence and the inclusion of trash cans (much like the one Alice would ride during Under My Wheels in the early 1970's.) Including early tracks such as Desperado, Street Fight and Gutter Cat Vs. the Jets completed the Alice's transformation back to those earlier days.

Certain new elements were brought into the show that fans in North America hadn't seen before, which made this tour definitely one to see. The transformation of Alice into "Killer Alice" before Ballad of Dwight Fry — with Alice being strapped-up by two, sometimes three people dressed as doctors and then his makeup smeared on his face (rather accurately, too) — was a striking part of the show and was continued into the subsequent tour. Alice's execution, however, was still missing from this tour. Perhaps the most interesting thing for fans of the mid-East and mid-West was seeing Alice play outdoor venues which (because he was on earlier in the evening) featured him performing in broad daylight, something rare for the fans who were used to seeing Alice on a darkened stage either inside or outdoors after dusk.

There were at least two shows on this tour when Alice performed a longer set list. The first was the show performed before the Scorpions tour actually commenced down at the Cabo Wabo Club in Cabo San Lucas, Mexico on June 2, 1996 — a concert that was filmed as a VH1 special and released on CD in mid-1997 as A FISTFUL OF ALICE. The other show was June 20, 1996 at the Ventura Theatre, Ventura, California, where the Scorpions didn't perform at all (Alice missed a subsequent Scorpions show in Bristol, Tennessee during late July.) These two shows featured songs not normally done on the tour including Bed of Nails, I Never Cry, Lost in America, and Clones (We're All). Clones (We're All) and Cleansed by Fire were both played at other shows, but not often enough to be considered regular parts of the tour. Be My Lover was also brought into the set list when the band played in the Detroit, Michigan area, while Cold Ethyl was added about midway through the tour.

Alice followed up the tour by taking a few months off before performing dates in the Detroit, Michigan area at the end of December to help ring in the new year. As it turned out, Alice enjoyed the 1996 tour schedule so much that he did a summer tour and New Year's tour again in both 1997 and 1998.

June 2, 1996 - Cabo Wabo Club, Cabo San Lucas, Mexico
    This show was performed before the start of the Scorpions / Alice co-headlining tour. The show was filmed and broadcast in 1997 on VH1 as a half hour special, and was recorded and released on CD and cassette as the official album A FISTFUL OF ALICE. See the album's entry in Part 1 of this chapter for more details about the show. How You Gonna See Me Now was rehearsed for this show, but not performed.
June 5, 1996 - University of Texas, El Paso, TX
June 7, 1996 - Austin, TX
June 8, 1996 - Alamodome, San Antonio, TX
    The show was recorded from the audience.
June 9, 1996 - Cynthia Woods Pavilion, Woodlands, Houston, TX
    The show was recorded from the audience.
June 11, 1996 - Starplex Amphitheater, Dallas, TX
June 12, 1996 - Little Rock, AR
June 14, 1996 - Tingley Coliseum, Albuquerque, NM
June 15, 1996 - Fiddler's Green Amphitheater, Denver, CO
June 16, 1996 - Wolf Mountain Amphitheater, Park City, UT

June 18, 1996 - Convention Center Arena, Tucson, AZ
June 19, 1996 - Universal Amphitheater, Los Angeles, CA
June 20, 1996 - Ventura Theater, Ventura, CA
   This was an Alice-only show. The Scorpions didn't appear. There was a longer set list, and the show was recorded from the audience.
June 22, 1996 - Irvine Meadows Amphitheater, Irvine, CA
June 23, 1996 - Compton Terrace, Phoenix, AZ
June 25, 1996 - Aladdin Theatre, Las Vegas, NV
June 26, 1996 - San Diego Sports Arena, San Diego, CA
June 28, 1996 - Cal Expo Amphitheater, Sacramento, CA
   The show was recorded from the audience.
June 29, 1996 - Shoreline Amphitheater, Mountainview, CA
   The show was recorded from the audience.
June 30, 1996 - Reno Hilton Amphitheater, Reno, NV
July 2, 1996 - Setland Arena, Fresno, CA
July 5, 1996 - Memorial Coliseum, Portland, OR
July 6, 1996 - The Gorge, George, Washington
July 7, 1996 - Pacific Coliseum, Vancouver, British Columbia
July 9, 1996 - Edmonton, Alberta, Canada
July 11, 1996 - Winnipeg Arena, Winnipeg, Manitoba, Canada
July 12, 1996 - Civic Center Arena, St. Paul, MN
July 14, 1996 - Marcus Amphitheater, Milwaukee, WI
July 16, 1996 - Riverport Amphitheater, St. Louis, MO
July 17, 1996 - Sandstone Amphitheater, Kansas City, MO
July 19, 1996 - Rosemont Horizon, Chicago, IL
July 20, 1996 - Polaris Amphitheater, Columbus, OH
   The show was recorded from the audience.
July 22, 1996 - Blossom Music Center, Cleveland, OH
   The show was filmed from the audience.
July 23, 1996 - Deer Creek, Noblesville, IN
July 24, 1996 - Riverbend Music Center, Cincinnati, OH
July 25, 1996 - Pine Knob Theater, Clarkston, MI
   The show was recorded from the audience.
July 27, 1996 - Val-Du-Lakes Amphitheater, Mears, MI
July 28, 1996 - Star lake Amphitheater, Pittsburgh, PA
July 30, 1996 - Molson Amphitheater, Toronto, Canada
July 31, 1996 - Sony / Blockbuster Entertainment Center, Camden, NJ
August 2, 1996 - Jones Beach Amphitheater, Wantaugh, Long Island, NY
August 3, 1996 - Great Woods Center, Mansfield, MA
   The show was recorded from the audience.
August 4, 1996 - Garden State Arts Center, Woodbridge, NJ
August 6, 1996 - Meadows Music Theatre, Hartford, CT
August 7, 1996 - Allentown Fairgrounds, Allentown, PA
August 9, 1996 - Washington, D.C.
August 10, 1996 - Virginia Beach Amphitheater, Virginia Beach, VA
August 11, 1996 - Walnut Creek Amphitheater, Raleigh, NC
August 12, 1996 - Lakewood Amphitheater, Atlanta, GA
August 14, 1996 - Riverfront Park, Charleston, WV
August 16, 1996 - North Americare Park, Buffalo, NY
   The show was recorded from the audience.
August 17, 1996 - Expo Grounds, Berthierville, Quebec, Canada

Tour Name: **NEW YEAR'S ROTTEN EVE 1996 Tour / WHIPLASH BASH**
Tour Period: December 28 1996 through December 31, 1996 in the Detroit, MI area.
Performers: Alice Cooper (vocals), Reb Beach (guitar), Ryan Roxie (guitar), Todd Jensen (bass), Jimmy DeGrasso (drums), Paul Taylor (keyboards and guitar.) Additional performers: Brian Nelson.
Opening Act: Local acts were normally used, if at all. Alice opened as co-headliner at the December 31, 1996 show with Ted Nugent.
Set List: Under My Wheels / Billion Dollar Babies / I'm Eighteen / Desperado / No More Mr. Nice Guy / Cleansed by Fire / Go to Hell / Poison / Be My Lover / Lost in America / Welcome to My Nightmare / Only Women Bleed / Feed My Frankenstein / Gutter Cat Vs. the Jets / Street Fight

/ Steven (instrumental) / Ballad of Dwight Fry / School's Out / Elected / Auld Lang Syne

In December 1996, Alice agreed to co-headline a concert which Ted Nugent did in the Detroit, Michigan area every year on New Year's Eve called the WHIPLASH BASH. Because it was Ted's party, Alice opened the show, but gave the audience a full show.

To get ready for the New Year's Eve show, and to make the cost of getting his band together worthwhile, Alice agreed to two other shows in the surrounding area — one in Saginaw, Michigan and the other in Toledo, Ohio. In fact, Toledo turned Alice's visit into a media event and the mayor of Toledo, Carty Finkbiner, announced that December 28, 1996 (the day of the concert in Toledo), was "Alice Cooper Day" as a way to apologize to Alice for an incident 23 years before which caused the cancellation of a show in Toledo after only a few songs.

The show remained much like the previous SCHOOL'S OUT tour, with little changed except for a couple of songs added or deleted from the set list. **Cleansed by Fire** was added, while **Cold Ethyl** was performed only in Toledo, and **Only Women Bleed** was not performed in Saginaw.

To celebrate the new year during the Detroit show (the actual WHIPLASH BASH), a giant cake was brought out during the **Elected** portion of the encore by a group of people wearing masks shaped like former Presidents and the current President (the Presidents had been a part of the show since the South American tour of 1995 when the band members wore the masks.) As the band played **Auld Lang Syne**, a greased-up, 500 pound woman in a bikini jumped out of the cake.

December 28, 1996 - Toledo Sports Arena, Toledo, OH
December 29, 1996 - Wendler Arena-Saginaw Civic Center, Saginaw, MI
    The show was recorded from the audience.
December 31, 1996 - Joe Louis Arena, Detroit, MI

Tour Name: **SCHOOL'S OUT FOR SUMMER '97**
Tour Period: The UK and European tour would run from June 20, 1997 through July 20, 1997.
Performers: Alice Cooper (vocals), Reb Beach (guitar), Ryan Roxie (guitar), Todd Jensen (bass), Jimmy DeGrasso (drums), Paul Taylor (keyboards and guitar.) Additional performers: Brian Nelson.
Opening Act: Unknown.
Set List: Under My Wheels / Billion Dollar Babies / I'm Eighteen / Desperado / Be My Lover / Lost in America / No More Mr. Nice Guy / Only Women Bleed / Halo of Flies / Poison / Nothing's Free / Cleansed by Fire / Go to Hell / Feed My Frankenstein / Gutter Cat Vs. the Jets / Street Fight / Steve (instrumental) / Ballad of Dwight Fry / School's Out / Elected

Since Alice didn't play Europe with the 1996 SCHOOL'S OUT tour, and had in fact not toured Europe since 1991, it was decided to return to the area in 1997. This wasn't only a chance to tour Europe again, but also a chance to warm up the band for the ROCK AND ROLL CARNIVAL tour that would commence in the US at the beginning of August. Both this and the North American tour were done in support of the A FISTFUL OF ALICE album that had just been released.

The European tour was essentially the same show (and the same stage set) as seen the previous year in the US with **Halo of Flies** being added into the mix. **Halo of Flies** became a standard on the 1997 and 1998 ROCK AND ROLL CARNIVAL tours.

Alice appeared in London, England on June 16, four days before the start of the tour in Germany, to take part in an autograph session at Tower Records in Piccadilly Circus.

June 20, 1997 - Gaswerk, Hamburg, Germany
    The show was recorded from the audience.
June 21, 1997 - Bospop-Festival, Weert, Holland
June 22, 1997 - Berlin, Germany
June 23, 1997 - Prague, Chez.
June 24 1997 - Warsaw, Poland
June 26, 1997 - Weiner Neustadt, Austria
June 27, 1997 - Budapest, Hungary
    The concert was filmed professionally and broadcast on European television.
June 29, 1997 - Antwerp, Belgium

June 30, 1997 - Le Bataclan, Paris, France
    The show was recorded from the audience.
July 1, 1997 - Le Bataclan, Paris, France
    The show was recorded from the audience.
July 3, 1997 - Civic Hall, Wolverhampton, England
    The show was filmed from the audience.
July 4, 1997 - Barrowlands, Glasgow, Scotland
July 5, 1997 - City Hall, Newcastle, England
July 6, 1997 - The Apollo, Manchester, England
July 8, 1997 - Astoria, London, England
July 9, 1997 - Astoria, London, England
    The show was filmed from the audience.
July 10, 1997 - Southampton Guildhall, Southampton, England
July 12, 1997 - Pyreness, Spain
July 15, 1997 - Rome, Italy
July 17, 1997 - Wettingen, Switzerland
July 18, 1997 - Munich, Germany
    The show was filmed from the audience.
July 19, 1997 - Balingen, Germany
July 20, 1997 - Loreley, Germany

Ticket for the June 23, 1997 show in the Czech Republic.

Tour Name: **ALICE COOPER'S ROCK AND ROLL CARNIVAL** (North America '97 Tour)
Tour Period: The North American portion of the tour (ROCK AND ROLL CARNIVAL) would run from July 30, 1997 through August 31, 1997.
Performers: Alice Cooper (vocals and guitar on I'm Eighteen), Reb Beach (guitar), Ryan Roxie (guitar), Todd Jensen (bass), Jimmy DeGrasso (drums), Paul Taylor (keyboards and guitar.) Additional performers: Brian Nelson, among others. Sheryl Cooper (performed on occasion.)
Opening Act: Slaughter, Warrant and Dokken, except where noted.
Set List: Hello, Hooray / Sideshow / Billion Dollar Babies / No More Mr. Nice Guy / Be My Lover / Lost in America / I'm Eighteen / From the Inside / Only Women Bleed / Halo of Flies / Nothing's Free / Cleansed by Fire / Poison / Public Animal #9 / Cold Ethyl / Unfinished Sweet / School's Out / Under My Wheels

This tour, sponsored by the rock music magazine METAL EDGE, was the first to really give fans a show based around THE LAST TEMPTATION album, encompassing a stage set that induced the feeling of a carnival sideshow, including a sideshow booth, a sarcophagus (for one of the acts listed on the canvas painting in the background) and a "high striker" (the test of strength with a mallet and a pole with a bell at its top.) Also featured were numerous extras dressed as clowns who harassed and were harassed by Alice and the band during the show. The clowns were also used to torment Alice later in the show by putting him into a demonic-looking wheelchair and smearing the "demented clown" makeup on him.

Additionally, the clowns were involved in creating Alice's first execution since the days of the TRASH tour. Throwing Alice into the sarcophagus, the clowns would seal it off and then shove several swords through the sides of the device. After doing so, the sarcophagus was opened to show a twitching Alice inside. The sarcophagus would then be closed again, only to be reopened to reveal no Alice, since he has now turned out to be one of the clowns. A classic magical illusion that worked very well on the concert stage.

In another development on this tour, Alice replaced the crutch used in I'm Eighteen (which had become a standard since the late 1970's) with a guitar — a surprise to many fans, since they had grow accustomed to Alice not playing any instruments during the show (besides a little bit of air guitar with the crutch during I'm Eighteen in earlier tours.)

The set list seemed a bit looser than on previous tours, and it wasn't unusual for Public Animal #9 to be played at different points in the show (sometimes after No More Mr. Nice Guy), or dropped altogether (along with Cleansed by Fire.) Sometimes Poison was also moved to the middle of the encore, in between School's Out and Under My Wheels.

July 30, 1997 - Sycuan Casino, El Cajon, CA
  This was the warm-up show for the tour, with Warrant and Loverboy opening, and was recorded from the audience.
August 1, 1997 - Marlboro Music Festival, Pershing Field, Fort Carson, CO
  This second warm-up show was actually part of a festival with Joe Walsh and Eddie Money. Alice's set was much like the abbreviated SCHOOL'S OUT SUMMER 1996 show for this one concert only.
August 2, 1997 - New World Music Theatre, Tinley Park, Chicago, IL
  First day of the tour proper. The show was filmed and recorded from the audience.
August 3, 1997 - Roy Wilkins Auditorium, St. Paul, MN
  The show was filmed from the audience.
August 5, 1997 - Pine Knob Music Theatre, Clarkston, MI
August 6, 1997 - Riverbend Music Center, Cincinnati, OH
August 8, 1997 - Eagles Ballroom, Milwaukee, WI
August 9, 1997 - Oakwood Theatre, Oakland, IN
August 10, 1997 - Buckeye Lake Music Center, Columbus, OH
  The show was recorded from the audience.
August 12, 1997 - Merriweather Post Pavilion, Columbia, MD
August 13, 1997 - Jones Beach Amphitheater, Wantagh, NY
August 14, 1997 - P.N.C. Bank Arts Center, Darien Lakes, NY
August 15, 1997 - Darien Lake Performing Arts Center, Darien Center, NY
  The show was filmed from the audience.
August 16, 1997 - Nautica Stage, Cleveland, OH
  The show was filmed from the audience.
August 18, 1997 - I.C. Light Amphitheater, Pittsburgh, PA
August 20, 1997 - LaCrosse Center, LaCrosse, WI
August 22, 1997 - Dallas Music Complex, Dallas, TX
August 23, 1997 - Retama Polo Grounds, San Antonio, TX
August 24, 1997 - The Woodlands, Houston, TX
August 26, 1997 - Mesa Amphitheater, Mesa, AZ
  The show was filmed from the audience.
August 27, 1997 - Aladdin Theatre, Las Vegas, NV
August 29, 1997 - Shoreline Amphitheater, Mountain View, CA
August 31, 1997 - Universal Amphitheater, Universal City, Hollywood, CA
  The show was recorded from the audience.

Handbill for the August 13, 1997 show in Wantagh, NY.

Tour Name: **ALICE COOPER'S ROCK AND ROLL CARNIVAL** (Australia '97 Tour)
Tour Period: The tour would run from September 5, 1997 through September 11, 1997 in Australia.
Performers: Alice Cooper (vocals and guitar on "I'm Eighteen"), Reb Beach (guitar), Ryan Roxie (guitar), Todd Jensen (bass), Jimmy DeGrasso (drums), Paul Taylor (keyboards and guitar.) Additional performers: Brian Nelson.
Opening Act: Unknown.
Set List: Hello, Hooray / Sideshow / Billion Dollar Babies / No More Mr. Nice Guy / Be My Lover / Lost in America / I'm Eighteen / From the Inside / Only Women Bleed / Halo of Flies / Nothing's Free

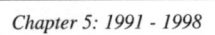

/ Cleansed by Fire / Poison / Public Animal #9 / Cold Ethyl / Unfinished Sweet / School's Out / Department of Youth / Under My Wheels

This was the same stage set and set list as the North America tour, with the addition of Department of Youth because it was a hit in Australia.

September 5, 1997 - Perth Entertainment Center, Perth, Australia
September 6, 1997 - Entertainment Center, Adelaide, Australia
September 8, 1997 - Entertainment Center, Melbourne, Australia
   The show was recorded from the audience.
September 10, 1997 - Boondall Entertainment Center, Brisbane, Australia
September 11, 1997 - Entertainment Center, Sydney, Australia

Tour Name: **NEW YEAR'S ROTTEN EVE 1997**
Tour Period: December 28 through December 31, 1997 in the Detroit, MI area.
Performers: Alice Cooper (vocals and guitar on I'm Eighteen), Reb Beach (guitar), Ryan Roxie (guitar), Todd Jensen (bass), Jimmy DeGrasso (drums), Paul Taylor (keyboards and guitar.)
Set List: Hello, Hooray / Sideshow / Billion Dollar Babies / No More Mr. Nice Guy / Be My Lover / Public Animal #9 / Be My Lover / Lost in America / I'm Eighteen / From the Inside / Only Women Bleed / Halo of Flies / Nothing's Free / Cleansed by Fire / Poison / Cold Ethyl / Unfinished Sweet / School's Out / Under My Wheels

Because of the success of the 1996 New Year's tour, Alice decided to once again return to the Detroit, Michigan area and perform in some smaller clubs. There were only three dates on the tour, and the band remained the same as it had been for the past year. At the first show in Merrillville, Indiana, an audience member was able to grab hold of the Ethyl mannequin and managed to de-wig the dummy before it was returned to the stage. Alice subsequently sang Cold Ethyl to a bald Ethyl at this one show.

Desperado, Clones (We're All) and Jailhouse Rock were performed at the New Year's Eve show in Detroit. Jailhouse Rock, one of the few cover songs Alice did in concert, became a welcome addition to the set list on the ROCK AND ROLL CARNIVAL 1998 tour the following year.

December 28, 1997 - Star Plaza Theatre, Merrillville, IN
   The show was recorded from the audience.
December 29, 1997 - Orbit Room, Grand Rapids, MI
   The show was recorded from the audience.
December 31, 1997 - State Theatre, Detroit, MI
   The show was recorded from the audience.

Tour Name: **ALICE COOPER'S ROCK AND ROLL CARNIVAL**
Tour Period: May 25, 1998 through June 7, 1998 in Europe and the UK. July 16, 1998 through September 6, 1998 in North America, with four additional dates in October 1998.
Performers: Alice Cooper (vocals and guitar on I'm Eighteen), Reb Beach (guitar, all except final dates in October), and Todd Jensen (bass.) Pete Friesen (guitar for all dates except June 19 through 22.) Ryan Roxie (guitar, replacing Pete Friesen from June 19 through 22, 1998.) Jimmy DeGrasso (drums up through June 22, 1998.) Eric Singer (drums, replacing Jimmy DeGrasso from July 16 through August 22, 1998.) Winston Watson (drums, replacing Eric Singer from August 22, 1998 onward.) Paul Taylor (keyboards and guitar for all dates except July 17 through August 1, 1998.) Derek Sherinian (keyboards, replacing Paul Taylor between July 17 through August 1, 1998.)
Opening Act: Unknown, usually local bands.
Set List: Hello, Hooray / Sideshow / Billion Dollar Babies / No More Mr. Nice Guy / Public Animal #9 / Be My Lover / Lost in America / I'm Eighteen / From the Inside / Only Women Bleed / Steven / Halo of Flies / Nothing's Free / Cleansed by Fire / Poison / Cold Ethyl / Unfinished Sweet / School's Out / Jailhouse Rock / Under My Wheels

Scorecards! Get your scorecards! You can't tell the players without a scorecard! Seriously, this was one tour that had even the die-hard fans trying to remember who played when and where on the tour. The 1998 tour was a continuation of the ROCK AND ROLL CARNIVAL tour from the previous year, with some different areas of both Europe and the US targeted for the tour this time around. It was also the first tour in quite a while to see the band members change, and was certainly a record setter for Alice in terms of so many changes in musicians.

The tour was originally to start May 24 with Ryan Roxie once again playing guitar, but at the last minute Roxie had to pull out because of other commitments. Replacing him was Paul Friesen, who hadn't played with Alice since the HEY STOOPID tour back in 1991. The May 24 concert was canceled to give Friesen another day to get ready for the tour, and Friesen played out the tour with the exception of three dates in June that took place in California where Roxie was able to perform.

Meanwhile, drummer Jimmy DeGrasso had to leave the band after the June 22 show in Del Mar, California to replace Nick Menza from the band Megadeth. With his leaving, Alice had asked Eric Singer (who had by this time left the band KISS) to perform in DeGrasso's place. Singer accepted — his first tour with Alice since the HEY STOOPID tour, where, ironically, DeGrasso had replaced him near the end of that tour. Singer, however, already had commitments to tour with Brian May in the fall and could only stay with Alice until the August 20 show at the House of Blues in Hollywood, California. Winston Watson, formerly from the Phoenix band Gentlemen Afterdark (who Alice had produced an EP for), took over for Singer from the end of August onward.

Paul Taylor has unable to play keyboards for Alice between July 17 and August 1, and was replaced by Derek Sherinian. Sherinian was another performer from the HEY STOOPID days (and before), so the line-up during this period was predominately that from the TRASH / HEY STOOPID years. Sherinian left the band after August 1 to get ready for a tour with his own band Dream Theater, and was replaced once again by Paul Taylor. The final show in October 1998, however, saw Sherinian once again playing keyboards for Alice.

Finally, not to be left out, Reb Beach is planning to replace George Lynch in the band Dokken. So, the final dates in October were done without Reb on guitar.

The tour itself was very much the same as the 1997 tour. In Europe, a snake owned by an Alice fan was used for the tour. The snake's name, Lady Macbeth, was later also given to the snake used for the North America tour. The latter snake became the star of the show during one of the House of Blues concerts in Hollywood by relieving itself while on stage with Alice. Evidently a first for any snake during an Alice show, it lead to the show being interrupted while the stage was cleaned.

Fans seem to agree that, during this tour, not only was Alice much looser than in the past, but his voice was stronger than ever. Most importantly, after all these years, Alice was still leaving the fans wanting more.

May 25, 1998 - Astoria, London, England
    The show was filmed from the audience. Back Yard Babies was the opening band.
May 26, 1998 - Astoria, London, England
May 28, 1998 - Haus Auensee, Leipzig, Germany
May 29, 1998 - Stahlwerk, Dusseldorf, Germany
May 30, 1998 - Music Hall, Hannover, Germany
June 1, 1998 - Stadthalle, Lichtenfels, Germany
    The show was filmed from the audience.
June 2, 1998 - Colosseum, Munich, Germany
June 3, 1998 - Maingauhalle, Kleinostheim, Germany
June 4, 1998 - Hamburg, Germany
    This show was supposed to be at Docks Konzerte in Hamburg, but moved to a different venue when Alex Van Halen was injured in the hall during a Van Halen concert sound check the night before by a piece of falling ceiling plaster.
June 5, 1997 - Beach Party Festival, Skive, Denmark
June 6, 1998 - Karlshamm Rock Festival, Kyrkhult, Sweden
June 7, 1998 - Rock Festival, Copenhagen, Denmark
June 19, 1998 - Konocti Harbor Resort, Kelseyville, CA
    The show was recorded from the audience.
June 20, 1998 - Konocti Harbor Resort, Kelseyville, CA
    The show was recorded from the audience.
June 22, 1998 - Del Mar Fair, Del Mar, CA
    The show was filmed from the audience.
July 17, 1998 - Chippewa Valley Rock Fest '98, Cadott, WI
    The show was recorded from the audience.
July 18, 1998 - The Checkered Flag, Appleton, WI
July 19, 1998 - Newport Music Hall, Columbus, OH
July 21, 1998 - State Theatre, Kalamazoo, MI

July 22, 1998 - Metro, Chicago, IL
July 23, 1998 - Medina Ballroom, Medina, MN
   The show was recorded from the audience.
July 24, 1998 - Rivercade, Chautauqua Park, Sioux City, IA
July 31, 1998 - Rock Mountain Music Festival, Labatt Blue Rock Fest, High River, Alberta, Canada
August 1, 1998 - Classic Rock Picnic, Minnedosa, Manitoba
August 6, 1998 - House of Blues, Myrtle Beach, SC
August 7, 1998 - House of Blues at the Tabernacle, Atlanta, GA
   The show was filmed from the audience.
August 8, 1998 - House of Blues, Orlando, FL
August 9, 1998 - Ruth Eckerd Hall, Clearwater, FL
August 18, 1998 - House of Blues, Los Angeles, CA
August 19, 1998 - House of Blues, Los Angeles, CA
August 20, 1998 - House of Blues, Los Angeles, CA
August 28, 1998 - Lulu's Nightclub, Kitchener, Ontario, Canada
August 29, 1998 - Michigan State Fair, Detroit, MI
August 30, 1998 - Vegas Kewadin Casino, Sault Ste Marie, MI
August 31, 1998 - Vegas Kewadin Casino, Sault Ste Marie, MI
September 1, 1998 - Stranahan Theater, Toledo, OH
September 2, 1998 - Nautica Stage, Cleveland, OH
   The show was filmed from the audience.
September 4, 1998 - Trump's Marina Casino, Atlantic City, NJ
September 5, 1998 - Trump's Marina Casino, Atlantic City, NJ
   The show was recorded from the audience, missing last three songs.
September 6, 1998 - Mohegan Sun Casino, Uncasville, CT
October 3, 1998 - Six Flags Astroworld, Houston, TX
October 4, 1998 - House of Blues, New Orleans, LA
October 5, 1998 - House of Blues, New Orleans, LA
October 24, 1998 - Phoenix State Fari, Phoenix, AZ

Tour Name: **Alice Cooper New Year's Eve Tour 1998**
Tour Period: December 28, 1998 in Robinsonville, Mississippi, December 30 and 31, 1998 in Florida. No other dates on the tour.
Performers: Alice Cooper (vocals and guitar on I'm Eighteen.) Todd Jensen (bass.) Pete Friesen (guitar.) Eric Singer (drums.) Lindsay Vannoy (keyboards.)
Opening Act: Unknown, normally local bands.
Set List: Hello, Hooray / Sideshow / Billion Dollar Babies / No More Mr. Nice Guy / Public Animal #9 / Be My Lover / Lost in America / I'm Eighteen / From the Inside / Only Women Bleed / Steven / Halo of Flies / Nothing's Free / Cleansed by Fire / Poison / Cold Ethyl / Unfinished Sweet / School's Out / Jailhouse Rock / Under My Wheels

Having found success with the New Year's Eve shows in the Detroit area in 1996 and 1997, Alice decided to do the same in 1998. The only difference was that the shows took place down South instead of in the icy cold of Michigan, Ohio and Indiana. The song list and stage antics were the same as on the CARNIVAL tour.

December 28, 1998 - Sam's Town Casino, Robinsonville, Mississippi
December 30, 1998 - Florida, Theater, Jacksonville, Florida
December 31, 1998 - Florida Theater, Pompano Beach, Florida

Part 4 — Films and Television 1991 - 1998

Although the 1990's have, so far, seen only three Alice Copper albums released (one of which was a live album), Alice has in the 90's made tremendous inroads into both the theatrical movie world and television — sometimes playing a different role, but normally playing himself. It was in the early 1990's that Alice made the film appearance for which he is probably best remembered, WAYNE'S WORLD. Alice made other appearances after this film, but the WAYNE'S WORLD role showed people in Hollywood what fans had known since the early days — that Alice didn't take himself too seriously.

Before WAYNE'S WORLD was a non-credited cameo appearance in FREDDY'S DEAD (the next-to-last NIGHT-

MARE ON ELM STREET movie), and for the video / television screen was the release of a full-length documentary on Alice's career, PRIME CUTS. Two music videos were also done for the HEY STOOPID album during that time, **Hey Stoopid** and **Love Is a Loaded Gun**. After this, it wasn't until the release of THE LAST TEMPTATION in 1994 that Alice starting being seen again on television, mainly for interviews or in the music videos created for the album. Also in 1994, Alice appeared in the movie MAVERICK, an update of the old television series. Alice played the town's drunk in the film, but his scene was cut and only the back of his head can be seen in the film.

Alice had better luck when he portrayed himself, as he did on the short-lived situation comedy from Gene Wilder on NBC called SOMETHING WILDER. Alice agreed to having his concert from the MONSTERS OF ROCK tour in 1995 filmed for South American television, and the following year his Cabo Wabo concert, recorded for A FISTFUL OF ALICE, was also filmed for a half-hour VH1 (MTV's sister channel) special.

Beyond this, Alice began making numerous appearances on television interview shows and doing commercials. For the longest time, the only commercial fans ever heard of Alice doing was the anti-drug radio spot (the infamous "take drugs and I'll cut off your puppy dog's tail" ad) from the early 1970's. As the 1990's progressed, Alice did more commercials, particularly for certain golf club manufacturers (mainly a company called Callaway for their Big Bertha clubs) which frustrated fans since they normally only appeared during golf programs and / or on the sports cable channels (so if you weren't a fan of golf or sports, you were pretty much out of luck.) Alice also did a great Australian commercial for an antacid called Rennie back in the mid-1990's. Perhaps the oddest commercial Alice did was an "infomercial" (the 30 minute / hour-long commercials for products normally shown late at night on television) for a CD player called the Fisher 24. Alice's part in the program featured himself and his mother in little skits about the CD player, Alice's music and his image.

With the upcoming release of the career spanning boxed set, it won't come as a surprise to see Alice in more television and film appearances in the near future. While we may never see THE ALICE COOPER SHOW ("Right here on our stage, here's Topo Gigio . . . ."), there's no doubt that Alice will continue to be a pleasant surprise on both the big and small screens for years to come.

As a side note, the early 1990's have seen some changes in the home entertainment medium, with the complete demise of Beta videocassette by 1990 in the US. This left VHS and Laser disc as the only ways to get a new movie or special for home viewing until about the mid-1990's. With advancements in the computer technology, it became possible to watch movies and specials on the home computer using a method called VCD (which uses MPEG-1 technology for its encoding.) The PRIME CUTS documentary was released in on VCD. Ironically enough, PRIME CUTS was also the first Alice-related video to be released on DVD (in 1998) — the technology that superceded VCD. With all of the computer video advancements that developed (and taken a chunk out of the Hollywood studios) Laser discs have begun their slow demise, much like the Beta Players before them. Even with all this advancement going on, the VHS videocassette recorder still remains the strongest unit in the group and all of the commercially available material listed before can be found on this format.

As for what the future of home entertainment holds, it's hard to say. Some are already suggesting products that will soon make DVDs outdated. Whatever new media emerge, in time there will no doubt be Alice material available on them.

Film Title:	**Hey Stoopid**
Film Type:	Music video.
Created:	Filmed March 1991 and shown on television music programs and channels like MTV.
Music:	Hey Stoopid

This was the first music video done for a single off the HEY STOOPID album. Alice and his band appear only periodically in the video. The concept deals with two teenagers facing the trials of life on a roller coaster. Ozzy Osbourne, who also sang backup on the song, appears briefly in the video.

Film Title:	**PRIME CUTS**
Film Type:	Documentary.
Created:	Filmed 1991 by Summer Place Productions for PolyGram Video. Produced by Charles Murdoch. Associated producer was Brian Nelson. Directed by Neal Preston. Released August 20, 1991 by Polygram Video on VHS videocassette.
Catalog No.:	083 631-3 (videocassette, US), CMP 6050 (videocassette, UK, released through Castle Music

Pictures), VAVZ 2127 (videocassette, Japan), VALP 3277 (Laser disc, Japan), BMG 21372313 (videocassette, Germany.)

After the success of the TRASH album in 1989-1990, this documentary was released directly to the home video market just as Alice was finishing up the OPERATION ROCK 'N' ROLL tour with Judas Priest in the US. Alice was also promoting the HEY STOOPID album (which is represented with a small in-concert clip during the documentary.)

The nearly 90 minute long special was a great treat for fans who had been waiting for a film such as this for years. Alice is interviewed in various locations and discusses his career, while film and video clips (many from rare performances, some even from appearances that fans overall had never heard of) are shown. Additional interviews are done with Bob Ezrin, Shep Gordon, Slash and Ozzy Osbourne to expand on certain elements of Alice's career.

The only disappointment (a disappointment that is purely typical on fans' part) is that only portions of the many film clips are shown, and not the whole performances (obviously the videocassette media creates length limits.) So, while the video packaging lists 23 songs in the documentary, many of these are just snippets and not the complete songs. However, unless PolyGram believed it could have sold a three hour long version of the same documentary, such editing is quite understandable and necessary. On the up side, the video does give fans a chance to see footage from two concert films that are rarely seen in excellent shape in the fan circles — GOOD TO SEE YOU AGAIN, ALICE COOPER and THE STRANGE CASE OF ALICE COOPER. See earlier chapters for more details about these two films.

As stated in the introduction to this section, PRIME CUTS was the first video to be released in the MPEG-1 format called VCD. It was also the first Alice-related music video to be released on DVD. The cover of the video has remained the same, the classic photo of Alice with a daisy in his hair and what looks to be Christmas wrapping around his arms and torso. In Europe, the video was released originally with a photo cover of Alice in concert wearing his traditional top hat and coat for School's Out. These early editions of the video were packaged and released in error and later editions of the European video have the traditional cover.

Video box for the US release of PRIME CUTS.

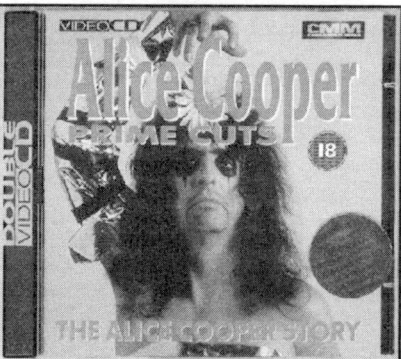

The UK VCD edition of the PRIME CUTS documentary.

The North American edition of the documentary contained additional footage of Alice discussing the careers of both Kane Roberts and Kip Winger. This footage, running about four minutes altogether, is missing from the European and Japanese editions of the documentary.

Overall, a very good, all encompassing documentary of Alice Cooper, and a great beginner's guide for fans just getting into Alice's material.

Film Title: **FREDDY'S DEAD: THE FINAL NIGHTMARE** (a.k.a. NIGHTMARE ON ELM STREET, PART 6: FREDDY'S DEAD)
Film Type: Full length movie.
Created: Filmed Spring 1991 and released September 13, 1991 by New Line Cinema. Directed by Rachel

Talalay. Written by Michael De Luca and Rachel Talalay. Released on video 1992 by New Line (catalog number TRN 4089) and on laser disc by Image on October 28, 1992 (catalog number 2169 LI.)

Alice appeared briefly in the latter part of the film. Alice's character is Freddy Kruger's guardian and is shown beating the teenage Kruger who takes the pain with pleasure. A portion of the movie was filmed in the gimmick 3-D process. When the film was released on video and shown on television the 3-D process was eliminated. However, a special edition of the laser disc did feature 3-D and came with a pair of 3-D glasses.

Film Title:	**IN CONCERT '91**
Film Type:	Concert performance.
Created:	Filmed July 21, 1991 at the Irvine Meadows Amphitheater, Irvine, California. Broadcast September 1991 on the ABC television network.
Music:	Go to Hell / School's Out / Hey Stoopid / Elected

Filmed during the first night of the OPERATION ROCK 'N' ROLL tour with Judas Priest, the program featured many songs from both Judas Priest and Alice, among others. This film is a good opportunity for fans to review what the show and stage looked like for the HEY STOOPID tour. The version of I'm Eighteen from this show later turned up as the B-side to the Love's a Loaded Gun single in the UK.

Video box for FREDDY'S DEAD.

Film Title:	**Love Is a Loaded Gun**
Film Type:	Music video.
Created:	Filmed August 1991 and shown on television music programs and channels like MTV.
Music:	Love Is a Loaded Gun

As with the Hey Stoopid video, Alice appears as a bit of a Greek Chorus to the drama being played out in the video itself. In Love Is a Loaded Weapon, Alice does eventually turn up within the story to resolve the story line. One of the more visually striking of Alice's music videos, it would be pushed further with the It's Me video released in 1994.

Film Title:	**HARD -N- HEAVY Volume 15**
Film Type:	Documentary.
Created:	Released on video cassette 1991 by MPI Home Entertainment (MP1678.) A production of Directors International Video.

A segment was filmed dealing with the making of the HEY STOOPID album.

Film Title:	**METAL HEAD VIDEO MAGAZINE Volume 6**
Film Type:	Interview.
Created:	Released on video cassette 1991 by Goodtimes Home Video.

Alice is interviewed about the just released HEY STOOPID album.

Film Title:	**WAYNE'S WORLD**
Film Type:	Theatrical film.
Created:	Filmed Fall 1991. Alice's sequenced filmed end of November 1991 at the Universal Amphitheater, Los Angeles, California. Released February 14, 1992 by Paramount Studios. Directed by Penelope Spheeris. Written by Mike Myers and Bonnie Turner. Released on video

1993 by Paramount (catalog number 32706) and laser disc by Pioneer in April 1994 (catalog number PLFEB 31331.)

Alice makes a brief appearances in this comedy based on Mike Myers' recurring character from his days on the NBC comedy series SATURDAY NIGHT LIVE. Myers and fellow SNL alumni Dana Carvey play two young guys who do a cable access program called Wayne's World.

Given a chance to go backstage at an Alice Cooper show, Wayne and Garth (Myers and Carvey) meet Alice and his entourage. Alice begins explaining the history of Milwaukee to the people backstage and an astonished Wayne and Garth. Feeling that they've taken up too much of his time, Wayne and Garth plan to leave, but Alice asks that they stay. Hearing this, Wayne and Garth fall to their knees and begin chanting "We're Not Worthy!"

The scene is one of the highlights of the film, which in all is clever and fun. There is also footage of Alice and the band performing **Feed My Frankenstein** on stage during the movie. If you look quickly, you can also see Alice's assistant, Brian Nelson, in the entourage backstage. The scene with Alice suddenly going into a history lesson of Milwaukee is a variation of an earlier SNL skit where the members of Aerosmith appeared on Wayne's World to discuss science and world events. The "We're Not Worthy" bit is also taken from an earlier Wayne's World skit where Wayne and Garth meet Madonna. This is not to slight Alice's work in any way, but just to point out Myer's tendency to reuse good material if given the chance.

The "We're Not Worthy!" chant continued to pursue Alice for years after the movie became a hit and he still runs into the chant from fans and non-fans alike in everyday events (including sporting events and at concerts.) As Alice related to PEOPLE Magazine in May 1992, after a year of people yelling "Hey, Stupid!" at him (because of the HEY STOOPID album), the "We're Not Worthy!" chant was a lot easier to take.

Film Title:	**CELEBRATION: THE MUSIC OF PETE TOWNSEND AND THE WHO** (a.k.a. CELEBRATION: THE MUSIC OF THE WHO and as DALTREY SINGS TOWNSEND)
Film Type:	Concert film.
Created:	Filmed February 26, 1994 at Carnegie Hall, New York City, New York. Directed by Michael Lindsay-Hogg.
Music:	Alice sings I'm a Boy.

This was a special concert put on to celebrate the music of the rock band, The Who and its main composer, Pete Townsend. The program featured Roger Daltrey singing most of the material, but a few guest vocalists were enlisted.

Film Title:	**Lost in America**
Film Type:	Music video.
Created:	Filmed March 1994 and shown on television music programs and channels like MTV.
Music:	Lost in America

The music video for the first single from THE LAST TEMPTATION album began with a clip of a young kid reading the Marvel comic book. This is the only color segment of the video besides a background montage of some of the comic book interior pages behind Alice in one portion of the video.

The black and white portion of the video with Alice and the band is excellent, with a knowing montage of television and film clips from the 1950's that counterpoint the lyrics to the song. The footage of the kid reading the comic is a bit of a waste, however.

Film Title:	**TOP OF THE POPS**
Film Type:	Performance appearance.
Created:	Filmed and broadcast May 19, 1994 in London, England for the BBC.
Music:	Lost in America

Alice appears on the program to sing the single from the (then) upcoming album THE LAST TEMPTATION. This was done during the promotional tour Alice did for the single and the album which found Alice touring Europe and Australia. The episode of TOP OF THE POPS featured Alice's snake introducing the show and some brief comedy bits where Alice hands his name over to Bruno Brooks, the announcer of the program, who ends up fighting the snake and is later seen with his clothes torn to pieces.

Film Title: **BIG BREAKFAST**
Film Type: Interview.
Created: Broadcast live on May 20, 1994 on the UK television.

Alice is interviewed by Paula Yates on this morning news program. The interview was in support of THE LAST TEMPTATION album.

Film Title: **NOISY MOTHERS**
Film Type: Interview.
Created: Filmed May 1994 and broadcast on British television on May 21, 1994.

Alice appeared to promote THE LAST TEMPTATION album. His interview was split into two parts on the program.

Film Title: **MAVERICK**
Film Type: Theatrical film.
Created: Filmed Spring 1994. Released June 1994 by Warner Brothers Studios. Directed by Richard Donner. Written by Roy Huggins and William Goldman. Released on video 1995 by Warner Brothers (catalog number 13374.)

Alice filmed a scene in this movie playing the town drunk. Alice's scene with Mel Gibson was cut from the movie, although you can still see the back of his head in a barroom scene. Okay, not that exciting, but if I don't mention it someone will complain that it should have been included in the book.

Film Title: **It's Me**
Film Type: Music video.
Created: Filmed June 1994 and shown on television music programs and channels like MTV.
Music: It's Me

One of the best music videos Alice has done is also his latest single, which was released from THE LAST TEMPTATION album in 1994. Alice is seen in two roles in the video: as himself and as the Showman (a.k.a. Killer Alice) from the album. The footage for the video is shot to look similar to that of the cover of the album. As stated before, an excellent video and a real shame that it didn't get shown more often than it did.

Film Title: **BRIAN CONLEY SHOW**
Film Type: Performance appearance.
Created: Filmed May 1994 and broadcast June 18, 1994 on UK television.
Music: Lost in America

Alice performed Lost in America.

Film Title: **SPACE GHOST: COAST TO COAST**
Film Type: Interview.
Created: Filmed February 1995 and shown March 12, 1995 on the US cable network, Comedy Central. Episode Title: Girlie Show.

Alice appears in a brief interview segment on this series. The show was based on the premise of 1960's cartoon superhero, Space Ghost, having his own interview show. The segments with Space Ghost and his cronies were done in limited animation, in which guests would appear on a television screen next to Space Ghost's desk.

While the program had numerous guests, the show was really based around Space Ghost and so the interviewees were normally only briefly seen, but it's a fun episode and a great series.

Film Title: **SOMETHING WILDER**
Film Type: Situation Comedy Series.
Created: Filmed January 1995 and shown March 12, 1995 on the NBC television network. Episode Title: Hanging With Mr. Cooper.

This was an unfortunately short lived situation comedy by actor / writer Gene Wilder. In the series, Gene plays a person who lives in a small town and works for his own advertising agency.

Alice appears as himself, and the episode deals with the noise and trouble Alice causes Gene when Alice moves into the house next door. In trying to get the noise turned down at the party over at Alice's house, Gene inadvertently ends up in a music video by Alice, which could cause trouble for Gene and his hope of landing an account that is suppose to give the town a "Norman Rockwell" small town feel.

Alice is great is the show, and the writing for once doesn't quite fall into the heavy stereotypical clichés of what a rock performer is like offstage. Alice has a lot of great lines and gets to sing a couple of times in the episode. Well worth checking out for Alice fans, if you can find a copy. Finally, while Alice calls another character Renfield, Alice's actual assistant doesn't play the part.

Film Title:	**MONSTERS OF ROCK**
Film Type:	Concert film.
Created:	Recorded September 7, 1995 in Santiago, Chile.
Performers:	Alice Cooper (vocals), Stef Burns (guitar), Paul Taylor (guitar), Greg Smith (bass), Jimmy DeGrasso (drums), Derek Sherinian (keyboards.) Additional performers: Brian Nelson and Sheryl Cooper (among others.)
Music:	Under My Wheels / Hey Stoopid / I'm Eighteen / No More Mr. Nice Guy / Desperado / Billion Dollar Babies / It's Me / Lost in America / Cleansed by Fire / Go to Hell / Devil's Food / Steven / Black Widow / Gutter Cat Vs. the Jets / Feed My Frankenstein / Only Women Bleed / Welcome to My Nightmare / Ballad of Dwight Fry / School's Out / Elected

This concert was filmed and broadcast as part of a MONSTERS OF ROCK special on South American television. The concert was then released on bootleg as ALICE COOPER GOES TO CHILE.

Film Title:	**Miller Beer commercial**
Film Type:	TV commercial.
Created:	Filmed 1995 and broadcast on commercial television in the UK in November 1995.

Alice appears as a guest in a parody of a talk show, which featured the real ad for the beer in the middle of the parody. Alice sings a song about a coat hanger and at no time actually endorses the beer in any way.

Film Title:	**TV-Shop commercial**
Film Type:	TV commercial.
Created:	Filmed and broadcast on commercial television in Sweden in early 1996.

Alice makes a brief appearance in this advertisement for a rock compilation CD.

Film Title:	**CONVERSATIONS WITH ANN LIGOURI**
Film Type:	Interview.
Created:	Filmed 1996 and broadcast May 7, 1996. Location of broadcast unknown.

Alice discusses his career and the upcoming tour on this program.

Film Title:	**PEARL**
Film Type:	Situation Comedy Series.
Created:	Filmed Fall 1996 and broadcast on the CBS television network on February 12, 1997. Episode Title: Write Stuff (Part One).

Alice appears briefly as a guardian angel in this situation comedy by Rhea Pearlman and Malcolm McDowell.

Film Title:	**AMERICAN MUSIC AWARDS**
Film Type:	Awards presentation.
Created:	Broadcast live on ABC television network on January 27, 1997.

Although for many years Alice was rumored to have spent time with Pat Boone in one context or another, this was one of the first times the two were paired together as they present an award on this program. Boone was also promoting his just released album NO MORE MR. NICE GUY, which also featured the song of the same name.

Film Title:	**A FISTFUL OF ALICE**
Film Type:	Concert film.
Created:	Filmed June 2, 1996 at the Cabo Wabo Club, Cabo San Lucas, Mexico. Broadcast on VH1 on August 12, 1997. A Perry Films, Inc. production, copyrighted 1997 by Hollywood Records, Inc. Produced by Robert Katz and Brian Brickman.
Performers:	Alice Cooper (vocals), Reb Beach (guitar), Ryan Roxie (guitar), Todd Jensen (bass), Jimmy DeGrasso (drums), Paul Taylor (keyboards and guitar.) Additional performers: Sammy Hagar (guitar on School's Out), Rob Zombie and Slash (both on Elected.)
Music:	School's Out / Billion Dollar Babies / I'm Eighteen / Poison / Elected

This was an edited version of the concert Alice did in Mexico released as the live album A FISTFUL OF ALICE. The show was finally broadcast on VH1 after the album had been released for about a month.

Sammy Hagar, who performed during the show, also introduces the program. Alice is also seen in interview bits shown before the commercial breaks in the program. While there have continued to be rumors of the entire concert being released on video, this half hour special is all that is currently available.

Film Title:	**TONIGHT SHOW**
Film Type:	Performance appearance.
Created:	Filmed July 31, 1997 and broadcast the same day on the NBC television network.
Music:	I'm Eighteen

Alice appeared on THE TONIGHT SHOW — his first in many years and the first time he appeared with Johnny Carson's replacement, Jay Leno. Alice appeared to promote A FISTFUL OF ALICE and performs I'm Eighteen with his band. The most noteworthy thing about the performance is the use of a guitar by Alice during the song. For many fans, this was the first time they had seen Alice with a guitar in his hands during a performance. Alice used a guitar from this point onward on I'm Eighteen when performing it in concert.

Film Title:	**RUPAUL SHOW**
Film Type:	Interview.
Created:	Filmed August 1997 and broadcast on MTV on August 14, 1997.

On this program that featured well known cross-dresser RuPaul, Alice appeared to talk about A FISTFUL OF ALICE.

Film Title:	**HALLOWEEN: THE HAPPY HAUNTING OF AMERICA**
Film Type:	Interview.
Created:	Released Fall 1997.

Alice appears briefly in this documentary about Halloween and haunted houses, discussing fear and the season.

Video documentary with comments by Alice.

Film Title:	**ALICE COOPER SCHOOL'S OUT '97**
Film Type:	Concert film.
Created:	Filmed June 27, 1997 in Budapest, Hungary and shown in the Fall 1997 on European television.
Music:	Under My Wheels / Billion Dollar Babies / I'm Eighteen / Desperado / Be My Lover / Lost in America / No More Mr. Nice Guy / Only Women Bleed / Halo of Flies / Poison / Nothing's Free / Cleansed by Fire / Go to Hell / Feed My Frankenstein / Gutter Cat Vs. the Jets / Street Fight / Steve (instrumental) / Ballad of Dwight Fry / School's Out / Elected

Recorded during the 1997 SCHOOL'S OUT tour in Europe, right before Alice began his ROCK AND ROLL CARNIVAL tour in the US. Alice can be seen performing as the Showman during a portion of the concert, as if continuing the "street fight" segment from the earlier SCHOOL'S OUT tour.

Part 5 — Books and Comics 1991 - 1998

Even with the Platinum success of TRASH, there wasn't much in the way of books or comic books published to discuss or cash in on Alice's success at the time. So, it was no surprise to fans that the period following that success also offered only a modest amount printed material. Alice's success with TRASH did lead to his history being updated in some of the rock music reference books, yet, even there, the research done normally stops at the release of THE LAST TEMPTATION and provides no further insight into projects that Alice has been associated with since then.

Magazine and newspapers articles and interviews have been plentiful, as throughout many periods of Alice's career, so there were still things in the press being said about Alice. Beyond these periodicals, however, there are only two major writing projects that have happened since 1991. One of these was the three part comic book series based on Alice's concept album THE LAST TEMPTATION. The comic, with the same title, was based on a story by Alice and writer Neil Gaiman and was issued by Marvel Comics in 1994 in both a mini-series format and as a book encompassing all three issues of the comic. The other major project was from Michael Bruce, the guitarist from the Alice Cooper Group. Bruce's project was an autobiography of his time before, during and after he performed with Alice (although the book mainly deals with his time in the group itself), called NO MORE MR. NICE GUY. The book was released in October 1996 and as of February 1999 is still available in some stores.

No doubt, with the release of the boxed set in 1999, and the promise of another studio album, there will be additional books (and maybe a comic or two) released to deal with the history and mania of Alice. Until that time, the definitive biography of Alice Cooper has yet to be written.

Book Title: **NO MORE MR. NICE GUY**
Published: Released in soft-back October 1996 by SAF Publishing Ltd., England. ISBN 0 946719 17 9. No hardback edition published.
Author: Michael Bruce, with Billy James.
Content: 149 pages, with black and white photos interspersed throughout the book. An autobiography by one of the members of the Alice Cooper group, dealing with his career before, during and after Alice.

After the breakup of the original Alice Cooper Group, Michael Bruce attempted to continue with a solo career, and with the band without Alice, as Billion Dollar Babies. By the early 1980's, Bruce had moved onto projects outside the music field and it wasn't until the early- to mid-1990's that he went back to performing on stage. With his return to the stage, fans of the original band began to ask him more and more about the Alice Cooper Group. It was then that Bruce decided to write a book about his time with the band.

The book, written with musician Billy James (a.k.a. Ant-Bee, whom Bruce had worked with musically), discusses his career before and after the Alice Cooper Group, however, most of the book deals with his time in the band from 1968 through 1974. It was the first time that anyone in the band besides Alice had talked about the Alice Cooper Group at such length, and many fans were happy to see the book. Fans were also just happy with the fact that there was finally another book out about Alice, period.

While a few fans have criticized the book as too one-sided about the split up of the band and about Alice,

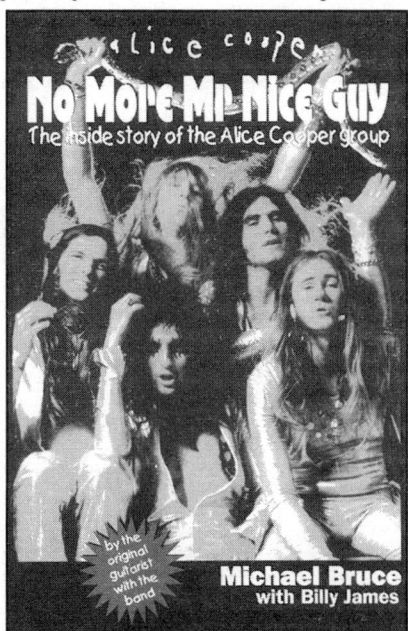

The NO MORE MR. NICE GUY book by Michael Bruce.

it is after all an autobiography, and is taken from just one participant's point of view. More important to the history of the band is Bruce's discussion of the many songs done during his time with them and background information on the tours and albums. On the other side of that same coin, however, there is a tendency (just as with ME, ALICE) on the publisher's part to rely on Bruce's memory concerning many things that are readily apparent to be slightly off or completely inaccurate (songs being released in the wrong time period and one glaring example of song titles from a bootleg album that were obviously incorrect.) That's not necessarily Bruce's fault, but more the result of the publisher not spending more time in proofreading the material before going to print (and, hey, I should know.)

Still, the book is a fun and fast read, with Bruce's writing style an easy-going experience. As for photos, while most of the material is from other sources (magazines, tour books, picture sleeves), there are several offbeat photos appearing as well.

The book was published in the UK and available as an import in other countries. Autographed copies of the book were also being sold for a time through Bruce's web site on the Internet.

Book Title: **ME & G.B.**
Published: Released in hardback, August 1998. No publisher listed.
Author: Edited by Paul Brenton.
Content: 124 pages, with color and black and white photos throughout the text. A look at the life of guitarist Glen Buxton through quotes and anecdotes of fans and friends who knew him.

Released in conjunction with the Glen Buxton Memorial Weekend held in Clarion, Iowa in August 1998, the book was to commemorate the life of Glen Buxton who passed away in October 1997. The book contained many photos of Glen throughout his life and included many photos of him with the Alice Cooper Group and the band's earlier incarnations. The initial printing of the book was 100 copies, with a second edition done in September for fans who couldn't attend the Memorial Weekend.

Book Title: **THE LAST TEMPTATION**
Published: Three-part comic book miniseries. Book I published May 1994. Book II published August 1994. Book III published December 1994. All three published by Marvel Music, a division of Marvel Comics. All three issues released in one paperback volume in 1995 as THE COMPLEAT ALICE COOPER.
Author: Written by Neil Gaiman, from a story by Neil Gaiman and Alice Cooper. Artwork by Todd Klein. Cover artwork (on all three issues) by Dave McKean. Colored by John Kalisz.
Content: Book I: "Act I: Bad Place Alone"
Book II: "Act II: Unholy War"
Book III: "Act III: Cleansed by Fire"
Plot: Steven, a high-school boy, is drawn into a theater run by the Showman (who looks mysteriously like Alice.) In the theater, Steven meets Mercy and is drawn into the show, which deals with the many horrors waiting for Steven in life. Steven is given an opportunity to join the show. After spending the next day being tormented by the Showman, Steven decides to return to the theater for the Grand Finale. Given the chance to either face the dangers and horrors of real life and death or merely to give up on life and no longer feel the pain, Steven must decide what to do.

This comic book series was created to help tell the story behind the music on THE LAST TEMPTATION album, and Alice had got Neil Gaiman to work on the story with him during the early stages of album production. Gaiman, a writer of novels, became well known for his work on a comic book series from Vertigo Comics (a division of DC Comics) called SANDMAN in the early 1990's — a series that was getting attention from peo-

The first issue of THE LAST TEMPTATION comic book.

ple who normally wouldn't read comics, including a large readership of women. Gaiman had also written horror tinged fantasy material including an excellent and funny book about the last days of the world called GOOD OMEN, and so was in the proper state of mind for a project of this sort with Alice.

Marvel Comics (who in 1979 had done an authorized Alice Cooper comic book for the FROM THE INSIDE album) produced the comic book series and the timing seemed to be perfect, not only for Alice's at the time yet-to-be-released album, but for Marvel as well. By the early 1990's Marvel had seen how well rock music oriented companies like Revolutionary Comics were doing with their unauthorized comics (including one on Alice, see Chapter 5, Part 5 for more details), and felt it was time that they got into the game. To do so, they developed their own line of comics called Marvel Music, that featured authorized biographical comics of many different performers along with fictional stories about performers as well (including a return of KISS in their own comic named KISSNATION.)

Marvel was notorious for becoming involved with a fad after its peak, when its death rattles had already been heard. It was a running joke among comic book fans that you could tell a fad was dead if Marvel based a character or comic around it (i.e. a disco-based superhero in 1980, etc.) Unfortunately, the same held true with the Marvel Music line of comics. By 1994, it was already apparent that the market was extremely limited and that sales were never as great as what some of the smaller companies would have had people believe. Marvel hedged and slowly began dismantling the line of comics even as a few reached the newsstands, including the first issue of THE LAST TEMPTATION and a biography on Bob Marley.

Alice fans could get the first issue of the comic series when it appeared since many stores carried the "limited edition" version of the album, which came with Book I of the comic book series. The comic book that came with the album featured the same cover as on the album itself, while the newsstand edition of Book I came with a different cover by the same artist, Dave McKean. Finding the second and third issue of the comic was much harder, because of the low distribution Marvel gave it, normally only appearing in stores specializing in comic books.

A collection of the three issues was finally released in 1995. In 1997 and 1998 autographed editions of the collection were available at Alice's concerts. There was also talk about a black velvet, hardback edition being produced, but this was never released.

As for the creativity behind the miniseries, Gaiman's writing is excellent and he manages to throw in several references to Alice's work outside of THE LAST TEMPTATION as well. Michael Zulli's artwork is very imaginative and is probably the finest presentation in a comic book of Alice in any form. It is excellent work by those involved and the comic book is worth having either as a stand alone series or as a complement to the album.

The second issue of THE LAST TEMPTATION comic book.

The third issue of THE LAST TEMPTATION comic book.

Part 5: Books and Comics

~~~ Chapter 6: "Luney Tune" ~~~

As can be seen in the previous chapters, Alice Cooper's career has included many official albums, singles, videos, and even books and comics. Still, these official projects are only part of the large volume of Alice-related material released over the years. This chapter examines some of the less common Alice-related material released, and may help fans better recognize albums that they may have seen in passing, but were unable to get any background on before buying.

The question that may occur to some readers at this point is — why bother? They may be thinking either: 1) If it has Alice on it, then it's worth getting, so who needs more info than that, or 2) If it's something that I already have on another album, then why buy the same track again? Frankly, the answer isn't that simple. As will be seen in Part 1 below, if a fan wanted to buy every variation of the TORONTO ROCK 'N' ROLL FESTIVAL concert (and, yes, there are fans this dedicated), they would end up with more than forty (and that's a low estimate) CDs, tapes and / or vinyl albums — all of which have wrong song title information and nearly all of which include two songs that were not even performed by Alice Cooper. More important, none of the albums from this show are considered to be part of Alice's official discography, but more details about that below.

The other side of the issue is helping fans find the best place to look for that elusive track that they wish they had, but don't know where to purchase. For example, if a fan wanted to get a copy of I Got a Line on You that Alice recorded in 1988, their initial objective would be to buy the soundtrack album for IRON EAGLE II. However, buying such an album (if one can find it) at the record store for full price is a lot to pay for just one track. Instead, this song can also be found on a couple of different singles and on two compilation albums — A NICE NIGHTMARE from 1997 and FREEDOM FOR FRANKENSTEIN from 1998. It's this knowledge that can help a fan get a better value for his money.

This chapter is presented in the following sections:
Part 1 — The 1969 Concert Albums
Part 2 — Compilation Albums (including "best of" packages)
Part 3 — Soundtrack Albums (including original recordings)
Part 4 — Guest Appearances
Part 5 — Performances by the Alice Cooper Group members
Part 6 — Bootleg Albums

Part 1 — The 1969 Concert Albums - Toronto Rock 'N' Roll Show and LIVE AT THE WHISKY A GO GO

In 1969, the Alice Cooper Group was on the threshold of getting its first national exposure. This came not only with the April release of PRETTIES FOR YOU, but also through a two month long cross country tour in promotion of the album and periodic performances across the country at rock festivals. The band also reached the big screen with a quick bit in DIARY OF A MAD HOUSEWIFE (see Chapter 2), while making an interesting splash at the Toronto Rock 'N' Roll Revival in September of that year. It was a big year for the band — maybe not in terms of money, but certainly considering the positive opportunities that were coming their way.

During that year, two of their shows were recorded with the knowledge of the band and their management. The first was the Whisky A Go Go show, which was recorded by Alice's label at the time, Straight / Bizarre, and the second was the Toronto Rock 'N' Roll Festival concert, which was recorded with permission from Alive, Alice's management. Oddly, although recorded in 1969, neither of these two recordings was released until the 1980's.

Album Title: ALICE COOPER AT THE WHISKY A GO GO 1969
Released: Recorded March 1969 at the Whisky a Go Go. Released February 1992 by Bizarre / Straight. Distributed through Rhino.
Catalog No.: R2 70369
Media: CD.
Song List: No Longer Umpire / Today Mueller / 10 Minutes Before the Worm / Levity Ball / Nobody Likes Me / B.B. on Mars / Sing Low, Sweet Cheerio / Changing, Arranging

Although actually recorded about six months before the Toronto show recordings, LIVE AT THE WHISKY A GO GO did not reach fan circles until 1989 when Rhino released a CD and cassette in America. The UK label, Enigma, who had also released CD versions of PRETTIES FOR YOU and EASY ACTION (as counterparts to Rhino's US release of the same CDs), was to have released the Whisky recordings as well, but plans were dropped with the demise of the label that same year. Edsel, another UK label, soon picked up where Enigma left off and released the album on CD, cassette and vinyl.

The recordings were done in the Spring of 1969 during a performance that was also an audition for Warner Brothers representatives (who, ironically, passed on the band at the time.) For contractual reasons, the recordings became the property of the Straight / Bizarre label that Alice Cooper was with from 1969 through 1971 (before being bought out by Warner Brothers.) Nothing more was heard about the recordings until two decades later.

The LIVE AT THE WHISKY A GO GO CD.

By 1989, Compact Discs had won the market battle over vinyl and many labels were re-releasing their artists' catalogs on CD. This was certainly true for Alice, thanks to the success of the 1989 studio album TRASH (a major hit for Alice's label at the time, Epic.) Warner Brothers took the opportunity to begin reissuing much of their Alice Cooper catalog on CD, while PRETTIES FOR YOU and EASY ACTION were licensed out to Enigma and Rhino for release in the UK and the US, respectively. Concurrently, both Enigma (and Edsel) in the UK and Rhino in the US were able to negotiate the release of the Whisky A Go Go recordings because of the reissuing frenzy.

As with the Toronto '69 recording listed below, the album released from the Whisky A Go Go show was not sanctioned or okayed by Alice or his management. On the other hand, Enigma did have the good taste to seek at least partial approval from Alice for the artwork used on the CD cover (the same cover used for the Edsel and Rhino releases.) Nevertheless, the album appears here, not as part of the official discography, because of Alice's lack of direct involvement with the project.

Nobody Likes Me didn't appear on PRETTIES FOR YOU, and until the release of this album in 1992, the only way to hear this lone track was to have the flexi-disc that appeared on the back of the KILLER tour book from 1971, or to find one of the numerous and horrible Toronto '69 albums listed below.

Notable Reissues:
Album Title: ALICE COOPER LIVE AT THE WHISKY A GO GO 1969
Released: 1992 by Edsel, UK.
Catalog No.: NEST 903 (vinyl) and NESTCD 903 (CD)
Media: Vinyl and CD.

This was a limited edition (reportedly only 1,500 copies) vinyl version of the album released in the UK.

Album Title: ALICE COOPER LIVE AT THE WHISKY A GO GO 1969
Released: 1992 by BMG, Australia.
Catalog No.: PSMCD 1231
Media: CD.

Released on the Australian MCA label, which Alice was on back in 1986 and 1987 for CONSTRICTOR and

RAISE YOUR FIST AND YELL.

Album Title: **ALICE COOPER LIVE AT THE WHISKY A GO GO 1969**
Released: 1992 by Bizzare, Japan.
Catalog No.: PSCW1081
Media: CD.

Japanese release of the album came with an obi.

Album Title: **THE TORONTO ROCK 'N' ROLL REVIVAL 1969, VOLUME IV**
Released: 1982 by Accord. Recorded September 12, 1969 at the Toronto Rock 'N' Roll Revival festival in Toronto, Canada.
Catalog No.: SN 7162
Media: Vinyl.
Song List: Ain't That Just Like a Woman / Painting a Picture / Group Instrumental / I've Written Home to Mother / Freak Out Song / Goin' to the River / Nobody Likes Me / Science Fiction

Ah, the infamous Toronto Rock 'N' Roll Revival recording. In September 1969, the Alice Cooper Group was asked to perform at the Toronto Rock 'N' Roll Revival festival in Toronto, Canada. This was a big event that included many famous performers of rock and roll music including the first public stage appearance of John Lennon outside the Beatles and the first stage appearance of a Beatle performing to a large audience in nearly two years.

Although **PRETTIES FOR YOU** was out by this time, the Alice Cooper Group was still relatively unknown outside of the Los Angeles area, so their impact on the audience was a bit mixed. The band was still going through a bit of an experimental musical phase at this point and the stage show was not as focused as it became over the next couple of years. That may be just as well, since other performers there that day were also experimenting (take for example the fifteen minutes plus version of **Don't Cry, Kyoko** performed by Lennon and Yoko Ono.) The Alice Cooper Group also performed as the backup band for Gene Vincent. In fact, Alice Cooper Group would dedicate **Return of the Spiders** to Vincent on their second album in 1970. Also at the concert were the Doors, Bo Diddley, Chuck Berry and Jerry Lee Lewis, among others. See the entry under tour dates in Chapter 2 for more info about the actual concert.

A recording of the event was made and pretty much locked away for years until 1982 when Accord decided to release a series of albums with performances from many of the people that were at the festival. A deal was struck with the owners of the recordings and the Alice Cooper performance was released as volume four in the series with original artwork by Steve Hunter (not the guitar player) that was reminiscent of the artwork used on the **SCHOOL DAYS** album released in 1973.

On the bright side, fans were happy to see such early material being released. The major problem and annoyance to Alice fans, however, was that many of the tracks were listed on the album cover with incorrect song titles, and two of the tracks (**Ain't That Just Like a Woman** and **Goin' To the River**) are not even Alice, but by another performer who also played at the festival. Speculation is that the performer was Ronnie Hawkins, who not only also appeared at the festival, but had both songs as part of his set list at the time. Members of Hawkin's own fan club believe the recordings to be him as well.

How do such mistakes come about? Two reasons: one, the release of the album was not officially sanctioned by the any of the original band members, or anyone associated with them; and, two, the people who put the album out couldn't be bothered to research the material to make sure that the tracks used were actually Alice Cooper. Nor could they be bothered getting song titles correct. All that mattered was that someone was in legal possession of the recordings from that show and they wanted to make some money off of them. In the grand tradition of bootlegs everywhere, a system of guesses was used instead. Perhaps it is just as well, in reflection, that the two Ronnie Hawkins tracks appeared, otherwise the album would have been less than 21 minutes long.

The actual song titles are:
Painting a Picture is really No Longer Umpire
Group Instrumental (a.k.a. A.C. Instrumental and An Instrumental) is really Lay Down and Die, Goodbye (portion only)
I've Written Home to Mother is really Lay Down and Die, Goodbye (portion only)
Freak Out Song is really Don't Blow Your Mind

Nobody Likes Me is Nobody Likes Me (the only one listed correctly on the album)
Science Fiction is really Fields of Regret

Don't Blow Your Mind and Lay Down and Die, Goodbye were both previously recorded by the band during their Nazz / Spiders days, with Lay Down ... being re-recorded for EASY ACTION in 1970, while Fields of Regret and No Longer Umpire appeared on the first album, PRETTIES FOR YOU. A studio version of Nobody Likes Me later turned up on the KILLER tour book as a flex-a-disc that could be cut from the book and played on a record player. A live cut of Nobody Likes Me also appeared on the 1992 release ALICE COOPER AT THE WHISKY A GO GO 1969.

With dismal sales, the interest in these recordings hardly registered on the scale. That would have been the end of the releases surrounding the Toronto show except for something that happened in 1985 — Alice came back big with He's Back.

As interest in Alice Cooper grew (and grew with a whole new generation of fans), the company that owned the tapes decided that it was a good idea to license the material to other companies. Unfortunately, this meant licensing the material to many different record companies and supplying these companies with the same incorrect information as used on the first release back in 1982. As the receiving companies didn't research the material that closely either (although there has been at least one exception — a company that announced on their album's sleeve that Alice Cooper did not perform two of the tracks on the album), the material keeps being reissued repeatedly with the same wrong information. To deceive fans further, the companies putting out these packages normally used photos of Alice from the 1970's up through to the present day, to give buyers the illusion that the album is both recent and different from all the other repackages crowding the store shelves.

As can be seen when examining the titles listed below, many have come out within the past ten years, and, no doubt, many more are sure to follow. Tracking down copies of the Toronto recordings can be "hit and miss" for collectors — while many turn up in record stores, mixed in with the official albums in the racks, it's just as likely that they'll be found in the $5 bins at the used record shops, or at the local gas station in the "buy 3 for $9.99" rack. Of all of these variations, none were approved, okayed or sanctioned by Alice or his management, thus, their appearance here.

THE TORONTO ROCK 'N' ROLL REVIVAL, VOLUME IV is of significance since it was the first of the albums to be released, and is the one that's normally referred to by other companies when packaging their own version of the recordings. If any of these Toronto show albums are to be considered collectible, it is this one and the colored wax vinyl edition of the album that came out soon afterward. Beyond these early releases of the material, a collector interested in items for resale should look elsewhere as this is truly an area where only the die-hard fans should venture.

The various reissues appear under a variety of names, most commonly as FREAK OUT or some variation on that name. Below is a group summary of the many different versions of this recording. It's safe to say that this listing is not all of the titles, merely a good number of them. For the convenience of collectors, all other variations of the Toronto '69 show are listed in alphabetical order.

Album Title: **AIN'T THAT JUST LIKE A WOMAN**
Released: 1994 by Music Reflextion, Israel.
Catalog No.: CD 1421.2005-2
Media: CD.

Album Title: **AIN'T THAT JUST LIKE A WOMAN**
Released: 1996 by Music Mirror, Czech. Distributed in Switzerland.
Catalog No.: 1021.2005.2
Media: CD.

Album Title: **AIN'T THAT JUST LIKE A WOMAN**
Released: July 15, 1996 by Music Mirror, Germany.
Catalog No.: MUMI 212005
Media: CD.

Album Title: **ALICE COOPER**
Released: by Object Enterprises, France. Release date unknown.

Part 1: The 1969 Concert Albums

Catalog No.: ONN 52
Media: CD

The cover is a photo of Alice in black leather and a black hat, holding a microphone in one hand and a knife in the other. Because the cover is blue and there is no title beyond that of Alice's name, some fans call this album THE BLUE ALBUM. Because of this, some discographies list both THE BLUE ALBUM and ALICE COOPER as two different albums. Lay Down ... is again listed as An Instrumental.

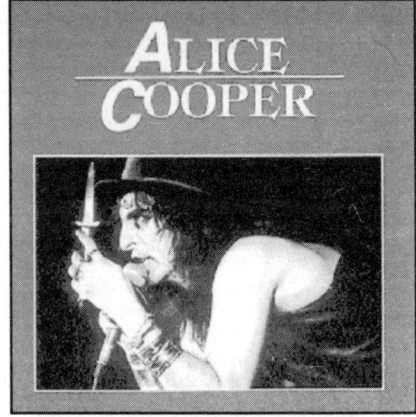

THE BLUE ALBUM - see entry for ALICE COOPER above.

Object Enterprises version on CD.
Also known as THE BLUE ALBUM in fandom.

Album Title: **EXPERIENCE**
Released: 1996 by Weton, Holland.
Release date unknown.
Catalog No.: EXPO 10
Media: CD

The photo of Alice in concert on the cover is from the HEY STOOPID tour. The CD was manufactured as a picture disc.

Album Title: **FREAK OUT (SSI 9934)**
Released: 1991 by Rock Classics, a division of Creative Sounds, Ltd., USA.
Catalog No.: SSI 9934 (CD) and SSI 3334 (cassette)
Media: CD and Cassette.

Weton version on CD.

Part of Lay Down ... is moved to after Goin' To the River and is listed as A.C. Instrumental.

Album Title: **FREAK OUT**
Released: 1993 by Pilz Entertainment, Inc.
Catalog No.: 449833-2
Media: CD.
Song List: Don't Blow Your Mind / Ain't That Just Like a Woman / Painting a Picture / Lay Down and Die, Goodbye (portion) / Fields of Regret / Goin' to the River / Lay Down and Die, Goodbye (portion) / Nobody Likes Me

The track listing order for this album is very different from what was used for most of the FREAK OUT albums listed here. The same track listing can also be found on the Omni entertainment FREAK OUT album. The Pilz Entertainment release came with the same photo cover found on the Creative Sounds FREAK OUT album.

Album Title: **FREAK OUT**
Released: 1996 by company unknown. Distributed in Denmark.
Catalog No.: MCPS RM 1532
Media: CD.

Came on a picture disc CD.

Another version.

Chapter 6: "Luney Tune"

Album Title: **FREAK OUT**
Released: Late 1980's by Omni Entertainment Group.
Catalog No.: 1204
Media: Cassette.

Same track listing as on the Pilz Entertainment FREAK OUT album. Same photo on the cover as on the Teller House FREAK OUT SONG album.

Album Title: **FREAK OUT / FREAK OUT SONG**
Released: 1995 by Excelsior, a division of Retro Music, Quebec, Canada.
Catalog No.: EXL10782
Media: CD.

Ain't That Just Like a Woman is moved to the end of the album. The cover of the album lists the title as FREAK OUT, but the actual CD says FREAK OUT SONG.

Album Title: **FREAK OUT SONG**
Released: 1982 by Tellerhouse Video products, Inc., USA.
Catalog No.: TEL-4007
Media: Cassette.

Don't Blow Your Mind is at the beginning of the album, while part of Lay Down ... is again after Goin' To the River. The cover is a photo of Alice holding a microphone.

Album Title: **FREAK OUT SONG**
Released: 1985 by Showcase. Copyrighted 1984 by Castle Communications, England.
Catalog No.: SHLP 115 (vinyl) and SHTC 115 (cassette)
Media: Vinyl. Cassette released 1985.

Same track order as on the Tellerhouse Video cassette release.

Album Title: **FREAK OUT SONG**
Released: 1994 by Retro Music, Canada.
Catalog No.: SLD13522
Media: CD.

And yet another version.

Same picture used on the cover as on the Excelsior release listed above. The cover lists the title as FREAK OUT SONG, but the spine of the CD says THE FREAK OUT SONG.

Album Title: **FREAK OUT SONG**
Released: July 14, 1995 by Prime Cuts.
Catalog No.: PRK 1352.1 (cassette) and PRK 1352.2 (CD)
Media: CD and Cassette.

Album Title: **FREAK OUT SONGS**
Released: early 1990's by Tec. , Japan.
Catalog No.: TECX 25287
Media: CD.

Prime Cuts CD edition.

Part 1: The 1969 Concert Albums

Thunderbolt version on CD.

Album Title: **HOME TO MOTHER**
Released: Release date and record company unknown.
Catalog No.: Unknown.
Media: CD.

Album Title: **LADIES MAN**
Released: 1987 and reissued 1988 by Thunderbolt, a division of Magnum Music Group, UK.
Catalog No.: THBM 005 (vinyl), THBC 005 (cassette), CDTHBM 005 (CD reissue from August 1988), and TDB 90 (CD reissue from September 5, 1995.)
Media: CD, Vinyl and Cassette.

There are two versions of the CD. The original version has the same cover as the vinyl release, while the reissue has a photo of Alice in leather holding a microphone. Fields of Regret is listed as Science Fiction for Alice and the instrumental portion of Lay Down and Die, Goodbye is listed as For Alice.

Shanghai Music version of LEGENDS on CD.

Album Title: **LEGENDS**
Released: 1994 by Shanghai Music Ltd.
Catalog No.: LECD 085
Media: CD.

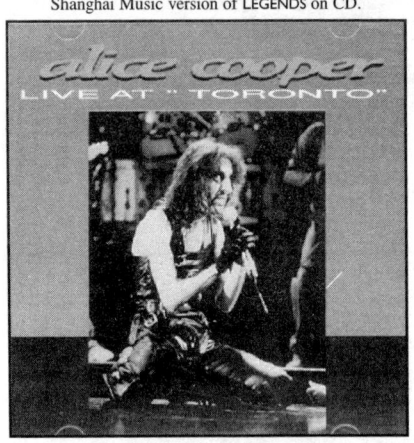

Peachtree Music version on CD.

Album Title: **LIVE AT "TORONTO"**
Released: 1993 by Peachtree Music, Inc. and Classic Sound, Inc., USA.
Catalog No.: Classic 7644
Media: CD and Cassette.

The cover is of Alice in concert in black leather and holding a microphone with the band in the background. This photo is from early in the 1978-79 MADHOUSE ROCKS tour and Alice is shown wearing a black athletic supporter cup instead of the familiar red one. Nobody Likes Me is listed as Nobody Like Me.

Album Title: **THE MAGIC COLLECTION**
Released: Released by Arc Records. Release date unknown.
Catalog No.: Unknown.
Media: Unknown.

Album Title: **MAGIC COLLECTION**
Released: Released by M&E, a division of Telesonic, Holland.
Catalog No.: MEC 949019
Media: CD.

Album Title: **MAGIC COLLECTION**
Released: Released by Magic Collect, UK. Release date unknown.
Catalog No.: Unknown.
Media: Unknown.

Album Title: **NOBODY LIKE ME**
Released: 1994 by MCPS, Europe. Licensed from the Long Island Music Company Limited.
Catalog No.: GAL 052
Media: CD.

The cover photo of Alice is from 1986. The title of the album is missing the "s" from NOBODY LIKES ME, although it appears correctly in the track listing. Goin' to the River and Ain't That Just Like a Woman are paired together at the end of the album, which may actually be a plus as neither song is by Alice and fans can merely skip over the end of the album instead of jumping around in the middle of the album to avoid them.

Album Title: **NOBODY LIKES ... ALICE**
Released: Release date and record company unknown.
Catalog No.: Unknown.
Media: Unknown.

Album Title: **NOBODY LIKES ... LIVE**
Released: September 14, 1997 by Going for a Song, UK.
Catalog No.: GOIN 071
Media: CD.

Album Title: **NOBODY LIKES ... ALICE, ALICE COOPER LIVE**
Released: Released by Going for a Song. Release date unknown.
Catalog No.: GFS071
Media: CD.

Album Title: **NOBODY LIKES ME**
Released: Released by Pulsar, France. Release date unknown.
Catalog No.: PULS010
Media: CD.

Album Title: **NOBODY LIKES ME**
Released: Released by Success Records. Release date unknown.
Catalog No.: 2157 CD.
Media: CD.

Different from the Pulsar release in cover artwork only. The Success release has a picture of Alice holding a microphone.

Album Title: **NOBODY LIKES ME (THE WORLD OF ALICE COOPER)**
Released: 1992 by Trace Records (a.k.a. Trace Trading), Holland.
Catalog No.: 0401272 (CD) and 0401274 (cassette).
Media: CD and Cassette.

Goin' To the River and Ain't that Just Like a Woman appear at the end of the album. The cover photo shows Alice singing into a cordless microphone as a red spotlight filters through his hair.

Trace Records version on CD.

Part 1: The 1969 Concert Albums

Album Title: **PAINTING A PICTURE**
Released: Release date and record company unknown.
Catalog No.: Unknown.
Media: Unknown.

Album Title: **ROCK AND ROLL REVIVAL: TORONTO '69**
Released: April, 1984 by Design, UK.
Catalog No.: PIXLP 3
Media: Vinyl picture disc.

Album Title: **ROCK LEGENDS VOLUME 2**
Released: Release date and record company unknown.
Catalog No.: Unknown.
Media: CD.

Album Title: **SCIENCE FICTION**
Released: 1985 and reissued 1988 by Golden Circle, Inc., USA.
Catalog No.: GC57531 (original cassette) and GC57531A (1988 reissue.)
Media: Cassette.

Ain't That Just Like a Woman and Goin' to the River do not appear on the album. Besides a different cover, the 1988 reissue is the same as the original 1985 Golden Circle release.

Album Title: **SCIENCE FICTION**
Released: Released by Music Otions. Release date unknown.
Catalog No.: Unknown.
Media: Unknown.

Album Title: **SNORTING ANTHRAX**
Released: March 23, 1998 by Dressed To Kill, UK.
Catalog No.: DRESS603
Media: CD.

Gold Circle cassette of the '69 Toronto show.

The cover is another concert photo of Alice from the wrong time period. This CD has the two non-Cooper tracks at the end of the album.

Album Title: **TORONTO ROCK 'N' ROLL REVIVAL 1969, VOLUME IV**
Released: 1982 by Breakaway Label, UK.
Catalog No.: BWY 70 (vinyl) and CC 70 (cassette)
Media: Vinyl and Cassette.

Album Title: **TORONTO ROCK 'N' ROLL REVIVAL 1969, VOL. IV**
Released: 1982 by Design Records.
Catalog No.: PIX LP3
Media: Picture disc Vinyl.

The A-side of this picture disc shows Alice with a giant tube of toothpaste. the B-side shows him with a snake wrapped around his head. Possibly the same album listed above as ROCK AND ROLL REVIVAL: TORONTO '69.

A-side of the picture disc from Design Records.

Part 2 — Compilation Albums

From I'm Eighteen onward, Alice Cooper has been one of the few lucky rock and roll performers to have had a series of outstanding hit singles over a period of years. More importantly, not only were these songs hits in the musical marketplace at the time of their release, but they have remained with us as classics referred to again and again over the years — perhaps not always by Alice, or in their original forms, but referred to nonetheless. Compilation albums are one of the ways that these songs end up being rekindled in our memories as time goes by.

Most compilation albums were available through mail order or from your local supermarket display through such companies as Ronco or K-Tel back in the 1970's. For kids wanting to hear the latest hits, but without the pocket money to buy all the albums that were coming out, these compilation albums were a way of hearing at least a few hit songs without going broke. If nothing else, they made it easier to plan the music at a party. And for the record companies that allowed the material to appear on compilation albums, it was a way to promote some of their performers in a cheap medium.

Warner Brothers was also doing compilation albums, with the emphasis on promotion and not much else. Over the years (and especially in the early to mid 1970's), Warner has released many promotional albums available only through mail order that featured tracks from many of their subsidiary labels. These albums, commonly called "samplers" (since they gave listeners a sampling of what the label had to offer), were normally double LPs that came in a gatefold cover which advertised the performers in lengthy biographical sketches with possibly a picture or two. Even with the Alice Cooper Group's first release, PRETTIES FOR YOU, Alice was no stranger to this type of promotion, as will be seen below.

A compilation album featuring a track from Alice.

A variety of compilation albums have been created over the years that contain material from Alice only. These compilations were released either by Alice's record label or through labels in foreign markets. This is especially common for artists in foreign markets, since many countries do not continuously keep a performer's catalog available for retail purchase. Compilation albums help attract interest in the artists as well as attracting additional dollars for the label with tracks that can be used again and again.

Confusion sets in for fans, however, when trying to figure out why many of these compilation albums are not considered part of the official discography listed in early chapters. Why is GREATEST HITS from 1974 listed with the official discography, while an album like CLASSICKS from 1995 isn't? The answer is simple — Alice was with Warner Brothers in 1974 and was directly involved with the release of GREATEST HITS, but he had left Epic by 1995 and was not directly involved with the release of CLASSICKS.

The collectibility of compilation albums is a fickle bird. Some collectors are not big on these albums since the material on them is rarely different from what can be found on the official full length releases. This is especially true with some "pure-Alice" compilations from Alice's label in the 1980's and 1990's. The other side of this issue is the fans who want to have anything released in connection with their favorite artists, and if a compilation album has a picture of the artist on the sleeve, then it's worth picking up. Also, you never know when a rare live or studio track may pop up on a compilation album unannounced.

Another compilation album featuring Alice Cooper.

While a variety of compilation albums are listed below, this is not to suggest that these are all of the compilation albums featuring Alice Cooper that have ever been released.

Album Title: **ZAPPED**
Released: 1969 by Bizarre.
Catalog No.: PRO 368
Media: Vinyl.
Song List: Titanic Overture and Refrigerator Heaven

This was a sampler album released by Frank Zappa's labels, Bizarre and Straight. The album was available through a coupon included on the paper sleeve of Straight and Bizarre albums released in the Winter of 1969, including PRETTIES FOR YOU. The cover shows a large black and white photo of Zappa.

ZAPPED, the first compilation album with material from Alice Cooper..

Album Title: **LOONEY TUNES**
Released: 1970 by Warner Brothers.
Catalog No.: Unknown.
Media: Triple Vinyl.
Song List: Return of the Spiders

A sampler album from Warner Brothers, this one was not directly from Straight or Bizarre, but rather an album featuring tracks from labels associated with or subsidiaries of Warner Brothers.

Album Title: **TOGETHER**
Released: 1971 by Warner Brothers.
Catalog No.: PRO 486
Media: Vinyl.
Song List: Long Way To Go

Another sampler album from Warner Brothers.

Album Title: **WARNER / REPRISE DISPLAY CASE VOL. 2**
Released: 1972 by Warner Brothers.
Catalog No.: PRO 508
Media: Double Vinyl.
Song List: Be My Lover

Another sampler album from Warner Brothers.

Album Title: **THE WHOLE BURBANK CATALOG**
Released: 1972 by Warner Brothers.
Catalog No.: PRO 512
Media: Double Vinyl.
Song List: Be My Lover (Side Two, Track 6)

As you can see by this point, Warner Brothers did many of these mail order sampler albums. Also included on the album were Todd Rundgren, Jethro Tull, Fleetwood Mac, T Rex and The William Tell Overture from the soundtrack of A CLOCKWORK ORANGE. A brief history of the band is given in the text inside the gatefold cover (although the band members are listed as artists who became musicians to extend their artwork), along with some positive critical reviews of the band. Album covers are shown for PRETTIES FOR YOU, EASY ACTION, LOVE IT TO DEATH (the non-censored cover, ironically enough) and KILLER.

Album Title: **FRUITY**
Released: 1972 by Kinney Music, West Germany, a division of Warner Brothers Reprise. Also released 1972 by Warner Brothers Reprise in the UK.
Catalog No.: K26005 (UK); no catalog number on the West German edition..
Media: Vinyl.
Song List: Under My Wheel (Side One, Track One)

This West German / UK vinyl release came in a specially designed round album cover, with a picture of a bowl full of fruit. The UK edition was also on the green Warner Brothers label, but came in a Reprise inner sleeve.

Album Title: **BURBANK**
Released: 1973 by Warner Brothers.
Catalog No.: PRO 529
Media: Double Vinyl.
Song List: Public Animal #9

Another mail order WB sampler album.

Album Title: **APPETIZERS**
Released: 1973 by Warner Brothers.
Catalog No.: PRO 569
Media: Double Vinyl.
Song List: Billion Dollar Babies

Another mail order WB sampler album.

Album Title: **DON KIRSHNER PRESENTS ROCK POWER**
Released: 1974 by CBS Records.
Catalog No.: P-12417
Media: Vinyl.
Song List: No More Mr. Nice Guy (Side One, Track Five)

Among other artists on the album are the Doobie Brothers and Black Sabbath (**Paranoid**.)

Album Title: **LISTEN TO THE MUSIC - 20 SMASH HITS**
Released: 1975 by Arcade.
Catalog No.: ADE P11
Media: Vinyl.
Song List: Teenage Lament '74 (Side One, Track Seven)

Album Title: **THE PEOPLE'S RECORD**
Released: 1976 by Warner Brothers.
Catalog No.: PRO 645
Media: Double Vinyl.
Song List: Go to Hell

One of the later Warner Brothers sampler albums. As the 1970's progressed, these samplers became less and less frequent.

Album Title: **PURE POWER**
Released: 1976 by Ronco.
Catalog No.: TV-2510
Media: Vinyl.
Song List: I'll Never Cry (Side One, Track Five)

The cover for ALICE COOPER GOES TO HELL appears as a small picture on the front cover of this compilation album, along with a picture of Alice on the back.

Album Title: **THE ROCK REVELATION**
Released: 1976 (possibly) by Warner Brothers.

Catalog No.: WB STMP 1 A
Media: Triple-Vinyl.
Song List: School's Out (Side One, Track Six)

Another in the long series of Warner Brothers sampler albums.

Album Title: **MUSIC MACHINE**
Released: Fall 1977 by K-Tel Records.
Catalog No.: TU 2568
Media: Vinyl, Cassette and 8-Track.
Song List: You and Me (Side Two, Last Track)

Also featured on this album were Wild Cherry, Foreigner, KISS, Abba, and Elton John. Robby the Robot from the film FORBIDDEN PLANET appears on the cover.

Album Title: **MONSTERS**
Released: 1979 by Warner Brothers Records.
Catalog No.: PRO-A-796
Media: Double Vinyl.
Song List: From the Inside (Side Four, Track Four)

MUSIC MACHINE, a K-Tel collection with You and Me.

Also featured on this WB sampler album were George Harrison, Bob Marley, Van Halen, Rickie Lee Jones, Chaka Khan and the Doobie Brothers.

Album Title: **COLLECTION**
Released: 1982 by Warner Brothers, Germany.
Catalog No.: WB 26 241 (vinyl) and 426-241 (cassette)
Media: Vinyl and Cassette.
Song List: School's Out / Elected / Billion Dollar Babies / Who Do You Think We Are / Teenage Lament '74 / Hello Hooray / Hallowed Be My Name / No More Mr. Nice Guy / I'm Eighteen / You Want It, You Got It / How You Gonna See Me Now / Killer

A "greatest hits" package from Germany that featured some songs not commonly seen, including Hallowed Be My Name and songs from the post-FLUSH THE FASHION period like Who Do You Think We Are. The cover of the album displays a photo of Alice from the same photo shoot that produced the photo found on the single for the German Talk Talk single released in 1980.

Album Title: **REMEMBER THE 70's, VOLUME 6**
Released: 1984 by Arcade.
Catalog No.: ADEHC 160
Media: Double Vinyl.
Song List: School's Out (Side Two, Track Seven) and Hello, Hooray (Side Four, Track One)

Album Title: **ROCK ANTHEMS II**
Released: 1986 by K-Tel.
Catalog No.: NE 1319
Media: Double Vinyl.
Song List: School's Out (Side One, Track Six)

Album Title: **ONES ON ONE**
Released: 1988 by BBC Records.
Catalog No.: REF 693
Media: Double Vinyl.
Song List: School's Out (Side Two, Track Four)

Album Title: **MASTERS OF METAL CRANKIN' UP 1970 - 1980**
Released: 1989 by JCI and Warner Special Products.
Catalog No.: JCD 4510
Media: CD.
Song List: Under My Wheels

Album Title: **MATERS OF METAL STRIKEFORCE VOLUME 2**
Released: 1989 by JCI and Warner Special Products.
Catalog No.: JCD 4541
Media: CD.
Song List: Give the Radio Back

Album Title: **MONSTER HITS**
Released: 1989 by CBS Records.
Catalog No.: CBS Hits 11
Media: Double-Vinyl.
Song List: Poison (Side Two, Track Six)

Album Title: **GLAM SLAM (NE 2434)**
Released: 1989 by K-Tel International (UK) Ltd.
Catalog No.: NE 2434 (vinyl), CE 2434 (cassette) and NCD 3434 (CD.)
Media: Vinyl, Cassette and CD.
Song List: School's Out (Side Two, Track Seven)

Released at a time in the late 1980's when nostalgia for the "glam" rock days of the early 1970's was nearing a peak, this album featured many artists that had major hits in the United Kingdom. This is to be kept in mind by American fans who pick up the double vinyl album, as certainly hearing two Gary Glitter tracks on the album is a bit perplexing (especially when neither is Rock and Roll, Part II.) Nor does the band 10cc readily come to mind when the term "glam" is spoken. Still, any album that contained Slade, Sweet, Suzi Quatro, and Sparks, along with Alice, on one album has to have something going for it. The album comes with a brief history of the songs and artists, including a couple of sentences about Alice. While the cassette version of this album (CE 2434) contains all 29 tracks from the vinyl album, the CD version (NCD 3434) only has 20 of the vinyl tracks.

GLAM SLAM cassette.

Album Title: **BEAST OF ALICE COOPER**
Released: 1989 by Warner Brothers, UK. Reissued May 19, 1998 by PID, Germany.
Catalog No.: WEA 241 781-1 (vinyl, UK), WEA 241 781-4 (cassette, UK) and WEA 241781-2 (CD, UK)
WAR 24178-1 (vinyl, Australia) and WAR 24178-2 (CD, Australia)
WE 833 / 2292-41781-2 (CD, France)
WPCR-1245 (CD, Japan)
2032 (CD 1998 German reissue)
Media: Vinyl, Cassette and CD.
Song List: School's Out / Under My Wheels / Billion Dollar Babies / Be My Lover / Desperado / Is It My Body / Only Women Bleed / Elected / Hello, Hooray / No More Mr. Nice Guy / Teenage Lament '74 / Muscle of Love / Department of Youth

A release from 1989 that's merely a repackaging of the 1974 compilation album GREATEST HITS with three additional tracks (two from the 1975 Atlantic Records' WELCOME TO MY NIGHTMARE album and one from BILLION DOLLAR BABIES.) While it's still a good collection of songs, fans may want to pass one or the other up.

WB compilation album BEAST OF ALICE COOPER.

The album cover shows Alice from his early position of tearing at his shirt during I'm Eighteen from the IN CONCERT television program. The album charted in Australia at No. 49.

Album Title: **PRINCE OF DARKNESS**
Released: 1989 by MCA.
Catalog No.: R163192 (vinyl), MCAD-42315 (CD), MCAC-42315 (cassette) released 1989 by MCA
MVCM 18534 (CD) released September 30, 1997 by MCA, Japan
MCBBD 4231 (CD) released October 3, 1997 by Universal, Canada
Media: Vinyl, Cassette and CD.
Song List: Prince of Darkness / Roses on White Lace / He's Back (The Man Behind the Mask) / Billion Dollar Babies / Lock Me Up / Simple Disobedience / Thrill My Gorilla / Life and Death of the Party / Freedom

A hasty repackaging of material from Alice's two MCA studio albums, CONSTRICTOR and RAISE YOUR FIST AND YELL. The track listing on this compilation is at least interesting, and includes a live version of Billion Dollar Babies. The downside of this is that the track listings on the album state the live track as recorded in 1976. This is definitely incorrect. The live track is actually from the 1981 French television special 16 TRACKS (normally called THE PARIS SPECIAL), and can also be found on the Teenage Frankenstein 12" vinyl single released in the UK. Artwork on the album's cover shows a portrait of Alice as a symbol on a playing card.

PRINCE OF DARKNESS album.

Album Title: **TO HELL AND BACK ALICE COOPER'S GREATEST HITS**
Released: 1989 by Hammond, Australia.
Catalog No.: HAM-115 (vinyl) and CAS-HAM-115 (cassette)
Media: Vinyl and Cassette.
Song List: Only Women Bleed / Department of Youth / Muscle of Love / Teenage Lament '74 / You and Me / Desperado / I'm Eighteen / Is It My Body / School's Out / Billion Dollar Babies / Go to Hell / I Never Cry / Wish You Were Here / How You Gonna See Me Now / Under My Wheels / (No More) Love at Your Convenience

It seems that the Australians really know how to put a compilation album together. You certainly have to give them a hand for the selection of songs on this album. At a time when some companies were just rehashing material from two albums, there's a bit more of a mix on this album.

Australian compilation alubum TO HELL AND BACK.

Album Title: **RAW Magazine #27**
Released: September 1989.
Catalog No.: 27
Media: Four-track EP.
Song List: I'm Your Gun

This was a special edition of Issue #27 of the heavy metal magazine RAW. Also included on the four track EP were Bad English and Living Colour. The packaging on the plastic sealed magazine states only the name of the performers and not the actual tracks on the EP.

Album Title: **WE WILL ROCK YOU**
Released: 1990 (?) by Thomsun, Australia.
Catalog No.: ENB-1746
Media: Cassette.
Song List: School's Out (Side One, Track Ten)

EP single that came with specially marked copies of issue #27 of RAW magazine.

For American tastes, this release seems fascinating in its selection of songs, with tracks ranging from Toto (Hold the Line) through Warrant (Cherry Pie.) The tapes are on 90 minute Thomsun cassettes and would actually make a good road trip tape for someone wanting to relive the 70's and 80's. The tape came in a pink plastic box that has a slip case area for the cassette. The cassette also came with a folded up lyric sheet for some tracks (School's Out is not included.) You can tell by the lyric sheet and the back of the cassette box that it was obviously printed in another country (probably Japan) and then sold into Australia. This was followed up by another Thomsun Original, ROCK BUSTERS.

Album Title: **ROCK BUSTERS**
Released: 1990 (?) by Thomson, Australia.
Catalog No.: ENB-1768
Media: Cassette.
Song List: Poison (Side Two, Track Three)

Packaged much like the WE WILL ROCK YOU collection listed above, this collection has many of the same songs as the previous collection. Still, a diverse group of performers, from Alice to Pat Benatar to Yes to Bad Company.

Two Thomsun cassette compilations featuring Alice Cooper tracks.

Album Title: **ELVIRA PRESENTS HAUNTED HITS**
Released: 1990 by Rhino Records.
Catalog No.: R2-71492 (CD) and R4-71492 (cassette)
Media: CD and Cassette.
Song List: Welcome to My Nightmare

A compilation album with horror movie host ("the hostess with the mostest") Elvira. The CD contains several additional tracks, but there is only the one Alice track on the album in either variation. Rhino followed this up with ELVIRA PRESENTS MONSTER HITS.

Album Title: **TWISTED METAL**
Released: 1990 by K-Tel Records.
Catalog No.: 782-2
Media: CD.
Song List: He's Back (The Man Behind the Mask)

Also included on this compilation were W.A.S.P., Ozzy Osbourne, Twisted Sister, Ted Nugent and KISS.

TWISTED METAL K-Tel album.

Part 2: Compilation Albums

Album Title: OPERATION ROCK 'N' ROLL
Released: 1991 by Columbia / Epic.
Catalog No.: ESK 5995 (CD) and EAT 4097 (cassette)
Media: CD and Cassette.
Song List: Hey Stoopid (Side Two, Track One)

Released in 1991 in support of the OPERATION ROCK 'N' ROLL tour that Alice was taking part in during the Summer of 1991. Also included on this promotional-only release are Judas Priest, Motorhead and Dangerous Toys. See Part 3 of Chapter 5 for more details about this tour.

Album Title: 70'S GREATEST ROCK HITS VOLUME 11: HEAVY HITTERS
Released: 1991 by Priority Records.
Catalog No.: P2 7055
Media: CD.
Song List: Only Women Bleed (Track Two)

This album also featured tracks from King Crimson, Edgar Winter, Mott the Hoople and Jethro Tull.

Album Title: BIZARRE SAMPLER
Released: 1991 by Rhino Records.
Catalog No.: PRO2 90086
Media: CD.
Song List: Reflected / Return of the Spiders / B.B. on Mars

Special promotional compilation from Rhino Records featuring three tracks from the Straight label Alice Cooper Group albums.

Video cassette version of the promotional cassette for the OPERATION ROCK 'N' ROLL tour.

Album Title: 80's GREATEST ROCK HITS VOLUME 9: ROCK HARD
Released: 1993 by Priority Records.
Catalog No.: P2 53733
Media: CD.
Song List: Trash

Priority Records compilation album featuring Trash.

Album Title: MASTERS OF METAL LIVE: THE 70's
Released: 1993 by JCI and Warner Special Products.
Catalog No.: JCD 4546
Media: CD.
Song List: Billion Dollar Babies

Album Title: WELCOME TO OUR NIGHTMARE
Released: 1993 by Triple X.
Catalog No.: 51109-2
Media: Double CD.
Song List: The name in parenthesis after each song title is the performer.
Reflected (Dramarama) / Levity Ball (Wallison Ladmoh with Paul Cutler and Don Bolles) / Refrigerator Heaven (John Trubee and the Ugly Janitors of America) / Lay Down and Die, Goodbye (Of Cabbage and Kings) / Caught in a Dream (Rubber City Rebels) / Black Juju (Lydia

Lunch and Rowland I. Howard) / Second Coming and Ballad of Dwight Fry (Bug Lamp) / Sun Arise (Flaming Lips) / Under My Wheels (Bulimia Banquet) / Halo of Flies (Haunted Garage) / Desperado (Chris Connelly) / Dead Babies and Killer (Shadow Project) / School's Out (Reverb Motherfuckers) / Generation Landslide (Claw Hammer) / Working Up a Sweat (Royal Court of China) / Teenage Lament '74 (Tyla) / Welcome to My Nightmare (Cold Ethyl with Steven Perkins) / Cold Ethyl (Carnival Art) / Only Women Bleed (The Hangmen) / Serious (Sloppy Seconds) / Pain (Duchess De Sade) / Clones (We're All) (They Eat Their Own) / Poison (Vandals)

Although not a true Alice compilation album, this tribute album is mentioned here since it's really a repackaging of Alice's many songs from over the years with other performers recording them. Probably some of the best known names on the release are Sloppy Seconds, They Eat Their Own and (of course) Miss Lydia Lunch. Another tribute album is set to be released in early 1999 by guitarist Bob Kulick entitled HUMANARY STEW. The new CD will have many familiar rock performers in the lineup and will be a must-buy for fans once it appears.

Tribute album WELCOME TO OUR NIGHTMARE.

Album Title: **70's GOLD**
Released: 1994 by Hollywood (CD) and Sessions (vinyl.)
Catalog No.: 174 (CD)
Media: CD and Vinyl.
Song List: I Never Cry (Track 25)

This massive 30 track collection also includes Abba, Blondie, Shaun Cassidy, K. C. and the Sunshine Band, and Leo Sayer.

Album Title: **FOUNDATION CD 10**
Released: May 1994 by Foundation.
Catalog No.: None listed.
Media: CD.
Song List: Unholy War

This CD, one of several put out by Foundation, was used as a method not only to promote Foundation, but also as a means to promote new releases from artists. Alice also is heard doing a brief interview before the track from THE LAST TEMPTATION album.

Album Title: **18 SCREAMERS FROM THE 70's**
Released: 1995 by JCI and Warner Special Products.
Catalog No.: JCD 3140
Media: CD.
Song List: No More Mr. Nice Guy

Album Title: **ELVIRA PRESENTS MONSTER HITS**
Released: 1995 by Rhino Records.
Catalog No.: R2-71778 (CD) and R4-71778 (cassette)
Media: CD and Cassette.
Song List: Feed My Frankenstein

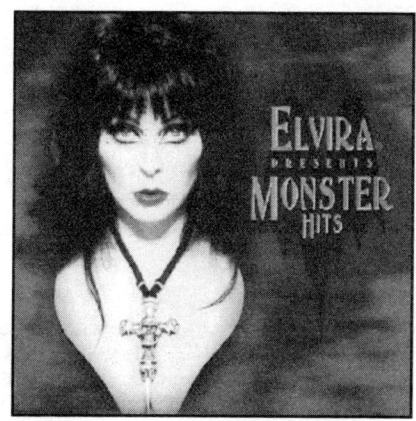

Rhino compilation featuring Feed My Frankenstein.

Part 2: Compilation Albums

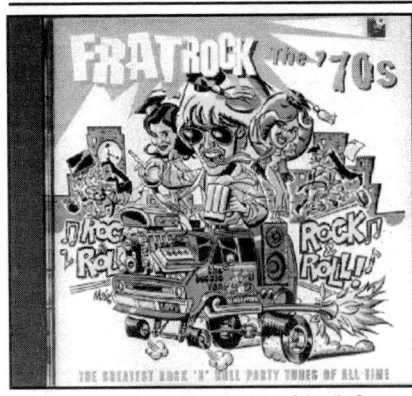

Album Title:	**FRAT ROCK THE 70's**
Released:	1995 by Rhino.
Catalog No.:	R2 72131
Media:	CD.
Song List:	School's Out

Album Title:	**WHO'S YOUR FAVE RAVE?**
Released:	1996 by Rhino Records.
Catalog No.:	R2-72819 (CD) and R4-72819 (cassette)
Media:	CD and Cassette.
Song List:	I'm Eighteen

A very odd placement of Alice's song in a package put together in connection with 16 Magazine. I'm Eighteen is featured along with Day Dream Believer, Follow the Boys and Mack the Knife.

Rhino compilation album featuring School's Out.

Album Title:	**THE ELECTRIC SEVENTIES**
Released:	1995 by Baby Boomer Classics and Warner Brothers Special Products.
Catalog No.:	Unknown.
Media:	CD.
Song List:	I'm Eighteen

Album Title:	**EPIC AUDIO BUYWAYS**
Released:	1995 by Epic. A division of Sony.
Catalog No.:	803 / 804
Media:	Cassette.
Song List:	Samplings on Side Two: Poison, I'm Eighteen and Fire

To entice customers into checking out some of the other artists Epic had in their stables, Epic came up with these "sampler" cassettes — sold (and sometimes given away) in record stores. The cassettes would normally have a few full tracks and then a few samples edited of other tracks from performers with albums available through Epic. The three tracks listed here are not the complete songs, but just portions of each.

WB compilation featuring I'm Eighteen.

Album Title:	**CLASSICKS**
Released:	Released September 5, 1995 by Epic. A division of Sony. Live tracks recorded December 14, 1989 at the Birmingham NEC, Birmingham, England.
Catalog No.:	SNY 67219.2 / ET 67219 (CD) and SNY 67219.4 / EK 67219 (cassette) released September 5, 1995 by Epic, US.
	9362-46079-2 (CD) released October 1995 by Epic, UK.
	SNY 67219.2 / ET 67219 (CD) and SNY 67219.4 / EK 67219 (cassette) released October 3, 1997 by Epic, Canada.
	SNY 480845 2 (CD) released September 1995 by Epic, Australia.
	SNY 480845 2 (CD) released February 6, 1996 by Epic, OES.
	ESCA 6232 (CD) released September 1995 by Epic, Japan.
Media:	CD and Cassette.
Song List:	Poison / Hey Stoopid / Love's a Loaded Gun / Stolen Prayer / House of Fire / Lost in America / It's Me / Under My Wheels (live) / Billion Dollar Babies (live) / I'm Eighteen (live) / No More Mr. Nice Guy (live) / Only Women Bleed (live) / School's Out (live) / Fire / It Rained All Night (only on ESCA 6232)

This is a mixture of a "live" album and a compilation album. Six of the fifteen songs on the album are actually from the video cassette ALICE COOPER TRASHES THE WORLD. There's a good photo of Alice from the proper time period on the cover of the CD, which included a sticker stating that several tracks were recorded live and being released (at least officially) for the first time. It Rained All Night was an additional track added to the Japanese release of this album. It can also be found on the Japanese version of HEY STOOPID and as

Cassette version of the BIZARRE ROCK compilation album.

Another Sony compilation album CLASSICKS.

the B-side for the US single of Hey Stoopid.

Album Title: **BIZARRE ROCK**
Released: 1997 by MCA.
Catalog No.: MCAC 20883 (cassette), MCAD 20883 (CD)
Media: CD and Cassette.
Song List: Prince of Darkness / Give the Radio Back / Freedom / Lock Me Up / Roses on White Lace / Not That Kind of Love / Teenage Frankenstein / Give It Up / The Great American Success Story / Trick Bag / Simple Disobedience / He's Back (the Man Behind the Mask)

Another MCA compilation album (released along with PRINCE OF DARKNESS in 1989 and HE'S BACK in 1997) made up entirely of tracks from the 1986 MCA album CONSTRICTOR and the 1987 MCA album RAISE YOUR FIST AND YELL.

Album Title: **...A NICE NIGHTMARE**
Released: 1997 by Sony Music Special Products.
Catalog No.: BT 28517
Media: CD and Cassette.
Song List: Hey Stoopid / I Got a Line on You / Bad Place Alone / Dangerous Tonight / Snakebite / Poison / This Maniac's in Love With You / Trash / Bed of Nails / Lullaby

First of the compilation albums to feature music from THE LAST TEMPTATION album (the 1998 album POISON would feature two more tracks from THE LAST TEMPTATION as well.) In fact, as expected, six of the ten tracks here can also be found on POISON.

Sony compilation album ...A NICE NIGHTMARE.

Album Title: **HE'S BACK**
Released: August 18, 1997 by BMG, Germany.
Catalog No.: 74321 47330 2
Media: CD.
Song List: He's Back / Freedom / Time to Kill / Prince of Darkness / Thrill My Gorilla / Teenage Frankenstein / Chop, Chop, Chop / Lock Me Up / Trick Bag / Step on You / The Great American Success Story / Crawlin' / Give It Up / Roses on White Lace / The World Needs Guts / Not That Kind of Love

As with PRINCE OF DARKNESS and BIZARRE ROCK, this is a compilation album that is made up of a few songs released as singles and an assortment of odds and ends from the two MCA albums CONSTRICTOR and RAISE YOUR FIST AND YELL. The cover artwork is a blue eye iris surrounded by fiery waves. Song titles are listed at the bottom of the cover, which is perplexing as the final one listed is U.V.A. This is actually an abbreviation of a German term that translate as "and many more . . ." and should not be viewed as meaning a song title itself. The cover folds out to show other albums available from the record company, while the back of the cover merely shows song credits.

Album Title: **HAVE A NICE DECADE**
Released: 1997 by Rhino Records.
Catalog No.: 72919
Media: 7-CD boxed-set.
Song List: School's Out

Special box set feature 160 songs from the 1970's, ranging from disco to hard rock and pop. There is only this one Alice track on the album.

HE'S BACK from BMG.

Album Title: **POISON**
Released: 1998 by Sony.
Catalog No.: CBU 67538
Media: CD.
Song List: Poison / Hey Stoopid / Only My Heart Talkin' / Bed of Nails / I'm Your Gun / Dangerous Tonight / Trash / Cleansed by Fire / Snakebite / Little by Little / Wind-up Toy / It's Me / Die for You / Spark in the Dark

Another in the endless series of compilations by both Sony and MCA where tracks from a small assortment of albums are salvaged to make another buck off of Alice's reputation. At least this one includes two tracks from THE LAST TEMPTATION, including the excellent Cleansed by Fire.

Album Title: **FREEDOM FOR FRANKENSTEIN**
Released: May 19, 1998 by Raven, Australia.
Catalog No.: RVCD-69
Media: CD.
Song List: He's Back (The Man Behind the Mask) / Teenage Frankenstein / Give It Up / Freedom / Lock Me Up / I Got a Line on You / Poison / House of Fire / Bed of Nails / Go to Hell (live) / Ballad of Dwight Fry (live) / Hey Stoopid / It Rained All Night / Feed My Frankenstein / Fire / Side Show / Sick Things (live) / Only Women Bleed / Wind up Toy (live)

FREEDOM FOR FRANKENSTEIN album.

Although this starts off like another MCA compilation, the album does eventually add up to something that fans would be interested in hearing. I Got a Line on You was only released as a promo-only single in the US and as part of an EP in the UK. It Rained All Night appeared on the Japanese version of CLASSICKS. Go to Hell and Ballad of Dwight Fry were recorded March 6, 1987 at the Cincinnati Gardens for the radio program SUPERSTAR CONCERT SERIES. Sick Things and the medley of Only Women Bleed and Wind Up Toy were from the September 1991 Electric Ladyland Studio recordings done for the Album Network, of which portions appeared with the Japanese edition of LAST TEMPTATION. While a couple of typographical errors occur in the 16 page booklet that comes with the CD, Andrew Carpenter does a good job in giving a brief history of Alice and the tracks on the CD. As always, the Australians seem to know things about putting together a compilation album that many other countries don't.

Album Title: **PARTY ROCK**
Released: October 27, 1998 by Rhino Records.
Catalog No.: 75544
Media: CD.
Song List: School's Out

Also featured on this album are Bad Company, Sweet, Foghat and Todd Rundgren.

Part 3 — Soundtrack Albums

Starting with DIARY OF A MAD HOUSEWIFE in 1969, Alice Cooper has made several appearances in the movies, normally in a singing role. However, only a few of these singing appearances have made it onto vinyl or CD. On the downside, that means fans are still waiting to hear official releases of Alice's two tracks from MONSTER DOG (the best things from that particular film.) On the other hand, it also means that no one has been subjected to Next, Next from the Mae West movie SEXTETTE on their turntable (at least, so far.)

Seriously though, it's surprising when you consider the number of soundtrack albums that have featured Alice's music over the years. Whether the track is just another reissue of School's Out — the most popular song of Alice's to appear in films — or a new one that has never been released on any official Alice albums (I Got a Line on You from IRON EAGLE II), there have been plenty of movie appearances.

Because several of these soundtrack albums have included either new songs or live performances, the listing below is in chronological order. Unless a song is new to the discography, no writer credits will be listed.

Album Title: MEDICINE BALL CARAVAN
(ORIGINAL SOUNDTRACK)
Released: 1971 by Warner Brothers.
Catalog No.: BS 2565
Media: Vinyl, Cassette and 8-Track.
Song List: Black Juju (Side Two, Track One)

Featured on the album as part of the live tracks taken from the film released under the same name, Black Juju is actually the studio recorded track from the LOVE IT TO DEATH album. Ironically, the movie itself contains the live version of this song.

The MEDICINE BALL soundtrack album.

Album Title: SGT. PEPPER'S LONELY HEARTS CLUB BAND: ORIGINAL SOUNDTRACK
Released: 1978 by RSO; reissued on CD April 21, 1998 by Polydor.
Catalog No.: RS-2-4100 (vinyl); 557076 (1998 CD reissue); AMLZ 66600 (UK release on A&M); RSO 2658 128 (French vinyl release) and RSO 3524 207 (French cassette release.)
Media: Vinyl, Cassette and 8-Track for 1978 release. CD and Cassette for 1998 reissue on Polydor.
Personnel: Alice Cooper, vocals. The Bee Gees, background vocals. Max Middleton, Keyboards and synthesizer. Robert Ahwai, guitar. Wilbur Bascomb, bass guitar. Bernard Purdie, drums and percussion.
Song List: Because (John Lennon and Paul McCartney) (Record Two, Side Two, Track Six; on the CD reissue, Disc Two, Track Six)

One of the few songs recorded by Alice for a movie that was exclusively picked up for the soundtrack album and has never appeared on an official Alice album. While hearing Alice bring a different interpretation to a Beatles track is interesting, it's a rather odd variation of the song. In fact, it's almost Residents in nature with the emphasis on the exaggerated vocalizations. Consequently, perhaps it's just as well that it's never appeared anywhere else. For more information about the movie, see Chapter 2. There's a small picture of Alice from the movie contained on the inside gatefold of the album.

Album Title: **ROCK N' ROLL HIGH SCHOOL ORIGINAL MOTION PICTURE SOUNDTRACK**
Released: 1979 by Sire Records.
Catalog No.: SRK-6070
Media: Vinyl, Cassette, 8-Track and CD.
Song List: **School's Out** (Side Two, Final Track)

This is one of the never ending soundtrack albums to use **School's Out** for context in the film. The soundtrack album is excellent, which is no surprise since the movie is a classic rock and roll film anyway. The version of School's Out used is from the original SCHOOL'S OUT album.

Album Title: **ROADIE (ORIGINAL MOTION PICTURE SOUNDTRACK)**
Recorded: 1980 at Cherokee Studios, Hollywood, CA.
Released: 1980 by Warner Brothers Records Inc.
Production: Produced, engineered and mixed by Todd Rundgren. Addition engineering by John Weaver.
Catalog No.: 2HS 3441 (vinyl) and 2X5 3441 (cassette); K66093 (2Hs 3441) (UK vinyl release)
Media: Vinyl and Cassette.
Personnel: Alice Cooper, vocals. Davey Johnstone, guitars. Kasim Sulton, vocals and bass. John "Willie" Wilcox, vocals and drums. Roger Powell, vocals and keyboards. Todd Rundgren, background vocals.
Song List: **Road Rats** (Side One, Track Four) and **Pain** (Side Three, Track Four)

This was the soundtrack album for the Alive Enterprises film, which also featured Alice in a small cameo role. The film, although not a hit, had a great soundtrack and this album is worth getting for the chance to hear some out-of-the-ordinary recordings by a group of major artists (including Cheap Trick's **Everything Works If You Let It**, which didn't appear officially anywhere else for years after the soundtrack's release.)

One of the unique things about this soundtrack album is Todd Rundgren producing the two Alice tracks, and having Todd Rundgren and his band, Utopia, back up Alice on the tracks as well. The two songs for this album were recorded with Rundgren in his typical role as producer, engineer and mixer to the production. It's a fascinating insight into how one performer interprets another, as Rundgren tends to be a heavy influence on recordings that he has produced. In fact, when FLUSH THE FASHION was reviewed by ROLLING STONE in 1981, one of the comments made by the reviewer was how much he enjoyed the Todd Rundgren-produced version of **Pain** on the ROADIE soundtrack over the one on FLUSH THE FASHION. Both songs were re-recorded for the album.

Road Rats originally appeared on the LACE AND WHISKEY album, while **Pain** showed up in 1980 on FLUSH THE FASHION. Both songs were part of the FLUSH THE FASHION tour that year as well. A portion of **Only Women Bleed** can be heard being performed in the film, but it doesn't appear on the soundtrack album.

The double vinyl album came in a gatefold sleeve that included one picture of Alice inside the gatefold cover.

Album Title: **ROADIE (ORIGINAL MOTION PICTURE SOUNDTRACK)**
Released: 1980 by Warner Brothers Records, Inc.
Catalog No.: PRO-A-861
Media: Vinyl.
Song List: **Road Rats** (Side One, Track One)

This was a single disc promotional album released to radio stations to help promote the movie and the soundtrack album of the same name. Of the two Alice tracks from the film, only **Road Rats** made it to this promotional album. Surprisingly enough, there is more production information given on the sleeve and label of this album than actually appears on the commercially released double vinyl set. Sound bites from interviews with Alice and others are included on this promotional version. The album came in a single sleeve, with no photo references to the film on the album cover.

Album Title: **HEARTBREAK HOTEL (ORIGINAL SOUNDTRACK)**
Released: 1988 by RCA.
Catalog No.: 8533
Media: Vinyl, Cassette and CD.
Song List: **I'm Eighteen** (Track Eight)

A rock and roll fantasy film about a family meeting Elvis. The studio version of **I'm Eighteen** appears on the soundtrack.

Album Title:	**THE DECLINE OF WESTERN CIVILIZATION, PART II: THE METAL YEARS (ORIGINAL MOTION PICTURE SOUNDTRACK)**
Released:	1988 by Capitol Records.
Production:	Track produced by Jim Faraci.
Catalog No.:	CDP-590205 (CD), C1-90205 (vinyl) and C4-90205 (cassette)
Media:	CD, Vinyl and Cassette.
Personnel:	Alice Cooper and W. Axl Rose, vocals. Slash, guitar. Izzy, bass.
Song List:	Under My Wheel

Alice appeared on camera in several interview segments of this movie, along with contributing a duet with Axl for the soundtrack. A short interview segment with Alice can be heard on the album as well.

Album Title:	**WES CRAVEN'S SHOCKER - NO MORE MR. NICE GUY - THE MUSIC (K-1 93233)**
Recorded:	1989 at Record Plant Recording Studios, Hollywood, CA.
Released:	1989 by SBK Records / Alive Records. Distributed by Capitol Records.
Production:	Mixed at Hit Factory Recording Studio, New York, NY. Produced by Desmond Child.
Catalog No.:	K-1-93233 (vinyl), K-2-93233 (CD) and K-4-93233 (cassette.)
Media:	Vinyl, Cassette and CD.
Personnel:	Alice Cooper and Mitch Pileggi, raps. Guy Mann-Dude and Vivian Campbell, guitars. Cornelius Mims and Rudy Sarzo, bass. Steve Deutsch, synths programming. Louis Merlino, Maria Vidal, Desmond Child, Kane Roberts and Michael Anthony, background vocals.
Song List:	Shockdance (Guy Mann-Dude, Desmond Child, Vivian Campbell and Kane Roberts) (Side Two, Track One)

This album was released in conjunction with the movie SHOCKER, a film by Wes Craven and created as the first film for a new franchise of movies like Craven's earlier NIGHTMARE ON ELM STREET films. While Craven had plans for future follow-ups with the character of Horace Pinker — a man electrocuted and then brought back from the dead as an entity living through electronics, among other things — the movie didn't do well at the box office and Craven moved onto other projects instead.

The soundtrack is interesting because instead of using a compilation of existing heavy metal tracks — which seemed to be the norm for horror movies at the time — Craven included Desmond Child in the project and enlisted the help of several heavy hitters in the metal field at the time to help.

Alice can be heard during the song **Shockdance** doing a rap with actor Mitch Pileggi as Horace Pinker. This song was co-written by one-time guitarist for Alice, Kane Roberts, who also participated in the recording of the track singing background vocals. Also on the track is Rudy Sarzo, who also played bass on Alice's track for the soundtrack of the movie IRON EAGLE II.

Alice also has co-writing credits for the song **Love Transfusion** (written with Desmond Child and Vladimir Matetski), which is performed by Iggy Pop on the soundtrack album. This song was written during the recording of the TRASH album.

While the subtitle of the movie is "No More Mr. Nice Guy" (a line that Pinker says in the film as well), this popular Alice song appears on the album done by the group Megadeth. A music video was also done to promote the movie using Megadeth's rendition of the song.

The CD version of this album has a catalog number of CDP 93233, but the actual disc states the catalog number as K2-93233.

SHOCKER soundtrack album.

Album Title:	**SHOCKER - NO MORE MISTER NICE GUY - THE MUSIC - A SHOCKING SAMPLER**
Released:	1989 by SBK Records / Alive Records. Distributed by Capitol Records.
Catalog No.:	DPRO-05316
Media:	CD.

Although the song featuring Alice from the commercially available soundtrack album doesn't appear on this promotional-only sampler, both the Alice co-written songs, Love Transfusion and Megadeth's version of No More Mr. Nice Guy appear here. It's also worth mentioning that the sampler's title is listed correctly above. "Mister" is spelled out instead of abbreviated. The track listing for the song is printed correctly, however.

Album Title: **IRON EAGLE II (ORIGINAL MOTION PICTURE SOUNDTRACK)**
Recorded: 1988 at One On One Studios, North Hollywood, CA.
Released: 1988 by Epic Records.
Production: Produced by Richie Zito.
Catalog No.: 45006 (CD), 45006 (vinyl)
Media: CD, Vinyl and Cassette.
Personnel: Alice Cooper, vocals. Adrian Vandenberg, guitar. Rudy Sarzo, bass. Mike Baird, drums.
Song List: I Got a Line on You (R. California)

A music video was done for this song from the soundtrack album, along with a cassette and 12" vinyl single. A 7" single was also released with this track as the A-side and Britney Fox's Livin' On the Edge as the B-side. I Got a Line on You was reissued on the compilation album A NICE NIGHTMARE in 1997 on both CD and cassette, and on the Australian compilation album FREEDOM FOR FRANKENSTEIN released in 1998. Otherwise, at the present time, the soundtrack album and the singles listed below are the only ways to obtain this song.

Single Title: **I Got a Line On You / I Got a Line On You**
Released: 1988 by Epic Records.
Catalog No.: 34-08114 (7"), EAS 1347 (12") and ESK 1355 (CD single)
Media: 7" Vinyl, 12" Vinyl and CD promotional single.

This is a promotional single for the song done by Alice on the IRON EAGLE II soundtrack album. The single comes in a plain black single sleeve with a white and red sticker advertising the song and the soundtrack album. This was a promotional item, and so was a bit harder to find than the 7" single with Livin' On the Edge on the B-side also released through Epic that same year. Since this was released in 1988, a year before TRASH, this single became the first official release from Alice on the Epic record label. He completed three full studio albums before leaving Epic in 1994. There was also a cassette release of this track through Epic, but there is no catalog number for the cassette.

Single Title: **I Got a Line on You / Livin' On the Edge**
Released: 1988 by Epic Records.
Catalog No.: 34-08114
Media: 7" Vinyl.

This 7" commercially available single featured Alice's track from the IRON EAGLE II soundtrack album on the A-side and Britney Fox with their own song from the soundtrack album on the B-side.

Single Title: **I Got a Line On You / I Got a Line On You**
Released: 1988 by Epic Records, Brazil.
Catalog No.: 52.160
Media: 12" Vinyl promotional single.

This is a promotional single for the song done by Alice on the IRON EAGLE II.

Album Title: **WAYNE'S WORLD: THE ORIGINAL MOTION PICTURE SOUNDTRACK ALBUM**
Released: February 18, 1992 by Warner Brothers.
Catalog No.: B00002LS9 (CD)
Media: CD and Cassette.
Song List: Feed My Frankenstein (Track Ten)

A soundtrack album for the movie that Alice will probably be best remembered for in years to come. Alice and his HEY STOOPID era band are seen in the film performing the song. See Chapter 6, Part 4 for more details on the movie.

The WAYNE'S WORLD soundtrack album.

Album Title: **DAZED AND CONFUSED**
Released: 1993 by The Medicine Label. Distributed by Giant Records. Manufactured by Warner Brothers Records, Inc.
Catalog No.: 9 24533-2 (CD) and 9 24533-3 (cassette)
Media: CD and Cassette.
Song List: School's Out (Track Three)

Another soundtrack release with School's Out on it. This soundtrack album also includes some good cuts from The Runaways, Sweet, Deep Purple and Rick Derringer. This is again the original track from the SCHOOL'S OUT album.

DAZED AND CONFUSED soundtrack album.

Album Title: **SONGS IN THE KEY OF X: MUSIC FROM AND INSPIRED BY "THE X-FILES"**
Released: March 19, 1996 by Warner Brothers.
Production: Produced and engineered by Rob Zombie, Terry Date and Charlie Clauser.
Catalog No.: 9 46079-2 (CD) and 9 46079-3 (cassette)
Media: CD and Cassette.
Personnel: Alice Cooper, vocals. Rob Zombie, vocals and all instruments.
Song List: Hands of Death (Burn Baby Burn) (Rob Zombie and Charlie Clauser)

With the cult success of the television series THE X-FILES, this album was produced to showcase both some of the music from the program — hence, it's appearance here rather than under compilations or guest appearances — and also new music based on characters and/or episodes from the series. Rob Zombie and Alice share vocals on this track.

SONG IN THE KEY OF X which featured Alice with Rob Zombie on one track.

Album Title: **JESUS CHRIST SUPERSTAR**
Released: April 16, 1996 by Jay Records.
Catalog No.: 1292
Media: Double CD.
Song List: King Herod's Song

See entry for HIGHLIGHTS FROM JESUS CHRIST SUPERSTAR below.

Album Title: **HIGHLIGHTS FROM JESUS CHRIST SUPERSTAR**
Released: October 7, 1997 by Polydor.
Catalog No.: 537686
Media: CD.
Song List: King Herod's Song (Track Fourteen)

In a rare appearance by Alice Cooper in a non-traditional role, Alice played King Herod in this CD adaptation of the rock musical JESUS CHRIST SUPERSTAR in 1996. This was done at the request of lyricist Tim Rice, who has been friends with Alice for some time. This production was recorded and released the same year by Jay Records.

King Herod's Song, while the comical highlight of the musical, is also disturbing in its sarcastic portrayal of Jesus in its lyrics. In fact, it's probably the most shocking song of the musical, and with that line of thinking, it was no wonder that Alice was drawn to it. However, it would have been more satisfying and rewarding to have seen or heard Alice in the role of Pious, which is not only a bigger part in the musical, but much more complex than Herod.

Part 3: Soundtrack Albums

The album did well enough that Polydor decided to release an edited version of the CD (reducing it to one disc) in 1997. Perhaps the most fascinating thing about the Polydor CD for Alice fans is the cover artwork, which, although not directly related in any way, is very reminiscent of work done for THE LAST TEMPTATION album. Well worth picking up, especially if you're a fan of the musical.

Part 4 — Guest Appearances

Over the years, Alice has made guest appearances on albums for other artists. With his distinctive voice and popularity, it is no wonder that he has been asked. Yet, it is not always his voice that has been the contributing factor to someone's album, there are several cases where Alice has co-written songs that have appeared on other albums as well.

Albums are listed in alphabetical order by artist.

Album Title: **Robin Beck - TROUBLE OR NOTHIN'**
Released: 1989 by Mercury, a division of Phonogram.
Catalog No.: 838 768-2 (CD) and 838 768-3 (cassette)
Media: CD and Cassette.
Song List: Hold Back the Night (Alice Cooper and Desmond Child)

Alice co-wrote this song on the Child-produced album. This album came out the same year as Alice's work on the Child-produced SHOCKER soundtrack and his own album TRASH, again produced by Child. Also performing on this album is Guy Mann Dude, who not only played on the Shockdance track from SHOCKER, but also enlisted Alice for a brief vocal appearance on his album in 1989.

The Robin Beck album TROUBLE OR NOTHING, featuring a track co-written by Alice.

Album Title: **Michael Bruce - IN MY OWN WAY**
Released: June 24, 1997 by One Way.
Catalog No.: 34486
Media: CD.
Song List: As Rock Rolls On (Michael Bruce) (Track Five)

Alice sang background vocals for his former band mate, Michael Bruce. This album was recorded in 1974 as the Alice Cooper Group began working separately on their own projects. As Bruce mentions in his book NO MORE MR. NICE GUY, the album was completed and a deal was set with Polygram in Germany, but there were no takers for the album in the US. Instead the album had to wait until 1997 when the One Way label picked up the recording for release on CD. Also featured on this album, among others, is Mick Mashbir on a variety of guitars.

Album Title: **Rick Derringer - IF I WEREN'T SO ROMANTIC I'D SHOOT YOU**
Released: 1978 by Blue Sky.
Catalog No.: JZ 35075
Media: Vinyl.
Song List: If I Weren't So Romantic (Alice Cooper, Bernie Taupin and Rick Derringer)

Alice contributed to the lyrics, co-written with FROM THE INSIDE collaborator Bernie Taupin. Music was written by Rick Derringer.

Album Title: **Guy Mann-Dude - SLEIGHT OF HAND**
Released: 1989 by MCA.
Catalog No.: MCAD-6324 (CD), MCA-6324 (vinyl) and MCAC-6324 (cassette)
Media: CD, Vinyl and Cassette.

Song List: On the Verge

Alice contributes vocals to this largely instrumental track. Actually, Alice only says two things during the entire song: "1, 2, 3, 4" (at the beginning) and "on the verge" (at the midpoint.) Guy Mann-Dude had also worked on the Shockdance track from the SHOCKER soundtrack album and played on the Robin Beck album which featured a song written by Alice.

Album Title: **Guns N' Roses - USE YOUR ILLUSION I**
Released: September 1991 by Geffen. Reissued by Mobile Fidelity in 1997 on CD.
Catalog No.: GEF-24415 (vinyl), GEFD-24415 (CD) and GEFC-24415 (cassette); 711 (1997 CD reissue)
Media: CD, Vinyl and Cassette.
Song List: The Garden (Side One, Track Five)

Alice provides additional vocals for this one track. Alice had previously recorded Under My Wheels with a few members of Guns N' Roses for the 1989 soundtrack to the movie DECLINE OF WESTERN CIVILIZATION, PART II: THE METAL YEARS (see the listing in the previous section.)

The Guns N' Roses album USE YOUR ILLUSION I which featured Alice on additional vocals.

Album Title: **Icon - RIGHT BETWEEN THE EYES**
Released: 1989 by Megaforce Worldwide, a division of Atlantic Records.
Catalog No.: 7 82010-1 (vinyl)
Media: Vinyl.
Song List: Holy Man's War (WE, Jerry Harrison, Tracy Wallach and Pat Dixon) and Two For the Road (Jerry Harrison)

Alice added minimal additional vocals to these two tracks.

Album Title: **Insane Clown Posse - THE GREAT MILENKO**
Released: June 24, 1997 by Hollywood Records. Later reissued on Polygram the same year.
Catalog No.: 162071 (CD, Hollywood) and 524442 (CD, Polygram)
Media: CD.
Song List: The Great Milenko

Alice provided a spoken piece during this one track.

Album Title: **Kane Roberts - KANE ROBERTS**
Released: 1987 by MCA.
Catalog No.: MCAD-5787 (CD), MCA-5787 (vinyl) and MCAC-5787 (cassette)
Media: CD, Vinyl and Cassette.
Song List: Full Pull (Alice Cooper and Kane Roberts)

Alice co-wrote Full Pull and does not appear on the album.

Album Title: **Kane Roberts - KANE ROBERTS PROMOTIONAL SAMPLER**
Released: 1987 by MCA.
Catalog No.: C-17441
Media: Cassette.
Song List: No songs associated with Alice.

This sampler cassette features only two tracks from the album, Outlaw and Out For Blood — neither of which had any involvement from Alice. What may be of inter-

Promotional cassette for Kane Robert's album, with the announcement to see Kane on tour with Alice.

Part 3: Soundtrack Albums

est to fans, however, is that the cassette cover states clearly that fans should "see Kane Roberts on tour with Alice Cooper."

Album Title: **Carol Bayer Sager - TOO**
Released: 1978 by Elektra.
Catalog No.: 151
Media: Vinyl and Cassette.
Song List: Shadows (Side One, Track Four)

Alice sang backing vocals on this one track.

Album Title: **Twisted Sister - COME OUT AND PLAY**
Released: November 1985 by Atlantic Records.
Catalog No.: 7 81275-1-E (Vinyl) and 7 81275-4-E (cassette)
Media: Vinyl and Cassette.
Song List: Be Chrool To Your Scuel (Dee Snider)

The Twisted Sister album COME OUT AND PLAY featuring Alice on one track

Alice shared lead vocals with Dee Snider on this track. A video was also done for the song featuring Alice, along with Twisted Sister, comedian Bobcat Goldthwait, famed makeup artist Tom Savini and a group of teenage zombies. Alice can be seen in the video wearing a variation of his outfit from the SPECIAL FORCES period, but with a return to the "Killer Alice" makeup (which he returned to for good with the release of CONSTRICTOR the following year.) It's this transitional phase that makes the clip a worthy addition to any Alice fan's collection (besides just being a very good song.)

Album Title: **Various Artists - FLASH FEARLESS VERSUS THE ZORG WOMEN, PTS. 5 & 6**
Released: February 1975 by Chrysalis Records. Reissued by CD by RPM Records in 1995.
Production: Produced by John Alcock. Alice Cooper's vocals produced by Bob Ezrin.
Personnel: I'm Flash - John Entwhistle, bass. Bill Bruford, drums. Robert A. Johnson, lead guitar. John Weider, guitar.
Space Pirates - John Entwhistle, bass. Justine Hayward, acoustic guitar. Kenny Jones, drums. Nicky Hopkins, piano. Steve Pettican, slide guitar. Keith - speaking part.
Catalog No.: CHR 1972 (US vinyl) and CHR 1081 (UK vinyl released in May 1975); and 5-022911-311476 (1995 CD reissue)
Media: Vinyl release, followed by CD release in 1995.
Song List: I'm Flash (Steve Hammond, Dave Pierce and Bob Pierce) (Side One, Track Two) and Space Pirates (Steve Hammond and Dave Pierce) (Side One, Track Five)

A curio for Alice fans especially as the album was a bit hard to find in complete form and for a cheap price. This was an album put together to showcase songs from a planned stage musical that was to parody the old FLASH GORDON serials much like ROCKY HORROR parodied old monster and sci-fi movies.

Together with an all-star cast of musicians (including John Entwhistle, Jim Dandy from Black Oak Arkansas, Justin Hayward of the Moody Blues, Carmine Appice, and Kenny Jones), Alice was enlisted, contributing vocals for the two tracks listed above. Since the album was recorded between October 1 and December 31 of 1974 and in various locations, Alice recorded his vocals separately in New York with Bob Ezrin producing. These recordings were then sent to be mixed with the

Chapter 6: "Luney Tune"

rest of the material.

The album originally came with a comic book that explained the structure of the musical (although the songs were placed in a different order on the album than in the comic book.) Finding copies of the vinyl album with the comic book is rare. Portions of the comic book were reprinted, however, when the album was reissued on CD in 1995 by RPM. There is a track difference between the US and UK vinyl versions of this album, with **Supersnatch** replacing **Georgia Syncopator** in the US version. However, since neither song has involvement from Alice, fans would probably be happy with either version (or the CD, which contains both songs.)

Although the musical saw the light of day briefly in 1981, both it and the album did rather poorly and have been mostly forgotten except by fans of those involved with the album. A promotional 7" single was released which featured **I'm Flash** on the A-side (with **Trapped** on the B-side) by Chrysalis under the catalog number CHS 2069.

Album Title: Various Artists - MERRY ARIZONA 2 - DESERT STARS SHINE AT CHRISTMAS
Released: November 1996 by United Cerebral Palsy.
Catalog No.: UPC 7 13914-0100-2 6
Media: CD.
Song List: Is There A Santa

A CD released to help raise money for cerebral palsy research using artists from Arizona. Alice loaned his vocal talents to this spoken word track based on an article that appeared in SPY magazine regarding the plausibility of Santa Claus. Since the CD was special sales release, it's becoming difficult to find in other areas of the country.

Part 5 — Performances by Alice Cooper Group Members

When Alice Cooper was started, it wasn't just a lead singer and songwriter named Alice, it was a group of five people who created the music and coexisted in the same space for many years before each going his own way. It's for this reason that the other four members of the Alice Cooper Group — Michael Bruce, Neal Smith, Dennis Dunaway and Glen Buxton — are presented here in their own section of this book detailing their contributions to music before and after their time in the band.

As many fans of the original band know, Michael Bruce has been the most prolific of the members, having recorded two albums, written a book, and performed tours extensively for the past few years. Both Neal Smith and Dennis Dunaway have done their share of performing as well, normally in collaboration with each other. This included Dunaway appearing on Smith's never released solo album PLATINUM GOD (see th entry below), and also as two parts of the band The Flying Tigers. Even Glen Buxton, who spent time away from music, returned in the mid-1980's to performing with his band Virgin, as well as occasionally popping up to perform with the other former band members.

While there are only a few albums to speak of here, there have been several concerts performed by the former members that have circulated on audio tape. There have also been a couple of bootleg albums released with former members on them: LIVE AT THE MASON JAR, a bootleg of Buxton's band Virgin, from Phoenix, AZ, and LIVE AT THE BARNABY'S CLUB with Dunaway's and Smith's band the Flying Tigers.

At the time that Alice's boxed set was first announced in 1993, there was talk of recording a new song for the album with all five of the Alice Cooper Group members. Unfortunately, the record label wasn't thrilled with the idea, and it was pushed onto the back burner. With the passing of Glen Buxton in October 1997, such plans can never be realized in the future.

Still, what of the other four members? As a matter of fact, on December 19, 1998 Alice met up with both Neal Smith and Michael Bruce at the public grand opening of Alice's restaurant (a combination rock and sports memorabilia bar and eatery) Cooper'stown in Phoenix, Arizona. Getting up on stage at the restaurant with both "Rockin" Reggie and a bass player form an Alice tribute band, the three former Alice Cooper Group members performed for the first time together since April 1974. Doing such songs as **Billion Dollar Babies**, **I'm Eighteen**, **Is It My Body** and **Desperado** (among others) without rehearsals, all who witnessed the event believed it to be a great show and a once in a lifetime opportunity.

Will it lead to something more than that? Only time will tell.

MICHAEL BRUCE:

THE RED HOUSE SESSION - A video of a concert performed by Michael Bruce with Richie Scarlet.

Single Title: **On A Day Like Today / A Man Like Myself**
Released: 1965 by Aster.
Catalog No.: A-WF-1 / 2
Media: 7" Vinyl single.
Personnel: Performed by Wildflowers. Michael Bruce (guitar, vocals.) Gary Dockery (bass.) Mike Miller (drums.) Gary Gilbert (keyboards.)

First single by Michael Bruce's band.

Single Title: **More Than Me / It Was Only Yesterday**
Released: 1965 by Aster.
Catalog No.: A-WF-3 / 4
Media: 7" Vinyl single.
Personnel: Performed by Wildflowers. Michael Bruce (guitar, vocals.) Gary Dockery (bass.) Mike Miller (drums.) Gary Gilbert (keyboards.) Mick Mashbir (additional guitar.)

Second single by Michael Bruce's pre-Alice band. By this time, Bruce had joined The Spiders and was working with both bands simultaneously. Bruce began calling himself Bruce Michael to keep some separation between the two groups. The two songs on this single also featured Mick Mashbir, who went on to work with the Alice Cooper Group between 1972 through 1974 and worked on Bruce's solo album IN MY OWN WAY.

Album Title: **SMOKIN' O.P.'S**
Released: 1970 by Palladium. Later reissued by Capitol on vinyl and CD.
Catalog No.: 1006 (Palladium vinyl) and CDP-99077 (Capitol CD.)
Media: Vinyl and CD reissue.
Personnel: Performed by Bob Seger. Bob Seger (guitar, piano, vocals.) Michael Bruce (guitar.) David Teegarden (drums, marimbas.) Jack Ashford (percussion, tambourine.) Eddie Bongo (percussion, conga.) Jim Bruzzese (percussion, tambourine.) Skip Knape (organ, bass, piano, keyboards.) Crystal Jenkins (vocals.) Pam Tood (vocals.)

Michael Bruce played additional guitars on the album for this other Detroit-based performer.

Single Title: **ON OUR WAY**
Released: 1972 by Westbound Records.
Catalog No.: 2010
Media: Vinyl.
Personnel: Performed by Teegarden & Vanwinkle.

Michael Bruce provided additional guitars and some vocals on this album. David Teegarden also appeared with Michael Bruce on the 1970 Bob Seger album SMOKIN' O.P.'S.

Album Title: **IN MY OWN WAY**
Released: 1975 by Polydor, Germany. Reissued June 24, 1997 on CD by One Way Records.
Production: Produced by Gene Cornish and Dino Danelli. Arranged by Michael Bruce, Gene Cornish, Dino Danelli, Mick Mashbir and Bob Dolin.
Catalog No.: Unknown (Polydor), 34486 (CD)
Media: Vinyl and CD reissue.
Personnel: Michael Bruce (guitar, vocals.) Gene Cornish (acoustic guitar, guitar, slide guitar.) Dino Danelli (percussion, drums.) Bob Dolin (piano, harpsichord, Hammond organ, Clavinet, Moog synthesizer and mellotron.) Ricky Fataar (drums) Bryan Garofalo (bass.) Mick Mashbir (acoustic guitar, guitar and slide guitar.) David Foster (piano.) Ed Black (steel guitar.) Additional vocals: Mylon LeFevre, Jackie Lomax, Gerry Beckley, Lynn Carey, Mickey McGee, Hunt Sales, Tony Sales, Timothy B. Schmit and Alice Cooper.
Song List: King of America (Bruce) / Lucky Break (Quinlan) / Friday on My Mind (Venda and Young) / In My Own Way (Bruce and Morris) / As Rock Rolls On (Bruce) / If the Sky Should Fall (Bruce and Morris) / So Far So Good (Holder and Lee) / Gotta Get Hold (Bruce) / Seems Like I Only Fool Myself (Bruce) / Morning Song (Bruce)

This was the solo project that Bruce worked on after the end of the 1974 South American tour with the Alice

Cooper Group. Included in the recording of the album were both Mick Mashbir (who had worked with Bruce's earlier band the Wildflowers, along with touring and recording with the Alice Cooper Group 1972 - 1974) and Alice Cooper (see Part 2 for more details about Alice's guest appearance.) An interesting additional performer on the album is Ricky Fataar, who has played with many musicians over the years, and was also a member of the Beatles parody group The Rutles. Gene Cornish and Dino Danelli had worked together previously as members of the band the Rascals.

Bruce had a deal for a release of the album through Polydor in Germany in 1975, but American distribution never came about, which delayed the release of the album in Germany for years. It wasn't until 1997 that the album was released in the US, on the One Way label who released it only on CD.

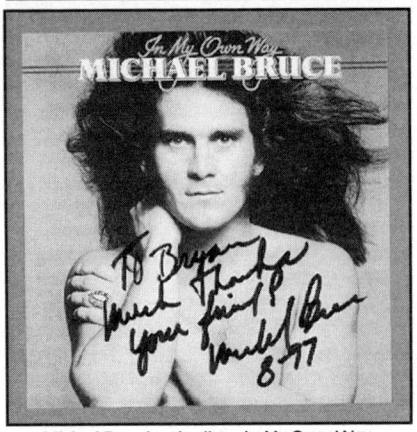

Michael Bruce's solo album IN MY OWN WAY.

When releasing the album, One Way went back to Bruce and asked if there was any additional material from the recording sessions that hadn't been used on the vinyl edition. One track, sung by Russell Morris, wasn't completed when the album was ready for release in 1975. Bruce finished the song and threw it into the re-release mix for "good measure." Several tracks from this album also appeared on the 1983 album by Bruce ROCK ROLLS ON.

Album Title: **BATTLE AXE**
Recorded: 1977 at Record Plant, New York City, NY.
Released: 1977 by Polydor.
Production: Produced by Lee DeCarlo and Billion Dollar Babies. Engineered by Lee DeCarlo, with assistance from Bill Freesh, Sam Ginsberg, Jay Krugman and Gray Russell. Mixed by Lee DeCarlo; later remixed by Jack Douglas. Mastered by Bob Ludwig at Masterdisk.
Personnel: Performed by Billion Dollar Babies. Michael Bruce (guitar, vocals.) Dennis Dunaway (bass and vocals.) Neal Smith (drums, percussion and vocals.) Bob Dolin (keyboards, synths and vocals.) Mike Marconi (guitar and vocals.)
Catalog No.: 6100 (original release), PD-1-6100 (Jack Douglas remix) and 2391625 (UK release)
Media: Vinyl, Cassette and 8-Track.
Song List: Too Young (Bruce, Marconi and Smith) / Shine Your Love (Bruce and Marconi) / I Miss You (Bruce, Marconi and Smith) / Love Is Rather Blind (Bruce Smith and Daye) / Rock and Roll Radio (Dunaway, Marconi, Smith, Jeffords and Douglas) / Dance With Me (Bruce and Marconi) / Rock Me Slowly (Bruce) / Ego Mania (Bruce, Dolin, Dunaway, Marconi and Smith) / Battle Axe (Bruce, Dolin and Dunaway) / Sudden Death (Dolin) / Winner (Bruce and Dunaway)

After roughly three years apart, Bruce, Neal Smith and Dennis Dunaway decided to get back together and form a band. Using the name Billion Dollar Babies, the band also enlisted Bob Dolin — who had toured with the Alice Cooper Group back in 1973-1974 — and a guitarist named Mike Marconi who had worked with Neal Smith on his 1974 solo project PLATINUM GOD. The idea was to produce an album that would lend itself to being used as the backbone of a theatrical tour, and the album finally produced really is a concept album just like in their previous days with the Alice Cooper Group.

The album's concept deals with a type of "Rollerball" (a science fiction film of the period that featured a roller derby-type sport fought in a warlike, brutal way) game of the future where music is used as a form of combat. The band had even sunk money into building a stage for the tour and designing a fight sequence near the end of the show.

The album was released but didn't fair well. A problem was also discovered with the original album that caused the needle to skip sometimes when the vinyl was played on a turntable, which caused several returned albums and a mad rush to have the album remixed to reduce the high end level of recording that caused the problem. This was when Jack Douglas was brought into the picture and he quickly reworked the album for a reissue.

Unfortunately, by that time, it was too late. With the album being remixed after it had already hit the shelves, the band needed to tour to promote it. The problem was, there were no albums on the shelves (since they had been returned), so there wasn't much interest from promoters. With no tour, there was no promotion from the label. When the album again appeared, the band was able to get was only a smattering of gigs. Since the concerts wouldn't allow the stage set to be used, because of cost, time and size restraints, the band rarely got a chance to use it.

It really is a shame because the album is fun to listen to and should have been a good seller. Bruce went back to performing solo and later used Too Young from this album on his next album, ROCK ROLLS ON, in 1983. Smith and Dunaway moved on to their own projects and turned up together on Buck Dharma'a album FLAT OUT in 1982, along with their work with the Flying Tigers in the late 1970's. All three got back together, along with Glen Buxton in 1994 to perform on the Ant-Bee album LUNAR MUZIK.

A promo sampler album was released for BATTLE AXE as well (catalog number PRO-022.) The sampler didn't have the same cover artwork as on the commercial album, and instead displayed a photo of the band members.

Album Title: **ROCK ROLLS ON**
Released: 1983 by Euro Tec Records.
Production: Produced by Michael Bruce and Bruce Caplin. Engineered by Shoes, Steven Escallier, Bill Freesh and David Palmer.
Personnel: Michael Bruce (guitar, vocals.) Mick Mashbir (guitar.) Ricky Phillips (bass.) Gene Cornish (bass.) Dino Danelli (drums.) Barry Brandt (drums.) David Foster (keyboards.) Bob Dolin (keyboards.) David Lindenmuth (vocals.)
Catalog No.: 4-27-1
Media: Vinyl.
Song List: Rock Rolls On (Bruce) / Gina (Bruce) / Too Young (Bruce, Marconi and Smith) / **Friday on My Mind** (Vanda and Young) / **Lucky Break** (Quinlan) / **In My Own Way** (Bruce and Morris) / **Do You Wanna Know** (Bruce and Smith)

Released in 1983, this was really a collection of material from Michael Bruce's first solo album, IN MY OWN WAY, and material from the BATTLE AXE album that Bruce did with Billion Dollar Babies. Many of the same tracks were used in creating the album, and only two of the seven tracks are new (Gina and Do You Wanna Know.) Do You Wanna Know was co-written by Neal Smith, an exclusive track to the album, which may be an additional incentive for fans to look for the album.

Rock Rolls On was originally recorded for the IN MY OWN WAY album under the title As Rock Rolls On and featured Alice on vocals. Alice's vocals do not appear on the updated recording on ROCK ROLLS ON.

A music video was produced in the late 1980's for the track Too Young. This video, produced by Telemusic

ROCK ROLLS ON album cover.

and directed by Rev. Ivan Stang (from the Church of the Sub-Genius), did not feature Bruce in it at all (except for his record being smashed at one point.) Instead, it told a conceptual story about a girl who is too young to drink, yet goes out and parties, gets in a car and dies. The end. The video was broadcast a few times here and there before disappearing.

ROCK ROLLS ON was the last full length solo album by Michael Bruce.

Album Title: **LUNER MUZIK**
Released: March 1998 by Divine Records, UK.
Personnel: Performed by Ant-Bee (a.k.a. Billy James.) Additional performers: Michael Bruce (guitar, bass, sitars, keyboards.) Neal Smith (drums.) Dennis Dunaway (bass.) Glen Buxton (bizarre guitar.)
Catalog No.: 20
Media: CD.
Song List: Snorks & Wheezes / Child of the Moon / Blew a Banana Thru the Sun / The One Who is Gold / Silicone Hump / Love is Only Sleeping / By-and-By I Touch the Sky / Diva Gliss (Are You Sirius?)

/ Tears That Fall Unto the Sky / Return of the Titanic Overture / Son of Snorks & Wheezes

This album featured the first reunion of four of the five Alice Cooper Group members since 1974. The album was created by Billy James, who goes by the stage name of Ant-Bee, a performer who has delighted in getting members of bands from late 1960's / early 1970's together to work on his projects. This has included members of the Mothers of Invention, the Alice Cooper Group, and performers from such bands as Soft Machine, Hawkwind, Yes and Focus.

All four former Alice Cooper Group members played on different parts of the album, but Michael Bruce not only played the most of the four, but also toured with Billy James after the album was completed. Bruce also contributed an early Alice Cooper song never recorded for the B-side of Ant-Bee's CD single for Child of the Moon (which also featured a live version of I'm Eighteen from 1995.) The song Come With Us Now was performed by the Alice Cooper Group back in 1969. Ant-Bee is currently working on another album and has already enlisted the help of Michael Bruce with a re-recording of the early Alice song Living.

The LUNAR MUZIK album with four of the five members of the Alice Cooper Group.

Additionally, a sequel to the early Alice track Titanic Overture called Return of the Titanic Overture was recorded for this album. This featured the former band members together in one place recording. The album also featured a track called By-and-By I Touch the Sky, which is broken down into movements that include a portion of Neal Smith's never issued album THE PLATINUM GOD. The movement is entitled The Platinum God Excerpts.

Album Title: **HERE TO RUIN YOUR GROOVE**
Released: 1996 by SPV / Rebel Records, Germany and Baloney Shrapnel Records, US.
Personnel: Performed by Antiseen.
Media: CD.

Michael Bruce played guitar on the band's cover of Sick Things.

GLEN BUXTON:

Album Title: **LUNAR MUZIK**
(See the entry under "Michael Bruce" for details.)

Buxton also did some work in the studio with his last band, The Buxton / Flynn Band, before passing away in October 1997. He also performed numerous times over the years with his band Virgin, and in other one-off situations (including a reunion show with Neal Smith and Michael Bruce just days before his passing.)

DENNIS DUNAWAY:

Album Title: **PLATINUM GOD**
(See the entry under "Neal Smith" for details.)

Album Title: **BILLION DOLLAR BABIES**
(See the entry under "Michael Bruce" for details.)

Album Title: **FLAT OUT**
Released: 1982 by Portrait.
Catalog No.: 38124 (vinyl) and PRT 477942-2 (CD)
Media: Vinyl and Cassette. Later reissued on CD.

Dennis Dunaway played bass on the track Born To Rock. Neal Smith played drums on Born To Rock (which he co-wrote) as well as That Summer Night. Buck Dharma is probably best known for his work with the band

Blue Oyster Cult. He also contributed a track, **Summa Cum Loud**, to the Deadringer album recorded in 1989.

Album Title: **ELECTROCUTION OF THE HEART**
Released: 1989 by Grudge Records.
Production: Produced, engineered and mixed by John Stronach, with assistance from Matt Lane. Mastered by Stephen Marcussen.
Personnel: Performed by Deadringer: Charlie Huhn (vocals.) Jay "Jesse" Johnson (acoustic guitar, guitar, and vocals.) Dennis Dunaway (bass and vocals.) Neal Smith (percussion, drums and vocals.) Joe Bouchard (keyboards and vocals.) Jeff Batter (keyboards.)
Catalog No.: 4512 (vinyl) and 4512-2-F (CD)
Media: Vinyl, Cassette and CD.
Song List: Everybody Rock (Smith, Bouchard and Dunaway) / When You're In You're In (Albert Bouchard and Debra Frost) / Love's a Killer (Smith, Bouchard and Dunaway) / Secret Eyes (Smith and Bouchard) / Balls Out (Jay Johnson) / Summa Cum Loud (Buck Dharma) / Double Talk (Smith, Dunaway, Bouchard and Johnson) / Dangerous Love (Charlie Huhn) / Bring on the Night (Johnson) / Unsung Heroes (Johnson)

Recorded in 1989, this album is a unique opportunity for fans to hear what type of work Dennis Dunaway and Neal Smith can do on their own. The album featured four tracks written by Neal Smith (three of which were also co-written by Dunaway), and both Smith and Dunaway performed continuously throughout the album. Also featured on the album is a track written by Buck Dharma, **Summa Cum Loud**. Both Dunaway and Smith performed on Dharma's 1982 solo album **FLAT OUT**.

Album Title: **LUNAR MUZIK**
(See the entry under "Michael Bruce" for details.)

Dunaway is also featured with Neal Smith in the band The Flying Tigers, which recorded some demos back in the late 1970's. Dunaway has also made one-off appearances since, normally with Neal Smith.

NEAL SMITH:

Album Title: **PLATINUM GOD**
Recorded: 1974 / 75.
Released: Never released.
Production: Produced by Jack Douglas.
Personnel: Neal Smith (drums and vocals.) Dennis Dunaway (bass.) Mike Marconi (lead guitar.) Stu Day (rhythm guitar.)
Song List: Holiday / Set Me On Fire / French Quarter / Baby Please Don't Stop / Platinum God

This was the solo project Smith worked on after the 1974 South American tour with the Alice Cooper Group. The project was never completed and only five finished tracks exist from the recording sessions. These tracks have appeared in fan circles.

Baby Please Don't Stop was rehearsed during the **MUSCLE OF LOVE** recording stages and a demo of it can be found circulating in fan circles. Pieces of **Platinum God** eventually appeared on the Ant-Bee album **LUNAR MUZIK** in 1998.

Guitarist Mike Marconi went on to work with Neal Smith, Dennis Dunaway and Michael Bruce in the band Billion Dollar Babies in 1977.

Album Title: **BEYOND THE VALLEY OF 1984**
Released: 1981 by Stiff Records. Reissued 1989 by PVC on CD, vinyl and cassette.
Catalog No.: 11 (Stiff vinyl), PVC-8929 (vinyl reissue), PVCC-8929 (cassette reissue) and PVCCD-8929 (CD reissue)
Media: Vinyl plus Vinyl, CD and Cassette reissue.

Neal Smith played some drums on this album by the infamous post-punk band, starring Wendy O. Williams. The album was later reissued with a reissue of the EP **METAL PRIESTESS**. The CD of this album is hard to find and quite collectible for fans of the Plasmatics.

Album Title: **FLAT OUT**
(See the entry under "Dennis Dunaway" for details.)

Album Title: **ELECTROCUTION OF THE HEART**
(See the entry under "Dennis Dunaway" for details.)

Album Title: **LUNAR MUZIK**
(See the entry under "Michael Bruce" for details.)

Neal Smith has worked with Dennis Dunaway in the band The Flying Tigers, who also recorded some demos back in the late 1970's. After Alice and Michael Bruce, Neal Smith has probably done the most in music since the days of the Alice Cooper Group, normally with Dennis Dunaway in some capacity.

Part 6 — Bootleg Albums

As with the compilation albums, when a band or a performer becomes popular, a good way to cash in on them is to release their music on a bootleg album.

So what is a bootleg album? The term "bootleg" is usually used in discussing albums and discs that contain material NOT found on any legitimate releases from a record company (who have the rights to the music.) This would include not only recordings left over from studio sessions over the years (including demo or alternative versions of songs), but also recordings of concerts.

While discussing bootlegs, we should also examine briefly two other types of albums that are closely associated with bootlegs and sometimes confused with boots — "pirated" and "counterfeit" albums. If someone takes an officially released album and reproduces its content and then sells this as a new album, then the album is considered to be a pirate (see the entry for the album EARLY HITS OF ALICE COOPER for an example of a pirated album.) If they take the same album and not only reproduce the material, but also the packaging, and then try to sell the product as the officially released item, then the album is considered a counterfeit. Counterfeiting normally occurs in foreign markets (Asian markets are notorious for counterfeits), although it does occasionally occur in the US. Normally, such out and out copying of official material is not found on bootleg albums, but just material that has not been heard before by the public at large.

Since most authorities consider these recordings to be unlicensed replication of copyrighted material, the selling of boots is illegal in most parts of the world. Some European and Asian countries still feature loopholes in their laws which allow some boots to be obtainable on the open market, but, with international copyright laws becoming more unified and universal, the number of countries that allow such practices are dwindling each year. Artists are also troubled by bootleg albums because the studio recordings saved from the trash bins and used on bootlegs are normally things that they considered not up to their own standards, so they aren't recordings that they wanted the general public to hear. Nor are the recordings from concerts always going to be a class A productions. While some are done from the sound board and with a true mix involved, most are from the audience with a person waving a little tape recorder and getting a lot of feedback from the speakers and from the drunken audience member next to the recorder screaming "Alice!"

Okay, it may not be quite that bad, but you get the idea.

The audience for bootleg albums tends to be the die-hard fans. As such, this is the most common argument in favor of bootlegs, since the people who buy them tend to be the ones who will buy EVERYTHING that has and will come out officially by the performer (even every single copy of the Toronto '69 show that they can find), and so the artist and record company aren't really losing any money in the long run. On the other hand, the people who release bootleg albums tend not to be fans at all. Although some people get involved in bootlegs for the love of the artist's work, most bootleggers are in the business to get a quick buck before they get caught by the record industry or the FBI. Boots are pressed by people with access to small pressing capabilities, with the number of copies pressed ranging from 50-100 for most bootleggers to 500-1000 for the richer and more well established record makers. Because of the illegal aspects of their products, bootleggers tend to release their albums with pseudo-information on the cover of the albums to divert attention away from themselves — wrong recording dates, a fake record company name, wrong country of origin and/or wrong country of release. Mainly this serves the purpose of confusing the fans more than the FBI or the Record Industry and should be kept in mind when reviewing the entries listed (since some dates may be off or nonexistent for this reason alone.)

Bootlegs came into fashion in the late 1960's and early 1970's, with a boom of the vinyl albums being released in the late 1970's through early 1980's. Early bootlegs were normally packaged in a single, plain, cardboard sleeve, with a photocopied 8 ½" by 11" piece of paper placed on top of the sleeve and shrink wrapped. As the 1980's progressed and collectors began to move towards CD, the production of the bootlegs became more glossy, with full color covers and added extras such as posters, etc. CD's became the norm for bootlegs by the late 1980's and earlier vinyl boots are becoming harder and harder to find.

Lastly, it's best for collectors to remember two things: many recording have been reissued and reissued again under different titles and labels over the years (the 1978 KING BISCUIT FLOWER HOUR radio special is the most popular Alice album among bootleggers, it seems), and, there is much fakery involved as well (see the entry for FEARLESS below for a prime example of this.) It's a seller's market, not only because these recordings sell at a premium, but because it's rare for a buyer to be able to go back to a seller and demand a refund for an illegally purchased item.

The bootlegs listed below are in alphabetical order (for easy reference when looking for particular titles.) To help fans looking for certain dates, we have attempted to list bootleg titles next to dates in the tour sections of the first six chapters. Due to the nature of the business, while several bootlegs are listed here, there is no claim made to suggest that these are all of the bootlegs available containing Alice.

Album Title: **1971 - EARLY A**
Released: 1976 by Quality Records, USA.
Recorded: 1971 in Cincinnati, Ohio by ABC Broadcasts for radio broadcast.
Catalog No.: Unknown.
Media: Vinyl.
Song List: Caught in a Dream / I'm Eighteen / Is It My Body / Sun Arise / Ballad of Dwight Fry / Black Juju

An early Alice bootleg that covers a variety of songs from the LOVE IT TO DEATH album (which makes it safe to assume that the recordings are actually from the 1971 tour in support of this album.) These tracks also appear on the boots ALICE IN ROCKLAND and PARRACIDAL SLUMBERS.

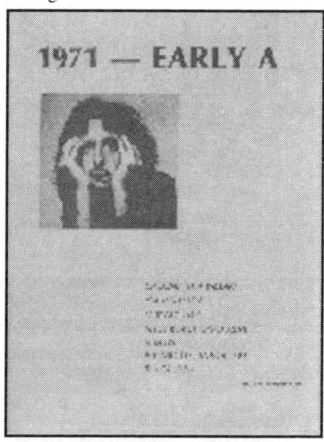

The 1971 - EARLY A bootleg album.

Album Title: **ALICE**
Released: April 1992 by Lobster Records.
Recorded: September 13, 1991 at Electric Ladyland Studios, New York City, NY.
Catalog No.: LOB 036
Media: CD.
Song List: No More Mr. Nice Guy / Billion Dollar Babies / Only Woman Bleed / Sick Things / Feed My Frankenstein / Cold Ethyl / Love's a Loaded Gun / I'm Eighteen / Go to Hell / School's Out / Hey Stoopid

This is some, but not all, of the tracks recorded for a radio special that was broadcast on October 31, 1991 via the Album Network. Several of these tracks later turned up with a special Japanese edition of THE LAST TEMPTATION CD on a bonus CD called LIVE AT ELECTRIC LADY (see that entry for details.) Missing from the recording, but appearing on the LIVE AT ELECTRIC LADY CD, is the track Poison. Several of these tracks also popped up on foreign 12" single releases during the 1990's.

The ALICE bootleg album.

Album Title: A-A-ALICE KILLERED
Released: Late 1970's by Sunrise Records.
Recorded: 1972 in Dallas, TX.
Catalog No.: 056B
Media: Vinyl.
Song List: Be My Lover / Yeah,Yeah,Yeah / I'm Eighteen / Is It My Body / Dead Babies / Killer / Long Way To Go / School's Out / Under My Wheels

Recorded during the KILLER tour.

Album Title: ALICE COOPER GOES TO CHILE
Released: 1997 by Kiss The Stone Records.
Recorded: September 7, 1995 in Santiago, Chile.
Catalog No.: KTS 512
Media: CD.
Song List: Under My Wheels / Hey Stoopid / I'm Eighteen / No More Mr. Nice Guy / Desperado / Billion Dollar Babies / It's Me / Lost in America / Cleansed by Fire / Go to Hell / Gutter Cat Vs. The Jets / Street Fight / Feed My Frankenstein / Only Women Bleed / Welcome to My Nightmare / Ballad of Dwight Fry / School's Out / Elected

Double CD set, with an in-concert photo of Alice wearing a bloody white top hat. Also referred to as ALICE COOPER GOES TO CHILE SANTIAGO, but the title of the CD is as listed above.

ALICE COOPER GOES TO CHILE.

Album Title: ALIVE COOPER - LIVE AT THE GARDEN
Released: 1994 by Sounds Alive, Germany.
Recorded: October 31, 1986 at the Joe Louis Arena, Detroit, MI.
Catalog No.: Unknown.
Media: CD.
Song List: Welcome to My Nightmare / Billion Dollar Babies / No More Mr. Nice Guy / Be My Lover / I'm Eighteen / The World Needs Guts / Give It Up / Cold Ethyl / Go to Hell / Ballad of Dwight Fry / Elected / Under My Wheels / Sick Things / I Love The Dead / School's Out

Bootleg recorded directly from THE NIGHTMARE RETURNS video cassette, which was a recording of this show from the tour of the same name. The CD is missing the also performed Teenage Frankenstein.

The LIVE AT THE GARDEN bootleg.

Album Title: ALICE COOPER TRASHES THE WORLD
Released: Mid-1990's by Birmingham and Diverse.
Recorded: December 14, 1989 at the Birmingham NEC, Birmingham, England.
Catalog No.: 90 444 (Birmingham vinyl release) and ACCD 01(Diverse CD release)
Media: Double-Vinyl and CD.
Song List: Trash / Billion Dollar Babies / I'm Eighteen / I'm Your Gun / Desperado / House of Fire / No More Mr. Nice Guy / Welcome to My Nightmare / Only Women Bleed / I Love The Dead / Poison / Muscle of Love / Spark in the Dark / Bed of Nails / School's Out

Taken from the same recordings that make up the bootlegs WAITING TILL THE EDGE KISS MY NECK and STREET TRASH with the deletion of both Hello, Hooray and This Maniac's in Love With You, but with the addition of Desperado. Diverse also released this as ALICE TRASHES THE WORLD.

As you'd expect, this is all just a variation of the ALICE COOPER TRASHES THE WORLD video cassette, which was recorded the same night as this bootleg. Consequently, the bootleg is also missing Ballad of Dwight Fry, Gutter Cat Vs. the Jets and Under My Wheels.

Album Title: **ALICE IN ROCKLAND**
Released: 1990 by Chapter One, Luxembourq.
Recorded: Tracks 1-6 recorded 1971 in Cincinnati, Ohio by ABC Broadcasts. Track 7 is a studio recording done in 1972 and released as a flexi-disc given away with copies of the February 17, 1973 issue of NEW MUSICAL EXPRESS.
Catalog No.: CO-25133
Media: Vinyl.
Song List: Side 1: Caught in a Dream / I'm Eighteen / Is It My Body / Sun Arise / Ballad of Dwight Fry / Black Juju / / Side 2: Slick Black Limousine

Although no listing is given for the exact location of the 1971 recordings found on the LP, these recordings are the same as found on the 1971 - EARLY A album released back in 1976. As mentioned above and elsewhere, Slick Black Limousine was recorded by the Alice Cooper Group back in 1972, but never released officially except as a flexi-disc included with a particular issue of the UK music newspaper NEW MUSICAL EXPRESS. This track will also show up on other bootlegs, normally when extra room on the disc or vinyl allowed the bootlegger to fill space.

The album, which was also released as a CD under the same catalog number through Chapter One, had a full color cover with a picture of Alice from the SPECIAL FORCES tour. The CD contains the track Second Coming, between Sun Arise and Ballad of Dwight Fry, although it's not listed on the album cover. Ballad of Dwight Fry is listed with the actor's name spelled correctly as Dwight Frye.

ALICE IN ROCKLAND bootleg.

Album Title: **ALICE N IAN 9-71**
Released: 1973 by Contra Band Records, USA.
Recorded: September 21, 1972 at the Hofstra University, Long Island, New York. Dubbed from the television series IN CONCERT.
Catalog No.: CBM 3908
Media: Vinyl.
Song List: I'm Eighteen / Gutter Cat Vs. the Jets / Killer / School's Out
            (all tracks, Side 1 only)

This is one of the earliest bootleg releases for Alice and the material comes directly from the IN CONCERT appearance done in 1972. Jethro Tull was also a featured guest on the program that night and Side Two has only the Jethro Tull tracks. These same tracks can also be found on several other bootleg albums needing filler material, including HELLO, HOORAY STARRING ALICE COOPER AT THE HOLLYWOOD BOWL 1972 and YOU'RE ALL CRAZIER THAN I AM (Trade Mark of Quality release.) The cover of the album featured pictures of both Ian Anderson (from Jethro Tull) and Alice.

ALICE N IAN 9-71 bootleg.

Album Title: **ALICE TRASHES THE WORLD**
Released: Late-1990's by Remember Gema.
Recorded: December 14, 1989 at the Birmingham NEC, Birmingham, England.
Catalog No.: 5242
Media: CD.
Song List: Hello, Hooray / Trash / Billion Dollar Babies / I'm Eighteen / I'm Your Gun / House of Fire / No

More Mr. Nice Guy / Welcome to My Nightmare / Ballad of Dwight Fry / Only Women Bleed / I Love The Dead / Poison / Muscle of Love / Spark in the Dark / Bed of Nails / School's Out

Taken from the same recordings that make up the bootlegs ALICE COOPER TRASHES THE WORLD, WAITING TILL THE EDGE KISS MY NECK and STREET TRASH with the deletion of both Desperado and This Maniac's in Love With You, but with the addition of Ballad of Dwight Fry.

As you'd expect, this is all just a variation of the ALICE COOPER TRASHES THE WORLD video cassette, which was recorded the same night as this bootleg. With this in mind, the bootleg is also missing Gutter Cat Vs. the Jets and Under My Wheels.

Album Title: **BABIES IN SCHOOL**
Released: 1987 by Snapshot Productions, Germany.
Recorded: May 10, 1978 in Saginaw, MI.
Catalog No.: 003
Media: Vinyl.
Song List: Under My Wheels / Billion Dollar Babies / I'm Eighteen / Is It My Body / Black Widow / You and Me / Only Women Bleed / Escape / I Never Cry / It's Hot Tonight / Lace and Whiskey / School's Out

This is another variation of the 1978 KING BISCUIT FLOWER HOUR radio program. See A BILLION $ SHOW for more details. You and Me is listed as What We Are Is What We Are.

BABIES IN SCHOOL bootleg.

Album Title: **BEST OF LIVE SERIES SAGINAW 1978**
Released: Mid-1990's by Best.
Recorded: May 10, 1978 at the Civic Center, Saginaw, MI.
Catalog No.: BOLS 010
Media: CD.
Song List: Under My Wheels / Billion Dollar Babies / I'm Eighteen / Is It My Body / You and Me / Only Women Bleed / Unfinished Sweet / Escape / Go to Hell / I Never Cry / It's Hot Tonight / School's Out

Another revamping of the 1978 KING BISCUIT FLOWER HOUR radio program.

Album Title: **BILLION DOLLAR KILLERS**
Released: Mid-1970's. Record Company unknown.
Recorded: July 23, 1972 at the Hollywood Bowl, Hollywood, CA.
Catalog No.: Unknown.
Media: Vinyl.

This album is another variation of the HELLO, HURRAY STARRING ALICE COOPER AT THE HOLLYWOOD BOWL album. See that entry for more details.

Official CD reissue of the King Biscuit Flower Hour 1978 Alice Cooper concert that has been released on several bootlegs over the years.

The Illustrated Collector's Guide To *Alice Cooper*   285

Album Title: **A BILLION $ SHOW**
Released: Early 1990's by Main Event.
Recorded: May 10, 1978 at Civic Center, Saginaw, MI.
Catalog No.: M-CD-016
Media: CD.
Song List: Under My Wheels / Billion Dollar Babies / I'm Eighteen / Is It My Body / You and Me / Only Women Bleed / Escape / I Love the Dead / Go to Hell / I Never Cry / It's Hot Tonight / School's Out

A shortened version of a show from the LACE AND WHISKEY tour. Because of the way the date for the show is given on the album, it's usually listed as being January 10, 1978. This show was recorded for radio broadcast for the KING BISQUIT FLOWER HOUR, and is merely a repackaging of that broadcast, which was aired on October 31, 1978.

Tracks from the KING BISCUIT FLOWER HOUR program can also be found on the following bootlegs: BABIES IN SCHOOL, LIVE IN USA 1978 / 1990, LIVE USA, NO MORE Mr. NICE GUY (Liveline Disc release), NO MORE MR. NICE GUY (Grapefruit release), NO MORE TEACHER'S DIRTY LOOKS, ONE HALLOWEEN NIGHT, SICK, THE KING SNAKE, THE NIGHT OF HALLOWEEN, and YOU'RE ALL CRAZIER THAN I AM! (Black Death label.)

Album Title: **CREATURES OF MY NIGHTMARES**
Released: 1991 by Flashback World Productions, Luxembourg.
Recorded: June 17, 1975 at the Los Angeles Forum, Los Angeles, CA for broadcast on THE KING BISCUIT FLOWER HOUR.
Catalog No.: Flash 09.90.0129-33
Media: CD.
Song List: Welcome to My Nightmare / Years Ago / No More Mr. Nice Guy / Billion Dollar Babies / I'm Eighteen / Under My Wheels / Cold Ethyl / Only Women Bleed / Devil's Food / Black Widow / Escape / School's Out / Department of Youth

This recording is missing Some Folks from the actual show. The cover is a badly hand colored WELCOME TO MY NIGHTMARE era photo shot of Alice in bed with the spiders all around him (the cover to THE NIGHTMARE video cassette.) As with the 1978 Saginaw, Michigan show, this concert was recorded for later broadcast on the radio program THE KING BISCUIT FLOWER HOUR, and, as with the 1978 show, numerous bootlegs have been made from this broadcast. Also released in a different edited (and shorter) form as SOLD OUT 1975 TOUR.

CREATURES OF MY NIGHTMARE bootleg.

Album Title: **EARLY ALICE**
Released: late 1970's by Quality Recordings Productions, USA.
Recorded: 1968 - 1971, location of recordings unknown.
Catalog No.: Unknown.
Media: Vinyl.
Song List: My Dog Spot / Nobody Likes Me / Return of the Spider / Ballad of Dwight Fry / Slick Black Limousine / Black Juju / Is It My Body

If you wanted to point to a particular bootleg album to show that sometimes bootleggers had no idea what they were doing, this would be a good example. Not only are many song titles listed incorrectly on the album (Ballad of Dwight Frye for Ballad of Dwight Fry, All My Own for Slick Black Limousine, Nobody Like Me for Nobody Likes Me and Last Juju for Black Juju), but the dates guessed at for the recordings are impossible. Although some of the songs are from a period that would present 1971, the band had moved away from songs such as Nobody Likes Me by this point in their career. It has been suggested that the version of Nobody Likes Me on this bootleg is actually from the flexi-disc taken from the back of the KILLER tour book, and this is quite possible. Fans may find the bootleg PARRACIDAL SLUMBERS of more interest, since it contains much of the same material and in a better format.

Part 6: Bootleg Albums

Album Title: **EARLY HITS OF ALICE COOPER**
Released: Late 1970's by Palm Tree Inc., USA.
Recorded: Between 1969 - 1971, location of recordings unknown.
Catalog No.: Unknown.
Media: Vinyl.
Song List: Mr. and Misdemeanor / Still No Air / Beautiful Flyaway / Return of the Spiders / Laughing at Me / Refrigerator Heaven / Shoe Salesman / Below Your Means

A questionable album made up of cuts from EASY ACTION and arranged in a different order. While not really constituting the requirements of a bootleg album (since it is neither live material nor unreleased songs), it's listed here because some fans may assume that this album is either a bootleg or an officially sanctioned album. In fact, the album really fits the requirements for a pirated album, since it's just an unauthorized reissuing of copyrighted material. Really just a good album to avoid altogether.

8-Track edition of EARLY HITS OF ALICE COOPER.

THE (EL PASO) SHOW vinyl bootleg album cover.

THE (EL PASO) SHOW boot on CD with a different cover.

Album Title: **THE (EL PASO) SHOW**
Released: 1982. Record company unknown. Later reissued on CD by Electric Pig in early 1990's.
Recorded: June 4, 1980 at the El Paso Coliseum, El Paso, TX.
Catalog No.: RR-BR-101 (vinyl); ERP 04 (CD)
Media: Colored Vinyl and CD.
Song List: Grim Facts / Go to Hell / Guilty / You and Me / Pain / Talk Talk / I Never Cry / I'm Eighteen / Gutter Cat Vs. the Jets / Clones / Nuclear Infected / Wish You Were Here

An early 1980's bootleg, THE SHOW is from one of the few early 1980's shows to appear on vinyl and has appeared in edited form on several other bootlegs including LIVE USA 1978 / 1980 and NO MORE MR. NICE GUY (Grapefruit label.) THE SHOW, however, is one of the few to feature at least twelve tracks from this particular concert.

Released on colored vinyl, the album was limited to 200 (some collectors say 100) vinyl copies and came in a photo cover very reminiscent of the FLUSH THE FASHION cover artwork. Electric Pig later reissued the album in the early 1990's on CD with a photo cover of Alice.

Album Title: FEARLESS
Released: 1979 by Trade Mark of Quality, USA.
Recorded: Recorded 1973 in the studio. No new recordings than can't be found on the Quadraphonic pressing of the BILLION DOLLAR BABIES album. Last track taken from the 1975 album FLASH FEARLESS VS. THE ZORG WOMEN.
Catalog No.: TMQ 72111
Media: Double-Vinyl.
Song List: Sick Things (mix 1) / Raped and Freezin' (mix 1) / Mary Ann (mix 1) / Hello, Hooray (mix 1) / Elected (mix 1) / Sick Things (mix 2) / Billion Dollar Babies (mix 1) / Raped and Freezin' (mix 2) / Unfinished Sweet / I Love the Dead / Elected (mix 2) / Hello, Hooray (mix 2) / Mary Ann (mix 2) / No More Mr. Nice Guy / Generation Landslide / Billion Dollar Babies (mix 2) / I'm Flash

Figuring that a sucker is born every minute, Trade Mark of Quality released this album in the late 1970's as being outtakes from the BILLION DOLLAR BABIES recording sessions. Actually, the recordings are remixed versions of tracks that can be found on the mid-1970's Quadraphonic release of the B$B album. Someone merely took the officially released album, mixed the cuts different a couple of times, and viola — a new bootleg. Actually, it comes close to being a pirated recording and quite surprising from a company who, at the time, was considered one of the top names in the bootleg field (but, then again, their reputation was changing at the time as well.) The two vinyl discs came in a blue and white cover with no information listed on the cover except the title. Track listings were included on a photocopied page inside the album cover.

Hello, Hooray is constantly misspelled as Hello, Hurray. I'm Flash is actually taken from an album that Alice help record in late 1974 (see the entry in Part 3 for more details.)

Certainly an album to avoid, unless one is a completist. These makeshift recordings have also appeared as the boots NICE GUYS SLEEP ALONE (vinyl release), LIVING NEXT DOOR TO ALIVE (CD release) and IN SESSION (CD release.)

Album Title: FUCK THE FASHION
Released: Early 1980's by Alice Super Sounds.
Recorded: Tracks 1 - 5 recorded March 26, 1973 at the Gardens, Boston, MA. Tracks 6 - 9 recorded March 30, 1969 at the Avalon Ballroom, San Francisco, CA.
Catalog No.: #18 (same as NO MORE MR. NICE GUY also release by Alice Super Sounds)
Media: Vinyl.
Song List: Hello, Hooray / Billion Dollar Babies / I'm Eighteen / Raped and Freezin' / Elected / Shoe Salesman / Still No Air / Levity Ball / Nobody Likes Me

Can't quite figure out if the bootlegger was trying to make some wry commentary on Alice's direction in the 1980's, or if he was just trying to rip off fans by making the album appear to be from a later period than the recordings actually are. Probably the latter. One of the few boots with material from the 1973 Boston show (although it's recorded from the audience.)

Album Title: GO TO HELL
Released: 1994 by Metal Mess.
Recorded: Listed as being recorded in San Diego, CA during a 1990 tour. Portions of this show are actually from the April 9, 1979 San Diego Sports Arena concert in San Diego, CA, which was used for the movie THE STRANGE CASE OF ALICE COOPER.
Catalog No.: MM 9212
Media: CD.
Song List: Welcome to My Nightmare / No More Mr. Nice Guy / Billion Dollar Babies / I'm Eighteen / Under My Wheels" / I Never Cry / Devil's Food / Black Widow / You and Me / Only Women Bleed / Go to Hell / How You Gonna See Me Now / School's Out

Although the packaging for this CD lists the recording coming from a concert in 1990, it's merely a reissuing

The GO TO HELL bootleg.

of the earlier NO MORE MR. NICE GUY CD from Liveline Disc. See that entry for more details about the recording.

Album Title: **HELLO, HURRAY STARRING ALICE COOPER AT THE HOLLYWOOD BOWL 1972**
Released: Mid-1970's. Record Company unknown, but probably Wizardo.
Recorded: First ten tracks recorded July 23, 1972 at the Hollywood Bowl, Hollywood, CA. Final six tracks dubbed from the television series IN CONCERT, which was recorded September 21, 1972 at Hofstra University, Long Island, New York.
Catalog No.: Not listed.
Media: Vinyl.
Song List: Public Animal No. 9 / Be My Lover / I'm Eighteen / Is It My Body / Halo of Flies / Gutter Cat Vs. the Jets / Street Fight / Killer / Long Way To Go / School's Out / I'm Eighteen / Gutter Cat Vs. the Jets / Street Fight / Killer / Elected / School's Out

Since the album is titled HELLO, HURRAY ... one would think that the song would appear on the album, and that the bootleggers would have spelled the title correctly. Incidentally, the version of Elected used during the IN CONCERT program was not a live track, but the studio version of the song played over a promotional film (an early music video.) The IN CONCERT tracks can also be found on the early boot IAN AND ALICE 9-71. This material was released in 1973 as YOU'RE ALL CRAZIER THAN I AM (Trade Mark of Quality label.)

The HELLO, HURRAY bootleg.

Album Title: **IN TORONTO 1973**
Released: 1977 by Wizardo Records.
Recorded: December 14, 1973 at the Maple Leaf Gardens, Toronto, Canada.
Catalog No.: Unknown.
Media: Vinyl.
Song List: Hello, Hooray / Billion Dollar Babies / I'm Eighteen / Big Apple Dreamin' / Muscle of Love / My Stars / Hard Hearted Alice / Unfinished Sweet / Sick Things / Dead Babies / I Love the Dead / School's Out / Working Up a Sweat

Incorrectly listed as December 18, 1973, this is a rare chance to hear something from the original Alice Cooper Group band on their last tour together.

Album Title: **THE KILLER TOUR**
Released: 1975. Record company unknown.
Recorded: 1972 at the Electric Ballroom, Detroit, MI.
Catalog No.: Unknown.
Media: Vinyl.
Song List: Public Animal No. 9 / Be My Lover / I'm Eighteen / Halo of Flies / Yeah, Yeah, Yeah / You Drive Me Nervous / Dead Babies / Killer / School's Out / Is It My Body

Although not the best sounding bootleg release that came out for Alice, it's a chance to hear rare songs from the KILLER album performed live.

THE KILLER TOUR bootleg.

Album Title: THE KING SNAKE USA 1969 / 1970
Released: 1990 by Liveline Disc, Italy.
Recorded: Tracks 1 - 4 recorded 1971 at the Paramount NW Theater, Seattle, WA. Track 5 and 6 are dubbed and remixed tracks from the BILLION DOLLAR BABIES quadraphonic reissue.
Catalog No.: LLR 059
Media: CD.
Song List: Is It My Body / Caught in a Dream / Second Coming / I'm Eighteen / Raped and Freezin' / I Love the Dead

Talk about false advertising in the title of an album. The first four tracks are from 1971, not 1969 or 1970, while the final two are not even live tracks, but the same remixed cuts from the B$B quadraphonic reissue made to appear like studio outtakes. Even FEARLESS and NICE GUYS SLEEP ALONE at least give you a full two vinyl discs of music with their cheating.

Album Title: LIVE AT THE GARDEN
Released: 1994 by Sounds Alive, Germany.
Recorded: Recorded for the SUPERSTAR CONCERT SERIES radio broadcast, March 6, 1987 at the Cincinnati Gardens, Cincinnati, OH.
Catalog No.: SA 24.010
Media: CD.
Song List: Welcome to My Nightmare / Billion Dollar Babies / No More Mr. Nice Guy / Be My Lover / I'm Eighteen / The World Needs Guts / Give It Up / Cold Ethyl / Only Women Bleed / Go to Hell / Ballad of Dwight Fry / Elected / Under My Wheels / Sick Things / I Love the Dead / School's Out

This is, surprisingly, one of the few bootlegs taken from a radio broadcast of a show from THE NIGHTMARE RETURNS tour.

Album Title: LIVE IN USA 1978 / 1980
Released: 1990 by Golden Stars.
Recorded: First twelve tracks recorded May 10, 1978 at the Civic Center, Saginaw, MI. Last ten tracks recorded June 4, 1980 at the El Paso Coliseum in El Paso, TX.
Catalog No.: GSCD 1109
Media: CD.
Song List: Under My Wheels / Billion Dollar Babies / I'm Eighteen / Is It My Body / Black Widow / You and Me / Only Women Bleed / Escape / I Never Cry / It's Hot Tonight / Lace and Whiskey / School's Out / Grim Fact / Go to Hell / Guilty / You and Me / Pain / Talk Talk / Gutter Cat Vs. the Jets / Clones / Nuclear Infected / Wish You Were Here

One of the never ending variations of the KING BISCUIT FLOWER HOUR show from 1978, this CD was also released through another company with just the Saginaw tracks and three additional tracks as just LIVE USA (see that entry.) The CD is, however, one of the few to be released with material from the FLUSH THE FASHION period. Saying that, however, many of these tracks also appear on the Grapefruit label CD NO MORE MR. NICE GUY (see that entry for more details) and twelve tracks from the El Paso show appear on the vinyl boot THE SHOW (see that entry.)

You and Me is given as What We Are Is What We Are in the track listings on the CD when it first appears during the Saginaw set, but is listed correctly for the El Paso portion of the CD. As this track's listing is the only one incorrect — and the only track appearing twice on the CD — it could be assumed that the mistake was an intentional way for the bootleggers to avoid admitting that one song appears twice on the CD. However, the track is also listed this way on the bootleg BABIES IN SCHOOL, so this may be the source that was used when compiling LIVE IN USA 1978 / 1980. Wish You Were Here, however, is listed as being the Pink Floyd song from the album of the same name, and song writing credits are given for that song instead of the Alice song. The cover art is of a hand holding an apple with a worm in it.

LIVE IN USA 1978 / 1980 bootleg.

Album Title:	**LIVE USA**
Released:	Early 1990's by LSD.
Recorded:	First thirteen tracks recorded May 10, 1978 at the Civic Center, Saginaw, MI. It is unknown when the remaining three tracks were recorded, most probably 1971.
Catalog No.:	LSD 152 062
Media:	CD.
Song List:	Under My Wheels / Billion Dollar Babies / I'm Eighteen / Is It My Body / You and Me / Only Women Bleed / Unfinished Sweet / Escape / I Love the Dead / Go to Hell / I Never Cry / It's Hot Tonight / School's Out / Second Coming / Ballad of Dwight Fry / Is It My Body (extended version)

The KING BISCUIT FLOWER HOUR 1978 show once again appears, only this time in a rather oddly packaged version. Instead of including more tracks from that concert on the disc where empty space seems to have been available, the record company instead decided to thrown in three tracks from the 1971 concert period. Reissued as LIVE USA through Imtrat (see next entry.)

Album Title:	**LIVE USA**
Released:	Early 1990's by Imtrat, Germany.
Recorded:	First thirteen tracks recorded May 10, 1978 at the Civic Center, Saginaw, MI. It is unknown when the remaining three tracks were recorded, most probably 1971.
Catalog No.:	IMT 900.021
Media:	CD.
Song List:	Under My Wheels / Billion Dollar Babies / I'm Eighteen / Is It My Body / You and Me / Only Women Bleed / Unfinished Sweet / Escape / I Love the Dead / Go to Hell / I Never Cry / It's Hot Tonight / School's Out / Second Coming / Ballad of Dwight Fry

The KING BISCUIT FLOWER HOUR 1978 show once again appears, only this time in a rather oddly packaged version. Instead of including more tracks from that concert on the disc where empty space seems to have been available, the record company instead decided to thrown in three tracks from the 1971 concert period. Ballad of Dwight Fry is not listed on the album, although it does appear as a track on the CD. Also released under the same title by LSD and with the 1971 version of Is It My Body.

Album Title:	**LIVING NEXT DOOR TO ALIVE**
Released:	1980's by Kiss The Stone.
Catalog No.:	KOS 003
Media:	CD.
Song List:	Elected / Hello Hooray / Generation Landslide (mix 1) / I Love the Dead (mix 1) / Billion Dollar Babies (mix 1) / Mary Ann / Raped and Freezin' / Billion Dollar Babies (mix 2) / Generation Landslide (mix 2) / Unfinished Sweet / I Love The Dead (mix 2)

Another FEARLESS remix variation of the Quadraphonic version of the BILLION DOLLAR BABIES album. See FEARLESS and NICE GUYS SLEEP ALONE.

Album Title:	**MAD HOUSE ROCK**
Released:	1991 by No Future Records.
Recorded:	Recorded April 9, 1979 at the San Diego Sports Arena concert in San Diego, CA, and used for the movie THE STRANGE CASE OF ALICE COOPER.
Catalog No.:	NFR-371
Media:	CD.
Song List:	From the Inside / Nurse Rozetta / The Quiet Room / I Never Cry / Welcome to My Nightmare / Billion Dollar Babies / Only Women Bleed / No More Mr. Nice Guy / I'm Eighteen / Wish I were Born in Beverly Hills / Devil's Food / Black Widow / Ballad of Dwight Fry / Got To Hell / How You Gonna See Me Now / Inmates (We're all Crazy) / School's Out

The MAD HOUSE ROCK bootleg.

Recording taken from the FROM THE INSIDE tour, this bootleg gets the names partially correct in several areas. Wish I Were Born in Beverly Hills is listed as Wish I Were Born, How You Gonna See Me Now is listed as How You Gonna See Me and Inmates is listed as In Mates. Photo cover of Alice (from the proper period of the recording) looking at his snake.

Album Title: **NICE GUYS SLEEP ALONE**
Released: Late 1970's by El Topo.
Recorded: Dubbed and remixed from the official quadraphonic version of BILLION DOLLAR BABIES. Final track dubbed from the FLASH FEARLESS VS. THE ZORG WOMEN album.
Catalog No.: No catalog number.
Media: Double-Vinyl.
Song List: Sick Things (mix 1) / Raped and Freezin' (mix 1) / Mary Ann (mix 1) / Hello Hooray (mix 1) / Elected (mix 1) / Sick Things (mix 2) / Billion Dollar Babies (mix 1) / Raped and Freezin' (mix 2) / Unfinished Sweet / I Love the Dead / Elected (mix 2) / Hello, Hooray (mix 2) / Mary Ann (mix 2) / No More Mr. Nice Guy / Generation Landslide / Billion Dollar Babies (mix 2) / I'm Flash

Simply a reissue of FEARLESS, which was nothing but a remixing of the quadraphonic reissue of BILLION DOLLAR BABIES to give the appearance of studio outtakes. Even Hello, Hooray is misspelled on the jacket, just as with the labeling for FEARLESS. The bootleg came on blue and green vinyl. This boot was later reissued as IN SESSION on CD in the late 1990's.

Album Title: **NIGHT OF THE HALLOWEEN MICHIGAN 9 / 9 / 78**
Released: Mid-1990's by Seagull Records.
Recorded: May 10, 1978 at the Civic Center, Saginaw, MI.
Catalog No.: SCD 024
Media: CD.
Song List: Under My Wheels / Billion Dollar Babies / I'm Eighteen / Is It My Body / You and Me / Only Women Bleed / Unfinished Sweet / Escape / Go to Hell / I Never Cry / It's Hot Tonight / School's Out

This bootleg lists the date of the show recorded for the KING BISCUIT FLOWER HOUR as being September 9, 1978 instead of the normally mentioned October 1, 1978.

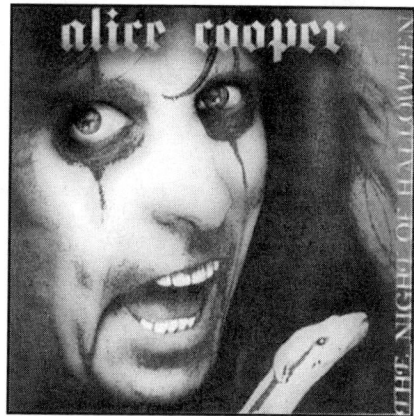

THE NIGHT OF HALLOWEEN bootleg.

Album Title: **NOBODY LIKES ME**
Released: 1991 by Beelzebub.
Recorded: July 14, 1990 at the Ellenfeld Stadium, Neunkirchen, Germany.
Catalog No.: 1991001
Media: Double-Vinyl.
Song List: Hello, Hooray / Trash / Billion Dollar Babies / I'm Eighteen / I'm Your Gun / Desperado / House of Fire / No More Mr. Nice Guy / This Maniac's in Love With You / Steven / Welcome to My Nightmare / Ballad of Dwight Fry / Cutter Cats Vs. the Jets / I Love the Dead / Poison / Spark in the Dark / Only My Heart Talkin' / Bed of Nails / School's Out

A terrible bootleg recording. Its only distinguishing feature is being pressed on colored wax. The labels used on the album featured skull artwork from the trash band SOD. The front cover is of baby heads with make-up. The album does include a rare chance to hear a live version of Only My Heart Talkin', though. Hello, Hooray was not performed the night of the concert and is instead a tape of the song played over the public announcement system before the show began.

Album Title: **NO MORE MR. NICE GUY**
Released: 1982 by Alice Super Sound.
Recorded: February 19, 1982 at the Glasgow Apollo in Glasgow, Scotland.
Catalog No.: #18
Media: Vinyl.
Song List: Who Do You Think We Are? / Go to Hell / Guilty / I'm Eighteen / Cold Ethyl / Only Women Bleed

/ No More Mr. Nice Guy / Clones / Under My Wheels / I Never Cry / Seven and Seven Is / Grim Facts / Pain / Billion Dollar Babies / Generation Landslide / School's Out

Not only a bootleg release for Alice at a time when not many were coming out, but also a release for a tour (SPECIAL FORCES) that is not normally heard from when dealing with bootlegs.

Album Title: **NO MORE MR. NICE GUY**
Released: 1993 by Liveline Disc, Italy.
Recorded: Tracks 1-4 and Track 7 and 8 recorded June 17, 1975 in Los Angeles, CA; Tracks 5, 6, and 9 - 11 recorded May 10, 1978 at the Civic Center, Saginaw, MI; and, Tracks 12 and 13 April 9, 1979 at the San Diego Sports Arena, San Diego, CA.
Catalog No.: LL 15466
Media: CD.
Song List: Welcome to My Nightmare / No More Mr. Nice Guy / Billion Dollar Babies / I'm Eighteen / Under My Wheels / I Never Cry / Devil's Food / Black Widow / You and Me / Only Women Bleed / Go to Hell / How You Gonna See Me Now / School's Out

NO MORE MR. NICE GUY bootleg.

For a bootleg that has a variety of material to choose from — after all, three concerts from three different tours and years are used — there's very little here that's of much consequence to the typical Alice fan. A much better CD would have consisted of the rarer live tracks from each show instead of the "greatest hits" package that occurs here. It's also worth noting that each show used has its official sources: THE KING BISCUIT FLOWER HOUR for Tracks 1 - 11, and THE STRANGE CASE OF ALICE COOPER concert film for the remaining tracks.

Fans interested in this CD may also want to look at the bootleg NO MORE TEACHER'S DIRTY LOOKS, which contains some different material from the same concerts. This CD was later reissued by Metal Mess in the same format and track listing under the title GO TO HELL. The Metal Mess disc is falsely listed as being from a show in 1990, but the dates listed above are correct. The cover of the album is a picture of a pig.

Album Title: **NO MORE MR. NICE GUY**
Released: Early-1990's by Grapefruit.
Recorded: First nine tracks recorded June 4, 1980 in the El Paso Coliseum, El Paso, TX; remaining tracks recorded May 10, 1978 at the Civic Center, Saginaw, MI.
Catalog No.: Unknown.
Media: CD.
Song List: Cold Ethyl / No More Mr. Nice Guy / Clones / Under My Wheels / Billion Dollar Babies / Who Do You think We Are? / Guilty / Seven and Seven Is / Grim Facts / I'm Eighteen / Is It My Body / You and Me / Only Women Bleed / Unfinished Sweet / Escape / I Love the Dead / Go to Hell / I Never Cry / It's Hot Tonight

Almost a counterpoint to the bootleg LIVE USA 1978 / 1980 (see that entry), this CD contains mainly the hits and a few tidbits of rare live tracks. While it does contain Seven and Seven Is, which doesn't appear on the LIVE USA 1978 / 1980 CD, the latter disc contains many more rare tracks than this one. Fans may be more interested in finding the bootleg entitled THE SHOW, since this has all twelve of the combined tracks from NO MORE MR. NICE GUY and LIVE USA 1978 / 1980.

Album Title: **NO MORE TEACHER'S DIRTY LOOKS**
Released: 1991 by Howdy Records, Germany.
Recorded: First thirteen tracks recorded May 10, 1978 at the Civic Center, Saginaw, MI; Tracks 14 - 17 recorded June 17, 1975 at the Los Angeles Forum, Los Angeles, CA; and, Track 18 recorded April 9, 1979 at the San Diego Sports Arena, San Diego, CA.
Catalog No.: Unknown.
Media: CD.

Song List: Under My Wheels / Billion Dollar Babies / I'm Eighteen / Is It My Body / You and Me / Only Women Bleed / Unfinished Sweet / Escape / I Love the Dead / Go to Hell / I Never Cry / It's Hot Tonight / School's Out / Welcome to My Nightmare / No More Mr. Nice Guy / Billion Dollar Babies / I'm Eighteen / How You Gonna See Me Now

Although the CD packaging lists some portions of this album being recorded in Los Angeles in 1979 and San Diego in 1980, both dates are incorrect. These recordings are actually from 1975 and 1979, respectively. Still, it's a chance for fans to hear recordings from three different tours and a few more rare tracks than can't be found on the Liveline Disc album NO MORE MR. NICE GUY (see that entry for more details.)

The Saginaw, MI material is another swipe from the KING BISCUIT FLOWER HOUR show with only I Love The Dead missing. The 1975 material is also from KBFH, while the 1979 material is from THE STRANGE CASE OF ALICE COOPER movie.

NO MORE TEACHER'S DIRTY LOOKS bootleg.

Album Title: **ONE HALLOWEEN NIGHT**
Released: 1978 by The Record Company and Westwood One
Recorded: May 10, 1978 at the Civic Center, Saginaw, MI.
Catalog No.: AC-01
Media: Multicolored-Vinyl.
Song List: Under My Wheels / Billion Dollar Babies / I'm Eighteen / Is It My Body / You and Me / Only Women Bleed / Unfinished Sweet / Escape / I Love the Dead / Go to Hell / I Never Cry / It's Hot Tonight / School's Out

This album is listed as the original Westwood One vinyl disc for the radio program that aired on radio stations using the Westwood One network on October 31, 1978. However, it should be pointed out that there are too many indicators on this album called ONE HALLOWEEN NIGHT to make it suspect, and possibly a bootleg. Westwood One normally didn't release their material in full color covers, nor were / are they known for releasing to stations multicolored vinyl for their radio shows (too much of an extra expense.) Also, I Love the Dead is missing from the track listing on the back of the album.

Still, ONE HALLOWEEN NIGHT is one of the few albums taken from the broadcast that includes all of the tracks used in the radio show. These tracks have been included on a variety of bootlegs over the years (see almost any other entry in this section for more details.) Both the KING BISQUIT FLOWER HOUR and the DIR Radio Network logos appear on the album cover.

Album Title: **PARRACIDAL SLUMBERS**
Released: 1972 (Trade Mark of Quality); 1973 (Wizardo); 1980 (The Amazing Kornaphone Label)
Recorded: Tracks 2 - 5 and 7 - 9 recorded 1971, possibly at Cobo Hall, Detroit, MI. Track 1 recorded 1971 and released as a flexi-disc on the back of the KILLER tour book. Track 6 recorded 1972 and released as a flexi-disc with copies of the February 17, 1973 issue of NEW MUSICAL EXPRESS.
Catalog No.: TMQ number is unknown; Wizardo number is unknown; TAKL 1932
Media: Vinyl (all three.) TAKL 1932 is on blue Vinyl.
Song List: Nobody Likes Me / Sun Arise / Caught in a Dream / I'm Eighteen / Is It My Body (extended version) / Slick Black Limousine /

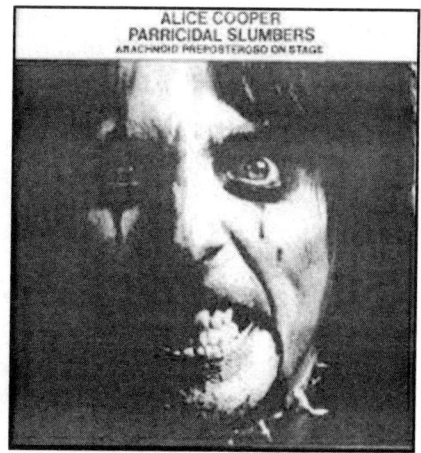

PARRACIDAL SLUMBERS bootleg.

Ballad of Dwight Fry / Black Juju / Return of the Spider

TMQ, Wizardo and TAKL are three bootleg companies that have had considerable ties between them, thus seeing this album be reissued over the years on each of these labels is understandable. Saying so, the track listing given above is for the 1980 TAKL reissue, and it's safe to assume that the 1972 TMQ version of this album is missing **Nobody Likes Me** and **Slick Black Limousine** as both were not released until late 1972 and mid-1973. Ballad of Dwight Fry is listed as **Ballad of Dwight Frye** and Slick Black Limousine is listed as **My Very Own Slick Black Limousine**. A rearranged version of this album, which also drops Slick Black Limousine, can be found as the vinyl bootleg PUKE ON A PIECE OF APPLE PIE.

Album Title: **PUKE ON A PIECE OF APPLE PIE**
Released: 1974 by Omi Productions.
Recorded: Recorded 1971, possibly at Cobo Hall, Detroit, MI. Final track recorded 1972 and released as a flexi-disc with the February 17, 1973 issue of NEW MUSICAL EXPRESS.
Catalog No.: OMI PROD. 09782
Media: Vinyl.
Song List: Caught in a Dream / I'm Eighteen / Is It My Body (extended version) / Sun Arise / Ballad of Dwight Fry / Black Juju / Slick Black Limousine

A variation of the earlier released Trade Mark of quality album PARRACIDAL SLUMBERS, it was also reissued under this earlier title two other times in the 1970's (both other times with the studio recording of Nobody Likes Me.) Still, can't beat that title.

Album Title: **SAGINAW, MICHIGAN 1978**
Released: Mid-1990's by Diverse.
Recorded: May 10, 1978 at the Civic Center, Saginaw, MI.
Catalog No.: CA 023
Media: CD.
Song List: Under My Wheels / Billion Dollar Babies / I'm Eighteen / Is It My Body / You and Me / Only Women Bleed / Unfinished Sweet / Escape / Go to Hell / I Never Cry / It's Hot Tonight / School's Out

Just another revamping of the 1978 KING BISCUIT FLOWER HOUR show. Also released by Manx Record Company.

Album Title: **SPIRIT OF HALLOWEEN SAGINAW 1978**
Released: 1991 by Oh Boy.
Recorded: May 10, 1978 at the Civic Center, Saginaw, MI.
Catalog No.: OHBOY 1-9090
Media: CD.
Song List: Under My Wheels / Billion Dollar Babies / I'm Eighteen / Is It My Body / You and Me / Only Women Bleed / Unfinished Sweet / Escape / Go to Hell / I Never Cry / It's Hot Tonight / School's Out

Just another revamping of the 1978 KING BISCUIT FLOWER HOUR show.

Album Title: **SICK**
Released: 1982 by Stellar Music.
Recorded: Recorded Tracks 1 - 3 recorded May 10, 1978 at the Civic Center, Saginaw, MI; Tracks 4 - 6, 9 and 10 recorded June 4, 1980 at the El Paso Coliseum, El Paso, TX; Tracks 7 and 8 recorded 1971 at the Paramount NW Theater, Seattle, WA.
Catalog No.: 5 MS-002-1
Media: Vinyl.
Song List: Under My Wheels / Billion Dollar Babies / Is It My Body / Pain / I Never Cry / I'm Eighteen / Caught in a Dream / Second Coming / You and Me

If ever there was a bootleg that tried to just make up information so that fans would be enticed, this is the one. Dates and locations are off in several places on the album cover. **Is It My Body** is listed as being recorded in 1969 in San Francisco, when it's actually a recording from 1978. **Pain** is listed as **I'm Your Pain** and all of the El Paso tracks are listed as being from 1981 instead of the proper year of 1980. **Caught in a Dream** and **Second Coming** are both listed as being from 1969 in San Francisco, when they're actually from Seattle, Washington in 1971 (in fact, both songs were not even recorded in the studio until 1971 for the LOVE IT TO DEATH album.)

The 1978 tracks are from the KING BISCUIT FLOWER HOUR show, and the El Paso tracks can be found on numerous other boots as well. More tracks from the Seattle, WA show can be found on the bootleg SNAKE, RATTLE AND ROLL. There is some speculation that Eighteen and You and Me are actually pirated recordings from the ALICE COOPER SHOW album. The record label on the vinyl states that the album is "Stellar Music Special Series 1 Show 2" and that it is of "San Francisco Bands (Pt. 1)."

The SICK bootleg.

Album Title: **SNAKE, RATTLE AND ROLL**
Released: 1990 by Bayfront Records.
Recorded: Tracks 1 - 7 recorded 1971 at the Paramount NW Theater, Seattle, WA; Tracks 8 - 13 recorded March 30, 1969 at the Avalon Ballroom, San Francisco, CA.
Catalog No.: AC 02 A-D
Media: Double Vinyl.
Song List: Sun Arise / Caught in a Dream / I'm Eighteen / Is It My Body / Second Coming / Ballad of Dwight Fry / Black Juju / No Longer Umpire / Reflected / 10 Minutes Before the Worm / Swing Low, Sweet Cheerio / B. B. on Mars / Fields of Regret / Nobody Likes Me / Don't Blow Your Mind (extended version)

This bootleg has a large number of errors in the track listings on the back of the album. The back of the album cover is also a photo of Alice in concert from 1987. Michael Bruce uses a photo of the back cover in his book NO MORE MR. NICE GUY as a reference to what the band played back in 1969 and 1971. It's quite surprising that he would use this as a reference since many of the song titles are incorrect for the last two sides of the album (every track has an incorrect song title, the real tracks are as listed above.) The version of Don't Blow Your Mind is a chance to hear the band do some extended experimentation.

Album Title: **"SOLD OUT" 1975 TOUR**
Released: 1975 by Wizardo Records.
Recorded: Recorded June 17, 1975 at the Los Angeles Forum in Los Angeles, CA. Final track dubbed for the television special THE NIGHTMARE, which was produced in 1975 for Canadian television.
Catalog No.: WRMB 327
Media: Vinyl.
Song List: Cold Ethyl / Only Women Bleed / Devil's Food / Black Widow / Escape / School's Out / Department of Youth / Ballad of Dwight Fry

From one of the better known labels of the 1970's, "SOLD OUT" is also one of the better known bootlegs of the period. Many of these same tracks also appear on THIS SWEET SICKNESS, WHEN NIGHTMARES TURN INTO DREAMS, NO MORE MR. NICE GUY (Liveline Disc label), and NO MORE TEACHER'S DIRTY LOOKS.

The "SOLD OUT" 1975 TOUR bootleg.

Album Title: **STREET TRASH**
Released: Early-1990. Record company unknown.
Recorded: December 14, 1989 at the Birmingham NEC, Birmingham, England.
Catalog No.: Unknown.
Media: CD.

Song List: Hello, Hooray / Trash / Billion Dollar Babies / I'm Eighteen / I'm Your Gun / House of Fire / No More Mr. Nice Guy / This Maniac's in Love With You / Welcome to My Nightmare / Only Women Bleed / I Love the Dead / Poison / Muscle of Love / Spark in the Dark / Bed of Nails / School's Out / Desperado

Also released as ALICE COOPER TRASHES THE WORLD and TRASHES THE WORLD, both with Desperado appearing after I'm Your Gun. This boot was also released, minus Desperado, as THIS SWEET SICKNESS, among others. Recorded from the same show used on the video cassette ALICE COOPER TRASHES THE WORLD.

Album Title: **THIS SWEET SICKNESS**
Released: 1986 by Promo Alice Cooper Nightmare Productions.
Recorded: Tracks 1 - 5 recorded June 17, 1975 at the Los Angeles Forum, Los Angeles, CA; remaining tracks recorded November 28, 1986 at the Apollo Theatre, Manchester, England.
Catalog No.: PRO-A-D 101
Media: Double Vinyl.
Song List: Welcome to My Nightmare / Billion Dollar Babies / No More Mr. Nice Guy / Be My Lover / I'm Eighteen / Give It Up / Cold Ethyl / Only Women Bleed / Go to Hell / Ballad of Dwight Fry / Teenage Frankenstein / Sick Things / I Love the Dead / School's Out / Elected / Under My Wheels / Welcome to My Nightmare / Years Ago / No More Mr. Nice Guy / Billion Dollar Babies / I'm Eighteen

The liner notes on the album are an attempt to make the album look as if it is some type of official — although promotional — release for Alice Cooper. It isn't. A photo cover shows Alice in concert with a baby carriage from the MADHOUSE ROCKS tour.

THIS SWEET SICKNESS bootleg.

Album Title: **TRASHES THE WORLD** - see ALICE COOPER TRASHES THE WORLD

Album Title: **UNDER THE BLADE**
Released: Late-1980's by Eighteen Records, England.
Recorded: November 23, 1986 at Wembley Arena, London, England.
Catalog No.: Catalog number not given.
Media: Vinyl.
Song List: Welcome to My Nightmare / Billion Dollar Babies / No More Mr. Nice Guy / Only Women Bleed / Elected / The World Needs Guts / Give It Up / Teenage Frankenstein / School's Out / Under My Wheels

One of the few bootlegs to have a track listing for Alice's typical introduction of the band during School's Out.

UNDER THE BLADE bootleg.

Album Title: **WAITING FOR THE EDGE KISS MY NECK**
Released: 1991 by Amazing Pig.
Recorded: December 14, 1989 at the Birmingham NEC, Birmingham, England.
Catalog No.: TAP-CD-9101
Media: CD.
Song List: Hello, Hooray / Trash / Billion Dollar Babies / I'm Eighteen / I'm Your Gun / House of Fire / No More Mr. Nice Guy / This Maniac's in Love With You / Welcome to My Nightmare / Only Women

Bleed / I Love the Dead / Poison / Muscle of Love / Spark in the Dark / Bed of Nails / School's Out

Also released as the bootleg STREET TRASH. The material is from the same show used for the video cassette ALICE COOPER TRASHES THE WORLD.

WAITING FOR THE EDGE KISS MY NECK bootleg.

Album Title: **WHEN NIGHTMARES TURN INTO DREAMS**
Released: 1990 by Oh Boy, Luxembourg.
Recorded: June 17, 1975 at the Los Angeles Forum, Los Angeles, CA.
Catalog No.: OH BOY 1-9071
Media: CD.
Song List: Welcome to My Nightmare / No More Mr. Nice Guy / Billion Dollar Babies / I'm Eighteen / Some Folks / Devil's Food / Black Widow / Steven / Welcome to My Nightmare (reprise) / Escape / School's Out / Department of Youth

Years Ago does appear on the CD, although it's not listed (it's used merely as a medley between songs.) The full color cover is of Alice from a much later period than 1974.

Album Title: **YOU & ME**
Released: Mid-1980's on vinyl (company unknown); reissued 1995 on CD by Golden Dragon Records.
Recorded: Recorded 1977. Exact date of recording unknown.
Catalog No.: HJLR 0011 (vinyl) and GDCD-0011 (CD)
Media: Vinyl and CD.
Song List: Escape / Go to Hell / I Never Cry / It's Hot Tonight / School's Out / Under My Wheels / Billion Dollar Babies / I'm Eighteen / Is It My Body / You and Me / Only Women Bleed / Unfinished Sweets

WHEN NIGHTMARES TURN INTO DREAMS bootleg.

Another recording from the LACE AND WHISKEY tour. The people behind this album managed not only to jumble the song titles around on the cover, but jumble around the order of the songs during the show. Billion Dollar Babies is listed as merely Billion, Is It My Body is listed as It Is My Body, You and Me and listed as You & Me, and Unfinished Sweet is listed as Unfinished Suite.

While the CD has Japanese and English writing on the cover, there is some speculation that Golden Dragon is not a Japanese release but from another country where making it look like a Japanese release is the norm (companies in Australia are notorious for doing this.) Since the original vinyl was produced in Korea, this may be the location of the subsequent CD reissue.

Album Title: **YOU'RE ALL CRAZIER THAN I AM**
Released: 1973 by Trade Mark of Quality.
Recorded: July 23, 1972 at the Hollywood Bowl, Hollywood, CA.
Catalog No.: TMQ 72012

Media:	Double Vinyl.
Song List:	Public Animal No. 9 / Be My Lover / I'm Eighteen / Is It My Body (extended) / Halo of Flies / Gutter Cat Vs. the Jets / Street Fight / Killer / Long Way To Go / School's Out / I'm Eighteen / Gutter Cat Vs.The Jets / Street Fight / Killer / Elected / School's Out

Also released as HELLO, HURRAY STARRING ALICE COOPER AT THE HOLLYWOOD BOWL 1972.

Album Title:	**YOU'RE ALL CRAZIER THAN I AM**	YOU'RE ALL CRAZIER THAN I AM (TMQ.)
Released:	Early-1990's by Black Death.	
Recorded:	Tracks 1 - 11 recorded May 10, 1978 at the Civic Center, Saginaw, MI; Tracks 12 - 14 recorded June 17, 1975 at the Los Angeles Forum, Los Angeles, CA.	
Catalog No.:	901201	
Media:	Colored Vinyl.	
Song List:	Under My Wheels / Billion Dollar Babies / I'm Eighteen / Is It My Body / I Love the Dead / Go to Hell / It's Hot Tonight / Devil's Food / Black Widow / Unfinished Sweet / Escape / Welcome to My Nightmare / Years Ago / No More Mr. Nice Guy	

You're all bootlegging what I am! Seriously, just another variation of the 1978 KING BISCUIT FLOWER HOUR radio show, along with three tracks from the 1975 Los Angeles Forum show. Other boots have more material from both shows.

The album comes with a black and white photo cover, with the front cover being of Alice bending over and looking into the camera, circa WELCOME TO MY NIGHTMARE. The back cover is five small photos of Alice, one with Dali and another with a snake. The vinyl is on red wax.

Well, my child, the story is over for tonight.

But, no matter, for I can see you are already on your way to where the Showman will take you away into another world.

So, as the lightning sickens the sky and the thunder rolls reality upon the world, let the Showman put on his show and make this world go away.

And let the music play.

Let the music play.

~~~ Chapter 7: Acknowledgments ~~~

As always, a book covering so much material and so many years is something that cannot be done by one person alone. In the time that it took to write this, there have been a variety of people who have helped me out in making the book the best reference guide to Alice Cooper that was possible. Some have come and gone, but there are a few that must be thanked individually.

First and foremost I want to thank Brian Gaddis for his continuous help and support on the project ever since I first contacted him months ago. Same goes for Si Halley (and his Alice Cooper Trivia File web site), Bryan Erickson, Tim Stradling and Davie Millar. All five allowed me to use information from them readily without any hesitation as to what I might do with it. All they cared about was a good book being produced about Alice and I hope I have lived up to their hopes.

Additional thanks must go to David Millar and Bryan Erickson for allowing me to use scans of merchandise from their web sites for use in the book. Without them allowing me to do so, the visuals in this book would be somewhat bare.

Kurt Scheinpflug was most helpful in filling in holes for the concert dates listed in the book, and I greatly appreciate his help. Kurt is still working on a definitive guide to all of Alice's concert appearances over the years and I wish him the best of luck with the project. Andy Michael was also helpful in providing a few concert dates.

I also wish to thank Gabor Kis and Brad Devine for additional bits and pieces that helped firm up a few entries for the book. Lee at Video Beat in Chicago, Illinois was also helpful in giving me a copy of the cover artwork for the video of STRANGE CASE OF ALICE COOPER. I was happy that they could find the time to do such a project for me and I only wish I was close enough to the store to go there more often.

Although he doesn't know it yet, Lee Davey and his web site "The Alice Cooper Ephemera Archive" was very beneficial to the book for verifying a few album releases and for the amount of magazine articles that were reprinted on the site. Between it and Si's site listed above, there was more than enough information to help me through the book.

Speaking of fans on the internet, one cannot forget the Sick Things. These fans have supported Alice through the years and, through Hunter Goatley's internet site, they have discussed many of the topics that I needed to research for the book. It would be impossible to name them all, but they know who they are and my wish is that this book will give them at least one or two things new to think about when discussing Alice's career.

I especially must thank Brian "Renfield" Nelson for listening to my ideas and his willingness to read through the text while I was writing it. It would have been easier for Brian to simply say "no" and move on, and there were times that we clashed a bit on what was to be said. Nevertheless, that is what is needed on a book like this and it would not have been as good as it is without his help (and anything good in it probably came as a result of Brian's read through.) Although the book is not official, Brian was willing to help out on the project, which just goes to show the level of gratitude Alice and his people have towards the fans.

Additional thanks to Brian Nelson again for the Alice photos used on the cover and elsewhere in the book. It was an extremely nice gesture on his part and much appreciated.

I wish to thank Jill for supporting me during the many days and nights that I've had to chain myself to the computer to work on this book. I also wish to thank the people where I work for putting up with me during this time, and thanks to my friends and family who put up with my talking endlessly about the book while working on it. I also wish to thank Ric Connors, Rob Godwin and everyone else at CGP for their willingness to jump on this project because I wanted to do it.

Finally, I wish to thank Alice. Just for being who he is and for putting out the music.

Dale Sherman
November 6, 1998

"This next song is called 18...brand new."

Lines form on the left and right
Lines form up and down
But I'm gonna stay in
The middle of town
I know where I belong

I'm 18 and I do what I want
18 and I get what I want
18 and I want what I want

I gotta get out of here
Mom and Dad's got me drinking beer

Don't need no biology line
I can make the math teacher any time
Cause she washes my clothes
Buys my wine, yeah
Any day it's many times

Cause I'm
18 and I get what I want
18, yes I want what I want
Don't you know I'm 18
And I gotta be
Gotta get away, gotta get away, hey yeah

Gotta get out of this place
Awww...
Don't be closing in and blowing in, yeah

(harmonica break)

I've been waiting for a very long time
I've been waiting to sing this song, yeah
I've been waiting on a bottle of wine and I
Think my time has come

Cause I'm
18 and I get what I want
Yes I'm 18
and I want what I want
Don't you know I'm 18
Gotta get away, gotta get away, gotta get away

I gotta get out of here
Mom and Dad's got me drinking beer

Yes I'm 18, yes I get what I want
Don't you know I'm 18
Gotta get away, gotta get away, gotta get away
No, no, and I gotta get away
No, no, 18, (18), 18, (18), 18
18 yeah
Don't like it when it's cold and hot
Don't like it when it's hot and cold
Like it in the medium, medium old
That's what I know it
(Ad lib "oh, oh"s and "yep, yep"s)
18, 18, 18
18, 18, 18
18, 18, 18
18, 18, 18
18, 18, 18, 18
Yeah, yeah, yeah, yeah, yeah, yeah, yeah, yeah, yeah, yeah, yeah
18, 18
I gotta be
18, 18
I gotta be
18, 18
Eight-t-t-t-t-t
Yeah

I'm Eighteen performed in 1970 at the Chicago Underground, Chicago, Illinois.

BLACK DIAMOND

THE BIOGRAPHY OF KISS (BOOK AND CD)

"... (Dale Sherman's) diligence and attention to detail is remarkable, making BLACK DIAMOND the bible for the KISS army."
 Ken Sharp
 THE ROCK REPORT

"... the committed will lap it up..."
 RECORD COLLECTOR

THE COLLECTOR'S GUIDE TO KISS (BOOK)

"I do believe this is the best KISS book I have ever read."
 KISS NEWS NETWORK

"In my opinion, this book is a straight forward, no holds barred, factual presentation of KISS."
 SHOCK ME

PRETTIES FOR YOU
ALICE COOPER
PRETTIES FOR YOU

The Alice Cooper Group.

EASY ACTION
ALICE COOPER
EASY ACTION

LOVE IT TO DEATH

Photograph by Ken Ballard

KILLER

SCHOOL'S OUT

Photograph by Ken Ballard

BILLION DOLLAR BABIES

MUSCLE OF LOVE

Photo by Brad Trevino

ALICE COOPER GOES TO HELL

Alice Cooper Goes to Hell

Photo By Ken Ballard

LACE AND WHISKEY

THE OUTSTANDING MYSTERY DISCOVERY OF THE DECADE

LACE AND WHISKEY

ALICE COOPER

THE ALICE COOPER SHOW

Photo by Ken Ballard

Photo by Ken Ballard

FROM THE INSIDE

FLUSH THE FASHION
ALICE COOPER '80
FLUSH THE FASHION

Photo by Ken Sallard

Photo by Ken Sallard

SPECIAL FORCES
ALICE COOPER

SPECIAL FORCES

Photo by Kevin Workman

Photo by Kevin Workman

ZIPPER CATCHES SKIN
ALICE COOPER

DADA
ALICE COOPER

CONSTRICTOR

Photo by Kevin Workman

Photo by Ken Ballard

RAISE YOUR FIST AND YELL

THE BEAST OF ALICE COOPER

Photo by Ken Ballard

TRASH

HEY STOOPID

Photo by Ken Ballard

Photo by Ken Ballard

THE LAST TEMPTATION

CLASSICKS

ALICE COOPER

Photo by Ken Ballard

A FISTFUL OF ALICE

ALICE COOPER
A Fistful of Alice

The Life and Crimes of Alice Cooper Boxset

Photo by Ken Ballard

Alice Cooper
No More Teacher's Dirty Looks

ALICE IN ROCKLAND

Photo by Ken Ballard

ALICE COOPER GOES TO CHILE

THE EL PASO SHOW
Alice Cooper
The El Paso Show

Photo by Ken Ballard

WHEN NIGHTMARES TURN INTO DREAMS
ALICE COOPER
WHEN NIGHTMARES TURN INTO DREAMS

MAD HOUSE ROCK

ALICE COOPER
MAD HOUSE ROCK

Photo by Ken Ballard

GO TO HELL

GO
TO
HELL

ALICE COOPER

THE COLLECTOR'S GUIDE TO HEAVY METAL

. . . for who can resist the unswerving majesty of the power chord? read about it, as we batter, praise, and otherwise penetrate the essence of over 3,300 bruising records comprising a large wedge of the world's Most Powerful Music. Designed to guide the discerning fan through the jungle of releases competing for your CD dollar. Hard Rock, Heavy Metal, Grunge, Thrash, Funk Metal, Black Metal, Death Metal, Euro Metal, Prog Metal, Punk, etc etc.

Includes an exclusive nineteen track Heavy Metal sampler compact disc.

'. . . Martin Popoff is to heavy metal what Hunter S. Thompson was to politics . . . this is a completists guide to Heavy Metal. By any definition . . . .'
Lollipop Magazine

"What a necessary brain stuffer this humungous belch of hard rock fan spoo is!"
Terminal City

LED ZEPPELIN The Press Reports

In "Led Zeppelin - The Press reports . . ." noted Led Zeppelin expert Robert Godwin has collected and reviewed over a thousand articles from around the globe. Reports of the band's activities from Tokyo to New York and from Sydney to London are compiled and collated in chronological order.

'. . . outrageously exhaustive . . .'
Guitar World

'. . . exceptional . . . a marvel of meticulous research . . .'
FMQB

"The Press Reports . . ." includes an exclusive interview compact disc with Jimmy Page from 1977 in which he discusses his amazing career as one of the world's top rock musicians.

Now available from Collector's Guide Publishing

The Pink Floyd Reference Encyclopedia

by Vernon Fitch

The Pink Floyd Reference Encyclopedia is an in-depth reference work covering all the people, places, and history of the musical group Pink Floyd. From the earliest days of the band to the present, this book explains the band from The Abdabs to Zee. Written by **Vernon Fitch** author of the web's leading Floyd site "The Pink Floyd Archives", The book also features an appendix of unique reference works including Books, Concert Dates, Discographies, Session Work, and more. The Pink Floyd Reference Encyclopedia is a must for every Pink Floyd enthusiast, from the casual fan to the obsessive collector.

The Pink Floyd Archives
E-Mail: PFArchives@CompuServe.com
WWW: http://ourworld.compuserve.com/homepages/PFArchives